The White Earth Tragedy

Melissa L. Meyer

The White Earth Tragedy

Ethnicity and Dispossession
at a Minnesota Anishinaabe
Reservation, 1889–1920

For Kent,
I could always count on you
to straighten me out before I went
totally awry.
Thanks for everything.
Melissa

University of Nebraska Press

Lincoln and London

The paper in this book meets the minimum require-
ments of American National Standard for Information
Sciences—Permanence of Paper for Printed Library
Materials, ANSI z39.48–1984.

Library of Congress Cataloging-in-Publication Data

Meyer, Melissa L. (Melissa Lee)
    The White Earth tragedy : ethnicity and
dispossession at a Minnesota Anishinaabe Reservation,
1889–1920 / Melissa L. Meyer.
        p.   cm.
    Includes bibliographical references and index.
    ISBN 0-8032-3154-7 (cl : alk. paper)
        1. White Earth Indian Reservation (Minn.)—
History.   2. Ojibwa Indians—History.   3. Ojibwa
Indians—Cultural assimilation.   I. Title.
E99.C6M46   1994
977.6′94—dc20   93-23456
                                                      CIP
Publication of this book was aided by a grant
from the Andrew W. Mellon Foundation.

For my mother, Helen L. Meyer,
and in memory of my father, Albert F. Meyer

And for Dr. Khalil Tabsh
and the 2 West nurses at UCLA Medical Center
for saving my daughter Tanis's life

Contents

Illustrations

Tables

Preface

To say that American Indians have not been integrated into American history is a profound understatement. Many standard textbooks explain the conquest and subordination of American Indians as a result of the inability of their primitive cultures to withstand the onslaught of civilization and modernization: just as wolves, bears, cougars, and other denizens of the forest lost their place to European settlers, so Indian people were doomed to fade before the advance of superior technology and democratic institutions. Equally debilitating is the romantic stereotype that casts Indian people as doing nothing more than acting in worshipful harmony with nature. Scholars have used simplistic brush strokes to paint life before European contact as the Eden of the Western Hemisphere. They explain subsequent interaction as a dualistic struggle between Western civilization and a world as yet untainted by industrial capitalism. The structure of this narrative tells us more about how Euroamerican intellectuals regard their own history than it does about American Indian experiences.

Certainly, some elements of this story line are inescapable. European nations did expand across the Atlantic, setting in motion processes that no indigenous group has been able to avoid. But the trajectory of history is not unilinear. The fortunes of specific groups may be plotted as stairways or roller coasters rather than continuous downward spirals. Although specialists in Indian history have made great strides in representing the diversity of Indian cultures and their many creative adaptations, the mainstream has remained stubbornly impervious to their insights. Indians are still portrayed as so weighted by a "traditional" ball and chain as to be unable to respond to their changing world at all, much less to devise their own solutions to the problems they faced. Most pervasive is the historically debilitating stereotype of helpless Indian victims with bulldozer tracks still visible on their prostrate bodies. These mythic renditions of U.S. history prevent American Indians from being understood as legitimate historical actors with logical, rational motivations for their behavior. They deny native people the reality of their histories and prevent their experiences, interactions, and contributions from being integrated into American history.

The story of the White Earth Anishinaabeg in the late nineteenth and early twentieth centuries is about nothing if not successful adaptation. Before the onslaught of deleterious legislation constructed by a coalition of timber and land corporations and their political friends, those who migrated to the White Earth Reservation in northern Minnesota had succeeded in adapting to new conditions brought about by encroaching loggers and Euroamerican settlers. Successful American Indian solutions are seldom spotlighted because corporate and political interests were usually even more successful in devising new strategies for divesting them of their land and resources. But the horrors of exploitation should not be allowed completely to overshadow the heroic efforts made by people to deal with the often harsh circumstances they faced.

Neither should obvious exploitation mask relationships within Indian groups that may have worked against their long-term success in maintaining maximum control over their lives and destinies. No Indian nation should be viewed as utterly homogeneous. That some Indian people chose to become capitalistic entrepreneurs who sacrificed group welfare to their own individual well-being is not palatable to those who resort to stereotypes to explain the course of history. Although historians have shown ethnicity to be a significant feature of Euroamerican history, they may be surprised to learn that it also figures prominently in American Indian history. This commonality indicates a fruitful direction for integration. Once we refrain from viewing Indians as exotic foreigners, many others will emerge.

I decided to embark on this study of the White Earth Anishinaabeg primarily to recast the narrative about American Indian adaptations during the period of land allotment and forced assimilation. As a beginning graduate student, I saw these coercive attempts to remake Indian cultures as some of the most intrusive and insensitive efforts ever undertaken by American reformers. How, I wondered, had American Indians ever managed to survive and retain any of their cultural practices? In the late 1970s the literature was so underdeveloped that the topic had not been addressed; only the details of policy formulation and implementation had been explored with very little attention given to Indian adaptations. Presuming that the theater of Indian-white relations was of paramount importance has blinded most scholars to the possibility that relationships among Indians may have been of equal or greater significance. I intended to provide a corrective by shedding greater light on American Indian social history during the late nineteenth and early twentieth centuries. However, what began as a community study soon snowballed into a more holistic history where economics and politics played central roles as well.

It had always been my goal to integrate my local case study into a larger theoretical framework. In my quest to understand why efforts by the White Earth Anishinaabeg to adapt to their new reservation were undercut, I found myself turning to the sociological realm of world-systems theory. I was initially surprised that reliance on a modified seasonal round had persisted into the twentieth century. At the same time, however, ample evidence indicated that it was rapidly being subverted. Why, I wondered, was dispossession delayed in northern Minnesota when Oklahoma tribes had been divested of their resources decades before? Exploring this question led me to the economic and political realms that are crucial for explaining White Earth's social history. Powerful forces were arrayed against the Anishinaabeg in their efforts to maintain their landed heritage—including capitalistic individuals among them. But circumstances allowed their opponents to succeed only by the early twentieth century.

Efforts to avoid stereotypes have convinced me that word choice and narrative structure make all the difference in the cast given to each story about American Indian history. Because of its connotation of immutability, I generally replace the word "traditional" with "conservative," indicating a more cautious approach to change and adaptation. When I do use "traditional" it simply means cultural patterns or customs from an earlier time. It should not be surprising that native groups, like all other human societies, were never static; change and adaptability are universal human traits. Certain leaders among the Anishinaabeg I have labeled "capitalists" because they engaged in market activities to turn a profit which they distributed narrowly to benefit their immediate families. Obviously, these individuals did not behave as venture capitalists who continuously reinvested their profits. Their involvement was more modest, but can accurately be described as capitalistic nonetheless, especially in comparison with more conservative reservation residents. My use of the terms "mixed-blood" and "full-blood" almost always reflects symbolic understandings rather than literal genetic labels. I elaborate on my argument in this regard in chapter 3.

Readers will not see the word "acculturation" on these pages. Acculturation fails to convey the remarkable creativity of native adaptations, because it implies that Indians discarded one cultural element after another for their American counterparts. Adaptation was generally a much more complicated creative process. Americans tend to think of "settlement" as a rather benign Ma and Pa endeavor. In reality, the expansion of market capitalism was spearheaded by fur traders, miners, loggers, speculators, and only later by settlers. I avoid referring to such abstract concepts as "modernization" or "progress" to explain the forces arrayed against the Anishinaabeg. Exploitation of Anishinaabe land and resources (and those of other native groups) helped the rest of the country to modernize and progress, but it impoverished Indian groups. Finally, I only use gender-referent pronouns when they are absolutely correct.

Modern orthographies translate "Anishinaabe/g" (the "e" ending is adjectival, the "g" form plural) as "Indian person." I use this native-referent term in preference to "Chippewa" or "Ojibwe" (Chippewa is simply a corruption of Ojibwe), the origins of which have been a matter of debate. Whether these names refer to a puckered style of moccasin construction, a story in which an enemy is burned until "puckered up," or the practice of making extensive pictographs, they are terms that outsiders would have used to describe the Anishinaabeg. I also use native-referent terms for the Dakota (Eastern Sioux), Odawa (Ottawa), and Mesquakie (Fox). However, in most other cases, I employ standard terms such as Iroquois and Cree to avoid undue confusion.

Before the early twentieth century, those who recorded Anishinaabe names tended to try to write them down as they heard them, resulting in various phonetic forms in the historical documentation. Slight nuances in how a name was recorded can result in completely different translations. On the advice of John Nichols, cocreator of the Nichols-Nyholm orthography (*Ojibwewi-Ikidowinan*), I selected a representative spelling of each Anishinaabe name that appears in the text for the sake of consistency. I routinely eliminate hyphens between syllables, provide an English translation if offered in historical documentation, and refer to individuals by their Anishinaabe name in the narrative if they regularly gave this as their name or were consistently designated as such. Names included in the endnote citations are spelled as they appeared in each document to enable them to be traced and perhaps accurately translated and spelled in accordance with modern orthographies in the future. Otherwise, all Anishinaabe words (other than proper names) have been spelled in accordance with the Nichols and Nyholm orthography, when possible.

It is very difficult to live in the Twin Cities area and not be aware of its very active, vibrant Indian community. I was a Ph.D. candidate at the University of Minnesota just as White Earth land claims were becoming a hot issue. After spending several months at the National Archives in Washington, D.C., photocopying documents, I realized how important they would be for those concerned with restoring the reservation land base. Upon my return, I contacted the grass-roots land claims group Anishinabe Akeeng and shared what I had found with them. Thus our reciprocal relationship began. As a graduate student and later as a professor at the University of Minnesota, I made several trips to White Earth Reservation with members of the land claims group and attended their meetings both at White Earth and in the Twin Cities area. These political activists know their history and federal Indian law very well and have discussed their work with my classes at the university and workshops at the Minnesota Historical Society. I gained insights from them and our conversations confirmed much of my interpretation. They have been enthusiastic about my research and publications; chapters of my Ph.D. dissertation were submitted to a congressional subcommittee in the course of reviewing White Earth land claims. I feel fortunate that my work has value for some White Earth descendants and that it serves some contemporary purpose rather than simply ending up on dusty library shelves.

Through these involvements I gained access to oral history collections compiled by Indian people in the 1980s. None of them were gathered by individuals trained in oral interviewing techniques; their efforts would not meet standards established by oral history associations. In conjunction with a project to produce histories of three reservations for high school students, the Minnesota Chippewa Tribe commissioned people to solicit responses from older reservation residents to a prepared questionnaire. Because the interviewers paraphrased respondents' answers I have not quoted them, although I do accept generalized events, trends, and processes indicated by their responses (I had access to these questionnaire responses through my participation as historian for the unpublished history of the White Earth Reservation). Members of Anishinabe Akeeng also taped interviews with older White Earth residents to document the history of reservation land fraud. Despite their obvious bias in phrasing questions, these tapes were of greatest value to me and I have quoted them freely. I have also used a number of interviews with White Earth descendants contained in the American Indian Oral History Project Component of the New York Times Oral History Program, even though most interviewees were too young to have lived through events at the turn of the twentieth century.

Portions of chapters 4 and 6 appeared in " 'We Can Not Get a Living as We Used To': Dispossession and the White Earth Anishinaabeg, 1889–1920," *American Historical Review* 96 (1991): 368–94, and portions of chapter 3 appeared in "Signatures and Thumbprints: Ethnicity among the White Earth Anishinaabeg, 1889–1920," *Social Science History* 14 (1990): 305–45. I am grateful for permission to reprint this material here.

I have incurred many debts in the course of researching and writing this book. Finally, I can acknowledge those who have contributed.

The collections and staffs of many institutions bear recognition. I worked most extensively at the National Archives, Washington, D.C., where Renee Jaussaud, Richard Crawford, Robert Kvasnicka, and Robert Fowler were most helpful at directing me through a mountain of material that I thought at times was insurmountable. I have worked for years at the Minnesota Historical Society Library and Archives, in St. Paul. Maureen Otwell's understanding of the ability of historical documents to educate has been an inspiration. Staff members of the society's Archives and Manuscript Division were always eager to help and took an interest in my research, especially Dallas Lindgren, Ruth Bauer, E. Hampton Smith, Steve Nielson, and Kathy Marquis. Bonnie Wilson, Dona Sieden, and Tracey Baker at the Audio-Visual Library cheerfully brought piles of photographs for me to look through and helped me achieve a tight deadline. Other institutions and their staffs were also helpful: the Kansas City Federal Regional Archive, Missouri; the National Cartographic Archives, Suitland, Maryland; the National Anthropological Archives at the Smithsonian Institution; the Becker County Historical Society, Detroit Lakes, Minnesota; the D'Arcy McNickle Center for the History of the American Indian at the Newberry Library, Chicago; Wilson Library at the University of Minnesota (especially the Government Documents section), the U.S. Department of Justice, Indian Claims Section, and the University Research Library and the American Indian Studies Center Library at the University of California, Los Angeles.

I thank the D'Arcy McNickle Center for the History of the American Indian at the Newberry Library for a predoctoral fellowship that supported this work, the University of Minnesota Graduate School for a doctoral dissertation fellowship, and the University of Minnesota College of Liberal Arts for research and travel funds. The Academic Senate at the University of California, Los Angeles, also provided research funds.

Thanks to John Howe, Paul Murphy, Russell Menard, Richard White, Donald Fixico, Tanis Chapman Thorne, Kenneth Lincoln, Frederick Hoxie, Raymond DeMallie, Martin Zanger, George Alter, Kent Smith, Walter Williams, Rebecca Kugel, Mary Yeager, Eric Monkkonen, Gary Nash, and Norris Hundley for offering insightful comments on the manuscript. Others offered encouragement along the way, among them Jean O'Brien, Janet Spector, Stuart Schwartz, Valerie Matsumoto, Sara Evans, and George Green. Vee Salabiye, librarian at the American Indian Studies Library at the University of California, Los Angeles, provided the unusual combination of expert bibliographic assistance, good-hearted friendship, and mirth. A cadre of research assistants ably plowed through censuses, tracked down bibliographic citations, and did preliminary literature surveys; among them Ann Caylor, John Olmsted, Kerwin Klein, Lance Kelley, and Nancy Shoemaker.

Many conversations with individuals with ties to White Earth have enriched this study. Thanks to Marvin Manypenny, John Morrin, Roberta Roy Brown, Dale Hanks, Holly Youngbear-Tibbets, Connie Ross Brandenberg, Winona LaDuke, Ray Bellcourt, Rich Bellcourt, Judy Fairbanks, Kimberley Blaeser, Donald Day, David Beaulieu, Gerald Vizenor, and Shelley McIntire for insights into their heritage and histories.

Thanks to my comrades who regularly participated in the Social History Brownbag Series at the University of Minnesota, who kept me thinking when the documents threatened to consume me, especially John Anfinson, John Campbell, Elizabeth Faue, Jon Gjerde, Clark Halker, David Howard-Pitney, Colette Hyman, Curt Johnson, Earl Lewis, Brent Olson, Edward Tebbenhoff, and Eileen Walsh.

Thanks to my family for continued support, though they often wondered what drove me in this endeavor: Albert F. and Helen L. Meyer, Diana D. Meyer, Leslie D. Stacey, Scott A. Sillett, and everyone else. My friend, Angela Campbell, helped extend my tight budget by offering her home to me during much of the time I spent in Washington, D.C. A special thanks to my husband, Russell Thornton, for love, support, and encouragement through the years, for reading and enthusiastically commenting on the manuscript, and for helping me to keep running to chase away the blues. Our daughter, Tanis, although too young yet to read this, drove home the reality that my students have such a hard time grasping. There is more to courage and heroism than fighting to the death. Making hard decisions necessary to keep the children alive and well is its own brand of heroism.

Finally, a very special thanks to the folks from Anishinabe Akeeng for their prayers and support. You have helped give this book meaning.

Introduction

In 1867, policymakers for the U.S. government and Anishinaabe leaders conceived of the White Earth Reservation in northern Minnesota as a place where the Indians might "conquer poverty by [their] own exertions." Eight hundred thousand acres that included prime farmland in the Red River Valley, valuable stands of pine timber, and lakes and streams supporting seasonal resources on which the Anishinaabeg had relied for generations seemed well suited to meet both subsistence needs and an evolving market orientation. Assimilationists had always thought of Indian reservations as temporary phases in a process whereby American Indians would meld completely into U.S. culture. In this bountiful, isolated area, federal officials hoped that the Anishinaabeg would be able to learn the ways of market farming and successfully "assimilate."[1]

The major focus of U.S. Indian policy in the late nineteenth century was on privatizing reservation resources. Eastern "humanitarians" directed the trend in a belief that inculcating the value of private property and market behavior would hasten Indians' assimilation. Since simply setting a good example for them had failed to achieve desired results, more forceful measures were apparently necessary. These people buttressed their faith in the almost magical ability of private property to transform Indians' collective values with a restriction protecting allotted land from sale or alienation for twenty-five years. Western politicians anticipated an economic windfall from "surplus" acres that would be opened after lands had been allotted and lent their support. These sentiments dovetailed to produce the General Allotment Act of 1887. Reservations nationwide were to be divided into privately held parcels of up to 160 acres each, with any remaining acreage opened to "settlement."

Before the act could be fully implemented, however, the direction of national policy shifted in two ways. First, because some Indians at White Earth and elsewhere clearly understood market values, it seemed patently "un-American" to regulate how they managed their allotted property. Policymakers thus sought some mechanism to free "competent" Indians from restrictions. Second, guarded optimism that most Indians could learn to function in a capitalistic economy gave way to pessimistic certainty that their inherent "backwardness" would prevent them from doing so. Social engineers reasoned that Indians had failed to assimilate because they were incapable of it. Policies promoting this end therefore were pointless. With these attitudes in place, the stage was set for local Euroamerican businesses and speculators to gain access to recently privatized resources. After the turn of the twentieth century, the vision of reservations populated by Indian landowners swiftly fell victim to the drive for the increasingly efficient incorporation of reservation resources into the rapidly maturing U.S. industrial capitalist economy. Allotment policy has been blamed for the rapid loss of reservation land in the early twentieth century, but, in truth, it never had a chance to succeed.[2]

Before Euroamericans rushed to acquire White Earth's resources, the Indians had successfully adapted to the reservation. It served as a haven of sorts and allowed immigrants to escape economic limitations of the forest and lake country of north-central Minnesota and to perpetuate their lifeways. Had they retained the land base, the White Earth Anishinaabeg might have continued to adapt.

It is important to emphasize how viable were Anishinaabe adaptations. Anishinaabe leaders and Indian Office officials alike acknowledged that Indians in northern Minnesota faced a growing subsistence crisis brought on by the expansion of market capitalism. Subsistence farming, wage labor, and marketing seasonal produce were Anishinaabe solutions. Managing their timber as a renewable resource would also have contributed to their strategies handsomely. "Settlement" did not threaten the Anishinaabeg as much as deforestation, environmental degradation, and declining animal populations did. Policymakers interpreted the crisis as the failure of an inherently backward culture to adapt to what Americans saw as "progress." From this viewpoint, assimilation would ensure the Anishinaabeg a place in the modern world. Native people knew that adaptation was their only choice, and they devised diverse strategies for its continuance. For many, the White Earth Reservation held out hope that they might, indeed, begin anew and regain an ample and secure livelihood in the north country.

But "assimilation" went awry for the Anishinaabeg, and corporate gain won out. Dispossession undercut a generations-old pattern of Anishinaabe self-support and flexible adaptation that had persisted into the twentieth century. Under the guise of "assimilation," U.S. government policies brought them increased poverty, disease, and diaspora.

The scenario is familiar—and not unique to White Earth. The expansion of Europe in the fifteenth century and the quest to obtain resources that fueled the industrial revolution set in motion similar processes around the world.[3] From the first decades of colonization, native North Americans struggled to maintain their autonomy, sometimes succeeding, often failing, and always adapting. As Euroamericans created societies of their own, they increasingly sought to incorporate or absorb the land and resources of Indian groups.[4] But the concomitant of incorporation for native people, one that world-systems theorists usually mention only in passing, was marginalization.

Although incorporation and marginalization affected all native groups in North America, the processes varied across time and space—probably in patterned ways. In general, utilizing or living near resources that were highly valued in the world economy and being located near a locus of strong state power meant that native groups soon felt the full impact of incorporation. State expansion and changes in technology, especially in transportation, enabled the resources of distant groups to be incorporated. Yet many factors could intervene to produce local variations in this pattern.

In 1988, Thomas D. Hall presented a comparative model of incorporation that emphasized a number of factors establishing parameters within which natives and Euroamericans interacted: the resources being exploited, the structure of the state government involved and its position in the world economy, the timing of incorporation relative to evolution of the world economy, and, the internal social organization of incorporated societies.[5] Ideally, facets of native cultures beyond social organization need to be included in the model, since native value systems and politi-

cal structures also influenced the outcome of their interaction with
Euroamericans.

For native groups that survived initial epidemics and depopulation,
ideological consensus facilitated political cohesion. The ability to present a unified front when dealing with Euroamericans enhanced a group's
power, adaptability, and autonomy. Attempts to forge alliances and con-
federations illustrate that some natives recognized this. Small groups and
those unable to mediate internal differences were at greater risk of Euroamerican domination. The point is presented most clearly by reference
to the extremes. Pueblo groups, for example, veritable theocracies in
which fused religious and political institutions ensured conformity to
group ideals, fared much better in their dealings with Euroamericans
than did the White Earth Anishinaabeg. At White Earth, profound factional divisions prevented concerted action at the very time it was most
necessary. Individualistic, capitalistic values proved to be divisive because they promoted accumulation of wealth by a few, greater distinctions among native social groups, and less homogeneity in values than
had previously existed. At times, political structures were manipulated
by those with capitalistic values and contested by those with concern for
a group's collective welfare. Either case paved the way for incorporation
of resources. Some groups, however, most notably the Pueblo peoples of
the southwest and Red Lake Anishinaabeg in Minnesota, managed to
maintain both their political cohesion and their land bases.[6]

The foregoing examples are merely suggestive, but they surely demonstrate that value systems and political systems merit inclusion in a
model of incorporation and marginalization. A more holistic approach to
native cultures will counterbalance the heavy emphasis Hall's model
places on the nature of states and the world economy. This approach
promises to provide a long-term comparative context that can reveal
both patterns and aberrations in the interaction between Euroamericans
and American Indians.

In this vein, the case-study approach offers an opportunity to examine
both the consequences of the expansion of market capitalism at a specific location and the objectives and decisions that Indian people forged
for themselves. Local case studies can expand, reinforce, or modify gen-

eral theories, while reminding theory builders that actual individuals seldom defined issues of importance in the same manner as academicians. These competing perceptions of reality should take on equal importance at the local level. In this fashion, the dignity of Anishinaabe historical actors can be maintained without losing sight of global and national patterns with which their experiences align.[7]

In the late nineteenth century, members of various Anishinaabe bands in northern Minnesota came together at the White Earth Reservation to establish themselves anew. They came in response to the 1867 Treaty, which created the reservation and the 1889 Nelson Act which attempted to concentrate all Minnesota "Chippewa" on one reservation and issue them privately owned allotments of land. During the early years of immigration, those who came focused their efforts on establishing their communities and economic livelihoods.

Those who came to White Earth between 1867 and 1906 comprised an interethnic social grouping, the components of which had evolved in Minnesota and Wisconsin as a consequence of frequent intermarriage between Euroamerican fur traders and local Indian populations. Conservative Anishinaabe bands located at a distance from fur trade outposts maintained a more subsistence-oriented way of life, while their mediator "cousins," analogous culturally to the Canadian Métis, participated more fully in the market economy. Neither group was "traditional" in the static, aboriginal sense. Both groups had adapted to altered conditions from a foundation of continuity with past cultural constructs. Members of both ethnic groups saw that White Earth offered them an opportunity to relocate and prosper.

These ethnic differences marked the genesis of community relationships at White Earth as reflected in settlement patterns, social and religious affiliations, household sizes, and surname frequencies. The terms "mixed-blood" and "full-blood" were used to distinguish between ethnic groups and became politicized as disagreement over management of reservation resources escalated.

In 1978, Robert F. Berkhofer, Jr., observed that historians knew relatively little about the cultural bases of political factions on reservations—whether they broke down according to "old politics of ins and outs, patronage distribution, and family affiliation."[8] His appraisal still applies not only to political factions, but to social and ethnic cleavages as well.

Historians have tended to interpret such internal differences by lumping them into dichotomous categories, paying little attention to their composition or to the historical processes from which they arose. Hence the literature is replete with references to traditionalists and progressives, Christians and pagans, and mixed-bloods and full-bloods.[9] But history does not unfold in fixed oppositional stages and the dichotomization of these terms, even if they were employed by historical participants themselves, reveals little about social processes. They indicate, instead, a recognition that intratribal heterogeneity was increasing, perhaps in patterned ways.

Although native people suffered much as a result of colonization, they also confronted new opportunities. One of the most significant was the opportunity to become actively involved in the market economy to some degree. Native responses to market opportunities varied greatly, and frequently included outright resistance to a process that threatened their notions of equity and concern for collective group welfare. If recent scholarship has demonstrated anything, it is that native cultures—their values, ethics, and world views—shaped Indians' involvement with Euroamericans and their responses to market opportunities.

Whether through trade mediation, cash-crop agriculture, or some other means, certain individuals within native societies eventually learned to function within market constraints and integrated basic capitalistic values into their decision making. Some members of native societies gradually became more individualistic and acquisitive in their outlook. Increasingly, they began to accumulate wealth and distribute it more narrowly to benefit their close families. The term "capitalistic" in this sense refers more to a basic value orientation rather than to the practice of reinvesting capital into business enterprises to generate ever-greater profits.

Ubiquitous dichotomous labels reflect the uneven and often conflict-ridden ways in which capitalistic values entered native societies. Avenues were numerous—intermarriage, education, and religion, for example—and varied considerably across time and space. Equally diverse were particular members of a society who were most receptive to these new values. A great deal of variance in local case studies must be antici-pated even as the expansion of market capitalism determined the overall trend. Even though polarized terms used to describe internal differences changed from reservation to reservation, parallels between groups sug-gest that their symbolic content may have been largely the same. The intrusion of market capitalism and the opportunities it presented to native people may bear primary responsibility for increasing social het-erogeneity among reservation populations. Recognizing dichotomous labels as symbols for patterned cultural differences can move scholars closer to discovering origins of increased heterogeneity within reserva-tion populations in the nineteenth and early twentieth centuries.

Ever-present dichotomous labels give the impression that some In-dians embraced U.S. assimilationist programs more readily than others. In some cases this was true, but it fails to capture the full picture. Acquisition of capitalistic values formed the very backbone of "assimi-lation" as policymakers construed it. However, some individuals had adapted to market conditions long before the United States had enough power to coerce cultural changes. Once U.S. Indian policy did take on such a coercive cast, native people approached assimilationist directives with their own objectives in mind, creating complex syncretic adapta-tions that policymakers had never dreamed of. The U.S. assimilation policy was just one arena of change. The major process with which they had to contend was the expansion of market capitalism. Native people adjusted their behavior to these changing circumstances they faced, as they had for centuries.

Anishinaabe Migrations and the Genesis of White Earth Communities

Introduction

Migration has always been a key component in Anishinaabe adaptation strategies. Their own oral tradition (now written as well) recounts the emergence of five original clans, Crane, Catfish, Loon, Bear, and Marten, from the Atlantic Ocean and charts their passage through the Great Lakes watershed to northern Minnesota, always following the shining vision of the *miigis* (a cowrie shell), which appeared to them in the western sky.[1]

Midéwiwin (Grand Medicine Society priests and priestesses) incised symbols on birchbark scrolls as mnemonic devices to aid them in ritualistically recounting these migrations.[2] Historical sources corroborate that various linguistically and culturally related bands came from the area surrounding what is now Sault Ste. Marie, at the outlet of Lake Superior between Michigan and Ontario, eventually to occupy sites in the northern Minnesota woodland.

Amalgamation, splintering, intermarriage, and ethnogenesis all accompanied the various phases of Anishinaabe migrations. The annual whitefish run at the Straits of St. Mary connecting Lake Superior and Lake Huron and periodic staging of the Feast of the Dead provided opportunities for proto-Anishinaabe bands to come together. Undoubtedly, marital relationships between these patrilineal, totemic descent groups established kinship ties that were reinforced at these gatherings. Iroquois aggressions and expansion of the Euroamerican trade in furs prompted their migrations north and south of Lake Superior. Many of those who followed the southern route converged at Chequamegon and

Keeweenaw peninsulas, on the south shore of Lake Superior, where a true Anishinaabe corporate entity arose. Year-round occupation there provided a more stable foundation for a common group identity. Intermarriage, religious ceremonies, and diplomatic and trade relationships with Euroamericans and other native groups integrated the disparate bands. However, these corporate communities did not persist; they splintered yet again, this time into bilateral bands that moved into northern Wisconsin and Minnesota and established linguistically and culturally related villages on the shores of larger lakes.

As Anishinaabe bands came to interact with Euroamerican fur traders, marital ties again cemented relations. Marriages and sexual relationships between Euroamerican traders and native women served as the nexus for cultural interchange. Individuals of mixed descent were likely to learn a great deal about their mothers' native cultures, and also to be steeped in the fur trade society of their fathers. As they proliferated in numbers, they formed a society of their own, based on their evolving position as cultural and occupational intermediaries. Through distinctive marital patterns and boundary-maintaining mechanisms, they increasingly came to identify themselves as people of mixed descent who shared a predominantly French heritage and maintained close affiliations with Indian relatives.

As overhunting, lumbering, and agriculture undermined the fur trade economy of the region, treaties with the U.S. government created reservations for the Anishinaabeg and opened land for American exploitation. The White Earth Reservation, established in 1867 in northern Minnesota held out the elusive ideal of an agrarian showplace in the north country. Convinced of its unlimited potential, U.S. policymakers embarked on a program of social engineering designed to concentrate all of the Anishinaabeg in Minnesota on the White Earth Reservation.

Splinter groups from across northern Minnesota elected to move to White Earth. The actions of Anishinaabe band members from various reservations reflected a long heritage of migration and flexible adaptation that allowed them to work out the best circumstances for themselves. Individuals of mixed descent who had grown up in and become adept at functioning within the fur trade society of the western Great Lakes now emphasized their ties with various Anishinaabe bands to secure the right to move to the White Earth Reservation as well. Their actions were in keeping with a long heritage of filling intermediary roles between Anishinaabe society and American society.

At White Earth, these disparate, but related, ethnic groups faced the prospect of amalgamation once again. As with all of their previous moves, this concentration effort entailed adaptation and cultural re-ordering—never a simple task. Individuals responded from the perspective and foundation of their own ethnic groups. And though political strife became a central facet of their corporate identity, they succeeded in becoming the "White Earth Band," and eventually the Indians of the White Earth Reservation.

The Emergence of a Tribal People

The people who would come to identify themselves as the Anishinaabeg had coalesced around the north shore of Lake Huron at the time of European contact around 1620. The Falls of the St. Mary's River, notable as a bountiful fishery, attracted disparate groups from the region, especially during the spring whitefish run. In the 1600s, the fishery "was to the northern Algonkians what the agricultural village was to the Iroquoians"; it was the main support of native people of the region—"the center of social life, and the base for political relationships," permitting settled village populations.[3] Recognizing this, early French explorers, harbingers of the more full-blown market trade in furs that was to evolve, termed the resident group "Saulteur," or "people of the Sault."

Harold Hickerson proposed that surrounding groups, organized in exogamous, patrilineal, totemic bands, were drawn to the Sault on a seasonal basis. Early Jesuits wrote of local groups that bore names very similar to later clan names among the Anishinaabeg. Hickerson summarized: "Thus, we read of the Ouasouarini . . . or fish phratry; the Nikikouet . . . or otter gens; the Amikouai or Amikwa . . ., indicating the beaver gens; the Atchiligouan and Outchougai . . ., either or both names associated with the heron gens . . .; the Marameg . . . or catfish gens; the Roquai or Nouquet . . ., or bear phratry or gens; and the Mantoue . . . or Mundua . . . associated with the marten gens." These groups of local kin appear to have been autonomous; observers described them as "occupying separate territories." In fact, the word *totem* is derived from the Anishinaabe word *doodem* or *oodena,* meaning town, village, or local group.[4]

Before 1640, local kin groups may have been autonomous politically, but they cooperated periodically on an economic basis and maintained affinal relationships between bands. Larger gatherings during the white-fish run required that people allocate prime locations for setting nets or spearfishing and otherwise respect each other's right to fish. They practiced bilateral cross-cousin marriage (marriage between children of opposite sexed siblings), which created, in anthropologist Fred Eggan's words, "multiple bonds between a limited group of relatives and maintain[ed] these from generation to generation." Furthermore, every seven or so years, Algonquians assembled for the Feast of the Dead, where they interred the bones of the deceased in a common ossuary. This ceremony served to focus the loyalties of related groups, redistribute goods, and perpetuate alliances. In 1660, Pierre Radisson participated in the ceremony with the Saulteur and related lineage bands and described a "banquett of kindred" where "marriages according to their country customs are made."[5]

Before the 1640s, natives of the Upper Great Lakes had begun to trade furs for European manufactured goods through Huron and Petun intermediaries, but such indirect contact had not yet had much impact on their customs. This was soon to change. In the late 1640s, efforts of the Neutral and later the Iroquois to expand their network of trading partners prompted major migrations west by groups in southern Michigan (Sauk, Mesquakie [Fox], Kickapoo, Mascouten, Miami, and some Potawatomi). Increasingly tribes were drawn into the fur trade orbit which created new political and economic circumstances and major cultural changes. Between 1648 and 1650, the Iroquois invaded Huronia, land of their most formidable trade rivals, and destroyed their villages thereby dispersing the Huron population. The Odawa (Ottawa) became closely affiliated with Huron interests and emerged as dominant intermediaries in the Upper Great Lakes fur trade. Further social and economic disruption followed as the French began to expand their fur trade interests by establishing new trading posts, forts, and missions through the 1690s.[6]

By 1660 the native people of Sault Ste. Marie had already begun to reorient themselves in response to fur trade opportunities. Totemic bands that had once converged at the fishery for the whitefish run amalgamated with the Saulteur. This was not a particularly difficult adaptation; after all, affinal ties linked bands and they had gathered annually at the fishery for some time. Emerging as a "pivotal trading locale," Sault Ste. Marie was transformed from a seasonal subsistence magnet to a more permanent commercial one.

This coalescence paralleled trends occurring throughout fur trade country. Continuing struggles between the Franco-Algonquian trade alliance and the Iroquois and their British suppliers set the stage for the convergence of tribal groups, traders, and missionaries at prime beaver areas, which became focal points for fur trade settlements. At times tribes and bands amalgamated, forming new group identities and directing their efforts more toward participating in the fur trade. Prolonged involvement in the fur trade led to reliance on European manufactured goods as native craft traditions and items of manufacture fell into disuse. These developments clearly benefited French economic and religious interests and were repeated as they extended their fur trade network further west.

The region around the south shore of Lake Superior was once characterized as a "beaver nursery." As such, it attracted both the French and the amalgamated bands that now formed the Saulteur. By about 1667, Jesuits had established their key Mission Saint Esprit at Chequamegon Bay. Odawa and Wyandot intermediaries had already gathered there by 1670, where they also fished, hunted on the nearby Apostle Islands, and cultivated corn. But extensive beaver trapping required establishing better relations with the Dakota to the south and southwest. French explorer and agent of empire Daniel Greysolon, Sieur du Luth (commonly known as Duluth) attempted to expedite such an arrangement at a general council at the west end of Lake Superior in 1679 by promising natives of the region to provide a reliable source of trade goods. From these negotiations a commercial alliance between the Dakota and the proto-Anishinaabeg took shape. It enabled the amalgamated bands from Sault Ste. Marie to begin to migrate south along the lake shore to Chequamegon and Keeweenaw peninsulas (see Map 1). As they embarked on this move, "the old local groups were well on their way to extinction as independent political bodies."[7]

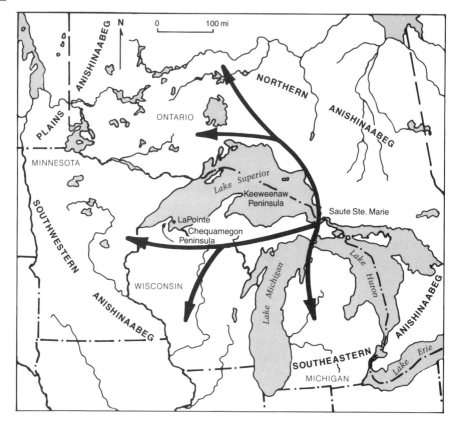

Map 1. Anishinaabe Migration Routes and Dispersal, c. 1840. Adapted from Robert W. Dunning, *Social and Economic Change among the Northern Ojibwa* (Toronto: University of Toronto Press, 1959, reprint 1972, 1974): 6–7.

The Dakota valued the proposed partnership with the amalgamated Saulteur; they would reap a more reliable supply of trade goods and also could depend on Saulteur neutrality in their wars with the Cree and Assiniboine to the northwest. Since game had grown scarce in the area surrounding Sault Ste. Marie, the amalgamated Saulteur welcomed the opportunity to hunt subsistence game on fresh land where intertribal conflict had created a sort of game preserve. They would also serve as trading partners (though not the only ones) for the Dakota, providing them with French trade goods in exchange for pelts. For their part, the French rejoiced at the greater supply of furs that establishing peace guaranteed.

Duluth encouraged intermarriage among the Dakota, amalgamated Saulteur, and Cree to cement the armistice. Not surprisingly (and not due to Duluth's exhortations), this actually occurred. After the Chequamegon settlement had been established for a generation, observers noted that the Dakota had intermarried in this area. And in the 1840s, William Warren, an Anishinaabeg of mixed descent who collected oral traditions from tribal elders, identified a particular group of Anishinaabeg in the eastern area of Minnesota as being of partial Dakota descent.[8] Sealing alliances by intermarriage has been a universal pattern in human history. There is no reason to imagine that native people of the Upper Great Lakes behaved any differently.

From their base at Chequamegon, amalgamated Saulteur hunters ranged into Dakota territory south and southwest of Lake Superior, obtaining subsistence game. It is likely that they also occasioned prairie and parkland areas beyond the coniferous forests surrounding Lake Superior, where elk and bison thrived. But it was an uneasy alliance; the circumstances promoting violent competition were as yet omnipresent. In the late seventeenth century, the proto-Anishinaabeg usually remained neutral, as promised, in the northern conflicts between the Dakota and Cree, but they were often at odds with the Mesquakie, who were sometimes allies of the Dakota. Then again, the amalgamated Saulteur might at times be Dakota allies or Iowa allies, against the Mesquakie, Mascouten, and Miami located to the south.[9]

Chequamegon village itself was about three miles long and two miles wide, strung along the lake shore. With the French Mission Saint Esprit,

Odawa and Wyandot residents, and the amalgamated Saulteur totemic bands, the polyethnic, multilingual Chequamegon population had much in common with other composite fur trade communities. The more sedentary pursuits of fishing and farming took place here, most likely under the direction of women. Amounts of corn and pumpkins culti-vated probably exceeded the products of later Anishinaabe farming ef-forts in the eighteenth century. As at Sault Ste. Marie, fish remained a crucial subsistence resource. By 1736, an estimated 150 able-bodied men or 750 to 1,050 people lived at Chequamegon, 40 able-bodied men or 200 to 280 people lived at Keeweenaw, and only 30 able-bodied men or 150 to 210 people remained at Sault Ste. Marie.[10] The migration was nearly complete.

Elders who spoke to William Warren described life at Chequamegon village as the golden age of the Anishinaabeg. Indeed, the amalgamated Saulteur who migrated here came together as a tribe and experienced a cultural florescence. Warren wrote that a "continual fire" was main-tained at their central town as a "symbol of their nationality." The discrete totemic bands that had converged at Sault Ste. Marie truly merged at Chequamegon; here the Anishinaabeg were born.[11]

The need to cooperate as intermediaries in the fur trade and as allies of the Dakota stimulated a cultural reordering. Inhabitants maintained the settlement year round, though band fragments still dispersed to hunt in winter. Sedentary village life provoked a gradual phasing out of both bilateral cross-cousin marriage and the Feast of the Dead. By creating reciprocal ties among a limited group of relatives, cross-cousin marriage hindered integration of the larger, more diverse population at Chequa-megon. It gradually became inoperative, with only remnant linguistic terms to suggest its earlier presence among the people of the Sault. Simi-larly, the Feast of the Dead was no longer necessary to unite disparate, but related kin groups, located as they were in larger settled villages.[12]

At Chequamegon, the Midéwiwin, or Grand Medicine Society, pro-vided religious confirmation of the nationalist movement behind the ethnogenesis of the Anishinaabeg as a tribe. Here the ceremonial healing complex reached its most elaborate expression. Priests and priestesses learned herbal and ritual remedies and were caretakers of Anishinaabe traditions, recounted orally with the aid of symbols incised on birchbark

scrolls. Initiates from all eight hierarchical ranks or degrees of the society were required to be present at the "national gathering" every year.
For this occasion, a large sacred wigwam was erected in the center of
town where Midéwiwin rites would be performed. Strong "bonds . . .
united one member to another" and provided spiritual leadership for the
stable, cohesive Chequamegon community that warranted a more elaborate priesthood. If tribal tradition was only nascent at Sault Ste. Marie, it
reached fruition at Chequamegon.[13]

Although French administrators responded to a glutted Montreal fur
market in 1697 by ordering the western posts to be closed, the 1713
Treaty of Utrecht ending Queen Anne's War made them reconsider. Fear
of British-Iroquois competition soon prompted them to shore up their
string of forts and posts in the western Great Lakes. France also felt
competition from new Louisiana trading outfits as *coureurs de bois*
(runners of the woods) attempted to open trade along the Missouri River.
Canadian-born French explorer and trader Pierre Gaultier de Varennes,
Sieur de la Vérendrye pushed west of Lake Superior in response to these
developments. He knew, however, that trading with the Cree would
anger their Dakota adversaries. By opening a post at Lake Pepin on the
Mississippi River French and French-Canadian traders intended to placate the Dakota by providing them with direct trading ties. Instead, the
traders inadvertently sabotaged the Chequamegon Anishinaabeg, leaving them with an even more "limited market for their trade commodities." The Dakota were none too pleased with the arrangement either.
Carefully displaying the heads of twenty-one men from La Vérendrye's
1736 expedition on beaver robes demonstrated their displeasure over the
fact that the French had chosen to supply arms to their Cree enemies.[14]

With the foundation for the always-fragile Anishinaabe-Dakota alliance fractured, the Anishinaabeg no longer had grounds for hunting in
Dakota territory. Their extreme dependence on subsistence game from
the area made them unwelcome competitors. When they attacked the
Dakota at Lake Pepin in 1736, the French deserted the post, fearful that
an all-out war might erupt. And this was only the beginning. As Chequamegon's commercial foundation collapsed, the Anishinaabeg embarked on a series of armed migrations that were to last for more than a
century.[15]

The Anishinaabeg only gradually abandoned the Chequamegon village. From Chequamegon, they launched acquisitive expeditions into the interior and then returned home. It provided a protective haven where they maintained sedentary village pursuits to support their outward thrust. Only by 1765, with the revival of the fur trade under British auspices after the French and Indian War, did it begin to diminish as the hub of Anishinaabe life. And even then, Alexander Henry still described it as a "metropolis," with fifty lodges housing 500 people.[16]

The resources of the deciduous forest transition area to the distant south and southwest of the Chequamegon village drew Anishinaabe hunters (see Map 2). The transition area extends across Minnesota in an arc running from northwest to southeast, forming an almost complete barrier between the coniferous forest and short-grass prairie. Its free-flowing streams and forest edge areas were ideal habitats for beaver, muskrat, and deer. Since it supported both subsistence game and furred game for trade, hunters were attracted to the area. It became a contested zone that Dakota and Anishinaabe hunters entered only at great risk, always prepared for war. Sporadic warfare between the two groups regulated exploitation of the transition zone by discouraging permanent habitation and creating a sort of game preserve. Periods of truce allowed intensified hunting and trapping, but this, in turn, led to resource depletion and increased conflict. The fact that bands of Anishinaabeg respected each other's fluctuating trapping areas, but not those of the Dakota, reflects their sense of ethnic solidarity. Between 1740 and 1850, traders repeatedly attempted to arrange truces between the Anishinaabeg and the Dakota so that beaver and muskrat in the rich deciduous forest transition zone might be intensively harvested. The ineffectual 1825 Prairie du Chien Treaty line was intended to eliminate conflict between the "Sioux" and "Chippewa" by establishing a boundary between them. The line ran the length of the transition area, bearing silent testimony to its pivotal role in the intertribal conflict.[17]

In their push to the interior of what is now Minnesota, the Chequamegon Anishinaabeg first established the villages of Lac Court Oreilles, Lac du Flambeau, Sandy Lake, and Leech Lake (see Map 2). Early on, the pattern of repeatedly extending their villages toward the hunting/war zones was established; hunting encampments frequently evolved into

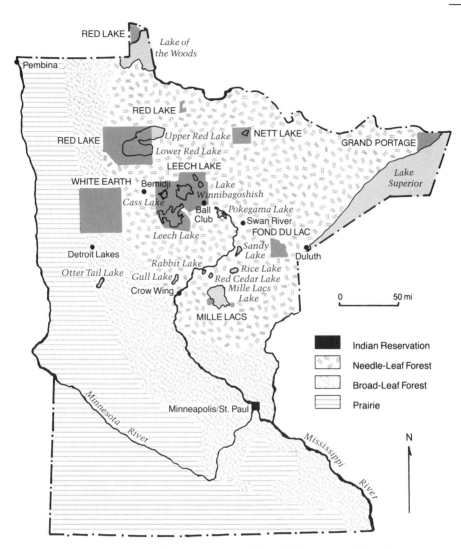

Map 2. Vegetal Zones in Minnesota. From Harold Hickerson, "The Virginia Deer and Intertribal Buffer Zones in the Upper Mississippi Valley," in Anthony Leeds and Andrew Vayda, eds. *Man, Culture, and Animals: The Role of Animals in Human Ecological Adjustments* (Washington, D.C.: American Association for the Advancement of Science, Publication 78, 1965).

permanent settlements. Several examples illustrate the pattern. Those who scored a decisive victory over the Dakota at Taylor's Falls in about 1675 pioneered a succession of villages throughout the St. Croix River watershed. Sandy Lakers founded on the border of what is now Minnesota and Wisconsin the following offshoot communities: Rice Lake, which evolved from an important ricing encampment; Pokegama Lake, further up the Mississippi River; Gull Lake, where resident hunters provisioned a trading post (Crow Island) at the confluence of the Mississippi and Crow Wing rivers; Rabbit Lake on the Rabbit River, a tributary of the Mississippi midway between Crow Island and Sandy Lake; Swan River north of Sandy Lake; Red Cedar Lake, not far from Sandy Lake and the Crow Wing-Mississippi junction; and eventually Mille Lacs, a large lake in central Minnesota that was formerly the site of a sizable Dakota village. Fluid village populations generally had strong affiliations with Sandy Lake as the parent community. The nativity of particular leaders sometimes confused contemporary observers and they often made reference to intervillage groups such as "Sandy-Gull Lake" or "Gull Lake-Swan River." By 1855, these villages had joined together to negotiate a treaty with the U.S. government in which they were represented as the "Mississippi Bands." Similarly, Leech Lake Pillagers established a spur community at Otter Tail Lake where all the sedentary signs of village life were evident by 1849, despite its vulnerability to Dakota hunting/war parties. Leech Lakers eventually expanded to Cass Lake, Lake Winnibagoshish, and White Oak Point in similar fashion.[18]

Villages, Hunting Bands, and the Crow Wing Connection

The Anishinaabeg who left Chequamegon were organized in bands of households that had become accustomed to village life. Since the amalgamated Saulteur bands had successfully integrated there, bands that initiated forays into the interior were composed of bilateral kin rather than unilineal descent groups. Bands usually consisted of a married couple in the prime of life, plus related kin, broadly defined: siblings (the Anishinaabeg reckoned that first cousins were siblings), children (those of siblings as well) and their families, elderly parents or grandparents, aunts and uncles, and friends and associates who were close enough to be considered fictive kin. Bands typically had a stable core of households

with more peripheral relatives who drifted in and out. Each househc
was a smaller agnatic extended family. Contemporary Euroameric...
traders, explorers, and missionaries tended to view male hunters who
acted on behalf of "tents" or "lodges" as heads of households, though
Henry Rowe Schoolcraft noted that, "the lodge itself, with all its arrangements, is the precinct of the rule and government of the wife." Women
decided where household members slept and stored their personal belongings and were often regarded as household leaders (usually when
men were dead or absent). Husbands had "no voice" in decisions regarding the lodge; Schoolcraft continued, "The lodge is her precinct, the
forest his." Households were discrete economic units that managed trade
accounts and debts and controlled usufruct rights and territorial alloca-
tions. They were never autonomous political units, being subordinate to
either bands or villages for most political decisions.[19]

Anishinaabe villagers made political decisions democratically, usually by the participants involved in major undertakings like hunting,
making maple sugar, or harvesting wild rice. Commonly, village councils
convened and deliberated matters of importance to all, such as making
alliances, going to war, or negotiating with various Euroamerican agents.
Even in this more formal context, no one exercised coercive control.
Leadership roles were determined in several ways. By the nineteenth
century some chiefs, or ogimaag (ogimaa, "chief; boss; king; authority")
in the Anishinaabe language, acquired their status through hereditary
channels. Men such as Eshkebugekoshe (Flat Mouth) of the Leech Lake
Pillagers, Waubojig (White Fisher) of the Lake Superior Anishinaabeg, or
Catawatabeta (Broken Tooth) of Sandy Lake achieved positions of prominence and then passed their position, and sometimes their name, to a
son. The case of Bugonaygeshig (Hole in the Day the Elder) of Sandy Lake
and then Gull Lake and Hole in the Day the Younger (Quewezaince) from
Gull Lake illustrates how this occurred. Quewezaince (Boy) assumed the
status and name of Hole in the Day (but not the name Bugonaygeshig)
upon his father's death. Certainly being born into a prominent family or
having a highly respected leader for a parent enhanced a talented child's
chances of following in their footsteps. Women of the lineage could also
assume positions of leadership and were usually referred to as "queens"
(ogimaakwe or "boss [female]; authority [female]; queen"). Some, like

Ruth Flatmouth (sister of Eshkebugekoshe) among the Pillagers, served as proxies for absent male relatives, but others were respected for their own capabilities.

Civil leaders achieved their status through their suasive skills as orators or negotiators and led decision making in civil affairs. A loose form of age-grading characterized Anishinaabe politics and civil leaders tended to be older men, the "gray-haireds," who let wisdom, patience, and level-headedness guide their actions. Conversely, warriors or war leaders typically were "younger men" or "hot heads," who were the first to defend and quick to seek revenge and pillage. Civil leaders generally acted as spokesmen and then warriors lent their support, but these two groups also had a tendency to form opposing factions, which Hickerson likened to "policy" (civil leaders) versus "action" (war leaders). Hickerson wrote that there was a "tendency for certain prominent war chiefs to shun leadership in civil affairs, including diplomacy, or have it denied them." Even so, these groups did not constitute institutionalized moieties, and some men evolved from warriors to civil leaders as experience tempered their enthusiasm for war and family life heightened their appreciation of peace. Eshkebugekoshe's case illustrates the fluid character of Anishinaabe leadership; he began what might have become a hereditary line, and was simultaneously a civil leader and a warrior. And he probably was not unique. The increase in warfare with the Dakota that attended the Anishinaabe advance into northern Minnesota called for more involvement of warriors (who were also hunters). Eventual dissatisfaction with the failure of the U.S. government to abide by treaty terms gave greater force to the position of war leaders, who became more potent rivals of civil leaders over time.[20]

Villages were composed of several bands organized in clusters of settlements. Each village was economically and politically autonomous; there was no overarching Anishinaabe "tribe" or "nation," though villages shared cultural and linguistic traits and were cross-cut by affinal ties and exogamous, totemic clans. Clan members could expect aid and hospitality from totemic relatives on an intervillage basis. Village members shared interests in common territories and resources, decided upon civil and military leaders and lent them their support, united against common enemies, negotiated together with external Euroamerican agents, and gathered together for Midéwiwin rituals. Villages were seats of sedentary pursuits where important economic activities were carried out. Task actors, predominantly women, regulated usufruct rights over fishing areas, wild rice fields, stands of maple and birch trees, and gardening areas. Each family that so desired received rights to gather resources from certain areas to ensure equitable access and adequate resource husbandry. War parties and hunting parties were recruited from villages and returned there when they accomplished their objectives.

Rituals of the Midéwiwin were celebrated at Chequamegon by newly assembled totemic band groupings. Thereafter, whenever each new village attained stability and population growth guaranteed a certain degree of security against conflict with the Dakota, an independent Midé priesthood was established. Until then, members of offshoot hunting bands returned to parent villages to observe Midéwiwin rituals. The Midéwiwin embodied the ultimate expression of new village identity.[21]

If villages represented settled life, hunting bands were the embodiment of mobility. Bands left the settled villages, most often in winter, to hunt and trap in contested areas closer to the Dakota. Groups were "small enough to subsist by hunting and gathering but large enough to furnish protection against hostile war parties and raids." Hunters cooperated to achieve greater efficiency; communal deer drives, deer impoundment, torch-light hunting, and joint bison hunts all ensured better results. Mobility and the dangers that accompanied permanent settlement inhibited the development of family hunting territories. Instead, band leaders allocated particular areas for individuals or small groups to use on an ad hoc basis. A variety of factors related to the habits of each animal species determined allocation patterns. The considerations involved in allocating beaver grounds where traplines could be used differed from strategies for most effectively hunting deer. In all cases, decisions were based on immediate, seasonal grounds, not on repeated use.[22]

Women played important roles in the hunting camps; a few even acted as skilled hunters. Priscilla Buffalohead elaborated, "Women built the lodges, spotted the game, butchered the meat; they processed the hides" both for clothing and for trade. They "fetched the venison and bear's meat from the woods" and played an important part in dividing the fruits of the hunt among relatives and friends. Traders also wrote of negotiating with both women and men for their furs, an indication that women exercised some ownership and distribution rights in what erroneously has been regarded strictly as a male domain.[23]

A regularly patterned round of seasonal harvesting activities integrated the functions of the villages and hunting bands and amply supplied subsistence needs except for brief periods of deprivation in late winter. Men and women, young and old, all served valuable functions in the seasonal round. The Anishinaabeg marked the passage of time by reference to the seasons and the skies.

Beginning in the fall, after ricing season, women wove new mats of bulrushes which were abundant in the lakes and streams. These mats replaced the sides of the wigwam, while mats woven of reeds covered the floor.

When the lakes froze, small groups of bilateral kin, the hunting bands, left for game areas. They carried with them new mats, a kettle, light food like rice and dried berries, and made a winter camp. Men shoveled snow away so that women could arrange the wigwams in a circle around a center fire where people cooked communally. Each wigwam also had a central fire over which large racks for drying meat rested.

Men made shorter trips to hunt game that contributed to their subsistence during the rest of the year, sometimes taking a sled with them to transport meat back to camp. More often, however, they returned with only a portion of the kill; women retrieved the rest. Nicholas Perrot described how a "young hunter brought his kill back to the lodge of his mother-in-law" who then divided it, making sure to give his own mother a substantial amount. Wives typically performed this function; this young man was performing bride-service. Customarily, each family hosted a feast with the first game killed; women then dried any meat not consumed for future use. Women also tanned the hides and furs that served as bedding and clothing and those intended for trade with Euroamericans. During the colder months, women busied themselves making fishnets of nettle-stalk fiber. Elders told stories and gave instruction in Anishinaabe values during the winter as well. Tales about the exploits of Nanabozho, the trickster, provided their audience with moralistic object lessons. During this period the men sometimes left for more distant hunting areas and stayed away for weeks at a time.

With the coming of spring, people left the winter camps, returned to the main villages, and immediately prepared to journey to the sugar bush. Sugaring leaders, usually women, allocated usufruct rights or rights of usage to a certain stand of maple trees to each household to which it returned annually. Birchbark and metal utensils were stored in a small lodge for future use in the annual sugaring process. During the year, people cached a store of food supplies nearby for use in the spring. The sugar camp soon became a bustle of activity. Women vigilantly kept the sap kettles boiling day and night until the thick syrup became granulated. They stored the sugar in birchbark cones and the upper mandibles of ducks' bills. Maple sugar (*ziinzibaakwad*) served as an all-purpose seasoning and as a confection. The Anishinaabeg regarded time spent at the sugar camp as one of the more pleasurable periods in the industrial year.

While women took primary responsibility for making maple sugar, some men spent time fishing with seines, hooks, traps, and spears. Fish served as an especially important food resource in the spring, but women exploited fish throughout the year, generally using nets that they constructed of nettle-stalk fiber and later of traders' twine. Pauline Colby, a missionary at Leech Lake, observed that "the woman that catches and cures the most fish is esteemed as the best provider, very much as we regard our housekeepers who have the largest store of pickles, preserves, etc." Fishing weirs in the rivers, as at a settlement on the Ontonagon River, could be focal points in themselves during the spring fish runs. In 1820, Schoolcraft exclaimed that "the number of sturgeon caught at this place [Ontonagon River] is astonishing, and the Indians rely almost entirely upon this fishery for a subsistence." By all of these means, the Anishinaabeg netted many fish which they both ate at once and cut into thin slices and dried for future consumption.

When they completed the sugaring process, families again returned to the villages to plant their gardens. Each family located its summer bark wigwam along the lake shore where it tended its own garden. Men broke additional ground every year to enlarge the garden, where women primarily cultivated corn, squash, and pumpkins. Colby described how with the assistance of older children, women completed the planting "in a few hours" in a "vein of gaity and frolic." Here again, women controlled "their own activities" and the products of their labor. Women took pride in these gardens; having "a store of corn" on hand helped them "to exercise [their] hospitality . . . in the entertainment of lodge guests." Although these subsistence gardens could grow to large sizes, the Anishinaabeg typically did not market the surplus they created. When the gardeners completed these tasks, Midé priests and priestesses gathered and requested a blessing for the garden from the *manidoo* or spirit.

Spring and summer signaled the onset of a series of gathering activities. Women and youngsters gathered berries of all sorts—blueberries, chokecherries, gooseberries, cranberries, and raspberries. They dried and ground most berries for storage, "boiling down" raspberries and spreading them to dry on pieces of birchbark. The Anishinaabeg gathered roots in the spring and basswood and birchbark in the summer. Herbal specialists selected medicinal plants in August once they had fully developed and most had blossomed.

At the close of the summer, thoughts turned to harvesting wild rice or *manoomin*. Highly nutritious, wild rice provided a significant proportion of Anishinaabe subsistence. Large groups gathered at the rice camps for the last time before bands dispersed for the winter. Ricing leaders, usually women as in other village economic endeavors, allocated a section of the rice field to each household to harvest, and everyone shared a tacit respect for these usufruct rights. Women of the household went to the fields in the summer to demarcate their area by tying some rice in sheaves and staking boundaries to show that they intended to harvest their area that year.

When the rice ripened, people gathered along the lake shores to begin the harvest. Women gathered rice in canoes often poled by men through the rice fields. They untied the sheaves, shook loose the ripe grains, and used poles gently to knock grains into the canoe. Since rice ripened gradually over a period of time, they repeated this process several times. They then spread the rice evenly on birchbark to dry, parched it in kettles, and pounded it to remove the husks. Winnowing came next, and men tread on the rice by "jigging" in clean moccasins. Afterward it was tossed on birchbark trays so that wind could carry away the chaff. The Anishinaabeg gathered successive harvests, accumulating great quantities of rice to last through the winter and beyond. Pauline Colby wrote that "a 'one sack of rice women' [was] looked upon as a very poor provider for her family." Despite the large harvests, they took only a portion of the total yield, encased some kernels in mud, and tossed them back into the water to ensure next year's crop.

After the wild rice harvest, each family group returned to its summer camp to harvest garden produce. By this time, many men had departed on their fall hunts, leaving the women and children to tend the gardens. Once this task was completed, women turned to fishing until the men returned and they all left for the winter camps.[24]

Throughout the course of a typical year, women spent more time cultivating and gathering plant resources and their activities kept them focused near lake environments. More of their gender-specific activities, especially child care and meal preparation, occurred on a daily basis. Women generally preferred working at provisioning activities in larger groups, although they frequently cooperated in households as well. All of this meant that women tended to remain near the village or base camp more than men. Men's gender-specific activities related more to animals and carried them farther away from the village or hunting camp for longer periods of time than women's tasks. Although men of a household had occasion to work together, they did so less frequently and in smaller groups than women. Primary responsibility for trade and diplomacy had rested with men, and this pattern continued once reservations were established. Men also provided for community defense, although external dangers posed less of a problem during the reservation era.

Although most tasks were associated with one specific gender, divisions were not hard and fast. In fact, men and women often worked side by side, taking responsibility for discrete tasks within a larger project. For example, men put together the frames for birchbark canoes, then women sewed the bark on with spruce roots and sealed the seams with pitch. Egalitarian relationships characterized Anishinaabe society and individuals might deviate from the general pattern without fear of recrimination.[25]

Although movement from one place to another characterized the overall seasonal pattern, stability in the timing and locations gave the annual cycle great continuity. The diverse resource base provided a hedge against failure of any one resource. Taken as a whole, this subsistence strategy particularly suited the north country of Minnesota. It had endured through generations and the Anishinaabeg adapted it to the needs of the Euroamerican fur trade.

The advent of the Euroamerican trade in furs and hides gradually transformed hunting from a subsistence activity to a commercial one. As native craft traditions were increasingly replaced by items of Euroamerican manufacture, Indians became dependent on trade goods that could only be obtained by exchanging furs and hides. Both the technology associated with the hunt and the time devoted to it intensified. This transformation did not happen overnight. Indeed, earliest exchanges involved manufactured items that had direct counterparts in Indian cultures. Only over time did Euroamerican traders succeed in introducing items that persuaded Indians to bring in ever more furs to trade. Despite the fact that most precontact Indian trade centered on ceremonial and political concerns rather than striking the best bargain, Indians eventually came to understand market terms.

Most furs for trade were taken during winter, when hunting bands dispersed from the villages. Traders extended credit to hunters for the guns, ammunition, and traps that they would need to have a successful season. Winter was a hide-processing season, with women's responsibilities spiraling. Some have suggested that an increase in polygyny attended the escalation of commercial hunting; multiple wives eased each other's work load and enhanced the status of their household by increasing the amount of trade goods available for distribution to their kin group. Hunters then visited traders in the spring to settle debts and obtain desired trade goods.

Fur traders who established posts in the western Great Lakes region faced long, unreliable supply lines, which prompted them to turn to their native trading partners for subsistence resources. Game, fish, wild rice, maple sugar, and other seasonal produce became marketable commodities in addition to furs and hides. This development created more opportunities for both women and men to barter products of their labor for Euroamerican manufactured goods that made the basic tasks of their lives easier.[26]

The relationship between the Anishinaabeg and Euroamerican traders involved more than a simple exchange of commodities. It involved a cultural exchange as well—one of the most intimate sort. Just as they had among the amalgamated Saulteur and among the Chequamegon Anishinaabeg, intermarriage and ethnogenesis characterized Franco-Anishinaabe relations in particular, and smaller numbers of Scots and British eventually followed the same pattern.

The French pioneered the structure that characterized trade with indigenous people of the western Great Lakes area. It was in place by the early eighteenth century and persisted through the British and American regimes with only slight alterations, until the fur trade economy bottomed out with the advance of lumbering and agricultural settlement. Historian Jacqueline Peterson described the following features of the system: acknowledgment of the importance of alliances with native trading partners based on honest bargaining and gift giving; licensing traders to control the amount of furs traded and the nature of relationships with native people; erecting posts to trade with Indians where they lived; using a bicultural, occupational class to travel and carry out daily relations with native trading partners; and winking at and sometimes encouraging extensive intermarriage with Indian women. As a consequence, a distinctive society arose in the area, complete with towns and villages where most economic activity focused on trade.

Peterson went on to discuss three types of "interrelated towns and villages founded by members of a 'fur trade society' prior to 1815," major "hubs" like Michilimackinac or Detroit, "smaller corporate trading towns" like La Baye (now Green Bay, Wisconsin), and "trading hamlets" like Crow Wing (Minnesota). When French and later British and Scotch fur traders married native women, they drew on the strength of kin ties to secure trading alliances. They and their métis (mixed-blood) offspring came to form a society of their own, relying on their bilingual, bicultural skills to mediate between conservative Indians and Euroamerican society. These people inhabited the network of fur trade towns. Almost all occupations revolved around trading furs; farmers were a rarity. Before 1790 when the ascendence of monopoly trade companies established a caste system based on both ethnicity and wealth, the towns had relatively few status distinctions. They drew their subsistence from the surrounding area, depending on their native kin for food and know-how, rather than relying on imported goods (except to trade). Not simply "an extension of French colonial culture," theirs was a syncretic culture in which they blended native and French elements to form a unique adaptation.

Not until the late eighteenth century did so-called "jack-knife posts," or "trading hamlets," as Peterson termed them, appear. These posts were small outlets where one trader or a few related trading families directed activities. Fur trade employees and their native and métis wives were "surrounded by a sea of Indian hunters and relatives" with whom "marital alliance[s] had been forged." Often these communities resembled "patriarchal fiefdoms" where small networks of "brothers, cousins, or fathers and sons" and their métis families lived. As the central economic activity, trade demanded ever-widening networks and expansion as game was depleted. Hence, the direction of growth was outward and tended toward the continual creation of new trading hamlets.[27]

The Anishinaabeg were most familiar with these sorts of trade communities. The Cadotte family, from which William Whipple Warren, the Anishinaabe historian of mixed descent, was descended, held sway at La Pointe and dealt extensively with the Chequamegon Anishinaabeg. Michel Cadotte, the family patriarch, married the daughter of *ogimaa* Waubojig, in archetypical fur trade fashion.[28] As the Anishinaabeg splintered and embarked on their interior migration, traders followed, establishing new posts at Lac Court Oreilles and Lac du Flambeau in present-day Wisconsin, Sandy Lake, and eventually Crow Wing in present-day Minnesota.

The Beaulieu family best illustrates this pattern. In 1804, Bazil Hudón dit Beaulieu, a fur trade employee of the Northwest Company from La Pointe, moved to Lac du Flambeau. He married Margaret or Ogemahge-shigoquay, a woman of Franco-Anishinaabe descent from farther east, in 1808, and his first son, Clement Hudón dit Beaulieu, was born three years later. Clement worked for a time in a store at La Pointe, before marrying Elizabeth Farling, who was the daughter of a German immigrant serving in the British army at Mackinaw and Nancy Frazer, a woman of mixed descent. No doubt while on a trip associated with his trading ventures, Clement met Elizabeth in Grand Haven, Michigan, where they wed. Elizabeth gave birth to their first son, Charles, at La Pointe. Clement moved his small American Fur Company Fond du Lac department store to Sandy Lake when treaty annuities (money, goods and services) began to be distributed there. Their fifth child, Julia, was born at Sandy Lake. Clement again shifted his base of operations to Crow Wing in 1837, still as part of the American Fur Company's Fond du Lac department. Their seventh child, Gustave H., was born in 1854 at Crow Wing, as were the rest of their children.[29]

In their parallel migration into interior Wisconsin and Minnesota, the métis perpetuated the pattern of simultaneous exogamy and endogamy. Early on, a *coureurs de bois* might marry a native woman which would help to secure trading alliances; later, he was likely to pair up with a métis woman who shared his own ethnic background. By the early 1800s, however, the pool of métis people in the western Great Lakes area was large enough to allow as much endogamy as exogamy in their marital choices. As trade with Euroamericans became increasingly ingrained in native economies, British and American traders wasted little time in giving gifts to lubricate the trade, and actions geared to nurturing trading alliances with native bands declined in importance. Major métis families that moved to Crow Wing, and eventually to White Earth Reservation, established fewer marital ties with the Mississippi bands of Anishinaabeg than they did among themselves.[30]

The Morrison family illustrates this composite pattern. William Morrison and his younger brother Allan were sons of a Scottish immigrant, Allan, from the Hebrides, and a French-Canadian woman (métis?) named Jane (or Jessie) Wadin. William had begun clerking in a Montreal store before he turned fifteen. At sixteen, his father apprenticed him to the Northwest Company and he left for Grand Portage, the Company's western headquarters on Lake Superior. In 1802, he was sent to Leech Lake and from there to an outpost on the Crow Wing River among the Pillager band of Anishinaabeg. They named him Shagahnansheence or "Little Englishman." His familiarity with the broad geographic area of northern Minnesota and its native people won him a promotion; he was placed in charge of a number of trading posts, with headquarters at Sandy Lake. William remained with the Northwest Company until 1816, when he received a better offer from the American Fur Company. He was placed in charge of the Fond du Lac department and remained there with John Jacob Astor's business until 1826, when he retired to buy an island in the St. Lawrence River, engage in farming for a while, and eventually settle in Berthier, Canada, where he became a merchant and served as a judge for the county court.

While William lived among the Pillager band of Anishinaabeg, he married a Pillager woman and fathered two boys and a girl. His wife's mother, in accordance with Anishinaabe custom, took care of the children after his wife died in childbirth. The children, therefore, were immersed in Anishinaabe culture as they were raised. Although Morrison tried to take his children with him in 1826 when he left Minnesota, their grandmother successfully hid them from him and retained custody. Later, his son, Joseph or Aygans, gained renown for attempting to persuade Hole in the Day not to carry out his threats to kill agency employees and traders in 1862 in collusion with Dakota leader Little Crow in the Dakota uprising to the south. Morrison's first marriage exemplifies the pattern of early métis exogamy.

William Morrison's second wife was the daughter of a trader named Roussain at Fond du Lac, Minnesota. She and William had no children of their own, but she had two sons and a daughter from a former marriage. Her first son joined William Fremont's expedition to the Pacific coast and settled in California, where he died in 1850. Her youngest son worked at jobs in Michigan, Illinois, Wisconsin, and Minnesota before he settled near the U.S.-Canadian boundary in the Red River Valley. He eventually became a member of the Territorial Legislature of Minnesota. The experiences of Ms. Roussain's sons are consonant with what elite métis men in the western Great Lakes might have expected; they were itinerant, but at the upper echelons of métis society. Morrison's second union with a métis woman typifies the dominant métis pattern in the western Great Lakes of endogamy in later marital choices.

William's brother Allan apprenticed with the American Fur Company for five years in 1821. He spent most of his time at Red Lake, Minnesota. In 1825, he married Charlotte Louisa Chaboullier, a métis woman "of culture and refinement" born at Old Fort William who became known as "the hostess of Crow Wing," by whom he had several children. His female children married either métis or Euroamerican men or did not marry; in no case did they marry Anishinaabe men. His son, John George Morrison, was born at Lake Winnibagoshish in 1843 while his father managed a trading post for the American Fur Company. After the Civil

War, in consideration of the fear inspired in white Minnesotans by the specter of a united effort between Little Crow and Hole in the Day, John George was placed in charge of a corps of scouts from Crow Wing to determine Anishinaabe sentiments.

During this time he married Margaret Elizabeth Fairbanks, daughter of Robert Fairbanks and Catherine Beaulieu. They had ten children, six of whom were born in Crow Wing, and four of whom were born at the White Earth Reservation. Later, John George himself moved to White Earth, and then eventually to the Red Lake Reservation in 1893. The families of Allan Morrison, Jr., and his son John George illustrate well the evolving pattern. Although they had kin ties with the Anishinaabeg through William's first wife, they and their children did not intermarry with local native bands; they married among métis families.

While there were certainly marital ties between métis of the western Great Lakes and the Minnesota Anishinaabeg, the ties among métis families were more prominent. The fact that Clement Beaulieu's grandmother was a sister of the grandmother (Nahgaunaush) of Wabonaquod or White Cloud (an important hereditary *ogimaa* of the Mississippi bands), made the two men cousins, reckoned according to Anishininaabe descent rules which defined first cousins and siblings as equivalent and applied the same kinship terminology for both. But these ties were few and rather "distant" even by Anishinaabe standards. Wabonaquod most frequently referred to the métis among his people as his "sons-in-law," a symbolic term emphasizing that their social and cultural origins lay elsewhere. Their fur trader forebears had married native women but had not become assimilated as Anishinaabeg; instead, they maintained their own distinctive ethnic identity. Marital bonds among métis families like the Beaulieus, Fairbanks, and Morrisons were far more numerous and culturally significant than their ties with the Anishinaabeg, as frequent discussions questioning whether they had been formally "adopted" into the group attest.[31]

Employees of the Northwest Company and, later, the American Fur Company pushed south from La Pointe, or the Fond du Lac district, and set up posts in the Crow Wing area. Allan Morrison and his brother William traded in the area as early as 1800. Others soon followed. John H. Fairbanks, Paul H. Beaulieu, and Clement H. Beaulieu were all affiliated with the American Fur Company. After the 1847 Treaty, the Crow Wing settlement was founded on the Mississippi opposite the mouth of the Crow Wing River. The following year, Charles W. Borup, as agent of the American Fur Company, sold all of its posts in the "Northern Outfit" to Charles H. Oakes. In the gulf of uncertainty created by this transaction, Franco-Anishinaabe trader Clement H. Beaulieu and Anglo-Anishinaabe trader John H. Fairbanks formed the "Beaulieu and Fairbanks" firm and became "the principal supplier of all the Chippewa Indian posts."

Many surnames among the population at White Earth derived from those who relocated to Crow Wing from the La Pointe area. Among them were Beaulieu, Beaupre, Bellanger, Dufort, Fairbanks, McDonald, McGillis, Montreuill, Morrison, and Warren. Establishment of the Chippewa Agency at the Gull Lake settlement near Crow Wing in the early 1850s also generated trade and agency business. Merchants, government employees, lumbermen, and missionaries took up residence as well. Added to the surnames in the White Earth population were Breck, Boutwell, Johnson, Jordain, Lynde, Parker, Peake, Richardson, Rohrer, Selkrig, Sloan, and Whipple. The surnames of residents of Crow Wing and Gull Lake formed a significant proportion of those at White Earth.

By 1850, a village had developed, replete with various trading posts, warehouses, saloons, and blacksmith shops. The Crow Wing area had matured into a bustling trade entrepôt astride a section of the Red River Trail network. The settlement served as the main depot for trade with the Anishinaabeg as well as a major crossing of the Mississippi River. The Woods Trail of the Red River Trail network passed through Crow Wing, where trader-merchants served the needs of the ox-cart travelers and nearby Anishinaabe communities. Ox-carts were constructed entirely of wood and leather, causing them to creak and shriek as they transported furs and commodities between St. Paul, Pembina, and the Red River Colony in Canada (travelers could hear them from miles away). Transplanted Lake Superior traders easily acclimated themselves to doing business with the northern Minnesota/Canadian ox-cart trade. The erection of Fort Gaines (later renamed Fort Ripley) in 1848 further encouraged Euroamerican settlement, providing protection and security.

Crow Wing, with its ethnically and linguistically diverse population, came to resemble other western Great Lakes trading communities. Traders and their métis offspring formed a society of their own, perpetuating their style of life through increased marital endogamy and continuing to mediate between conservative Anishinaabe bands centered around Gull Lake and the surrounding fur trade society. To the ear of a traveler, the place sounded like a "Babel of mixed races and tongues." In a sense, the Crow Wing and nearby Gull Lake communities continued a pattern already well established throughout the Great Lakes watershed.

In the mid-1840s, the economy of north-central Minnesota began to shift from fur trading to lumbering. The lucrative trade in furs suffered as animal populations dwindled. Economic attention shifted from the forests' animals to the trees themselves, as the St. Croix triangle and Minnesota's northeastern "arrowhead region" felt the lumbermen's axes. Sawmills mushroomed and "voyageurs became lumberjacks." Residents succeeded in establishing Crow Wing County in 1857, with Crow Wing Village as the county seat. Former traders served in all important county government positions, perpetuating their positions of prominence in the local area. During the height of the regional lumber industry, a group of surveyors and speculators made their base at Crow Wing, among them Clement H. Beaulieu and Hole in the Day the Younger. These resourceful individuals made their livelihoods by mediating between the Gull Lake Indian community and the larger world. In addition, they were attuned to national and local legislation and exhibited creativity in their attempts to turn a profit. This cadre of traders, merchants, lumbermen, and speculators clearly understood how the market operated.[32]

Indians in the area had altered their practices by hunting more intensively and selling foodstuffs to traders, but they continued to rely on the products of their environment. Métis trader-merchants encouraged them to continue in these pursuits. A symbiotic relationship persisted between them, as it had during the heyday of the fur trade, and they profited from their mutual association. These trader-merchants and their Anishinaabe clientele transplanted the way of life they had evolved to the White Earth Reservation. The social and economic patterns later evident at White Earth had congealed here in the 1850s and 1860s.

Treaties and Anishinaabe Identity

The expansion of the U.S. market economy brought burgeoning white settlement to the western Great Lakes by 1820. Most important, the advent of cash-crop agriculture and livestock production would force the

Anishinaabeg to make more radical adjustments than the trade in furs and commodities had ever demanded. Facilitating this transition was the paramount concern of the U.S. government; avoiding conflict with the region's indigenous inhabitants was an important, but secondary, goal. As historian Reginald Horsman observed, native people received "as much justice as was compatible with the wholesale acquisition of land."

After an unsuccessful attempt to deal with native groups as conquered nations after the Revolutionary War, the United States adopted a heritage of treaty making from preceding European nations. Typically, treaties promised money, goods, services, reservations of land, and certain rights to resources in return for specific cessions of land and professions of peaceful intentions. Such federal legislation as the 1787 Northwest Ordinance, the Indian Trade and Intercourse Acts, and the Marshall trilogy of Cherokee decisions prescribed the relationship between Indians and the U.S. government; treaties further refined the details.[33]

Anishinaabe social and political organization confounded U.S. policymakers. Besides recognizing autonomous villages and their off-shoot hunting bands, the Anishinaabeg also distinguished regional differences among themselves based largely on geography, environment, and concomitant cultural features. Mississippi River bands were termed "Ke-che-se-be-win-in-e-wug (Great River men)." "Mun-o-min-ik-a-sheenh-ug (Rice makers)" described those who lived in the St. Croix River drainage. Villages around Leech and Otter Tail lakes, some of the earliest to contest with the Dakota, were "Muk-me-dua-win-in-e-wug (Pillagers)." Those located between the "Great River men" and the "Ke-che-gum-me-win-in-e-wug (Men of the Great Water)," who lived on the shores of Lake Superior near present-day Duluth, were "Be-ton-uk-eeng-ain-ub-e-jig" or "Those who sit on the borders." Far to the north on Lake Superior lived the "Sug-waun-dug-ah-win-in-e-wug (Men of the thick fir woods)." Much farther north were the "Omushke-goes (Swamp-people)." Sometimes treaty negotiators targeted groups that conformed roughly to these divisions, but often they did not. In fact, some treaties established "bands" and "nations" whose entire legitimacy rested on nothing more than the paper on which the treaties were written.[34]

Substantial land cessions began with the 1837 Treaty negotiated at St. Peter's, the first treaty to recognize the rights of the "Chippewa Nation" to cede portions of Minnesota and Wisconsin. The 1837 Treaty did not differentiate between the various bands located throughout this vast area, commonly referring to them collectively as the "Chippewa Nation." While the terminology bore little relation to political reality for the Anishinaabeg, the "nation" nomenclature would later weigh significantly as present-day descendants press their claims in the courts.

Geographic location continued to determine the band aggregates targeted for negotiations by the U.S. government. The 1842 Treaty of La Pointe divided the "Chippewa Nation" into the "Chippewa of the Mississippi" and the "Lake Superior Chippewa." The presence of valuable deposits of copper and iron on the north shore of Lake Superior prompted policymakers to attempt to isolate native people of this area in negotiations. Their proximity in the Mississippi headwaters area brought the Mississippi and Pillager bands together as a focus for further treaty cessions. Similarly, the Pembina and Red Lake bands came to be closely associated. Even though these particular divisions best suited the aims of the U.S. government, the rights and responsibilities attached to them took on meaning for the people associated with each treaty. Well into the twentieth century, and even after band members had scattered over several reservations, band leaders would make reference to these treaties as they continued to look after their rights and tried to hold the U.S. government to its end of the bargain. The Anishinaabeg regarded treaty affiliations as being of the utmost importance. Band leaders spent considerably more time attempting to persuade the U.S. government to live up to its treaty obligations than in trying to dissolve the relationship already cemented.

Through a negotiation process that often placed them at a disadvantage, the Anishinaabeg relinquished the larger portion of northern Minnesota between 1837 and 1883. Land cessions concentrated Anishinaabe bands onto progressively smaller areas of land, while permitting them to continue to exploit ceded lands for subsistence purposes in much the same manner as they always had. With the apparent continuation of usufruct regulations as they understood them, it may have seemed to the Anishinaabeg that little had really changed.

The 1854 Treaty of La Pointe established the first "reservations" for the Lake Superior bands, and underscored their separate status from the

Mississippi bands in diplomatic relations with the U.S. government. The U.S. policymakers built provisions into treaties to foster the "civilization" of the natives. Having located their own culture at the apex of a universal scale of human civility, they incorporated their ideas about "progress" and social evolution into treaties with Indian groups. Treaty terms included agricultural accouterments and educational provisions to aid the Anishinaabeg in achieving the yeoman farmer ideal. Earliest treaties contained only modest versions of these provisions; most of the people living within the vast areas "ceded" scarcely felt their effects.

Over the years the assimilative thrust of the treaties became more evident. Negotiators promised increasing amounts of money and services designed to reach more people. Voluntary allotment provisions offered the potential to farm privately owned plots of up to eighty acres of land to those willing to undertake the agrarian experiment. Policymakers believed that these provisions would induce individual Indians to "progress" one more increment along the idealized pathway to "civilization" that they envisioned. "Civilization," in the American vein, was to compensate for land cessions.

The Anishinaabeg retained the right to hunt and gather their livelihood from the lands they "ceded" and may have believed that treaty provisions gave the U.S. government the same sort of usufruct privileges that they respected among themselves. From an Anishinaabe perspective, as long as the floral and faunal resources remained accessible to all, how much could it matter that the United States "owned" the land?

But the 1854 and 1855 treaties ushered in a new era. These treaties not only brought substantial land cessions to the Anishinaabeg, but also greatly altered conditions of life. Previously, they had been acquainted with the few Euroamericans who lived among them in their country. Now "strangers" were everywhere. Lumbermen, farmers, and petty merchants swarmed onto ceded lands without regard for the Anishinaabe population around them. The greater proximity of Euroamericans reignited episodes of epidemic diseases. Not only did a smallpox epidemic in 1854 force people to disperse into the bush to save themselves, but venereal disease and alcohol abuse debilitated them. The Reverend Breck, a missionary, wrote that "Crow Wing has only thirty-two dwellings, but there are seven whiskey shops." He described how the Leech

Lake Pillagers carried "five to ten gallon kegs" from Crow Wing "on their shoulders." Small wonder that John Johnson Enmegahbowh, an Odawa Episcopal missionary among the Anishinaabeg, proclaimed Crow Wing "Whiskey City."

The 1855 Treaty established the first reservations for the Mississippi and Pillager bands. Although band leaders had come to believe that treaty provisions would aid them in adjusting to altered conditions of life, the treaty signers suffered reproach. Eshkebugekoshe's horse met death at the hands of young men from Leech Lake, acting in symbolic protest. Even Hole in the Day the Younger was rebuked, despite the growing popularity of his action-oriented approach among the younger element of the bands.

Other disturbing features of treaty relationships were also coming into focus. Regardless of how carefully band leaders saw to their concerns in treaty negotiations, congressmen frequently altered the versions they finally passed. And fulfillment of even those altered treaty provisions was problematic at best. If Congress failed to appropriate funds, annuity payments could not be made. This problem was chronic and complaints about past-due sums of money were regular features of any new negotiations. Annuity fraud also took the form of collusion between agents, who ordered goods at inflated prices, and contracters, who supplied inferior merchandise. The "Indian ring" profited at the expense of treaty beneficiaries. All of these developments demonstrated to the Anishinaabeg their growing subordination to the U.S. government.[35]

Beginning in 1837, treaties with the Anishinaabeg also included substantial amounts of money to pay off what were termed "traders' debts." Supposedly, these moneys were slated to offset debts that the Anishinaabeg had amassed with various traders, whose names were usually appended to each treaty. But Anishinaabe leaders felt that they had cause to protest; sometimes the amounts of money were extraordinarily high— $50,000 in the 1855 Treaty alone. Whether these debts were legitimate or not, U.S. negotiators knew that it was important to curry the favor of traders, who were often of mixed descent; they could smooth the bargaining process with their native associates.

Treaties also increasingly evidenced the evolving relationship between the Anishinaabeg and their métis cousins. Although blood status had traditionally meant little to the Anishinaabeg, Indian leaders and federal authorities directed special treaty provisions toward the Anishinaabeg's "half-breed" relatives. Earliest terms provided money to be distributed among "half-breeds," many of whom belonged to trading families. Later treaties encouraged "half-breeds" to take allotments on the ceded lands or the public domain, away from the tribe. Policymakers expected these individuals to sever their tribal ties and journey further down the idealized yellow brick road to assimilation. Some of those who took advantage of these early allotment provisions eventually moved to the White Earth Reservation.

Issuance of "half-breed scrip," as these early allotment provisions were termed, accomplished far different goals than policymakers originally had in mind. In 1863, the Commissioner of Indian Affairs decided that residence among the Anishinaabeg at the time of the 1854 Treaty did not determine "half-breeds'" eligibility to take scrip. This broadly construed ruling allowed land speculators an entrance into Anishinaabe ceded lands. Speculators advertised the benefits to be gained and attracted people with marginal ties to the Anishinaabeg to come from all over Minnesota, Wisconsin, and as far away as the Red River Colony in Canada to claim scrip. An 1871 congressional investigation revealed how speculators had located the scrip on valuable pine and mineral lands. The métis trader Clement H. Beaulieu located his land scrip in the village of Crow Wing, as did other speculators such as Allan Morrison, John Fairbanks, Charles Borup, C. C. Andrews, J. R. Moulton, and Hole in the Day the Younger, who opportunistically bought up "half-breed scrip." Traders of mixed descent who fully understood how the market operated always availed themselves of opportunities like those posed by the issuance of "half-breed scrip."[36]

But these were not the opportunities pursued by most Anishinaabeg. As game diminished, Euroamerican settlement increased, and the U.S. government continued to renege on its treaty obligations, civil leaders sought to strengthen their farming efforts. Protestants who had proselytized among them had always urged them to begin to farm for the market instead of for their subsistence alone. Now, with a subsistence crisis at hand, they ventured to reach out to a new breed of missionaries—Episcopalians who employed native ministers and seemed to behave as the Anishinaabeg thought allies should.

Missionaries with the American Board of Commissioners for Foreign Missions and their early Episcopal successors, James Lloyd Breck and Ebenezer S. Peake, failed because of their insensitivity to Anishinaabe customs. However, with the conversion of John Johnson Enmegahbowh, the Episcopals found a man who worked hard to understand and live in accordance with Anishinaabe values. Although he was of Odawa descent, he grew up in a Christian Anishinaabe village in Canada. These villagers had found that embracing Methodism while carefully maintaining elements of their Anishinaabe heritage allowed them to pull themselves back from the morass of alcoholism and poverty. In the 1830s they allied with the Methodists with the aim of spreading their message of hope to other native communities. Enmegahbowh joined this effort. Historian Rebecca Kugel described their training program: "First they worked as interpreters at mission stations, then as schoolteachers and assistants; finally, after some formal religious education, they became qualified as missionaries."

Enmegahbowh came to the United States in 1834 as a mission interpreter. Within the next ten years, he married the niece (Biwabikogizigokwe or Iron Sky Woman) of Bugonaygeshig (Hole in the Day the Elder) and his brother Strong Ground, important leaders at Sandy Lake, thereby establishing a primary affinal relationship with the Mississippi bands. At his urging, the Episcopalians established the St. Columba Mission at Gull Lake in 1852. Enmegahbowh himself became an Episcopal deacon in 1859.

Enmegahbowh's understanding of Anishinaabe values emphasizing generosity, sharing, and reciprocity enabled him to interact effectively with band members. As he generously gave of his own personal belongings and resources, he differentiated himself from other Euroamerican missionaries who had come before. Several important band leaders were especially drawn to Enmegahbowh's message: Wabonaquod (White Cloud), son of Waubojig (White Fisher), who inherited his father's position at Gull Lake and evolved as the most prominent leader of the Mississippi bands; Minogeshig (Fine Day) and Iahbay (Buck) from Mille Lacs, where desperate conditions brought by close contact with Euroamericans made the farming option seem especially attractive; Mezhucegeshig (Horizon) a lesser leader from Rabbit Lake, whose wife and two children had converted to the Episcopalian religion before him; and Gull

Lakers Nabunashkong and Manidowab, both of whom had had strong ties with Hole in the Day the Younger and often supported his more militant brand of politics. None of these men evinced a great deal of enthusiasm for the Episcopalian religion. Instead, they hoped that intensified farming efforts would help rejuvenate their communities and they respected the lessons that Enmegahbowh had earlier learned from the Canadian Anishinaabeg.[37]

At this point, several issues converged. As pressures on the Anishinaabeg mounted, their subsistence crisis worsened. Lumber companies in particular, with their ties to political interests in the state, pressed for access to the timber on Anishinaabe ceded lands and reservations. Politicians were apt to be responsive. At the same time, the influential Episcopal Bishop Henry Benjamin Whipple, who had long been a voice for reform in Indian affairs, began to argue that the Anishinaabeg of north-central Minnesota should be relocated to an area of greater agricultural potential where they might be sheltered from the negative aspects of involvement with Euroamericans.

The plan to concentrate various Anishinaabe bands together on one reservation first surfaced in the 1864 Treaty with the Mississippi, Pillager, and Lake Winnibagoshish bands (an earlier treaty drafted in 1863 was quickly aborted). Policymakers focused on the Leech Lake area for their concentration plan. However, the lack of suitable agricultural land at Leech Lake sent them searching for a new location for their experiment. The 1867 Treaty with the Mississippi bands established the White Earth Reservation in an effort to increase the amount of fertile farming land at the concentration site. The Gull Lake band, located near the confluence of the Mississippi and Crow Wing rivers, became the target for policymakers' experiment in social engineering. The U.S. commissioners persuaded the Mississippi bands to cede land around Leech Lake set aside by the 1864 Treaty in exchange for a reservation with greater agricultural potential, even though their jurisdiction over the land was questionable. After negotiations, Indian leaders and U.S. officials focused on the White Earth Reservation to carry out their plans.

Treaty provisions established the skeletal assimilation framework that the U.S. government intended the Anishinaabeg to follow. The 1867 Treaty mandated allotment provisions, but structured them in a novel way. Cultivating 10 acres of land would entitle an individual to title to 40 acres. Increasing the acreage they cultivated would allow each Indian to accumulate up to 160 acres. Lands so held were to be exempt from taxation or attachment for debt and could only be sold to another Anishinaabe with permission from the Secretary of the Interior. These allotment measures were intended to promote industry and to reward individual efforts.

Policymakers buttressed the assimilation program by agreeing to provide financial support for agricultural implements, breeding stock, both saw- and gristmills, schools, medical care, and annuities. Terms of the 1867 Treaty limited eligibility for these benefits to those "mixed-bloods" who actually lived among the Anishinaabeg on one of their reservations. The 1867 Treaty, then, narrowed the field of participants and outlined specific components of the assimilation program.[38]

The 1868 Removal to White Earth

The Gull Lake band's migration to the White Earth Reservation might have occurred rather uneventfully had it not been for the murder of Hole in the Day the Younger, a controversial figure. His father, Bugonaygeshig, or Hole in the Day the Elder, a respected civil and war leader, and uncle, Strong Ground, a war leader, both originally from Sandy Lake and then Gull Lake, were not above advocating a militaristic course of action when circumstances warranted. Increasingly, this approach worked in the mid-nineteenth century; contests first with the Dakota and then with the ever-unreliable U.S. government brought honor and respect to successful young warriors above and beyond that which they would normally have been accorded. Hole in the Day the Younger, a charismatic man typically clad in a green blanket, black waistcoat, pink calico shirt, beaded leggings and moccasins, and feathered headdress, parlayed the skill of combining civil leadership with militarism into what amounted to a career.

While some respected band leaders turned to the Episcopalian farming program to help them out of their dilemma, Hole in the Day staged confrontations with local Euroamericans and, by association, the U.S. government. Not content to acquiesce in sending petitions and entreaties to government officials, only to be ignored, he commanded attention.

In 1862, his carefully coordinated attacks on symbols of American domination, the St. Columba Mission and the registry office where land claims were filed, coincided with Dakota raids in the southern part of the state that escalated into what became known as the "Sioux Uprising." It was a gamble that the shrewd leader transformed into a major coup—at least as far as his relationship with the U.S. government was concerned. He outmaneuvered Commissioner of Indian Affairs William Dole and his troops when they made a special detour just to meet with (and capture) him. The fiery leader's actions prompted the Minnesota State Legislature to appoint a special commission to negotiate a settlement with him. Among its members were Governor Alexander Ramsey and Senator Henry M. Rice, attesting to the seriousness accorded to Hole in the Day's demands. Despite his volatility—behavior that other Anishinaabe leaders felt compelled to dissociate themselves from—his actions brought results. Supplies were forthcoming and treaty provisions were more generous when Hole in the Day was in charge. Rather than being punished for his extreme tactics, he was rewarded. Consequently, he had no reason to tone down his approach.[39]

Instead of relying on demanding Episcopalian missionaries, Hole in the Day forged alliances with local traders who had influential ties to political and business leaders across the state. Although this worked to his advantage time and again, it was also to be his literal undoing. Playing political brinkmanship meant that he might go over the edge.

Hole in the Day had curried favor with local traders of mixed descent such as Clement H. Beaulieu and John Fairbanks. As skilled mediators with a far-flung network of associates, they were as useful to him as he was to them. For their part, the métis traders needed the aid of a powerful band leader to succeed in having suspicious trade debts written into treaty provisions. They also found Hole in the Day to be an effective ally in staving off the attacks of Episcopal band leaders who would have liked for them to be evicted from the area because of their whiskey peddling and general bad influence. Their relationship was a symbiotic one.

Many Anishinaabeg recognized the close ties between Hole in the Day and the métis traders. They frequented each other's homes and socialized together at saloons on occasion. Reportedly, Hole in the Day regarded them as "his own sons" and they looked on him as "their chief."

The métis traders had been added to the annuity rolls of the Mississippi bands at Hole in the Day's request.

However, for reasons that are not entirely clear, Hole in the Day firmly opposed inclusion of "French-Canadian mixed-bloods" who had made their homes at Crow Wing in the removal to the White Earth Reservation. Conflict between them had been brewing for several years before the 1868 removal. Hole in the Day believed that the "white men of Crow Wing" were responsible for a suspicious fire that destroyed his two-story home at Gull Lake in 1862. Shortly thereafter, they came to blows. One day Maheengaunce, a politically active member of the Mille Lacs band who eventually moved to White Earth, saw Hole in the Day come out of a Crow Wing saloon with a blackened eye that was swollen shut. "See what my relations, the mixed bloods, were doing to me. I can hardly see," Maheengaunce heard him say. He went on, "Wait awhile. I shall get back at them. . . . After awhile they will not receive their annuity payments any more." Indignant at the treatment he had received, Hole in the Day resolved to "use the butcher knife" to sever ties that métis traders hoped to establish with the reservation that he claimed responsibility for creating. Maheengaunce testified that the flamboyant leader declared that he "wasn't going to allow them to come on this reservation."

Moving to White Earth was important for the métis traders at Crow Wing. Initially they had opposed the White Earth concentration plan; removing the Gull Lake band would eliminate most of their clientele. Failing in this, they determined to make the best of the situation. They had pinned their hopes for renewing their economic niche as mediators on White Earth; the denouement of the fur trade in northern Minnesota left them few other options. They had not counted on Hole in the Day and his boastful decree.

Not so mysteriously, perhaps, Hole in the Day was soon found dead by the roadside one August evening in 1868 after he had ridden off to try to renegotiate the 1867 Treaty. The assassination party was rumored to have consisted of Leech Lake Pillagers. Many had reason to want Hole in the Day dead. For some, murdering him may have assuaged their anger and jealousy over his extravagant accumulation of wealth. He owned two homes, land, had several wives (a daughter of an important leader from each of four Mississippi band villages and a white woman, Helen Kater, whom he had recently married while on a trip to Washington, D.C.); he employed a bodyguard/interpreter; had finagled his own annuity written into the 1867 Treaty; and was rumored to have stashed a "pot of gold" somewhere near Gull Lake. The murderers stripped the chief and took his possessions (including a gold watch that they later tried to sell to Julia Warren Spears, sister of Anishinaabe métis historian William Warren), and then robbed his home, terrifying his family in the process. These were sure signs that they resented his materialistic lifestyle. Leech Lake Pillagers resented his arrogance in agreeing to a cession of land located near their reservation in 1864. And for the métis traders and their relatives, Hole in the Day's death cleared the way for them to perpetuate their roles as cultural brokers and join in the exodus to White Earth.

Rumors about motives behind Hole in the Day's murder abounded, but many individuals reiterated one particular story. Kahgegayaush, a Gull Laker who moved to White Earth six years after the first removals, testified that métis trader Clement H. Beaulieu, Agent Ruffee, and Beyuneesh summoned himself and three other Indians (Kahbenungweway, Kayquaygegahbow, and Chinggwabay) to come to a place where "lots of others," among them métis traders John G. Morrison and Robert Fairbanks, had gathered. There they were each promised $1,000, a house, a team of horses, and chief's status if they killed Hole in the Day. When Kahgegayaush was denied half up front, he refused, saying, "I can't do that . . . cut out the person's life for nothing." Had they come up with the payment, however, he would have obliged. Obviously he held no deep reverence for the controversial *ogimaa*.

Mezhucegeshig, a minor Rabbit Lake leader who grew to prominence at White Earth, told a similar tale. Approximately seven years after the assassination, seven men came to him as their "uncle," confessed to killing Hole in the Day, complained that "there was some promises made to them to be paid," and identified Clement H. Beaulieu as the person who made the promises. The allegations surprised Mezhucegeshig because he had thought, as had many others, that Clement and Hole in the Day had gotten along well. Nonetheless, two of the men were his nephews and he advised them to "let it go . . . for fear that there shall be an outbreak, and your relatives will be killing one another on this reservation."

Regardless of the veracity of this, or any other, story, it is important for understanding future White Earth politics to emphasize that this is what people insisted had happened. Believing that Clement H. Beaulieu and métis trader John Fairbanks had resorted to hiring assassins made Mezhucegeshig ever-vigilant of any association with them. Hole in the Day's murder kindled suspicion and hard feelings between people who moved to the White Earth Reservation.[40]

Gull Lake leaders who had opposed Hole in the Day took heart at the prospect of moving to the White Earth Reservation. Their community had fractured during the 1850s and 1860s. Unable to contain his influence, important band leaders like Bad Boy and Buffalo had sought refuge among the Mille Lacs Anishinaabeg. They and their constituents refused to return to Gull Lake even to receive their annuities; they took them separately until they moved to White Earth. Even Enmegahbowh, his mission utterly sacked during the 1862 hostilities, left to join his closest Gull Lake associates at Mille Lacs. A coalition of Gull Lake leaders, many of those who most resented Hole in the Day, hoped to reestablish their community at White Earth, with the aid of their Episcopalian allies.

Even so, the first group of emigrants reflected the symbiotic society that had evolved in the Crow Wing and Gull Lake vicinities. Ignoring Hole in the Day's admonitions that he would personally kill the first person to leave for White Earth, the vanguard set forth on 4 June 1868. Truman Warren, descended from the La Pointe Cadotte family and brother of Julia Spears and William Warren, was hired by the U.S. government to oversee the removal. He assembled about two hundred people at the "Old Agency" and left, leading a "long train of ox teams." Paul H. Beaulieu served as interpreter and the first government farmer. Wabonaquod, Nabunashkong, and Manidowab, all respected Mississippi band *ogimaag*, were among the first party to depart. Nabunashkong, or Isaac Tuttle, who was "a brave as well as a chief," led the way in defiance of his old ally, Hole in the Day.

Hole in the Day had opposed commencing the migration until the U.S. government built houses for the immigrants and constructed a sawmill and gristmill; he hoped to renegotiate the treaty before it was too late. He worried that the emigrant Anishinaabeg might suffer a difficult first year if these essential obligations went unmet. As it happened, his concerns were well founded. The Indians camped in tents and wigwams near the eventual location of the Indian Agency, because few houses were ready in time for cold weather. Truman Warren was forced to distribute rations on a weekly basis because the immigrants had arrived too late to plant gardens. That year the Christian Anishinaabeg lived like their ancestors, harvesting a bumper crop of wild rice, fishing as if their lives depended on it, and bagging large numbers of ducks, geese, and prairie chickens. They were hired by the U.S. government to build the very houses that had been promised to them upon arrival. But adversity tends to bond people together, and the newly arrived immigrants rallied and named their reservation *Gahwahbahbigonikah*, or White Earth, for the white glacial loess found beneath the black surface soil.

The Episcopalian Gull Lakers were not the only immigrants to move to White Earth. Government employees who directed the removal were descended from métis traders; more individuals of this ethnic group followed. Hole in the Day was murdered in August 1868 and the métis migration to White Earth began shortly thereafter. After her home in Little Falls burned to the ground, Julia Warren Spears left her position as matron at the Leech Lake boarding school to go to White Earth in 1870 at the behest of her brother Truman. Her sister, wife of the White Earth government carpenter, accompanied her. William Warren's adult children and their families, and the families of Frank Campbell, Robert Fairbanks, and Frank Roy also migrated. Several traders, George Fairbanks, William McArthur, Clement H. Beaulieu, and George Morrison, came early on and engaged in a brisk trade for animal pelts in an area that had not yet been overhunted. John George Morrison waited until 1874 to move—until after Hole in the Day's murder. Chain migrations characterized the entire thirty-five-year migration to White Earth; the métis experience was no exception to this pattern.[41]

Agent Edward P. Smith reported only 550 migrants in 1872, when the White Earth Agency was established. By 1875, the total population had increased to around 800, with some supporting themselves comfortably through farming. Episcopal missionary Joseph Gilfillan estimated that between one-third and one-half of the population were "mixed-bloods," who "kept coming" from "all parts of northern Minnesota and Wisconsin," perhaps a thousand or more who were all Roman Catholic. Located on the reservation were a sawmill and gristmill, three schools, and several Christian churches. Representatives of the U.S. government believed their assimilation efforts were paying off.

Population increased dramatically in 1876 to 1,427. Residents from the Gull Lake community had continued to dribble in over the years. However, most of the new immigrants belonged to the Otter Tail Pillager and Pembina bands. The Otter Tail Pillagers, an off-shoot of the Leech Lake band, had scattered over the countryside south of White Earth, living off the land. The Pembina band, closely affiliated through treaties with the Red Lake band, hailed from the vicinity of Turtle Mountain in North Dakota and had been involved in the buffalo hide trade with their métis relatives. Congress mandated that these bands be removed to White Earth and appropriated $25,000 to purchase one township of land near present day Mahnomen for the Pembina band. The Mississippi band accepted $25,000 to incorporate the Otter Tail Pillagers into their band as fully participating members. The Otter Tail band received no separate plot of land, though many concentrated near Pine Point.[42]

U.S. Policymakers and the Concentration Solution

Even though the 1867 Treaty guaranteed the Mississippi band that the White Earth Reservation would belong to them forever, land pressures from outside interests increased. Concerned humanitarians responded to this threat by devising ways to protect the White Earth land base.

Beginning in the 1860s, wheat farming in Minnesota increased dramatically and had become firmly entrenched in the southern part of the state by the 1880s. Easy land acquisition through the Homestead Act encouraged American and foreign-born settlers to locate in Minnesota. The expansion of railroads to the west and northwest and the emergence of Minneapolis as a great milling center stimulated settlement of the fertile Red River Valley, an excellent area for wheat production. Technological advances in the milling process kept wheat the dominant cash crop throughout the late nineteenth century. The ascendancy of wheat coincided with the peak period of logging the great stands of red and white pine in northern Minnesota. The forests of North America had long furnished the needs of the burgeoning Euroamerican population. Lumbermen from Maine and Michigan turned to the forests of Wisconsin and Minnesota in the decades following the Civil War. Conservation did not emerge as an ethic until late in the century, after the dangers of unimpeded resource exploitation had become painfully obvious. Lumber companies found ways to decrease competition and secure the most favorable terms for themselves. After logging the St. Croix triangle and the arrowhead region northeast of Duluth, railroads and loggers pushed further west and surveyed the bounty of the eastern townships of the White Earth Reservation. Soon pressures mounted to open uncultivated land at White Earth to Euroamerican settlement.

A group of settlers from the Red River Valley threw their support behind any plan that would open White Earth lands to them. Caring little for the assimilation experiment, they clamored for satisfaction, charging that the "toiling pioneers" needed White Earth's resources "to aid them in their work of developing the great Northwest." Episcopal Bishop Henry S. Whipple was especially concerned for the White Earth Reservation; the St. Columba Mission was his favorite project. He responded to mounting outside pressure to open White Earth to Euroamerican settlement with a campaign to save the reservation. In addition to writing letters to Minnesota congressmen, he devised a plan to concentrate all Minnesota Anishinaabeg on the White Earth Reservation. Allocating the entire land base to individual Indians would eliminate any argument that White Earth land lay unexploited and thereby save the reservation. At least he hoped it would.[43]

On 15 May 1886, Congress appointed a commission to negotiate with all of the "Chippewa" bands in Minnesota, except Red Lake, for a consolidation arrangement. Bishop Whipple served as one of three members of the Northwest Indian Commission, and traveled with them to discuss the concentration plan with leaders of each band.

White Earth residents feared that a large influx of their poorer relatives would pauperize their reservation. The commissioners tried to allay their worries, promising to "make everyone rich" upon arrival by supplying land, animals, wagons, tools, homes, and supplies for two years until the Indians became self-supporting. Those who had immigrated under the 1867 Treaty would receive the full 160 acres promised to the newcomers rather than being required to fulfill 1867 Treaty provisions regarding land acquisition.

Each of the Minnesota Anishinaabe bands hesitated to enter into new negotiations when earlier promises made by the U.S. government had gone unfulfilled. The Leech Lake, Cass Lake, Lake Winnibagoshish, and White Oak Point bands especially resented a series of dams built on the Mississippi River by the U.S. Army Corps of Engineers to hold back spring floodwaters that threatened to destroy the Falls of St. Anthony, the locus of Minneapolis's milling industry. Flooding caused by the dams had destroyed substantial wild rice fields, cranberry marshes, and low-lying meadows, for which the Indians had received no compensation. The Mille Lacs band refused to consider removal at all, insisting on their right to occupy their reservation under the 1863 Treaty. No amount of persuasion by the commissioners could induce more than a few to consider the move. The Northwest Indian Commission filed its report in 1887, but negotiations stalled out in Congress. However, the concentration plan contained therein contributed much of its substance to the 1889 Nelson Act.[44]

The push to concentrate the Minnesota Anishinaabeg on the White Earth Reservation culminated in the 1889 Nelson Act. In 1889, the Anishinaabeg occupied twelve reservations in northern Minnesota that had been established through various treaties. Agents and policymakers considered White Earth to have the greatest agricultural potential and continually pointed out how bleak economic conditions were elsewhere. Although outside business interests continued to urge that White Earth be opened to Euroamerican settlement, those who hoped to assimilate the Anishinaabeg saw White Earth as a panacea for what they termed "Minnesota's Indian problem."

The 1887 Dawes Act, or General Allotment Act, threatened reservation land nationwide. In part, it promoted the U.S. government's assimilation campaign by mandating that tribal land be allotted to individual Indians in parcels of up to 160 acres. Supposedly, respect for private property would replace communal bonds and hasten Indians' progress toward the yeoman farmer ideal. Holding allotments in trust for twenty-five years would allow Indians to learn to regard land as real estate and manage their own affairs before they would be allowed to sell the land or be required to pay property taxes. These alterations in reservation land tenure were aimed at the ultimate incorporation of reservation land and resources into the American economy. But to say that policymakers were overly optimistic about the impact this would have for native peoples is putting it mildly.

Another component of the Dawes Act reflected the demands of outside business interests. Lands that remained after all individuals received allotments were to be sold on the open market to would-be settlers. Revenue generated by land sales would finance the U.S. government's assimilation programs.

Humanitarians concerned with assimilating Indians and westerners who coveted reservation lands compromised to pass the Dawes Act. Special enabling legislation carried the Dawes Act into effect for each reservation nationwide.[45]

The 1889 Nelson Act brought the Dawes Act to bear on the special situation of the Minnesota "Chippewa." Under the act, the Anishinaabeg were to cede all reservations in the state except White Earth and Red Lake and relocate to the White Earth Reservation to farm individual land allotments; Red Lake Indians would take allotments on their own reservation. All agricultural lands remaining after allotments had been made would be sold for $1.25 per acre under the Homestead Act. Valuable timberland made the Anishinaabe situation different from most other reservations. Rather than being allotted, the pine lands would be appraised and sold in forty-acre plots at public auction. A three-member commission would negotiate with each band and have responsibility for compiling censuses, taking votes, securing removals, and making allotments. The commissioners would oversee expenditures from the "Chippewa in Minnesota Fund," in which the proceeds from land and timber sales would be deposited. The fund would draw interest in the U.S. Treasury for fifty years and yield annual per capita payments. Curiously, the Nelson Act also contained a provision allowing individuals to take allotments on their own reservations, effectively undermining the consolidation plan. No rationale explained this clause, which effectively made relocation voluntary. The Nelson Act mandated sweeping changes in Anishinaabe polity in northern Minnesota. Most important, creation of the "Chippewa in Minnesota Fund" conveyed a shared right in a common fund to all Anishinaabe people on their scattered reservations. Prior to this time, each band and reservation claimed special rights vis-à-vis

the U.S. government stemming from their individual treaty relationships. The "Chippewa in Minnesota Fund" became a focus for pan-
reservation Anishinaabe political identity, a development that U.S. policymakers had not anticipated. Once again, U.S. policy influenced how
various Anishinaabe groups identified themselves. The legislative man-
date may not have had much relation to reality for Indian people at the
time it was passed, but over the years diverse immigrants would agree
that they belonged to the White Earth band and reservation leaders from
across the state would pursue their claims to the "Chippewa in Minnesota Fund." Passage of the Nelson Act, then, marks a watershed for
White Earth, for the General Council of the Chippewa (formed in 1913),
and for the Minnesota Chippewa Tribe, which came into being only in
the 1930s.[46]

Negotiations of the U.S. Chippewa Commission

The U.S. Chippewa Commission quickly made arrangements to begin
negotiating by mid-June of 1889. Anishinaabe men at each reservation
assembled to meet with the commissioners and selected one or more
primary spokesmen to represent their concerns. In keeping with their
familiar style, older men served as head *ogimaag*, striving to achieve a
balance of interests to retain the support of the "young men." Band
members usually respected the wisdom of the "gray-haired" and recognized the benefits of keeping the "hot-headed" younger men in check.
Most band members paid ritualistic homage to appointed spokesmen
before venturing their own opinions. Wayway from Red Lake insisted
that he wanted to "follow the example of the old chief" because he had
"too much respect for [his] relatives" to say "anything in opposition."
This form of political organization reflected earlier leadership patterns
based both on consensus and flexible age-grading.

Reservation leaders everywhere confronted U.S. Chippewa commissioners with the same concerns they had expressed to the Northwest
Indian Commission. Repetitive negotiations for concentration in the
face of unfulfilled treaty obligations and outstanding debts insulted their
authority. Anishinaabe leaders continually embarrassed the commissioners, who were unable to justify Congress's past actions.

Red Lake leaders were the first to complain of past injustices and to object to new proposals. Their cooperation was crucial because the sale of their large reservation would provide most of the revenue for the "Chippewa in Minnesota Fund." Commissioners reported that the allure of Nelson Act benefits enticed the necessary majority. However, Red Lake leaders expressed profound displeasure with the bill in other forums. That all of the Anishinaabeg statewide would share the proceeds from the Red Lake Reservation seemed unfair. They also opposed dissolving their tribal relations, realizing that they would lack political power without some form of organization. They persisted in their resolve against both allotment and discontinuing their tribal ties for many years to come; their decisive stance resulted as much from U.S. policy as it did from their own domestic concerns.

Next, White Earth leaders had to be convinced that the Nelson Act would not harm them. White Earth leader Joseph Charette (Wainjemah-dub) immediately complained to the commissioners that, "We should come to an understanding about this old debt before entering upon any new and complicated arrangement." White Earth leaders had good reason to be wary of the commissioners' assurances; already, promised funds had not materialized, mills and plows had fallen into disrepair, and fields lay fallow for want of seeds and teams. The United States had not proven itself trustworthy. Band members worried most about the likelihood of an immediate cession of land. They had become accustomed to threats to the reservation land base. Gus Beaulieu, son of métis trader Clement H. Beaulieu, heatedly argued that "there should not be a single solitary foot" disposed of by sale, but was reminded of the ultimate "authority" of the United States. The commissioners rebuked Beaulieu with paternalistic rhetoric and demanded that the Indians acquiesce in a cession "for your own safety and protection." Eventually the commissioners persuaded Wabonaquod, the most respected White Earth *ogimaa*, that selling the timberlands would provide the capital necessary to develop their resources. Although he felt too old to benefit much from the act himself, he believed that if he "was a young man" he would "overflow with joy and . . . profit by the opportunities now offered." With this rationale, he urged his tribespeople to take advantage of the Nelson Act, especially its educational and economic benefits.

The commissioners encountered the same "embarrassment which . . .

Table 1. U.S. Chippewa Commission: Census Totals and Votes for
Acceptance of Nelson Act, 1890

Band	Total Population	Adult Men	Adult Men Assenting to Removal	Percent Assenting
Red Lake	1,168	303	247	82
Pembina (White Earth)	218	83	77	93
White Earth Mississippi	1,169	284	270	95
Gull Lake	277	61	57	93
White Oak Point	661	176	172	99
Mille Lacs	895	213	189	89
Leech Lake	1,141	324	217	67
Otter Tail (White Earth)	657	164	144	88
Cass Lake	241	67	65	97
Lake Winnibagoshish	169	45	40	89
Grand Portage	294	73	72	99
Bois Forte	743	228	211	93
Fond du Lac	671	157	123	78

Note: Compiled from census and vote totals of U.S. Chippewa Commission,
"Report of the U.S. Chippewa Commission," p. 9.

too often attends our negotiations with the Indians" at all of the interior Minnesota reservations. Unfulfilled treaty obligations continued to hamper progress on the new Nelson Act negotiations. However, a more fundamental obstacle was the bands' opposition to removal. Many members of the Leech Lake and Mille Lacs bands, in particular, resisted the concentration plan and resolved "to remain at the place of [their] nativity." But having observed how traditional deference operated in the councils, the commissioners proceeded to take the censuses and votes (see Table 1), confident that winning the leaders' consent was all that was necessary.

A number of factors convinced individuals to agree to the Nelson Act. Generous provisions for allotment and agricultural assistance appealed to those who hoped to try their hand at farming. Others saw land titles as a way to protect the remaining reservation land base from trespass. However, the commissioners admitted that they would never have secured

Anishinaabe approval of the Nelson Act without the unexplained clause allowing individuals to take allotments on their own reservations.[47]

The 1889 Nelson Act Immigrants

Most Anishinaabeg of northern Minnesota resisted removal to White Earth, preferring to take allotments where they lived. While some, like the Leech Lake Pillagers, took allotments at home, others, the Mille Lacs band especially, felt steady, increasing pressure to remove. By 1900, 1,198 people of Anishinaabe descent had availed themselves of the option to relocate to White Earth. Many more, however, chose to remain where they were (see Map 2).[48]

Anishinaabe leaders throughout northern Minnesota understood that the 1889 Nelson Act gave them the option of remaining on their own reservations rather than removing to White Earth. Wherever the U.S. Chippewa Commission and their educated métis employees traveled, they encountered organized opposition to removal. "Kickers," who resisted these new policies, forced commissioners to concentrate on persuading individuals to move and to postpone making allotments.

The U.S. Chippewa Commission targeted the Mille Lacs band, more than any other, for intensive removal efforts. White squatters had encroached on their reservation and areas where they harvested resources and regarded the Mille Lacs Indians as obstacles to Euroamerican expansion. The band members were subjected to many abuses, but nonetheless chose to stay put.

The Mille Lacs band resolved to remain on their reservation with as much dedication as local Euroamericans who wanted them evicted. The "chiefs," the "headmen" or "bears," and the "young men's party" persuaded an assembled council to resist removal unless all three "parties" agreed to it. Removal agents sought out families in the remote reaches of the bush to explain the benefits to be gained. They financed trips to White Earth so prospective immigrants could see its advantages for themselves. Despite such costly, labor-intensive efforts, only a few Mille Lacs Indians agreed to remove.

When efforts to secure voluntary compliance failed, the U.S. Chippewa Commission turned to more forceful measures. Complaining that "something stronger than mere coaxing must be done," the chairman of the commission recommended that the Commissioner of Indian Affairs withhold annuities legally due to the Mille Lacs band and pay them only at the White Earth Reservation. Policymakers hoped that such coercive measures would force the recalcitrant Mille Lacs Indians to travel to White Earth to be paid, whereupon they might be induced to remain.

Mille Lacs leader Waweyeacumig (Round Earth) upbraided the Indian Office for having "deliberately denied us a right which we had under the law" and upheld a resistance effort that was to last for many years. Neither withholding their annuities nor appropriating $40,000 to finance their removal persuaded more than 125 to leave by 1904. However, the commissioners were so tirelessly zealous in their efforts that the Mille Lacs band comprised the third largest band at White Earth by 1907 (see Figure 1).[49]

Members of the Pillager and Mississippi bands at Leech Lake, Lake Winnibagoshish, Cass Lake, and White Oak Point had no intention of leaving, nor were they happy about the idea of taking allotments at home. Federal authorities did not duplicate their heavy-handed tactics in the vicinity of Leech Lake; the poor agricultural potential of the land probably worked to the benefit of those who opposed removal. As the commissioners relented and began to issue allotments, they found that Indians in the Mississippi headwaters area had "banded and determined not to make any selection of land." Their organized resistance efforts paid off. While those who voluntarily migrated formed a substantial proportion of the White Earth population, many more decided to remain where they were.[50]

Anishinaabe intransigence prolonged the commissioners' work and they assessed all the escalating costs against the "Chippewa in Minnesota Fund." In the hope that potential immigrants would hasten their decision, the Indian Office imposed a deadline of 1 October 1894 for all removals. Criticisms from reform organizations such as the Indian Rights Association succeeded in reducing the size of the commission in anticipation of its dissolution and stemming the "waste of tribal funds."[51]

Vague legislative terms created confusion about who was entitled to partake in the benefits of the 1889 Nelson Act. On 24 May 1895, the Assistant Attorney General ruled that a "Chippewa Indian" must be of

"Removals" from the Mille Lacs Reservation pose with their *ogimaa* Waweyeacumig (Round Earth, back row, fourth from right) at Big Elbow Lake around 1905. Waweyeacumig and his wife Nawajibigokwe (Woman dwelling in the midst of the rocks, standing, second row, third from right) were both fourth-degree Midé priests. Their removal agent is seated in front next to the little boy standing with beaded sash and bag. *Photo courtesy of Minnesota Historical Society.*

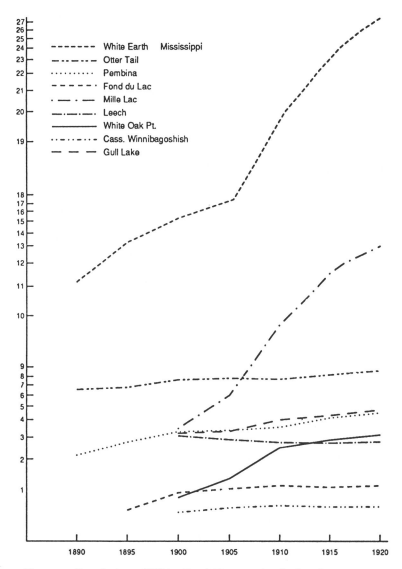

Figure 1. Population of White Earth Reservation by band, 1890–1920. Compiled from Bureau of Indian Affairs censuses, White Earth Reservation, 1890–1920, at five-year intervals.

"Chippewa Indian blood"; must have a recognized connection with one of the bands in Minnesota; must have been a Minnesota resident when the act was passed; and must move to one of the reservations with the intention of residing there permanently. The opinion discriminated against the children of Anishinaabe women who married U.S. citizens after 9 August 1888 denying them rights under the Nelson Act. The ruling also extended Nelson Act benefits to those who had received "half-breed scrip" under the 1854 and 1855 treaties. This meant that recipients of land scrip could legally receive a total of two and in some cases three allotments of land all told. Many individuals of Anishinaabe descent throughout the western Great Lakes area could therefore claim rights under the Nelson Act. These decisions eased the work of the U.S. Chippewa Commission by clarifying questions of entitlement.[52]

In the years immediately following 1889, those who immigrated to the White Earth Reservation appreciated what the Nelson Act had to offer. The year 1891 witnessed the largest influx of immigrants. A secondary peak occurred around 1893 and 1894 and reflects the impact of the October 1894 deadline for removal established by the Indian Office; apparently it had the desired effect and encouraged indecisive families to move. After 1894, migrations dropped off dramatically, increasing only slightly after 1898 (see Figure 2).

The removal experience of most bands differed from the overall migration pattern; only the Mille Lacs band replicated the larger pattern, albeit on a smaller scale. These variegated patterns reflect the nature of the overall removal experience. For most, removal occurred within the context of band, community, and kin. Chain migrations of groups of kin characterized the removal as related groups left together at nearly the same time, accounting for peaks in reporting statistics. The particular removal experience of each band accounts for the wide variations in migration patterns.[53]

The majority of new Nelson Act immigrants settled in the eastern lake country. As is typical of chain migrations, groups of Indian immigrants joined friends and family at the various settlements. The Mille Lacs Indians who formerly lived at Chief Megesee's village had "children or other relatives residing there," and considered this factor in their decision to remove. Charles H. Beaulieu welcomed chain migrants be-

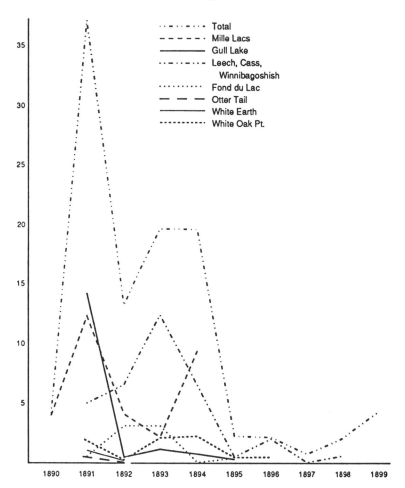

Figure 2. Annual removals to White Earth by band, 1890–99. Compiled from the Chippewa Commission, 1890–99. Reprinted by permission from Melissa L. Meyer, "Signatures and Thumbprints: Ethnicity among the White Earth Anishinaabeg, 1889–1920," *Social Science History* 14:3. Copyright 1990, Duke University Press, Durham, N.C.

cause they eased his task as allotting agent. Persuading a key individual to remove could ensure that several families would follow. For example, Mozomonay's half-brother promised that "the moment any one of his relatives remove he will follow." The absence of relatives at White Earth similarly impeded removals.

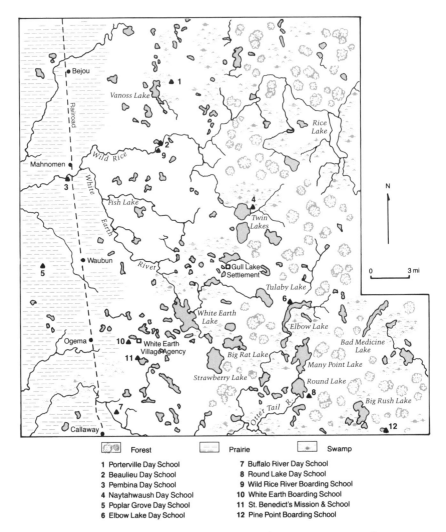

	Forest		Prairie		Swamp

1 Porterville Day School
2 Beaulieu Day School
3 Pembina Day School
4 Naytahwaush Day School
5 Poplar Grove Day School
6 Elbow Lake Day School

7 Buffalo River Day School
8 Round Lake Day School
9 Wild Rice River Boarding School
10 White Earth Boarding School
11 St. Benedict's Mission & School
12 Pine Point Boarding School

Map 3. White Earth Indian Reservation. By Melissa L. Meyer. Based on "Map of White Earth Indian Reservation, as existing at the passage of the Act of Jan. 14, 1889," Forestry and Grazing Division, Minnesota, Folder 6, National Cartographic Archives, Washington, D.C.

Members of the Mille Lacs band generally preferred locating at Wild Rice River (or Beaulieu), Twin Lakes, and Elbow Lake, while those from the Leech Lake area settled with their Otter Tail Pillager relations at Pine Point. In this fashion, settlement patterns perpetuated band affiliations. On the other hand, not all band members settled together, which fostered a commingling of those who shared a similar economic orientation. Other settlements that drew a substantial number of immigrants where the Dam, the Gull Lake Settlement, Buffalo River, Rat Lake, Fish Lake, and White Earth Village (see Map 3).

Indians from the vicinities of Leech Lake and Mille Lacs were regarded as being among the most conservative of the interior Anishinaabe bands that migrated to White Earth. Indians from these bands formed the bulk of the immigrant population after 1889. That they chose to locate in areas where they might perpetuate the type of life to which they were accustomed should not be surprising.

Return migration complicates interpretation of aggregate migration statistics. Close affinity between Indian people in northern Minnesota fostered frequent visiting and population movement. Statistics on the phenomenon of return migration do not exist, but some evidence suggests that it was not uncommon. Individuals traveled between their old and new residences—a natural pattern within the context of community and kin. Some removed temporarily to acquire benefits under the Nelson Act, only to leave soon thereafter. The promise of rations persuaded some to relocate only on a short-term basis. Others selected land parcels at White Earth, returned home, "and have not been there since." Agent Simon Michelet described how young men left to work in "the grain fields of North Dakota and the lumber camps of Minnesota" because there was "not enough work . . . on the reservation to give employment to all." Thus, a number of factors promoted unrecorded migration away from the reservation.[54]

Persuading Anishinaabeg to move to White Earth was only the beginning of the removal process. Organizing the whole process in terms of finances, goods, and personnel posed an administrative nightmare. The U.S. Chippewa commissioners had to allot the land and set up each family that came to White Earth. People who moved later in the year, too late to plant and harvest a crop, required greater assistance. Transporting families and their household possessions and securing subsistence sup-

plies and other issues provided wage labor for individuals at White Earth
and generated revenue for businesses in the surrounding region. Warehouses held a small supply of subsistence rations purchased on the open
market that could be doled out at any time, but farm implements and
livestock had to be purchased in the neighboring area upon the immigrants' arrival. Commissioners arranged for issues of horses, oxen, cattle,
wagons, sleighs, plows, and other agricultural implements as well as
flour, sugar, pork, tea, and other subsistence goods. The agent kept more
expensive items such as farm equipment aside to be shared cooperatively
between several families. Building houses for those who removed to
White Earth consumed large amounts of wood products. At the agent's
request, a temporary sawmill was erected at Twin Lakes to manufacture
lumber, shingles, and laths. This practice made use of Anishinaabe resources, avoided the cost of procuring them from outside the reservation,
and provided wages for Anishinaabe men. Employees hired by the U.S.
Chippewa Commission broke ground for gardens and farms and assisted
the new arrivals in plowing and planting. Tasks associated with the
removal effort were manifold.

Although the commission hired a corps of assistants to administer
their duties, problems inevitably arose. Immigrants who arrived at White
Earth only to find that their houses had not been built faced the prospect
of returning home, sometimes at their own expense. Unbroken fields,
inadequate farm implements, and delays in receiving supplies convinced
some that the removal experiment was unreliable and contributed to
return migration. Unforeseen delays at times left individual families
waiting for funds that had been guaranteed. The U.S. Chippewa Commission chairman pleaded with the Secretary of the Interior that "rations to
these Indians in the dead of winter is a matter of no little importance."
Fortunately their continuing reliance on the seasonal round helped to see
them through the crisis.[55]

Allotments were not made in accordance with Nelson Act stipula-
tions; opposition to removal postponed assigning allotments far beyond
the time anticipated by the Nelson Act. Then in 1891, Congress reduced
allotment acreage across the country from 160 to 80 acres. Many Anishinaabeg protested what they regarded as land theft and refused to take
80-acre allotments. Those who accepted the reduced acreage often did so
with economic gain in mind. Taking what amounted to first choice of

the richest land on the reservation gave them an economic advantage which in no way jeopardized their chances of acquiring additional acreage in the future. Mississippi band chiefs could be persuaded to acquiesce to 80-acre allotments in 1892 only after repeated assurances that they would soon receive 80 more acres.

The technicalities associated with making allotments were confusing, especially for inexperienced Indians who were unfamiliar with surveyors' methods and markers. Agents who had to mediate conflicting claims over surveyed boundaries complained that "each Indian has to be shown his corners." The U.S. Chippewa Commission also spent a good deal of time changing allotment selections. Once they arrived at White Earth and took up residence, recent immigrants sometimes decided that a different location better suited their needs.

Abundant land lessened potential conflicts that might have arisen over competing allotment claims. Longer-term residents claimed selections they had already developed, choosing additional acreage to comprise the total permitted. Although government employees constructed houses for immigrants on their allotments in an effort to influence residence patterns, it is not clear that they were effective. That agents continually attempted to persuade Indians to move onto their allotments indicates that many had chosen not to do so.

Assigning allotments began in 1891; 65 percent had been recorded by 1895. By 1900, a total of 4,446 allotments had been made. However, these statistics more accurately reflect bureaucratic success at recording allotment assignments than actual residence patterns. The agent listed only 300 families living on their allotments in 1893.

Certainly, different aims motivated individuals in their allotment selections. Some cared only about living near kin in an area where they might perpetuate their traditional pursuits and located near settlements in the eastern forest and lake country. Those who conceived of land in market terms selected agricultural or timbered allotments of the greatest monetary value. Historians may never be able to discern with any precision why individuals acted as they did.[56]

Conclusion

Even a short historical survey amply demonstrates that migration and cultural reordering figured prominently among Minnesota Anishinaabe adaptation strategies. They adjusted to each new situation from the context of the one preceding. In this sense, neither their migrations to the White Earth Reservation nor the adaptations they undertook there were without historical precedent.

In each instance, the circumstances differed. Seasonal migrations characterized life prior to contact with Euroamericans. Even then, marital ties cemented interband alliances. The fur trade offered opportunities for material enrichment as it stimulated the integration of previously autonomous bands into an incipient body politic first at Sault Ste. Marie and then at Keeweenaw and Chequamegon peninsulas. On the south shore of Lake Superior, the Anishinaabeg coalesced as a corporate group. Religion and social structure bent to accommodate their evolving needs.

When shifting trade relationships and resource needs demanded, the Anishinaabeg aggressively pushed into interior Minnesota to maintain access to the rich parkland zone that they had been privy to as allies of the Dakota. Again, they modified their social structure, splintering into bilateral hunting bands and then consolidating at a series of villages much smaller than the Chequamegon center.

They also forged trading partnerships with French and later Scottish and British fur traders. Here again, intermarriage sealed these affiliations and the offspring of these unions created a unique métis society throughout the western Great Lakes region. Members of this bicultural, occupational class continued to stay closely associated with their native relatives, mediating between them and Euroamerican society.

As the costs of commercial hunting and encroaching loggers and settlers caught up with them, the Anishinaabeg devised ways to cope. Hole in the Day's strategy of staging carefully orchestrated militant demonstrations against erratic U.S. policies and other band leaders' efforts to ally with Episcopalian missionaries and adopt more intensive farming techniques were essentially flip sides of the same coin. As "civil leaders" sought to contain the influence of those who had no qualms about resorting to armed aggression (such tactics threatened peaceful village life), they simultaneously had to recognize that militance extorted concessions. Those who advocated belligerence gained the upper hand in the mid-nineteenth century because conditions warranted it. As pressures mounted, villages fractured, and Gull Lake leaders especially sought solutions. A concentration plan focusing on the White Earth Reservation emerged under these circumstances. The U.S. policymakers and Anishinaabe leaders agreed that moving farther away from Euroamerican settlement just might help them adjust (and provide land for Euroamerican settlement as well).

Each migration phase that brought the Anishinaabeg into interior Minnesota had been prompted by different circumstances. They adjusted to these challenges with great creativity ranging from amalgamation to intermarriage and ethnogenesis. They were, in effect, especially skilled adapters—and they would prove this once again at the White Earth Reservation.

$$\text{л}2\text{л}$$

Signatures and Thumbprints

Community and Ethnicity

at White Earth

Introduction

White Earth's variegated ecosystem enabled residents to pursue multiple strategies for securing their livelihoods. Indians intent on seasonal harvesting concentrated their efforts in the eastern forest and lake country. Lands in the mid-section of the reservation and to the west drew those who cared to try their hand at farming on a larger scale. In addition, cultural brokers, those who mediated between Indian communities and the dominant white society, concentrated in the central part of the reservation. In this sense, the White Earth environment eased transplantation of a rejuvenated version of the society that had evolved near the Crow Wing and Gull Lake communities.

By 1900, those who had migrated to White Earth within the past two decades had evolved a society based on band ties and residence patterns. Having located in different parts of the reservation, Mississippi, Otter Tail, and Pembina band leaders pursued separate concerns stemming from past treaty relationships even as they shared concern for the welfare of their reservation. Their lifeways and leadership patterns reflected this.

Immigrant Anishinaabe bands integrated themselves into this existent social order. They tended to maintain band ties, social roles, and leadership roles after removal to White Earth. Drawn largely from more conservative interior Minnesota bands, most opted to join family and kin in the settlements in the eastern forests.

Life patterns of the conservative Anishinaabeg carried them in different directions than the métis mediators. Members of the two groups had only fleeting associations. Residence patterns separated them, and they socialized largely within their own distinct ethnic groups. Anishinaabeg from more conservative interior Minnesota bands generally practiced the Midéwiwin religion or attended syncretic Episcopal mission services, while those of Franco-Anishinaabe descent tended to be Catholic. Métis children more often received training at regional and national boarding schools and at schools on the reservation. Investigators frequently complained that students with very little Indian "blood" filled the schools, excluding many "full-blood" children. Thus, in many spheres, paths of the two ethnic groups at White Earth crossed only infrequently.

The Environment

Most of Minnesota's geography and topography bear the effects of massive continental glaciation. The state's many lakes and small hills formed as the glaciers receded northward, draining and depositing till. White Earth Reservation lies in a transition area characterized by several glacially created features. The western part of the reservation lies on the flat plain of the glacial-epoch Lake Agassiz. The Red River flows northward to Hudson Bay through this ancient glacial lake bed. The Alexandria Moraine extends into the central part of White Earth, accounting for the many small lakes in this area. The Wadena drumlin area abuts White Earth on the south. Pine Point, an elongated hill in the far southeastern portion of the reservation, is a drumlin deposited by the retreating glacier. This glacial topography influenced subsequent ecological developments.

The Red River Valley consists of a vast prairie, its borders coterminous with the earlier shore of the glacial-epoch Lake Agassiz. Streams run west to the Red River, draining the area rather than producing bogs or swamps. Before agricultural development, short grasses covered the prairie which, with interspersed pockets of oak savanna, created excellent conditions for grazing animals including bison. The flood plain of the Red River contained some of the richest soil to be found anywhere, a fact that would attract many European immigrants in the late nineteenth and early twentieth centuries.

At the prairie's edge, a narrow band of hardwood forest eventually gave way to a climax pine forest. The deciduous forest in northwestern Minnesota boasted a great wealth of tree species, with oak often predominating over large tracts, and it formed almost a complete barrier between the coniferous forest and the prairie. The coniferous forests of Minnesota were relatively uniform throughout. Very few deciduous trees were interspersed, with the exception of white birch. The poor soil of the coniferous forest hindered agriculture, but the extensive forests of red and white pine fueled the lumber industry in Minnesota in the late nineteenth and early twentieth centuries.

The deciduous forest and its edges supported more diverse animal life than either the prairie or the coniferous forest, which hosted only small populations of game animals. Edge communities harbored a greater number of species and population density than the ecotonal communities flanking them. Since White Earth straddled two edge communities, the prairie-deciduous forest and the deciduous-coniferous forest, a diversity of plant and animal life could be found there. Anishinaabe herbal specialists from across northern Minnesota recognized the lushness of the White Earth environment and journeyed there to gather plants in August once they had blossomed and reached their greatest potency. The deciduous forest ecotone provided excellent habitat for deer and other hoofed animals that required the browsing conditions that the coniferous forest could not sustain. In addition, the streams, lakes, and swamps supported moderate populations of beaver and muskrat, animals valued for their pelts. For several generations, Anishinaabeg and Dakota had clashed at sites along the transition zone edge communities throughout Minnesota, both contesting for unrestricted access to its abundant resources and trade opportunities. The popularly known "War between the Chippewa and Sioux" clearly had an ecological basis. The generations-old conflict had created a buffer zone between the two groups where humans dared not settle and game flourished. Immigrants to White Earth profited from the diversity and abundance of resources in this previously uninhabited transition area.

White Earth represented the best scheme that social engineers then had to offer for assimilating the Anishinaabeg. At heart, U.S. policymakers contemplated nothing less than the wholesale replacement of native cultures with a romantic version of the Jeffersonian agrarian ideal, the small-scale yeoman farmer. Assimilationists believed that their goals would be achieved through changes in land tenure arrangements, coupled with educational programs designed to ensure conformity to the American ideal. To them, reservations were a temporary phase in a process of bringing the Indians to meld completely with the dominant white society.

The U.S. policymakers and Anishinaabe leaders had the foresight to straddle White Earth Reservation on the three ecozones of the prairie-deciduous forest and coniferous-forest transition area. The forest and lake country to the east supplied marketable timber and a greater proportion of subsistence resources while fertile prairie land to the west in the Red River Valley offered better opportunities to engage in agriculture. Clearly, White Earth did not resemble the arid reservations of the west where harsh environments consigned assimilationists' plans to failure from the start. In this sense, White Earth's ecosystem sustained diversity, allowing residents freedom to choose among a number of options for making a living. If the U.S. government's programs of assimilation had a chance to succeed anywhere, White Earth should have become an experimental showcase.[1]

Economic Indicators of Ethnic Differences

Agriculture was the backbone of the U.S. government's assimilation campaign. Social engineers envisioned Indians becoming self-sufficient tillers of the soil, producing a specialized cash crop to sell on the market. By all accounts, those who embarked on the Episcopalian farming experiment succeeded in the early years. Enmegahbowh, who followed the first group of immigrants after Hole in the Day was killed, gloried in the metamorphosis, saying, "I have never seen them so willing & ready to work & cultivate the soil." When Julia Warren Spears arrived in 1870, she was "much surprised" at the changes in people she had known all her life. "When they left they were heahhens [sic] and wore blankets, long hair and feathers and painted their faces, and now . . . they were dressed like white men, hair cut and no paint on their faces."[2]

In 1873, the Episcopalian Indians at White Earth further demonstrated their commitment to the alliance by staging a pageant for visiting Episcopal Bishop Henry Whipple. Whipple, an influential man both within the Episcopalian church hierarchy and in national political circles involved with Indian affairs, had always taken a special interest in the White Earth experiment. He was an ally worth cultivating. Wabonaquod narrated the spectacle that unfolded. First, he portrayed "in glowing terms" how abundant their lives had been before the whites appeared. The lakes were "full of fish" and the woods were "alive with deer and elk." They were "virtuous and happy." At this point, a man and woman stepped out on the church porch "splendidly dressed" in "beads, belt, pouch, leggins [sic], embroidery, etc." to illustrate their good fortune in days gone by. Wabonaquod went on to recount how they had "sunk lower and lower" after "the white men" came. Now at the church door stood a man and woman "clad in a few old wretched tatters" with "shreds of blankets" that "flopped about their naked limbs." The ogimaa turned to them with a flourish and demanded to know who they were. In answer, the man gave the ogimaa a sidelong look, "took a whiskey bottle from his bosom," and "took a long loving draught." Thereupon, fearing that he would consume it all, the woman "snatched it and put it to her mouth." Once they crawled away, Wabonaquod went on to praise the "new era which had dawned upon them," since Bishop Whipple had come among them. Now the couple appeared dressed in "citizen's clothes." Having made their point, the players from all three eras emerged to stand side by side for the bishop's approval. Next, no less than sixteen men stepped forward to be baptized, kneeling down to have their scalp-locks cut off. The Episcopalian Anishinaabeg knew how to use a symbolic cross-cultural metaphor to safeguard the loyalties of their allies.[3]

Most Anishinaabeg kept substantial gardens. However, concentrating their efforts on producing a cash crop for the market did not appeal to them. They did intensify their farming efforts, but maintained a commitment to cooperative techniques, and showed "no disposition to enlarge their farms" once they had attained the desired subsistence level. Indians in the east grew corn and only small amounts of wheat, evidence that they were not responding to escalating market prices. Instead, they took care of their subsistence needs and were satisfied with what they had accomplished. This approach to farming persisted among conservative Indians into the twentieth century. Early Indian immigrants, who would come to be known as the "Old Settlers," borrowed from the Episcopalians rather than assimilating to their program. They understood that cultural metaphors expressed deeply held values. Just as "eating from the same dish" and "smoking the same pipe" symbolically signified their alliance with the Dakota, "shaking hands" and especially "taking hold of the plough" represented not their capitulation, but their compact with the Episcopalians on their own terms.[4]

The strategy of subsistence farming made the most sense for more conservative Anishinaabeg who had no way to obtain operating capital independently. Conditions at White Earth worked to the detriment of even ambitious and enterprising farmers. The north country climate, with its long, cold winters and violent hail and wind storms, could destroy several successive crops. Sizable, diversified operations would be necessary to absorb these costs. Livestock production required laying up tons of hay and large barns to feed and shelter stock through the winter. In addition, the Indian Agency was understaffed and undercapitalized for the kind of ambitious agricultural programs with which it was entrusted. Episcopalian missionaries bemoaned the Indians' apparent apostasy and withdrew their support and the U.S. government was not forthcoming with financial aid, causing Wabonaquod to complain that they "had no funds to do the work with." Considering the large distances involved and the few unpaved roads, it was "impossible for two farmers [Agency employees hired to teach farming] to give the necessary instructions" in farming techniques. More expensive farm implements were loaned to Indians on a cooperative basis, making it difficult to meet intensive demands at harvest time. Facilities and outmoded equipment fell into disrepair. By 1887, the sawmill and gristmill built in association with the 1868 removal were inoperable. Before 1905, no replacement gristmill existed on the reservation, raising costs by forcing farmers to travel thirty to forty miles for both mills and markets. Wabonaquod wondered, "Whose fault was it, . . . the Indians . . . or the Government in failing to allow us to repair the mills, which are so essential to our welfare." All of these liabilities made it difficult for conservative Anishinaabeg to rally to Agent Robert M. Allen's quixotic charge "not to be disappointed at the failure of even two crops, but to work faithfully on."[5]

Only those who conducted operations on a scale large enough to compensate for periodic crop losses and higher transportation costs could sustain successful farming endeavors. Individual success stories existed.

Table 2. Land under Cultivation by Indians, White Earth, 1887–1904

Year	Acres	Year	Acres
1887	5,703	1894	9,125
1888	5,778	1899*	1,990
1889	5,846	1900	6,000
1890	7,542	1901	6,025
1891	6,715	1902	6,075
1892	8,269	1903	6,075
1893	8,448	1904	6,075

*Between 1895 and 1898, figures for the "Chippewa in Minnesota" were aggregated, making it impossible to derive statistics for White Earth alone.
Source: Taken from the Annual Reports of the Commissioner of Indian Affairs.

Many recognized Ishquaygahbow as a successful "full-blood" farmer, who raised a surplus to sell. But most market farmers tended to be wealthier innovators of mixed descent who took advantage of allotment provisions and relied on wheat production to create prosperous enterprises. More often than not, they located their farms in the western portion of the reservation. Benjamin L. Fairbanks, son of métis trader George Fairbanks, got a foothold on the White Earth Reservation in this fashion before opening his general store. As early as 1885, the agent at White Earth observed that fully 75 percent of the harvest was "raised by mixed blood Indians." Of the 52,000 bushels of wheat raised on the reservation in 1887, "mixed bloods" raised 46,000 bushels while "full bloods" raised only 6,000. By 1901, Agent Michelet found that the Indians had "not taken advantage of this fine farming land"; instead, those of mixed descent predominated among "Indian farmers" at White Earth. Clement H. Beaulieu affirmed that "what was raised was raised by the mixed bloods and the whites who have intermarried with our people." Weather, undercapitalization, and long, cold winters hindered agricultural efforts by all but those of substantial means. However, agents glossed over these differences in their reports, making no distinctions between social groups.[6]

Acres of land cultivated by Indians steadily increased from 1887 to 1894 (see Table 2) with principal cash crops of wheat, oats, potatoes, and later, flax, all of which increased in value. But between 1894 and 1904, acres under cultivation declined and leveled off, even though the number of Indians living on their allotments increased from a mere 52 in 1889 to 730 by 1904. Despite the downward trend, federal authorities pointed to these figures as evidence of the success of the U.S. government's assimilation programs.[7]

On 1 September 1904, the Minneapolis, St. Paul, and Sault Ste. Marie Railroad, a spur of the Great Northern Railroad, began regular daily train service running north-south through the western part of the reservation. By 1905, eight grain elevators were built at the various railroad stations, prompting the agent to predict good times for Indian farmers. He hoped that the reduction in marketing costs would encourage Indians to grow more grain. But for those who lived in the eastern section of the reservation, distances remained great. The arrival of the railroad did nothing to increase their incentive to farm for the market.

While land was abundant and under Indian control, those who cared to engage in market agriculture at White Earth might succeed if they were capable of supplying operating capital themselves. Only a limited sector of the White Earth population made this type of commitment. When Congress passed legislation between 1904 and 1907 allowing alienation of the land base, many of these market farmers would find their efforts undermined. Later statistics would reflect this.

Successful cash-crop farmers had always been the exception rather than the rule in the eastern forest and lake country. The continued integrity, viability, and flexibility of the traditional seasonal round provided Indians an economic alternative with the advantage of a familiarity born of generations of experience. Those who pursued market agriculture in the west pioneered an innovative economic strategy that remained inaccessible and often undesirable to those in the east.[8]

The emphasis policymakers and missionaries placed on market agriculture should not obscure the fact that the Anishinaabeg had in no way abandoned the seasonal round. Most observers failed to appreciate its abiding integrity and viability. Since they did not consider seasonal resources to be agricultural produce, U.S. Indian agents and investigators took infrequent notice of wild rice, game, fish, or maple sugar yields in their annual statistics. Such figures were at times reported for the Leech

Lake area, but never for White Earth. For these reasons, it is impossible to ascertain statistics for the amount of produce the Anishinaabeg harvested from their environment. John Rogers, who grew up in the bush at White Earth at the turn of the twentieth century, reported that his family harvested a hundred pounds of wild rice in a typical year. A number of families gathering such amounts could lay up quite a store. Indeed, Episcopalian missionary Joseph Gilfillan argued that the Indians "got hold of a great deal more money in the course of the year than the average white farmer," and that it was "a mistake to try to force them to be farmers only." As long as they had recourse to the seasonal round, the Anishinaabeg could sustain themselves when farming failed. It served as the cornerstone of autonomy for the White Earth Anishinaabeg in the late nineteenth and early twentieth centuries.[9]

At each stage of the annual cycle of provisioning activities, family followed family "twenty or perhaps fifty miles and back" to group camps, no one wishing to be left behind. Missionary Pauline Colby described how "several households . . . joined forces and the cavalcade start[ed] on a laborious but very congenial campaign." Before they left, they turned their cows and pigs loose to fend for themselves. Some walked and some rode in pony-drawn wagons, carrying just a few blankets and pots and pans. Upon arrival at the group camp, people pitched tents and erected temporary shelters. These large assemblages of people abided by a time-honored system of respecting usufruct rights well into the twentieth century.[10]

These activities routinely interfered with U.S. educational programs. In the spring, Viola Cook, superintendent of the Wild Rice River School at Beaulieu, complained that "sugarmaking vacation caused the usual delay in returning." In the latter part of July and August, M. S. Peticolas, the female industrial teacher, noted as she made her rounds in 1896 that "blueberry season" had "rendered the work light . . . taking so many from home." The onset of ricing season regularly delayed the start of the school year in the fall and often prevented children of conservative parents from securing places. Seasonal gatherings were recognized social events and *The Tomahawk*, a newspaper published at White Earth by former métis trader Gus Beaulieu, frequently noted that "most of the Indians are out for the harvest," or "the sugarmakers have returned from

An Anishinaabe man poles while a seated woman uses ricing sticks to knock ripened kernels of wild rice into the canoe at Flat Lake. *Photo by Kenneth Wright, St. Paul, courtesy of Minnesota Historical Society.*

An Anishinaabe couple at their sugar bush camp boil maple sap to make sugar. By 1920, when this photograph was taken, men had assumed a more prominent role in making maple sugar. Joe Big Bear stands to the right. *Photo courtesy of Minnesota Historical Society.*

their sugar camps." Obviously, agriculture was not the only economic activity on the minds of White Earth residents.

Many observers downplayed the significance of the seasonal circuit, failing to realize that it was the economic backbone of the Anishinaabe economy. They regarded its components as part of the "heathen," "pagan," "uncivilized" complex that they believed comprised Anishinaabe culture. The U.S. assimilation programs intended to undermine and eradicate the seasonal round, offering an overly romanticized version of the American agrarian ideal in its stead.

But the adaptability of the seasonal round enhanced its long-term survival. In 1902, Special Agent Charles McNichols went against the grain when he observed that "no Indians are better situated for securing a part of their subsistence by old-time Indian methods." Conservative

White Earth residents continued to adapt the seasonal round and incorporate new elements that they found beneficial.[11]

Selling seasonal produce on the market fit easily into this framework. Indians sold wild rice, maple sugar, berries, ginseng, snakeroot, fish, hides, and game to local merchants, who then sold the produce to their clientele. They also sold items of their own manufacture. Merchants regularly advertised to buy and sell these products in *The Tomahawk*: Robert P. Fairbanks, a licensed government trader, offered "Cash paid for Hides, Fur, and Country Produce," and "Indian Fancy Work a Specialty"; Louisa J. Lynch, another licensed trader, similarly hawked "All Kinds of fresh fish and game kept in season," "Indian Beads Silk and Fancy," and "Needle Work, a Specialty."[12] As they had done during the heyday of the fur trade, the Anishinaabeg continued to sell seasonal produce and craft items on the local market.

John Rogers or Wayquahgishig recounted numerous instances in which his relatives at White Earth traded seasonal resources for food and manufactured items in nearby towns. While ice fishing, they threw fish "on the ice" until they were "frozen as hard as cordwood sticks." Once they had "five or six hundred pounds," they took them to "town and sold" them, always keeping enough for their "immediate needs." Rogers remembered that berry picking was so fruitful that "besides the supply for our own use and canning we sold many a bushel." Native women "found a ready market [for blueberries] in the not too distant towns, and [got] a fair price." A market for wild rice also existed, so that when they were "blessed with a good crop" they always "gather[ed] some rice to sell." Over the winter, even small children "kept busy making pretty baskets with the intention of taking them out to sell them when the right time came." Generally, they kept enough of each resource for their subsistence needs and then sold the rest on the market.[13]

Gathering and selling snakeroot illustrates how the Anishinaabeg learned to integrate their traditional seasonal pursuits into the market economy. Herbal specialists among the Anishinaabeg had long recognized the medicinal properties of Seneca snakeroot (*Polygala senega L.*), calling it *bi'jikiwuck* or "cattle medicine." They made a decoction from it for coughs, colds, convulsions, and in combination with other plants for heart trouble, treated sore throats with an infusion from its leaves, and used it to destroy swallowed water bugs. American pharmacists also came to value snakeroot primarily as an expectorant and cough remedy, creating a market for it. Local merchants, like Sylem Fairbanks, advertised "Market Prices paid for Ginseng, Snake Root and Furs." Indians obliged, gathering far more than they needed for their own medicinal needs. Wagoosh, a young man who was courting John Rogers's sister, introduced him to snakeroot, telling him that "the prices . . . are going to be high." Once Rogers learned the technique of digging roots, there was no stopping him. Soon he and his brother "were bragging over our speed in pulling the snake root" and making it a "contest to see who would get the biggest root for his sack." Wagoosh also taught Rogers's family how to market snakeroot by escorting his mother to town to exchange it for a "goodly supply of groceries." After that, he and his family "dug snake root every day, making several trips to town with it—so we always had a good supply of edibles." Snakeroot had become a significant source of income, and the Anishinaabeg learned how to get the best price for it. Some observers regarded collecting snakeroot and ginseng (*Panax quinquefolius L.*) as a demeaning way to make a living. For the Anishinaabeg, however, it provided yet another source of income that was easily integrated into the seasonal round.[14]

Although many observers commented that game in the area had grown scarce, products of hunting and trapping still formed a significant part of Anishinaabe subsistence. Prime furred animals, beaver, mink, and otter, had grown scarce in the immediate area and Indian men went fifty or one hundred miles to trap muskrats and other small animals, often earning a hundred dollars or more a month. John Rogers learned to hunt from Wagoosh, his prospective brother-in-law. On one trapping expedition, Rogers alone bagged three muskrats, a small mink, and an otter that were worth "fully $80" to a merchant in Brainerd; each member of the party had snared an equal amount. Individuals still sold muskrats, and sometimes more valuable pelts, on the market even though the most lucrative period of the fur trade in the area had passed.[15]

Deer and moose, animals that contributed more directly to subsistence, may have actually increased in numbers due to nearby logging activities. Clearing forests created the open, browsing conditions that these cervines favored. John Rogers and his family never experienced game shortages. As a skilled hunter, Wagoosh exchanged venison for some wild rice that his soon-to-be mother-in-law had gathered. Reverend Gilfillan marveled that moose meat and venison were available all winter long for as little as five cents a pound. As late as 1905, the Board of Fish and Game Commissioners reported a regular "ring" that hunted deer and moose illegally. "Poachers" either sold meat directly to local schools or to traders who distributed it to schools and more distant eastern markets. Such an operation required a substantial amount of moose and venison in excess of subsistence needs. Hunting continued as a valuable economic activity, netting a surplus to be sold on the market.[16]

Wage labor also provided a limited source of income open primarily to young men. Like many others, John Rogers traveled west to hire himself out in the wheat fields of the Red River Valley; he received "ten dollars a month and room and board" and worked on a farm "all through the winter and on into the summer." Others worked in lumber camps in northern Minnesota. Though they often went unenforced, regulations gave preference to Indian labor on the "Chippewa ceded lands." Periodically, *The Tomahawk* reported that "a number of the boys have left to work on the drive." The availability of wage labor provided young Indian men with an alternative to the hunting and trapping lifestyle that eased the transition they faced. Finding new roles by working for wages, they minimized the social dislocation they might otherwise have felt and still continued to contribute to the annual subsistence cycle.[17]

Administration of the agency and mission complexes also provided opportunities for wage labor and generated a significant cash flow. Ambitious assimilation programs undertaken by the U.S. government created a limited number of positions for manual laborers as well as those with a more specialized education. Teamsters hauled supplies from neighboring towns for the agency and schools. Upkeep and maintenance of agency buildings, building and repair of roads and bridges, and sawing lumber and constructing homes for immigrant Indians all presented periodic opportunities to work for wages. Women worked as cooks, seamstresses, and laundresses in the schools. When less-educated Indians were hired to work at the agency, they filled those sorts of manual labor positions.[18]

The Indian Office usually recruited physicians and most schoolteachers from outside the reservation. However, Indians often filled skilled positions as interpreters, teachers, police, government farmers, and occasionally found employment in temporary positions generated by the removal and allotment processes. More often, educated Indians of mixed descent who spoke English, understood U.S. institutions and the agency bureaucracy, and lived near the agency filled positions requiring a greater degree of skill.[19]

Favoritism played an important role in hiring because the agent and the Indian Office appointed individuals to agency positions. Although smaller population centers such as Pine Point and Wild Rice River (or Beaulieu) offered a few jobs, most employees were drawn from the vicinity of White Earth Village, where the agency was located. This created inequality of opportunity, prompting complaints about inequity to be voiced along band lines due to the nature of settlement patterns on the reservation. Those in the eastern section of the reservation perceived themselves to be disadvantaged both in terms of employment and in terms of the benefits that White Earth Village received. Early on, such remote settlements as Pine Point lacked a blacksmith, hospital, and even a road to connect them with the agency. This inequality contributed to a growing competition between groups on the reservation.[20]

Cutting "dead and down" timber also afforded employment to those who applied to cut it under federal legislation. Agents recommended this policy to salvage marketable timber that had been damaged by wind storms or fires. Individuals either cut the timber themselves or contracted to have a lumber firm do the work. Over the years, agents recommended that sawmills be established at the site of logging operations to provide Indians with wages. During its existence, the dead and down logging policy provided much needed employment for Indian men, it being "almost the only labor performed by them during the winter months."[21]

The "fancy work" that White Earth merchants advertised was produced by Indian women who availed themselves of an opportunity that was rather unique to the Anishinaabeg. When Sybil Carter, an Episcopalian missionary, arrived at White Earth in 1886, she was "struck with pity for the women whose lives were spent in futile ill-paid work." She began teaching women affiliated with the Episcopal mission to make a form of "needle point" lace, made of "very fine thread, sometimes as fine as 1000,

Anishinaabe men working for wages at the U.S. Government Sawmill at White Earth Agency in about 1872. Here White Earth timber was manufactured into wood products to be used for building houses and reservation structures, upkeep and maintenance of the agency, and issues to residents. *Photo by Hoard & Tenney, Winona, courtesy of Minnesota Historical Society.*

sometimes, 300 or 200" gauge. Using her church network, Carter succeeded in persuading women of means from the eastern United States to form the "Ladies of the Lace Association" and underwrite her new project until it could become self-supporting. She found a ready market for the lace that Anishinaabe women made and was able to expand the operation, at the women's request, first to Wild Rice River, then to Leech Lake and Red Lake. Eventually Carter brought in other Episcopalian

An Anishinaabe family hauling logs across a frozen lake with a horse-drawn sleigh in about 1920. *Photo courtesy of Minnesota Historical Society.*

women to take over the reservation enterprise to free her time to buy supplies and to market lace across the country.

Indian women walked great distances to the missions to participate in this new industry. They especially appreciated "the opportunity of earning" in late winter when their stock of stored "fish, potatoes, dried corn and berries . . . [was] beginning to dwindle." Earning money from selling lace "enable[d] them to buy the flour, pork, tea, sugar and tobacco from the half breed traders." After they had learned the technique, they were permitted to do piece work in their homes, though missionaries initially feared they would dirty the lace. Anishinaabe women welcomed the convenience of home work, and it never took on the sweat shop proportions of the early industrial revolution. At times, it chagrined missionary overseers that native women took "their own time in doing it"; no matter how pressing the order was, they saw "no need for haste unless they [were] in immediate need of the shonia (money)." Nevertheless, Indian women took great pride in their craft. As "the younger set who had been educated in the government school translated and explained" how the lace they made was "worn by great ladies, and went into beautiful homes to make them more beautiful," they responded with "gratified smiles and exclamations." Despite their obvious pride, it is doubtful, however, that these women had internalized the class dimensions of this arrangement.

The lace-making endeavors lasted until Sybil Carter died in 1909. All her tireless efforts had failed to make the industry self-sustaining. Without her well-connected network, her marketing know-how, and the Ladies of the Lace Association's New York showroom, the enterprise languished and Anishinaabe women lost this creative opportunity to earn cash.[22]

The White Earth Anishinaabeg also made use of money and services available to them from the U.S. government. Most continued to receive annuities legally due to them through treaty rights. In addition, the Nelson Act entitled individuals to per capita payments from the "Chippewa in Minnesota Fund." Goods and services included among removal benefits also contributed to the domestic economy.

The promise of a regular annuity payment complemented the old relationship between traders and Indians; traders simply extended credit to Indians on the strength of their annuity payment instead of their trapping returns. The arrangement became more reliable, reducing uncertainty for traders and reinforcing existent patron-client relationships. Although, as Joseph Gilfillan described, "every Ojibwa goes in debt to his trader just as deeply as he will allow him," Indians felt comfortable as participants in a system with which they had long been familiar. In 1902, Special Agent Charles S. McNichols observed that the "licensed traders . . . are not complying with the rules . . . in the matter of posting prices." As in the past, the system was still subject to abuse as some traders took advantage of monopolistic conditions by inflating their prices and refusing to post them. However, as long as Indians could procure the goods they needed, the relationship continued as a mutually profitable, symbiotic one. The Anishinaabeg complained more about U.S. government policies than about the traders' behavior.[23]

After 1902, policymakers restricted Indians' access to the proceeds of the sale of their land and timber. Instances of fraud and their belief that Indians were incapable of managing money prompted their actions. They relied instead on appointed guardians to manage individual funds for minors and "incompetents." Waushkesid Agustin criticized the autocratic manner in which "Mr. Niles" was appointed to administer his younger brother's and sister's funds because "he is interested in bank (*sic*) that are connected in . . . trying to buy our land and is a speculator." True to Agustin's depiction, Acting Commissioner of Indian Affairs C. F. Larrabee simply dismissed his concerns. Indians were surprised and dismayed to find their requests for access to their individual accounts limited to ten dollars a month. People who desired more money had to apply to the agent and explain their reasons.[24]

Although policymakers intended these guidelines to provide protection so that funds would not be "squandered," the results did not always conform to expectations. Indians sought access to their funds for a variety of reasons. Some planned capital investments; others, especially the elderly, had subsistence needs. Ahbowegeshig (Warm Day), an Otter Tail band leader from Pine Point and grandson of the *ogimaa* Minogeshig (Fine Day), believed it to be entirely reasonable for those who were unable to work "on account of sickness" to be "enabled to buy the necessaries of life with the proceeds of [their] timber." The U.S. authorities, however, did not agree. Agents frequently regulated access to individual accounts as a means of social control. "Competence" to manage one's funds became secondary to compliance with U.S. Indian policy directives in determining which requests gained approval. Special Agent McNichols admired Agent Michelet's policy: "If an Indian applies for any favor his [Michelet's] first question is 'Do you live on your allotment?'" If not, it was useless for the applicant to request anything. Agents refused to give Indians their annuity payments if they had not been vaccinated or if they had not "legally" married. Any previous infraction might be summoned up to deny an Indian's request.[25]

Despite such restrictive monitoring of their individual funds, the Anishinaabeg manipulated governmental institutions to suit their own purposes. Since direct requests for their funds produced negligible results, they resorted to subterfuge. They worked "all kinds of games on the government doctor to get sick rations," or on school personnel "to get clothing for the children." School superintendents knew that offering meals in day schools would attract more conservative Indians. Parents who worked in logging camps during the winter relied on boarding schools where children could "have advantages which [could] not be had in the camps." Indians schemed to secure a greater share of what they knew to be their own resources.[26]

The U.S. government's restrictive policies gave métis cultural brokers much about which to complain. Safeguarding tribal resources was one thing, but increasingly intrusive U.S. policies were something that no one had counted on. When leaders had agreed to the Nelson Act, it had seemed much like another treaty. They had not agreed that the Indian Office should have iron-clad control over all their tribal funds and assets. The lessening of autonomy that accompanied the Nelson Act had been unannounced and unanticipated. Métis elite at White Earth were approaching the zenith of their economic success and power. That they should suddenly be forced into a position of wardship was more than they could bear. Their denunciations of Indian Office policy fairly well crackled with their anger and indignation. Their opinions usually found voice in *The Tomahawk*, published by the Franco-Anishinaabe Gus Beaulieu. They charged that the government held Indian people in an anomalous position, "recognizing them as independent" in a limited sense, while holding them "in subjection and subservancy [sic]." In the name of its motto, "Truth before Favor," *The Tomahawk* steadily maintained a critical posture toward the Indian Office, monitoring Anishinaabe affairs across the state. Its writers advocated lessening restrictions imposed by the Indian Office to allow Indians "the right to use their own judgments" so that they might become more self-reliant. Between 1902 and 1906, most White Earth residents agreed that the Indian Office held too tight a rein on Indian economic activities and they chafed under the yoke of federal guardianship.[27]

A small group of individuals descended from unions between French and British fur traders and native women gained their livelihoods independently as entrepreneurs. As the days of large, monopolistic fur trading companies in Minnesota passed, they suffered dislocation and struggled to maintain their status and involvement in the local and regional economy. In the past they had proven their appreciation of land as real estate and made profitable decisions about their holdings. When they received "half-breed scrip" under the 1854 Treaty, some located their parcels of land in Crow Wing Village, capitalizing on the bustling Red River ox-cart traffic by speculating in land. They were some of the first to claim land allotments under the 1867 Treaty and would come to make lucrative decisions about later allotments. All told, these "French-Canadian mixed-bloods," as they were termed, received more allotments of land than any other category of Indians.[28]

Many former traders from Crow Wing and their offspring became merchants, real estate agents, and lawyers at White Earth. Such businesses as the merchant establishments of B. L. Fairbanks, Robert P. Fairbanks, L. L. Lynch, and Ed Leecy, Theodore Beaulieu's real estate office, the Hotel Leecy, and Gus Beaulieu's newspaper *The Tomahawk*, were situated in White Earth Village, further contributing to its economic ascendancy on the reservation. Their economic success, measured by the standards of U.S. society, set them apart from most of the White Earth Anishinaabeg.[29]

Their familiarity with U.S. institutions enabled Indian Office employees and entrepreneurs of Euro-Anishinaabe descent simultaneously to perform useful mediating services for the Indian communities and to make substantial financial gains for themselves. The location of their businesses in the mid-section of the reservation reflected their mediating roles in geographic terms. Delegates and representatives from White Earth who closely monitored congressional activities to safeguard Anishinaabe resources were usually drawn from this group and band chiefs. In one sense, they served as a protective buffer, insulating more conservative Anishinaabeg from direct interaction with representatives of American society. As long as their involvement produced beneficial results, their accumulation of wealth was tolerated as simply a "different" way of life that distinguished them from "Indians." Some even held them in esteem. All of these individuals served as effective cultural brokers.

Life for Indian women of mixed descent in the western part of the reservation resembled that of other rural women. They tended subsistence gardens near their homes as their husbands and sons engaged in market agriculture, worked for wages, or managed their business concerns. Their energies were focused on the domestic scene, preserving and

Theo. H. Beaulieu's real estate office at White Earth in 1908. *Photo courtesy of Minnesota Historical Society.*

B. L. Fairbanks Company General Store at White Earth sometime between 1910 and 1915. *Photo courtesy of Minnesota Historical Society.*

The office of *The Tomahawk* was conveniently located next to the Land Office, easing Gus Beaulieu's multifaceted business dealings. *Photo courtesy of Minnesota Historical Society.*

canning produce, sewing clothing, caring for children, and otherwise running their households. Their activities created a stable base from which their husbands might move in larger economic and political circles if they chose. Their extrahousehold involvements tended to center on church-related social activities, with many of them practicing Catholicism. They coordinated social events like dances and picnics associated with the church and expressed concern for the moral order of the community. Extramarital affairs especially angered them, posing a threat to the stability and security of their lives. Boundary-maintaining mechanisms were reflected in marital choices as those of mixed descent tended to marry within their own group.[30]

While Métis people in western Canada suffered discrimination and poverty after the diaspora that followed in the wake of the 1885 rebellion led by Louis Riel, a Métis leader who challenged Canada's land policy, at White Earth these people, who shared cultural roots with the nationalistic Canadian Métis, attained social, economic, and political ascendancy. They considered themselves and their families the "better class" of people on the reservation and maintained only minimal associations with people of the eastern forests.[31]

Political Leadership Patterns

By 1900, many avenues existed by which political leaders might gain status among the White Earth Anishinaabeg. Key band leaders still acquired their positions through hereditary channels, but the difficult transition period created opportunities for new sorts of leaders to emerge as well. Individuals with diverse skills who could provide much needed guidance in directing Anishinaabe adaptations might find themselves called upon to perform as leaders.

Until his death in 1898, most reservation residents deferred to Wabonaquod (White Cloud) as the paramount *ogimaa* at White Earth. He inherited this position as the eldest son of Gull Lake *ogimaa* Waubojig (White Fisher) and was performing as a respected leader by 1867. He had been among the first to reach out to the Episcopalians for aid in enhancing Anishinaabe farming skills and enthusiastically supported the move to White Earth in an effort to revitalize their economy. Upon "conversion" he adopted the name D. G. Wright after an Episcopalian benefactor, though he seldom used it. During his lifetime, the Anishinaabeg were increasingly drawn into the orbit of the U.S. government. Treaty provisions became ever more intrusive until U.S. administrators began dictating complicated legislative terms aimed at assimilating Indians and changing their culture. Wabonaquod did not speak English and was forced to rely more and more on the mediating skills of bicultural métis brokers to negotiate a course through the myriad demands of the United States, the details of which often eluded him. As he addressed the U.S. Chippewa Commission, he was aware of his limitations: "We have passed many sleepless nights; many have done their best to understand this act [the 1889 Nelson Act], but I and many others do not yet fully understand it, not having the benefit of education." By the 1890s, Wabonaquod had "converted" to Catholicism, perhaps symbolic of his need for a close association, an alliance of sorts, with the métis brokers. He was correct in determining that a more thorough understanding of American culture was necessary to negotiate the best terms for his people. However, this also signaled his waning effectiveness as a leader. By the time of his death, Wabonaquod was more of a figurehead, a symbol of an earlier autonomous era, than a leader who brought results.[32]

Others also claimed hereditary rights to act as leaders. Everyone agreed that Waweyeacumig (Round Earth) of the Mille Lacs band had inherited his position as *ogimaa* from his "parents" (not his father alone). He continued in this capacity at White Earth, behaving generously toward his constituents as was appropriate for someone of his stature. Wiese of the Pembina band was also consistently recognized as the head leader. Mezhucegeshig (Horizon, or Light Reaching to the Ground all around) of the Mississippi band was the eldest son of Quewezaince (Boy), a famed warrior from Rabbit Lake. He had been attracted to the Episcopalian farming program, adopted his seldom-used conversion name, A. T. Twing, and acquired 160 acres at White Earth by cultivating them under the 1867 Treaty terms. Although he was considered a minor leader who counted only 50 people in his band, he rose to such prominence at White Earth that by 1908 Reverend Joseph Gilfillan described him as "the present Head Chief of the Ojibways . . . the only living man descended from a long line of Chiefs." In fact, Mezhucegeshig's forebears had not been so illustrious, but he functioned as such an effective *ogimaa* that the requisite past was embellished if not invented outright. As such, he is a good example of flexible Anishinaabe leadership criteria. Anyone who hoped to gain support for their cause turned to Mezhucegeshig as a paramount leader second only to Wabonaquod while he was alive. Ahbowegeshig (Warm Day) of the Otter Tail band of Pillagers also reached into his past to garner greater credibility for his leadership claims. Realizing that his father Cahbemahbe's status did not bolster his position, he made reference to his grandfather Minogeshig (Fine Day) of the Mille Lacs band who had performed as a noteworthy leader for many years. All of these men met fairly traditional Anishinaabe standards for leadership and were quite active and visible in White Earth politics.[33]

Various treaties entitled each band to certain rights and benefits from the U.S. government. Band leaders and their constituencies interceded to safeguard these rights by petitioning assorted government officials. Pembina band leaders repeatedly pressed for the right to participate in distributions of funds to the Red Lake band and to the Turtle Mountain band, pointing to former treaties to justify their claims. Otter Tail Pillagers from Pine Point keenly felt that their settlement was excluded from the benefits enjoyed by those who lived at White Earth Village close to the agency. They requested their own blacksmith because the distances involved prevented them from using the blacksmith at Wild Rice River. Combinations of bands also expressed common concerns. The Gull Lake, Mille Lacs, and White Oak Point bands allied, calling themselves the White Earth Mississippi bands and requested that delegations be allowed to represent their concerns in Washington, D.C. Band protests against infractions of treaty terms were common. In a sense, U.S. policymakers inadvertently helped to perpetuate band ties by failing to honor treaty rights.[34]

Maintenance of old band ties in some ways worked against reservation unity. Unequal distribution of funds for reservation improvements fostered discord as more distant settlements vied for funds with White Earth Village. Special treaty rights pitted the Mississippi bands, as the original negotiators of the 1867 Treaty, against the Otter Tail Pillager and Pembina bands, which had not been in residence at the time. The Mississippi bands often argued that provisions for 160-acre allotments should apply to "the Mississippi band only" and that members of other bands should receive only 80 acres apiece. Inevitably the concerns of different bands at times diverged and could inhibit political cooperation across band lines.[35]

There were times, however, when various bands at White Earth could agree and cooperate for common purposes. On occasion, interband councils decided whether applicants were eligible for enrollment. They concurred most frequently about financial matters, especially in their support for per capita payments and criticisms of the manner in which the Indian Office managed their accounts.[36]

Yet despite occasional cooperation across band lines, the band remained the primary unit of political identity before 1907. While all band leaders made reference to White Earth as their reservation, a reservation-based political consciousness had yet to supplant earlier band ties. The coalescence of bands to become the White Earth Anishinaabeg awaited the rise of land fraud as a political issue.

Individuals knew to which band they belonged, and who their band leaders were. They belonged to the Mille Lacs band or the Otter Tail Pillager band or the Leech Lake band—political groupings derived more from geographic location than the personage of a particular leader. And when U.S. agents created new leaders to facilitate their programs, the Anishinaabeg easily identified these people too, sometimes according them respect, and sometimes paying them no mind whatsoever. Removal agents received instructions that "each chief to be recognized must have at least 50 members in his band." Allotment registries filed with the Crookston Land District of the General Land Office recorded no fewer than eighty "chiefs" among the White Earth bands, with twenty for the tiny Leech Lake removal band alone. Clearly, all such "chiefs" could not have had relevance for White Earth residents, but these sorts of fictions aided the U.S. Chippewa Commission in achieving the largest possible number of removals. Similarly, Indian men who supported changes envisioned by U.S. policymakers might also find themselves elevated to leadership status by external authorities. Mezhucegeshig remembered several occasions on which U.S. officials "made . . . quite a number of chiefs," among them "Pay-kin-ah-wash, Nay-tah-waush, No-kaince, O-zow-wah-ge-shig, and O-ge-mah-wah-je-wabe." To underscore their status, they were taken to New York City, where "the President of the U.S. put medals on them." Mezhucegeshig went on to speak of Indian leaders "electing" men such as Benjamin Casswell, John Hanks, Nezho-cumig, and Joseph Charette (Joseph Critts or Wainjemahdub) as chiefs because "other Indians would follow [them] in industrial pursuits." Joseph Charette himself attested to this, saying, "The white people made me a chief. . . . It was through some Indian agent, and they forwarded it down to Washington, and they accepted me that way." Ever humble, he admitted that he had "always been a brave in the past"; the Indians recognized this by giving him a feather to commemorate his brave deeds, while the United States awarded him a Grand Army button for his service in the Civil War.[37]

Determining band membership suffered from a similar sort of bureau-

cratic nonchalance, creating "bands" on paper that bore little relation to
those that functioned in reality. The enrollment process did not operate
according to fixed rules and considerable folklore surrounds the manner
in which individuals attained enrollment as "Chippewa Indians of Minnesota." Indians testified that band leaders had placed their friends on
the rolls or people for whom they "felt sorry." Liquor sometimes eased
the process. Some charged that individuals with little or no valid claim
had been rounded up in Minneapolis and St. Paul and added to the rolls.
Members of the U.S. Chippewa Commission enrolled individuals originally affiliated with Lake Superior and Wisconsin bands (some came to
call them the "Lake Superior mixed-bloods"), even though they had
received explicit instructions not to do so. Clement H. Beaulieu, a prominent trader of mixed descent originally from Lac Courte Oreilles, Wisconsin, based his right to enrollment at White Earth on unrecorded ad
hoc arrangements made under the 1854 Treaty allowing Lake Superior
and Wisconsin band members residing at Sandy Lake and Crow Wing essentially to switch band affiliations and collect their annuities where
they lived, instead of traveling the long distance to La Pointe. Enrollment decisions made in this fashion would soon come under question.
Through this type of piecemeal process, ultimately approved by external
authorities, the "bands" took shape.[38]

Federal officials also intended to restrict the roles of leaders whom
they had helped to create. Leaders, hereditary or those created by U.S.
officials, faced almost certain opposition from the Indian Office as they
asserted what they believed to be legitimate claims. Commissioner of
Indian Affairs W. A. Jones informed Temperance Chief that "the Department does not want Indian delegations here." Agent Michelet disappointed a council that had met at Wild Rice River in 1902 by advising
them that the Indian Office felt it unnecessary for them "to employ
attorneys in the settlement of their affairs with the government." The
Indian Office would process all complaints itself thereby circumscribing
the activities of Anishinaabe leaders at White Earth.[39]

The U.S. officials usually viewed these sorts of "official" leaders as
the most legitimate Anishinaabe representatives, even as they belittled
their positions. New circumstances created new criteria for leaders,
which was in itself within standard Anishinaabe means for determining
leadership.

The alliance that Gull Lake leaders forged with Episcopalians produced native ministers, many of whom became spokesmen for measured, purposeful change—especially through farming and church attendance. In a manner reminiscent of hereditary lines of descent, a number
of sons of important band leaders studied for the ministry, were ordained
as deacons, and opened missions of their own among the Anishinaabeg.
These native ministers became important leaders in their own right, and
were most effective at mediating between Episcopalian church leaders
and other Anishinaabeg. They were attuned enough to their native kin to
voice authentic Anishinaabe concerns, but also advocated adaptation
along agrarian and educational lines.

In 1852, Episcopalian missionary James Lloyd Breck opened a mission
and school at Gull Lake, where he brought several Indian boys to be
educated in Euroamerican ways. Samuel Madison (Nabiquan or The
Ship), son of Shaydayence (Little Pelican), head Grand Medicine man of
the Anishinaabeg, was among them. Although Shaydayence did not
"convert" to Christianity until he was sixty-four years of age, he became
quite devout and wanted his son to have all the knowledge of both whites
and Indians when he succeeded him. Breck was driven from Gull Lake in
1857 for his failure to abide by Anishinaabe ethics and went to Faribault to establish the Shattuck Boarding School where he housed thirty
to forty Anishinaabe scholars, Samuel Madison among them. In 1873,
Madison moved to the White Earth Reservation to be trained for the
ministry by Reverend Gilfillan. He was ordained as a deacon in 1876
along with two others at the St. Columba Mission at White Earth, and
then left within the year to found a new mission at Red Lake. His career
path was not unique.

Three sons (Fred Smith, George Smith, and John Coleman) of Crow
Feather, Hole in the Day's head warrior, also became ordained as deacons
and played prominent roles as spokesmen, as did Charles T. Wright
(Nashotah or Twin), son of Wabonaquod (White Cloud), George B. Morgan (Kahkahcun), son of Mille Lacs leader Iahbay (Buck), and George
Johnson, son of John Johnson Enmegahbowh. Only a few native ministers, Mark Hart (Obimweweiash or Sailing along with a Thundering
Sound), Louis Manypenny, Duane Porter, and Joseph Wakazoo had no
kinship ties to prominent Anishinaabe band leaders. Clearly, succes-
sional leadership roles were passed from important band leaders to their

Episcopalian sons in much the same way that semihereditary lines of descent had operated in the past. Most of these native deacons were sent away from the White Earth Reservation to establish new Episcopalian missions elsewhere. Crow Feather's sons, Fred Smith, George Smith, and John Coleman, and the orphan Mark Hart for a time, officiated at Red Lake, traveling about in very difficult weather to persuade members of the most conservative Anishinaabe band in the state to come to their Christian church. Charles Wright and Mark Hart moved to Leech Lake, and Charles Wright eventually settled at Cass Lake. Only two men with kin ties to the White Earth Anishinaabeg, George Morgan, son of Mille Lacs leader Iahbay, and George Johnson, son of Enmegahbowh, remained at White Earth after their ordination. The others who ministered to the White Earth population came from more distant locales: Louis Many-penny, who frequently performed as an interpreter and had charge of the church at Twin Lakes, hailed from Wisconsin; Duane Porter, minister at Mahnomen, originally came from Pine City in the Snake River area; and Joseph Wakazoo was from Michigan. Native proselytizing efforts toward their kinfolk throughout Minnesota drained effective leadership away from the White Earth Reservation. Some of these men, Charles Wright and Fred Smith in particular, were often listed among important peti-tioners and resolution signers, but, more often than not, their day-to-day concerns lay elsewhere and their absence for much of the time under-mined their credibility, much to the detriment of the White Earth politi-cal scene.[40]

Women's groups associated with the Episcopalian missions also pro-vided leadership, especially in the sphere of social welfare. Charles Wright's wife, referred to as Mrs. Nashotah, often served as a go-between for female missionaries who hoped to broaden their influence. Mission-aries frequently turned to the Women's Auxiliary and the lace makers to help popularize new programs such as hospitals and old folks' homes. Pauline Colby, an Episcopalian missionary, evinced a special concern for the elderly, believing that they were the "greatest sufferers by this on-ward sweep of progress." She appealed to the Women's Auxiliary to allay suspicions that these institutions were places where people went to die, saying, "You know they will come if you say it is all right." Once persuaded that these efforts were sincere, the sick and elderly did, indeed, come, though they did not simultaneously reject their own medicinal practices.[41]

Although men more frequently assumed prominent political roles, Anishinaabe women were far from absent. Women of important hereditary lineages might be considered "queens" or *kitchiogimakwe*, the female equivalent of a head chief or *kitchiogima*. "Old Mon-i-do-wub," or Odubenaunequay, who was most likely a sister of Manidowab, was one such "old queen" of the Mississippi band who was prominent at White Earth. The suffix *equay*, a phonetic representation of *ikwe* or *akwe*, meaning "woman," indicates that several women signed the Nelson Act agreements and were listed among "band chiefs" who removed to the White Earth Reservation. They might be termed "queens" or "first" or "second" band queens. Five of thirteen identifiable women on these lists were named Wahbonequay, which an interpreter translated as "White Hair," no doubt an equivalent female reference to the tendency toward age-grading in determining leadership. Major John Howard, agent at White Earth, informed government visitors that "a great many of them [women] . . . attend . . . councils . . . [and] sometimes they are heard." Indian Office investigators were repeatedly surprised at how vocal native women were in their behind-the-scenes lobbying activities, occasionally speaking up in the councils themselves. Inspector James McLaughlin was amazed to find that "old full-blood Indian woman [*sic*] manifest such a deep interest," serving as proxies for absent male relatives and signing agreements in their own right without objection from the assembled men. Unaccustomed to women's participation in political affairs, U.S. commissioners reported that they allowed women to sign the agreements only "at the request of the chiefs," oblivious to the fact that a few of those "chiefs" were women.[42] It would appear that U.S. society did more to restrict the roles that Anishinaabe women might assume than did the Anishinaabeg.

Students who returned from national boarding schools such as Carlisle (Pennsylvania) and Hampton (Virginia) were also prepared to perform as particularly effective mediators. Benjamin Casswell, Margaret Warren, Isabel Schneider, and others served as both interpreters and teachers, positions for which their education had well prepared them for. Ben Casswell served as principal of the Cass Lake Boarding School and was active politically as both a representative and an interpreter for the "Full Blood Faction." Also an interpreter, Isabel Schneider had strong convictions about fairness and refused to witness the minutes of meetings where she felt Gus Beaulieu and Ben Fairbanks had manipulated unsuspecting Indians. Similarly vexed by Gus's skilled maneuvers, members of the Graham Commission, appointed by Congress in 1911 to investigate charges of land fraud at White Earth, turned to Margaret Warren, relying on her honesty. Especially as métis cultural brokers came to be distrusted, these "returned students" played increasingly important roles as cultural mediators.

The political involvement of individuals of mixed descent complicated matters. Individuals of mixed parentage had "followed the trading enterprise" and made homes in composite fur trade "hamlets" near the Anishinaabeg. This miscegenation, a consequence of frequent unions between Indian women and traders, originated during the early years of the fur trade. Though genetic distinctions meant little to the Anishinaabeg, women who married Euroamerican men broke the patrilineal clan line. Patrilineal descent systems meant that children without Anishinaabe fathers had no institutionalized role within the clan structure. Because the clan system was flexible, native communities easily accommodated these children. However, the cultural orientation of métis parents meant that they were also likely to send their children away from the reservation to acquire a more formal education. Many moved temporarily to larger Minnesota towns or to eastern cities where they either boarded at schools or lived with relatives while they attended.[43] As early as 1838, Julia Warren Spears accompanied her mother and five siblings to Clarkson, New York, where her "Grandfather Warren" lived. She and several of her brothers and sisters remained to attend Clarkson Academy and the Oneida Institute near Utica. Her sister Mary attended school in Ohio to train to become a teacher, and her sister Sophia went to boarding school at Belle Prairie near Little Falls, Minnesota. In 1840, "Uncle Robert" Fairbanks was sent to Fredonia, New York, to attend school. John Carl, who was by his own accounting "more white than . . . Indian," attended Haskell Institute in Lawrence, Kansas, the University of Minnesota, and nearly graduated from the University of Kansas at Lawrence with a degree in law. The Beaulieu brothers were also better educated than most; Gus first had a private tutor, then attended Sinsinewaymound College, and finally left St. John's College, near St. Cloud, Minnesota, at the age of nineteen; Clement studied to become an Episcopalian minister. As late as 1913, Clement still felt that his daughter would receive a better education in the Twin Cities, and he placed his two allotment tracts in trusteeship to pay for it. When they returned to the Anishinaabeg, these young metis adults found that their training had prepared them to mediate between the two ethnic groups, much as their fathers and mothers had done before them.[44]

The careers of some of these individuals read like updated versions of mediating roles their parents had played in fur trade society. Benjamin L. Fairbanks's father was trader George Fairbanks and B.L., as he was called, spent his childhood at Leech Lake, steeped in fur trade culture. George and B.L.'s uncle Robert were the first traders at the White Earth Reservation, where they moved when B.L. was a boy. During his early adult years, B.L. successfully farmed at White Earth, where he lived with his wife Sarah (nee Dufort) with whom he had eight children, four boys and four girls. B.L.'s older brother George had operated their father's trading post after he died. After his brother's death, the White Earth trading post and all its goods burned, prompting B.L. to build his own "General Store" and become a merchant himself. By 1913 he owned three stores, one at White Earth, one at Red Lake, and one at Beaver Dam, and owned 20,000 acres of what had once been allotted land. His reputation as the wealthiest man on the reservation extended far beyond its boundaries.[45]

In 1913, Theodore H. Beaulieu, Gus's cousin, made his living by farming, dealing in real estate, and "now and then [he did] some writing for the papers and magazines for pastime." Acting as a realtor probably brought him his greatest profits as he explained how he bought and sold lands, "not only here [at White Earth], but elsewhere . . . in Milaca Point, Pine County, in Canada, and . . . in Oregon." The jobs he performed prior to this vocation illustrate perfectly the mediating roles of these transplanted cultural brokers. Theo. H., as he frequently referred to himself, worked in the government service for many years. He began as census enumerator and allotting agent for the U.S. Chippewa Commission as they persuaded various Anishinaabe families across the state to move to White Earth. Then he worked in the agency office under Major Sutherland and Agent Michelet "looking after the affairs of the Mille Lacs Indians," who had moved there. Next he was transferred to the field service "looking after the nomad Indians . . . those that were not left on the reservation, but who were entitled to remove there and take up their allotments." He was given charge of making up the annuity rolls and then spent three years registering allotments in the land department. Finally, he took over as superintendent of the White Earth Boarding School between 1879 and 1882. Theo. H. Beaulieu was a highly respected reservation leader and, although he shared their criticisms of the way the Indian Office managed Anishinaabe affairs, he worked hard to dissociate himself from the activities of members of his ethnic group that he considered to be exploitative and self-aggrandizing, especially those of his cousin Gus. His efforts must have paid off. Naomi Warren Ladue remembered, "I think Theodore Beaulieu worked more for the benefit of the people, as a whole. I think Gus [Beaulieu] worked more for his own, and Ben [Fairbanks] was a lot that way too."[46]

Gustave H. Beaulieu, born in 1853 at Crow Wing to Clement H. and Elizabeth (nee Farling) Beaulieu, became the most influential (and notorious) métis cultural broker at the White Earth Reservation. Although his parents wanted him to become a priest, Gus left college at nineteen to become, first, a member of a surveying party, and, then, assistant timber agent for the Northern Pacific Railroad Company. After traveling for a number of years, he decided to return to the White Earth Reservation and made his living first by hauling lumber and then by venturing into the "photograph business" for a short time. In 1886, he initiated the first newspaper at the White Earth Reservation, *The Progress*, with the primary purpose of monitoring the management of Indian affairs by agents and the U.S. government. At the same time, he was appointed U.S. deputy marshal in 1879 where he served for eight years before he was transferred to the U.S. Attorney's Office, where he served for ten more years as an interpreter and clerk. After his resignation in 1897 to "look after Mille Lac interests," he devoted all of his time to overseeing the interests of the "Chippewa Indians of Minnesota."[47]

The paternalistic manner in which the Indian Office controlled Anishinaabe tribal funds annoyed métis cultural brokers. Gus, in particular, became a veritable thorn in the side of every agent and Indian Office inspector as he criticized their policies at every turn. The Commissioner of Indian Affairs refused to allow the Anishinaabeg any role in managing their tribal or individual resources and slated their funds to be used for programs that the Indians adamantly opposed. Taking his position of authority to heart, Agent Timothy J. Sheehan determined to defuse Gus's influence by confiscating his printing press and, as C. D. O'Brien described, "disposed of [Gus's] newspaper with an ax." Gus sued him in federal court and won. Not to be so easily dissuaded, Gus later reconstituted the newspaper in 1902, naming it *The Tomahawk*, and true to its motto, "Truth before Favor," continued his surveillance of Anishinaabe affairs.[48]

Gus H. Beaulieu and others like him found power in their roles as cultural brokers. They were often present as interpreters at political and diplomatic gatherings and, through their linguistic skills, controlled the exchange of ideas and information. Their formal education and experience enabled them to understand treaty and legislative negotiations, the intentions of the U.S. government, and the potential consequences of policies. Together with band leaders, they sought to safeguard their tribal and economic interests. Merchants and mediators among them, like B. L. Fairbanks and Gus H. Beaulieu, enjoyed patron-client relationships with Indian people and received not only payment but, sometimes, political support in exchange for their credit and services. Their leadership style reflected their ethnic heritage of brokerage, rooted in Great Lakes fur trade society, and stronger adherence to market values. Often their services were indispensable in the struggle to preserve Anishinaabe resources and to combat U.S. paternalism.[49]

Beyond protecting Anishinaabe resources vis-à-vis the U.S. government, however, their interests often diverged from those of more conservative Anishinaabeg. Aggressively accumulating individual wealth was part of their personal agenda and their experience in fur trade society enabled them to gain the best advantage within the context of the U.S. market economy. Their greater wealth and close association with state politicians increased their visibility and power, but also made them vulnerable to criticism at home. When they pursued individual interests that conflicted with collective interests that more conservative Anishinaabe also sought to safeguard, they were sure to draw censure.

In 1915, Robert G. Beaulieu stands to the right in the press room of *The Tomahawk*, a weekly newspaper founded by Gus H. Beaulieu in 1902. *Photo courtesy of Minnesota Historical Society.*

Despite marked ethnic boundary-maintaining mechanisms, marriage relationships, reckoned by Anishinaabe rules, had created far-flung kinship ties between Lake Superior and Wisconsin band descendants and those who had legitimate rights to reside at White Earth. Gus Beaulieu's grandmother and Wabonaquod's mother were cousins, for example. Similarly, Hole in the Day's father and Gus Beaulieu's grandmother were first cousins. As noted earlier, Wabonaquod symbolically called these intermarried métis his "sons-in-law." In a similar vein, Mezhucegeshig referred to Clement H. Beaulieu as his "brother" since their mothers were sisters. It was upon these kinship ties that the matrix of power relationships within the multiethnic Mississippi band rested.[50]

Ethnic differences, reflected in different orientations to market behavior, were evident at an early date. Even though he recognized the kinship relationship, Wabonaquod was also well aware of the advantages that those who understood U.S. institutions might arrange for themselves, complaining, "Those who can talk the best get the seed-grain first. . . . When there is anything issued, . . . it is issued to our sons-in-law . . . the whites who are intermarried with our families. . . . Those who are so solicitous for their own interests and . . . have more foresight than we."[51]

Although Wabonaquod recognized the positive role that educated "mixed-bloods" played in protecting Anishinaabe resources, theirs was at times an uneasy partnership. He complained that "in some matters I am a perfect slave of . . . those I call my sons-in-law . . . they always coerce me into it."[52] Ambivalence characterized Wabonaquod's attitude toward his "sons-in-law," and he always anticipated unacceptable behavior from them. Yet, band, kinship, and political ties kept them closely affiliated. Wabonaquod believed that increasingly complex Anishinaabe relations with the U.S. government only heightened their dependence on the métis cultural brokers and he hoped to make the best of the situation. His death in 1898 would seriously undermine the so-called Lake Superior mixed-bloods' position on the reservation.

The rights of the Lake Superior mixed-bloods had been questioned since the establishment of the reservation in 1867. Hole in the Day had opposed their efforts to move to White Earth and many believed that this had figured in his murder. Over the years, the Indian Office received complaints from band leaders that Indians from Lake Superior and Wisconsin bands had been wrongfully included among those entitled to reside at the White Earth Reservation. In 1889, four Mississippi band leaders, Mezhucegeshig, Joseph Charette, Paykinahwaush, and Ojibway urged the Commissioner of Indian Affairs to take a closer look at the Beaulieu family's right to live at White Earth. Paykinahwaush complained that "the chiefs and Indians do not want . . . Clem. H. Beaulieu nor Theod. B. H. Beaulieu to have anything to say in our business." Joseph Charette concurred, insisting that "this man [Clement] does not belong on the reservation." In 1893 and again in 1896, Anishinaabe leaders protested decisions of the U.S. Chippewa Commission in enrolling those whose rights they now challenged, but they were not taken seriously. Many of those in question had been among the earliest migrants to White Earth and had acquired land through the 1867 Treaty and 1889 Nelson Act provisions. Some had been prominent spokesmen during negotiations with the Northwest Indian Commission and the U.S. Chippewa Commission. Nonetheless, concerned leaders admitted that they had not paid close enough attention at these critical junctures and continued to reiterate their complaints.[53]

Since the inception of the reservation in 1867, powerful patron-traders of mixed descent, like Clement and Gus Beaulieu and Benjamin L. Fairbanks, had managed to exert a great deal of political influence on the reservation. The "Beaulieu-Fairbanks gang," as some called them, dominated self-proclaimed "elective" council meetings at White Earth from the 1890s to around 1910, when the factional dispute escalated.

They scheduled councils conveniently for themselves, always at White Earth Village, publicizing them through their newspaper, *The Tomahawk*, without concern for the extent of its circulation. Sometimes "the tribal councils were not in fact held"; instead, "a small party of Beaulieu's friends and followers went from place to place," counted those to whom they spoke, and tried to pass off their opinion as the result of a council. When a majority threatened to vote independently, the reservation "bosses" resorted to what Agent John Howard called "the spring-wagon method of holding councils," where they used wagons and drivers to round up eligible voters from around town to stack the deck in their favor. The ringleaders bullied speakers at council meetings and, through manipulations of parliamentary procedure and rules of order, refused to recognize those whose opinions ran counter to their own. Unable to comprehend these procedural quirks, James Bassett complained that "whenever a full blood wants to say anything the President raps the table on them." Isabel Schneider, an interpreter, refused to affix her signature to the proceedings of a council held at White Earth Village on 15 March 1909 because, "Resolutions . . . were railroaded through . . . and the Indians were bewildered in the council." She complained that "the Indians did not understand that . . . their sentiments should have been expressed by their standing up or holding up their hand." These political power brokers even scheduled their 1910 council meeting during the June 14 Celebration, a time of festivities, to serve as a smokescreen for holding their own personal meeting that they could then pass off as a representative council.[54]

Their strategies for domination could also extend far beyond the bounds of mere manipulation. Suspicion of outright fraud was implicit in "full-blood" leader Mezhucegeshig's complaint that his name had been added to "mixed-blood" petitions without his knowledge. Government officials could anticipate becoming targets for trumped-up allegations as part of the métis cultural brokers' "organized propaganda to . . . try in every manner to make life a burden for them." Lumber company owners, aided by Gus Beaulieu and B. L. Fairbanks, were not above using monetary bribes "to keep prominent Indians who might stir up trouble quiet." And Ben Fairbanks used his influence as a merchant "to coerce Indians of the various reservations to the support of their designs" by withholding credit from those who were not forthcoming with political support at election time.[55]

Through strong-arm tactics of this nature, the métis cultural brokers selected themselves as representatives and delegates for the reservation and widely claimed that their views reflected the majority opinion. They achieved success through a shrewd blend of personal charisma, expertise in the methods of "boss" politics, and the application of pressure to their clients to gain support. Their ties with Mississippi band leaders and their early activities in championing the defense of Anishinaabe resources helped their cause. However, their complicity in future land fraud dealings in conjunction with their domineering behavior would irreparably damage their reputations.

Religious Patterns

Ethnic differences evident in leadership patterns were also reflected in religious affiliations at White Earth. Native religious practices persisted while Catholic and Episcopal missionaries worked among the White Earth population. Earlier interdenominational conflicts dissolved into a peaceful, harmonious relationship after 1889, as missionaries ministered to congregations that were largely segregated along ethnic lines.

The Episcopalians operated four churches, three schools, and a hospital at White Earth in 1894. The main mission was St. Columba located at White Earth Village; there were additional churches at Pine Point and Wild Rice River. In 1887, John Johnson Enmegahbowh explained that Episcopal mission activities attracted more "full-bloods" or conservative interior band members than the Catholic religion did. Enmegahbowh

The choir gathers on the steps of the St. Columba Episcopalian Church in about 1910. *Photo by J. Johnson, Detroit Lakes, courtesy of Minnesota Historical Society.*

White Earth girls in their classroom at the St. Benedict's Catholic School at the agency, about 1900. Euroamerican traits show clearly in many of the girls' faces. *Photo courtesy of St. Benedict's Convent Archives, Minnesota Historical Society.*

boasted that he had financed the church, capable of seating 600, and had won 100 "communicants," but by 1894 the Episcopalians had attracted only about 300 adherents. Despite these low figures, the Episcopalians had succeeded in establishing an institutional infrastructure that blended better with native Anishinaabe religious practices. In fact, some suggested that the hybrid Episcopalian congregations evolved in areas where there were no Midé priests, filling a need for more conservative people. The St. Columba Mission itself was transplanted from Gull Lake to White Earth in the first migrations in 1868. In 1894, eight of nine Episcopal clergymen were of Indian descent and Sunday services were "conducted in both English and Chippewa." Episcopal parishioners learned to sing standard Christian hymns in the Anishinaabe language. Even though their membership totals remained low in relation to the overall population, Episcopal methods reflected tolerance, flexibility, and the use of native personnel and the Anishinaabe language. The Episcopalians had greater success in blending elements of the new ways with the old to produce a syncretic religion based on both that proved more attractive to conservative Indian people who were inclined to sample Christianity.[56]

When they first came to White Earth in response to requests from the resident métis population, Catholic missionaries encountered a substantial Catholic population. In fact, referring to them as "missionaries" is a misnomer. The many French-Canadian and métis descendants of fur trade society had brought a heritage of Catholicism with them to the reservation. Catholic priests had only to minister to the resident population rather than seek converts. James S. Woodward, physician at White Earth in 1887, observed that Catholics kept proselytizing to a minimum, urging them "but very little to come to the Catholic church."

In 1890, the Benedictine order of the Catholic church operated a mission and a contract boarding school for orphaned girls at White Earth Village. By 1894, the agent at White Earth estimated that the Catholics ministered to 1,200 "communicants." Before 1900, an itinerant Catholic priest traveled a circuit to the northwestern Minnesota reservations and included a stop at the heavily Catholic Pembina settlement at White Earth. By 1900, "daughter parishes" had been established in a variety of locations on the reservation, including Wild Rice River (Beaulieu),

Mahnomen, Ponsford (Pine Point), Naytahwaush (Twin Lakes), Waubun, Calloway, and Ogema. All but three, Ponsford, Wild Rice River, and Twin Lakes, were located along the railroad in the western part of the reservation where those of Franco-Anishinaabe heritage congregated. Catholics outnumbered Episcopalians at White Earth even before a permanent Catholic church had been established there, so that priests and nuns seldom extended their religious pursuits beyond the doors of the mission.[57]

The Midéwiwin or Grand Medicine Society represented the most hierarchical, organized expression of Anishinaabe spirituality. This religious complex and healing society was transplanted to the White Earth Reservation along with the earliest immigrants and persisted into the twentieth century.

The Anishinaabeg attached great importance to interpreting dreams. Each individual possessed two "souls," one of whom traveled at night, living the dreams. Having two souls made communication possible with the *manidoog* (spirits; singular form is *manidoo*) and the souls of all nonhuman persons ("plants, animals, and natural entities"). A matrix of *manidoog* inhabited the Anishinaabe world, which was like "a muskeg floating in a lake. Below the water was another flat earth; above was the dome of the sky on which a third world was located." *Manidoog* lived everywhere and behaved much like humans, but possessed greater power. None was preeminent, but six were important: (1) the Four Winds, who governed weather and the seasons; (2) the Underwater Manidoog, composed of both the horned serpent and underwater lion, who controlled all game and determined the water conditions of lakes and streams; (3) the Thunderbirds, who ameliorated the negative powers of the Underwater Manidoog, controlled birds, and "manifested themselves through thunder and lightning"; (4) the Owners of various animal species who regulated hunting success; (5) the Windigo, a giant ice cannibal who threatened during starving times; and (6) Nanabozho, the central culture-hero and trickster who created the world and enabled humans to hunt. Visions experienced during puberty revealed guardian spirits that provided guidance throughout life and reinforced the individual's role in the whole of the circle of life. This cosmogony emphasized "being" and "right living." "Good" behavior ensured individual control and harmony with the *manidoog.* "Wrong" behavior could bring recrimination in the form of sickness. Disease then, served as a check on social deviance.[58]

Most disease was believed to stem from an unbalanced relationship between hunters and animals. According to one story, when humans abrogated their friendship with animals by killing too many, the mosquito and fly were sent to cause illness in retribution. Nanabozho took pity on humans and taught them herbal cures. Diseases could also be caused by *manidoog*, witches, the dead, soul-loss, powerful religious leaders, and a breach of Anishinaabe ethics.[59]

In this arena, Mide practitioners could be of aid. Frances Densmore wrote, "Health and long life represented the highest good to the mind of the Chippewa, and he [*sic*] who had knowledge conducive to that end was most highly esteemed among them." Midé priests and priestesses, having learned their calling through special dreams, intervened to mediate between individuals and the *manidoog*. Once admitted, lodge initiates elected to work their way through an internal hierarchy of four ranks. Many failed to attain the uppermost ranks due to the expense involved in amassing the necessary presents and preparing feasts. A potential member paid requisite fees for the privilege of spending years learning the "secrets." When the period of preliminary instruction ended, initiates hosted a feast and distributed presents that they had worked for years to accumulate. These materialistic aspects of the Midéwiwin were engendered by increased wealth stemming from the trade in furs. Because of its oceanic origin, the symbolic *miigis* (cowrie shell) eventually had to be procured through traders. Furthermore, commercial trade gave potential initiates the means to accumulate the fees necessary to move from one rank to the next. Midé specialists possessed knowledge of herbal medicinal properties and healing remedies and performed healing ceremonies when so called upon. Typically those in need offered some sort of compensation to the priests and priestesses for their services. Midé members also preserved their traditions by incising them in hieroglyphs on birchbark scrolls that recounted the genesis and migrations of the Anishinaabeg, the organization of the Midéwiwin, and the proper course for initiates to follow to achieve each successive level. Spiritual leaders convened the Midé membership periodically, and kept its rituals and traditions in deepest secrecy. In 1890, anthropologist Walter Hoffman predicted the demise of the Midéwiwin through "the death of their aged predecessors" and "the adoption of new religions," but by 1910 ethnographer Frances Densmore named sixteen practitioners who continued to offer their services. Since she merely gathered songs from these people and made no effort to be comprehensive, it is safe to assume that other Midé practitioners existed as well. By the time of Densmore's later 1928 ethnography, the Midéwiwin was still conspicuous at White Earth.[60]

Those who believed in and practiced Midé rituals faced a period of transition. The U.S. assimilation programs worked to undermine native religious practices and align individuals with a Christian denomination. Administrators made special efforts to win school children to the Christian faith, requiring that they attend some church service on Sundays.[61]

However, the experiences of John Rogers reveal that many still called upon the medicine men and women in times of sickness. During Rogers's adolescence, three of his siblings died. Each time, the Midé healers came to minister to the dying child. Rogers's religious indoctrination at boarding school confused him, so that "it was sometimes hard to understand all [that his mother] said about the 'Great Spirit.'" When his brother Ahmeek died, his mother expressed her sorrow from the context of an Anishinaabe world view, explaining that "sickness and troubles . . . c[a]me upon our people" when they departed from the teachings of the Great Spirit. Rogers resolved his dilemma when he himself fell seriously ill and prayed to the Great Spirit, whom he felt would understand better than a Christian god. "Thus it was that I remembered the teachings of my Indian people."[62]

Many children who were subjected to more than one religious philosophy probably experienced spiritual confusion similar to John Rogers's. Whether they resolved their conflicts in the same manner cannot be known. Most likely, responses ranged along a spectrum, with most individuals producing a syncretic solution for themselves—one that blended elements of both the old and the new. These aspects of individual ideology and spirituality remain the most private of matters. Evidence regarding these spheres of life seldom makes its way into standard historical sources. While historians may attempt to read further meaning between the written lines, they must also leave these historical actors with their dignity, by admitting that some elements of the past may never be known in their entirety.

Educational Patterns

The introduction of formal, institutionalized educational instruction in the knowledge and values of American society had profound effects among the White Earth Anishinaabeg. Members of White Earth's two ethnic groups made decisions concerning their children's education that were based on their different cultural orientations. Before sustained interaction with Euroamericans, Anishinaabe children had received training in appropriate gender roles through their families and bands. Attending school daily, especially at distant boarding schools, disrupted this pattern. People of dual heritage who were descended from fur trade society were more likely to have attended school themselves and to seek the opportunity for their children. These different choices reflected and perpetuated ethnic divisions at the reservation.

In 1890, four boarding schools existed at White Earth: the White Earth Boarding School and St. Benedict's Orphan School at White Earth Village; the Pine Point School; and the Wild Rice River School. Together their combined average attendance surpassed 200. Religious societies contracted to operate all but the White Earth Boarding School. This situation was short-lived, however. Sentiments in favor of separating the church-state partnership and a growing anti-Catholicism in the nation at large converged to prompt the U.S. government to move toward secular education. By 1892, the only contract school remaining was the Catholic orphanage; the U.S. government operated the others. An Episcopal mission school taught fewer than 20 children.

In 1895, the government opened a day school at Twin Lakes with an average attendance of nine. Policymakers saw day schools as a way to allow Indian students to commute, thereby creating more room in the boarding schools for children from more distant areas. By 1902, other day schools had been established at White Earth Village, Porterville, and Pembina. Besides these reservation schools, older children from White Earth also attended schools in the regional area, such as Flandreau in South Dakota and St. John's in St. Cloud, Minnesota. A limited number attended far-off eastern boarding schools such as Carlisle and Hampton.

Teachers complained that siphoning off older, more-educated children in this manner left them with the dull task of introducing young children to the rudiments of the English language without the reward of watching them progress.

The instruction children received at these schools emphasized basic competence in reading, writing, and arithmetic, along with chores designed to instill in them the habits needed for an agricultural lifestyle. Typically, students spent half the day in classes, and half the day working at tasks that contributed to the upkeep of the school. Each school maintained gardens and livestock to expose youngsters to the trappings of the agrarian ideal. Boys tended the garden and livestock, chopped and fetched firewood, carried water, and otherwise assisted in heavier manual labor. Girls learned domestic skills of cooking, cleaning, laundering, and sewing. Besides lessons and chores, Indian students were subjected to heavy doses of U.S. patriotism and the "habits of industry." School personnel emphasized order, neatness, and punctuality, training children to answer to bells and march in step, "even to the smallest mite."

The changes involved with attending school, especially for Indian children raised in a conservative fashion, could be wrenching. With heartfelt empathy, teachers and superintendents described the homesickness children suffered during their first days at school. Besides the trial of leaving their close-knit family group for the first time, Anishinaabe children encountered an all-out cultural assault. Teachers forbade the children to speak their native language, forcing them to converse only in English. Authorities cut the boys' hair and assigned English names to be used in place of Indian ones. Not surprisingly, some children fled such repressive places, only to be met with corporal punishment upon their return. Others adjusted more easily. Those whose cultural practices already more closely resembled those of Euroamerican society fared better, but individual preferences played a role as well. Evangeline Critts Fairbanks, who attended White Earth Boarding School said that "it didn't bother me," but "my sister didn't . . . like . . . it because she ran away once. I never did; it seemed like it was fun." At White Earth, the student body was characterized by more cultural homogeneity than at eastern boarding schools, and soon after the initial trauma, most children who stayed found some solace in each other.

In the early 1890s, some parents from the eastern forests did "all they [could] to keep their children away" from the boarding schools and took "great satisfaction" in hiding those who ran away. Long absences from the family, sometimes amounting to years, disrupted the seasonal round, when children were a "great help to their parents." Some Indians moved closer to the boarding schools to breach the distances between themselves and their children. It would take time for them to regard formal education as an asset.

By 1895, many Indians sent their children to school "without any compulsion," but superintendents complained of their inability to accommodate all children of school age. The schools were "always crowded" and school administrators routinely had to "refuse places to many." School supervisors made recurrent requests for additional schools so that "many Indian children can be taken in and educated that have never been to school." So, despite the fact that schools were typically filled to capacity, hundreds of children were effectively denied access to an education.

School administrators responded to this situation by admitting more children than the schools could optimally hold. Children slept several to a bed and shared sanitary facilities meant for a much smaller number. Conditions such as this fostered the spread of disease, the constant scourge of boarding schools. Torn between the desire to educate as many as possible and the need to maintain some standards of cleanliness and health, teachers recommended reducing admissions, although they found it difficult "to refuse to take a child who is sadly in need of clothing, food, and instruction." Although administrators counted on new school facilities to alleviate this problem, they were not forthcoming and overcrowding remained endemic.

Inadequate school facilities lessened the need for stringent measures to enforce attendance. Runaways and delinquents simply created spaces that others quickly filled. Therefore, those who objected to attending school enjoyed the freedom to do as they pleased. While teachers applied strict discipline in the schools, apparently large numbers of children escaped its impact.

Both choice and circumstance excluded more conservative Indian children from school. Shifts in educational policy promoted sending older, more educated children to off-reservation boarding schools and establishing day schools for children, typically of mixed descent, who lived close enough to commute. These changes should have opened more space for Indian children, but the schools still failed to meet the demands of all who sought admission. Since ricing season overlapped with the onset of the school year, Indian children from the eastern forests were almost sure to arrive too late to find vacancies. Parents who least understood Euroamerican institutions were slowest to apply for school admission. Consequently, "the ones most needy [were] the ones left out."[63]

White Earth Indians reacted to the prospect of sending their children to U.S. boarding and day schools in patterned ways reflecting their ethnic affiliations. Those who regarded this form of education as a priority, particularly descendants of the bicultural, métis ethnic group, applied promptly and sent their children regularly. They supported establishing day schools and later championed integrating Indian children into predominantly white public schools, where the curriculum afforded a better education. Others who objected to the prospect, often the more conservative Indians, either stayed away or were refused admittance. Once they came to approve of formal education, they more often supported the "Indian schools," despite the poorer quality of education, as places where their presence was not greeted with scorn and derision. In this fashion, experiences with institutionalized schooling reinforced the segregation of ethnic groups at White Earth.

John Rogers's experience with schooling may or may not have been typical. His mother recognized the cultural assault that her children had endured during the six years they had attended reservation boarding school and resolved to reacquaint them with Anishinaabe ways. Having been separated from their mother for six years, only the oldest daughter retained any knowledge of the Anishinaabe language and translated conversation for all the others. Their mother set about to teach them how to "set rabbit snares and deadfalls" and how to set traps for larger game. She also insisted that they use only their Anishinaabe names. His sisters became Mindi and Bishiu, his brother Ahmeek, and his own name, WayQuah, meant "dawn of day." Despite six years of concerted effort to eradicate his Indian heritage, WayQuah never did forget the old ways.[64]

The Spectrum of Ethnic Band Differences

Ethnic differences characterized White Earth social relations. Immigrants who came in response to the Nelson Act perpetuated the east-west settlement pattern, with most joining relatives in the eastern forests (see Map 2). Two distinctive cultural patterns persisted. Residential, marital, religious, and educational choices acted as boundary-maintaining mechanisms reinforcing these divisions. As the twentieth century wore on, these basic ethnic differences would come to eclipse band ties as the primary determinants of reservation social affiliations.

Use of the terms "mixed-blood" and "full-blood" was widespread among reservation residents despite a dramatic decline in the number of individuals enumerated in censuses as genetic full-bloods. The U.S. and Bureau of Indian Affairs (BIA) censuses for the White Earth Reservation reveal 44 percent full-bloods in 1900, 15 percent in 1910, and less than 1 percent by 1930.[65]

Instead of reflecting actual genetic heritage, the terms "mixed-blood" and "full-blood" encapsulated perceptions of ethnic differences that Indians observed among themselves. They distinguished between the symbols by referring primarily to cultural attributes, though they also made reference to genetic characteristics. Hairstyle, clothing, type of house, cultural practices, and, most important, economic ethics, all contributed to the ethnic symbols that reservation residents used to differentiate among themselves. Participants and observers alike consistently described full-bloods as "poor" Indians, concerned only with their subsistence and distributing resources equitably. Mixed-bloods were "shrewd," understood how the market operated, and accumulated material wealth. Before the involvement of key leaders of mixed descent in land fraud, the term "mixed-blood" carried few of the pejorative connotations that it later came to bear. Only U.S. policymakers interpreted the terms genetically; Indian definitions revolved around cultural characteristics that eventually came to include a political dimension.

When asked to define "mixed-blood" and "full-blood" precisely, Indian informants often had difficulty responding. The Anishinaabe word for mixed-blood is *wiisaakodewikwe* (female) or *wiisaakodewinini* (male), translating roughly to "half-burnt-wood-man or woman." Reverend Baraga explained that "they call the half-breeds so, because they are half-dark, half-white, like a half-burnt piece of wood, burnt black on one end, and left white on the other."[66] Rules for determining descent were not concrete. The common denominator in all definitions of "mixed-blood" was some admixture of white "blood," reflecting a common folk notion that blood transmitted characteristics particular to a certain human group. An individual could be a "little mixed blood" or "nearly white." Generally, informants agreed that the term "half-breed" signified equal parts of white and Indian blood. As such "half-breeds" were a subclass of mixed-bloods that had been more numerous during the fur trade era. Aside from these commonalities, an individual's identity rested on the observer's interpretation.

Many informants cited genetic characteristics in their attempts to describe mixed-bloods and full-bloods. For some, physical features were the most distinguishing characteristics. Full-bloods were more darkly complected, had straight black hair, dark brown eyes, and no body hair. Mixed-bloods had lighter skin, brown, sometimes curly hair, and lighter eyes; men grew facial hair. However, Anishinaabe informants understood that these general characteristics served only as guidelines, since some genetic variations occurred naturally.

Despite their reference to genetic attributes, informants most often relied on cultural characteristics to distinguish between mixed-bloods and full-bloods. Clothing was a telltale feature. When asked if an acquaintance was a mixed-blood, Kechemahquah thought, "He would have looked that way if he had pants on, but . . . he wore [a] breech cloth clear up to his death."[67] Similarly, Wahwayzhooquay identified a group of men as full-bloods, saying, "They would have had hats if they were white." Another clue for her was that "they would wear pants; and white collars" if they were mixed-bloods.[68]

Other distinguishing cultural features surfaced as well. When asked whether he had ever lived at his grandfather's house, Aydowahcumigoquay protested that "he did not have any house—he was an Indian."[69] Mezhucegeshig's explanation of his friend's religious conversion illustrates how one's status as a mixed-blood or full-blood could change with cultural preferences: "He was a very old Indian. He was a full blood Indian but when he adopted the church, why he felt as though he was a

Frenchman. He acted as one."[70] Most agreed that mixed-bloods with white fathers possessed no *doodem* (totem or clan affiliation), because *doodemag* were inherited through the paternal line. Baybahdaungay-yaush fastened on this attribute to describe a woman she knew, saying, "I believe that she was an Indian because she had a dodaim [*sic*]. Indians have dodaims [*sic*]."[71] Atypical marriage patterns might produce mixed-bloods with *doodemag*, but these cases were exceptions. Confronting such a case confused Gahmahnahchewahnay. He claimed that the people in question were not "regular Indians." "They didn't look like it, but the only peculiar thing about them, they had a dodaim [*sic*]. . . . Perhaps they just assumed it as being their dodaim [*sic*]."[72] Through comments such as these, the cultural or ethnic content of the mixed-blood and full-blood symbols emerged.

As White Earth residents made clear, the cultural content of these ethnic symbols revolved around differences in lifestyle. Shinowwaince bristled at the suggestion that his friend Minogeshig might have been a mixed-blood: "He wore two braids; had linen leggings on, and he was a fourth degree member of the grand medicine. . . . He used to build a tee-pee . . . and call other warriors to follow him. . . . Are those the deeds of a mixed-blood? I used to see him swallow bones . . . in his incantation for eliminating sickness. . . . Is this the practice of a mixed blood?"[73] Obviously, Shinowwaince did not think so. George Morrison explained that those who wore breech cloths and blankets, lived in wigwams, and associated primarily with others like them were considered to be full-bloods, "not on account of their blood . . . it was their way of living that regulated that."[74] Cultural affiliations and way of life made all the difference. Baybahdaungayaush was asked if a person with only a small amount of white blood who lived as an Indian would be called a mixed-blood. He answered, "No, because he would be poor, and he just would look after what he wants to eat . . . to subsist."[75] Residents had evolved a melange of cultural characteristics to differentiate between ethnic groups on the reservation.

Marital preferences also reflected the marked ethnic differences between mixed-bloods and full-bloods. Genealogical research into the backgrounds of several prominent mixed-blood families revealed very few marriages between mixed-bloods descended from Lake Superior bands and Mississippi band members. When asked if his former father-in-law had been white, Mezhucegeshig quickly dismissed the idea, saying, "If he had white blood his daughter would have had white blood and she wouldn't have liked me, and she wouldn't have married me." These patterns arose during the fur trade era when intermarriage between French, Scotch, and English fur traders and native women produced a large population of individuals of mixed descent. These bicultural people then evolved into a unique métis society, creating the Great Lakes fur trade network and maintaining their distinctive cultural attributes ultimately through marriage with people like themselves. Mezhucegeshig cast further light on these preferences and patterns: "When a white man gave a child to an Indian woman, the usual thing was that when the child was born the man would go away and leave the woman to take care of the child, but when a white man married a mixed-blood he would stay." He explained that whenever an Indian woman had a child that "no one claim[ed] . . . it was always laid to the Frenchmen." White Earth residents described marital preferences as endogamous boundary-maintaining mechanisms, reinforcing ethnic differences. Mezhucegeshig denied that mixed-bloods who lived at La Pointe married Indian women: "They didn't marry Indian women. They married mixed-bloods."[76]

Marital patterns reinforced and maintained ethnic differences among the White Earth Anishinaabeg that were recognized by the natives themselves. Mahdosayquay reflected on mixed-bloods' ethnic characteristics that many recognized: "They were Indians, but they were different . . . a different class of people." Older White Earth residents remembered the days of their youth when blood status meant little. Many Indians from interior Minnesota bands firmly believed that earlier in the century, they had never seen a mixed-blood—only people like themselves. They realized that mixed-bloods had proliferated throughout the north country because of their trading ties. Mahdosayquay could tell a mixed-blood from a full-blood by sight when she "saw them at Crow Wing."[77]

The Crow Wing connection, where many former traders and their offspring developed close relationships with the Mississippi bands, remained prominent in people's minds. They identified Crow Wing as the point from which people of mixed descent had entered the population and continued to grow in numbers. Like many others, Kezhewash testified that mixed-bloods had not lived among the Indians when she was a young woman: "They came around when they began to have annuity payments."[78]

Prominent métis trader Clement H. Beaulieu accounted for his family's presence among the Mississippi band in a similar fashion. Lake Superior band members living at Sandy Lake or Crow Wing would have had to travel long distances to receive their annuities. Beaulieu explained how this difficulty was remedied: "I joined them under the Treaty of 1854. . . . We were allowed to go either with the Mississippi Chippewas or with the Lake Flambeau Indians . . . and from that time I have always been with the Chippewas of the Mississippi."[79] However, the 1854 Treaty itself mentions no such provision.

Anishinaabe use of the term "mixed-blood" suggests that its meaning was evolving as Indians adapted to the increased presence of people of mixed descent and to changes in their lifeways. "Mixed-blood chiefs" were included among signers of several treaties. Proliferation of clans and ogimaag indicates a changing social structure. Some suggest that the appearance of the Eagle clan for those of Anglo-Anishinaabe descent and the Maple Leaf clan for those of Franco-Anishinaabe descent represented attempts to accommodate doodem-less mixed-bloods with clans of their own. Along social and demographic lines, the Anishinaabeg were facing a time of transition.[80]

If the labels "mixed-blood" and "full-blood" accurately identify basic cultural differences between White Earth residents, individual behavior ought to reflect this. The relative proportion of French or English surnames as opposed to Anishinaabe names can serve as a very rough indicator of each band's cultural orientation (see Table 3). In this context, anglicized names indicate a more innovative choice of names, while Indian names reflect more conservative ones. They also reflect the degree of intermarriage with Euroamericans.

Names listed on Bureau of Indian Affairs censuses do not necessarily reflect individuals' choices. Anishinaabe names could change during an individual's lifetime. Initially, children might be named after a peculiar incident at their birth or some special power possessed by another Indian ("namesake names"). As they grew, names might be added or completely changed. Furthermore, the anglicization process was not uniform: some

Table 3. Anishinaabe versus English Names, 1890–1920

	FdL	P	M	GL	WOP	C&W	OT	ML	LL
1890									
% Anishinaabe	–	30	25	–	–	–	84	–	–
% English	–	70	75	–	–	–	16	–	–
N	–	218	1107	–	–	–	652	–	–
1900									
% Anishinaabe	3	11	14	28	72	57	70	50	75
% Both	3	–	.7	.3	3	6	–	–	2
% English	93	89	86	71	25	37	30	50	23
N	91	318	1544	336	88	51	741	323	309
1910									
% Anishinaabe	2	5	5	12	30	16	42	45	43
% Both	–	.3	3	3	9	6	10	8	15
% English	98	95	92	85	61	78	48	47	42
N	111	361	1995	401	259	63	744	990	277
1920									
% Anishinaabe	.9	2	2	6	13	16	16	24	19
% Both	.9	3	3	7	13	18	22	19	29
% English	98	95	95	88	74	66	62	57	52
N	113	472	2764	469	315	61	886	1308	281

Key: FdL = Fond du Lac band
P = Pembina band
M = Mississippi band
GL = Gull Lake band
WOP = White Oak Point band
C&W = Cass Lake & Lake Winnibagoshish bands
OT = Otter Tail Pillager band
ML = Mille Lacs band
LL = Leech Lake band
Source: Bureau of Indian Affairs Censuses, White Earth.
Note: By "Anishinaabe names" I refer to names recorded in the native language without surnames.

translated their Anishinaabe names into English and added an English first name; some took their *doodem* (clan) name as a family name; nicknames stuck; lumber company employers and school officials assigned names arbitrarily; and names were misspelled and mistranslated phonetically. In addition, names recorded in censuses often are nothing more than Anishinaabe words meaning, for example, "woman" (commonly rendered as *equay*, though *ikwe* would be more correct) or "boy" (commonly rendered as *quewezaince*, though *gwiiwizens* would be more correct). Individuals might possess both an English name and an Anishinaabe name, which could be used interchangeably. Many factors combined to create the census listings. But any problems with the censuses apply equally to all bands. Resulting surname patterns complement other social and demographic patterns that differentiated bands at White Earth.[81]

The breakdown of bands at White Earth by surname frequency reflects differences in the duration and intensity of their involvement in Great Lakes fur trade/métis society. Centered at a long-established fur trade depot on the St. Louis River, the Fond du Lac band stood at one end of a spectrum of surname frequencies. The Pembina band, an offshoot of the Turtle Mountain métis population in North Dakota and closely affiliated with the Canadian Red River Colony, exhibited characteristics similar to the Fond du Lac band. The White Earth Mississippi band regularly placed third after these two bands in the proportion of anglicized surnames. The White Earth Mississippi band consisted of an amalgamation of social groups. In the earliest migrations to White Earth, a large number of métis descendants of fur traders from Crow Wing and Lake Superior and Wisconsin bands of Anishinaabeg joined the more conservative Mississippi band centered at Gull Lake. As such, both patterns were reflected in the White Earth Mississippi band. The mixed-bloods predominated, however, causing characteristics of the Mississippi band to resemble more closely those of the Pembina and Fond du Lac bands; they shared common origins in fur trade society (see Table 3). The Fond du Lac, Pembina, and Mississippi bands continually exhibited higher proportions of French and English surnames.[82]

Conservative Anishinaabe bands from more isolated locations in Minnesota's interior retained their Indian names longer. Despite the overall trend toward increasing anglicization of names, the Leech Lake, Otter Tail, and Mille Lacs bands maintained higher proportions of Anishinaabe names. In the past, their seasonal existence at interior Minnesota lakes circumscribed their interaction within Great Lakes fur trade society. While they engaged in trade, intermarriage occurred on a more limited scale among them than among bands located near major trade entrepôts such as Crow Wing, La Pointe, and the Red River Colony.[83]

The patterning of bands within this spectrum of surname frequencies does not represent a hard-and-fast categorization of bands by cultural characteristics. Several bands lie in a middle zone and exhibit some individual variation. Yet it is clear that specific bands continually occupied upper and lower limits, establishing the pattern. Because the Fond du Lac, Pembina, and Mississippi bands consistently had higher proportions of French and English surnames as opposed to the Otter Tail, Mille Lacs, and Leech Lake bands, it is correct to say that naming patterns at White Earth reflected cultural differences between bands.

Age pyramids showing the distribution of names illustrate the anglicization process (see Figures 3, 4, 5, and 6). In 1890, the White Earth Mississippi band showed a 75 percent majority of French and English surnames. Only a small, shrinking core of Indian names remained. By 1920, Anishinaabe names had all but disappeared. Some older residents took their Indian names to the grave; fewer children were identified officially by their Anishinaabe names. The pattern of names in the Otter Tail band replicates this larger trend but reveals an earlier stage in the process: 84 percent Anishinaabe names in 1890, 38 percent by 1920. When members of interior bands did adopt surnames, they were more likely to use Anishinaabe ones, like Wadena or Gahbow, or to anglicize Anishinaabe names, producing family names like Rock, Squirrel, Skip in the Day, or Skinaway. The anglicization process at White Earth reflected ethnic differences.

The average size of households also varied among White Earth bands. The spectrum of household sizes at White Earth corresponds in its basic configurations to the spectrum of surname frequencies (see Table 4). With some annual variation, diagnostic bands at the upper and lower ends of the spectrum remain the same. Bands with a longer history of

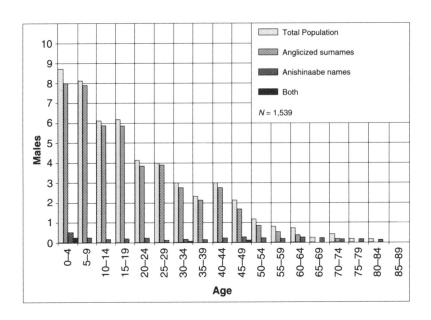

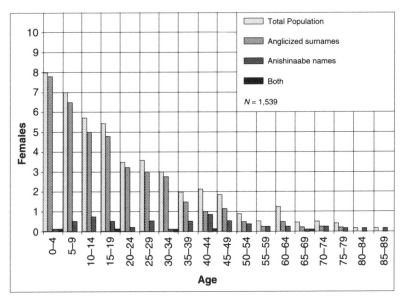

Figure 3. Age structure and patterns of names: Mississippi Band, 1900. Compiled from the Bureau of Indian Affairs, 1900.

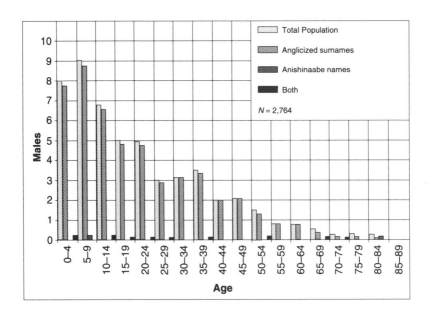

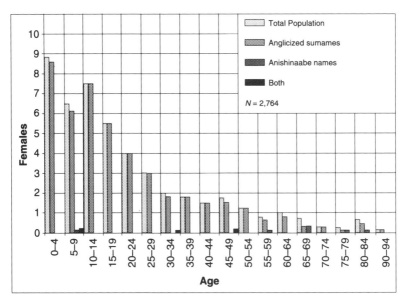

Figure 4. Age structure and patterns of names: Mississippi Band, 1920.
Compiled from the Bureau of Indian Affairs, 1920.

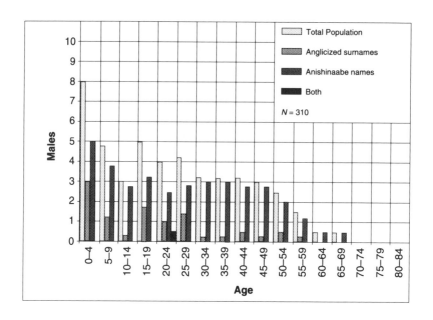

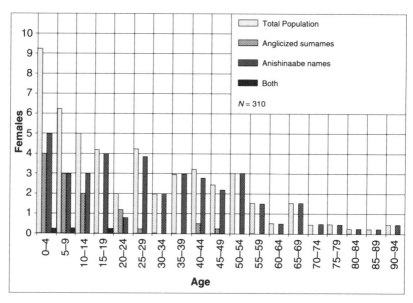

Figure 5. Age structure and patterns of names: Leech Lake removals, 1900. Compiled from the Bureau of Indian Affairs, 1900.

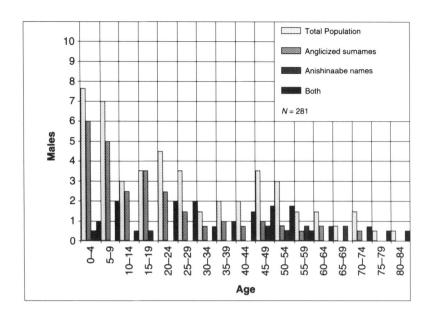

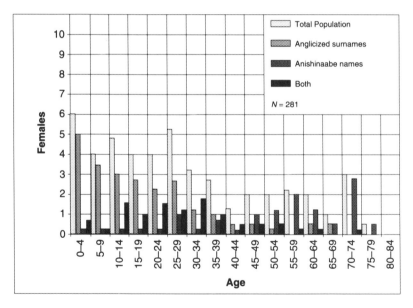

Figure 6. Age structure and patterns of names: Leech Lake removals, 1920. Compiled from the Bureau of Indian Affairs, 1920.

Table 4. Mean Household Size, by Band, White Earth Reservation, 1890–1920

Band	1890	1900	1910	1920
Fond du Lac	–	5.3	5.3	7.5
Pembina	4.9	5.7	6.0	7.0
White Earth Mississippi	3.8	5.0	5.0	5.0
Gull Lake	–	5.1	4.6	5.3
White Oak Point	–	4.6	4.5	5.4
Cass Lake & Winnibagoshish	–	4.6	6.3	7.6
Otter Tail Pillagers	4.2	4.4	4.2	4.8
Mille Lacs	–	5.1	4.9	4.7
Leech Lake	–	4.4	3.7	4.9

Source: Bureau of Indian Affairs Censuses, White Earth Reservation, 1890–1920. Reprinted by permission from Melissa L. Meyer, "Signatures and Thumbprints: Ethnicity among the White Earth Anishinaabeg, 1889–1920," Social Science History 14:3. Copyright 1990, Duke University Press, Durham, N.C.
Note: Solitary individuals have been omitted.

participation in Great Lakes fur trade/métis society tended to have larger households. Cultural differences between bands were reflected in the reservation's social structure.

None of these rough measures alone can be considered conclusive, although recurrence of established patterns through several measures enhances their reliability. Bureau of Indian Affairs censuses for White Earth cannot be used to construct reliable age structures in the years after about 1910, when out-migration escalated, but they can help to establish patterned interband differences. When information derived in this fashion complements interpretations drawn from literary sources, the reliability of both is strengthened.

Ethnic Patterns of Socializing

Socially, members of each ethnic group affiliated largely among themselves. Most social occasions were essentially segregated.

The seasonal round offered countless opportunities for socializing. Larger social groupings that gathered for weeks at a time for sugaring

Anishinaabe men gamble on the outcome of the moccasin game, a sleight-of-hand game where players guess which moccasin hides a stone (about 1920). The game was a prominent feature at annuity payments, the June 14 Celebration, and other social gatherings. Benjamin L. Fairbanks observes from the right rear. *Photo courtesy of Minnesota Historical Society.*

in the spring and ricing in the fall made these especially festive occasions, where social ties were reinforced. Besides these regular events, conservative Indians also participated in a complex of visiting and dancing both within the reservation and throughout northern Minnesota and the eastern Dakotas, traveling "a hundred miles or more to visit another band of Chippewas or . . . to visit the Sioux two or three hundred miles away." Gambling and give-aways were prominent activities at dances. Skilled Anishinaabe gamblers sometimes spent the entire summer seeking out gaming opportunities. The moccasin game, a sleight-of-hand game, went on "day and night for three or four days." Give-aways enhanced the reputation of givers, served as occasions for redistributing material possessions, and were accompanied by socializing with family and friends. Dancing, visiting, and gambling formed important elements of a social complex that persisted among more conservative White Earth residents.[84]

Cultural brokers of mixed descent who opted for a lifestyle more closely tied to the market economy were also involved in a visiting complex. Some socialized with relatives on nearby reservations, but they also journeyed more frequently to larger towns and cities, sometimes purely for social reasons but just as often to take care of business interests. The "Local and Personal" column of *The Tomahawk* frequently chronicled their comings and goings.[85]

Those who lived at White Earth Village, the location of the agency, tended to affiliate more often among themselves due both to proximity and their overall cultural orientation. They included Euroamerican agency employees among their friends and held their dances, characterized by more formal "bowery" dancing to music provided by a local band, at the White Earth Hall. White Earth villagers hosted parties for each other at private homes, where they played cards and "games, music and refreshments were the order of the evening." Agency employees happily participated in these social activities, noting with approval that the "mixed-bloods" were the "better class" of Indians on the reservation. Oscar Lipps, newly appointed superintendent of the White Earth School and fresh from a reservation in the Dakotas, found that White Earth Villagers resembled those in any average white community: "To one whose work has been among the 'wild' Indians, it is very difficult to realize that this is actually an Indian reservation." Social activities among the cultural brokers of mixed descent bore little resemblance to the social complex of more conservative Anishinaabeg. Separate social activities helped to maintain cultural boundaries that distinguished ethnic groups on the reservation.[86]

Although separated by many cultural facets, members of the two ethnic groups were drawn together by two annual events. The annuity payment served as a magnet for most White Earth residents. Also, the June 14 Celebration of White Earth's creation in 1867 played an integrating role. Nevertheless, each ethnic group left its distinctive stamp on these interethnic social events.

Every year, federal agents distributed money and goods due the Anishinaabeg through treaty rights. Payment usually occurred in October, barring unforeseen delays caused by inclement weather or congressional failure to appropriate funds. More Indians assembled for festivities associated with the annuity payment than at any other time of year. Drums associated with traditional singing and dancing could be heard from a distance, and participants visited stores, gambling places, and the dance all in turn. Indians of all ages from both ethnic groups socialized with kin and renewed friendships.

Métis merchant-traders frequented the paying places, waiting outside for those to whom they had extended credit; the annuity payment was an obvious occasion when the merchants' presence might remind native people of their debts before other attractions lured them to spend their newly acquired cash. The system of credit operated rather informally. As noted earlier, most Indian clients regularly carried a debt load, making an occasional payment to ensure that they would continue to receive credit. This system, which was partially of the Indians' own making, served their needs, allowing them to acquire credit while they met their obligations gradually. Merchant-traders benefited by keeping their clients beholden to them. Merchants displayed their wares at the time and place of the annuity payment, which conveniently took place near their establishments. What better time for Indians who had just received a sizable amount of money to purchase a sewing machine, a horse, yard goods, or groceries? In fact, the annuity payment was ripe for any cash transaction; saloons and gambling houses also profited. Again, both ethnic patterns were reflected in the activities that occurred in conjunction with the annuity payment.[87]

The June 14 Celebration of White Earth's founding drew people from all over northern Minnesota and the Dakotas in addition to White Earth residents. The Anishinaabeg looked forward to the annual visit of the Dakota and Nakota and made preparations to host them; they organized planning meetings and solicited donations for the feast, encouraging Indians to assume financial responsibility for the festivities themselves. The U.S. policymakers supported the event, hoping it would instill reservation pride among its diverse residents.

A typical June 14 Celebration followed an established pattern of events. Before the appointed day, 150 to 200 visiting Dakota and Nakota assembled in encampments at the celebration grounds in White Earth Village. At dawn, the "Grand Celebration began with the firing of the federal salute, signalling the onset of the festivities." The parade that

Members of both ethnic groups at White Earth, as well as visiting Dakota, gather in 1910 for the June 14 Celebration of the founding of the reservation. *Photo courtesy of Minnesota Historical Society.*

followed symbolically recounted the most significant happenings that had contributed to White Earth's establishment and prosperity. Representing Indians of the past, riders in warrior costumes, astride brightly decorated ponies, pranced past the crowd of spectators, keeping time to the beating drums in the "Grand Aboriginal Parade." They reminded onlookers of a time when the Anishinaabeg had been in more direct control of their political lives and diplomatic relationships. (By the twentieth century, threats of war had all but disappeared, but Indians fondly remembered their more autonomous past.)

Next, participants staged a "PEACE MEETING between the SIOUX and CHIPPEWA," bringing to a symbolic end the generations-old conflict that had by then attained almost mythic proportions in the folklore of the Anishinaabeg, the Dakota, and Minnesota society at large. Although conflict between the two nations was never as all-encompassing as folklore had it, the presence of Dakota friends and relations underscored the significance that mending their differences had for them.

Following the reenactment of the peace meeting, the "survivors of the first arrivals" in 1868 filed past and were honored by the crowd. Having persevered through the difficult early years, these "old settlers" were accorded the status of veterans who had endured weighty sacrifices on behalf of generations to come. The parade concluded with current White Earth residents representing "Indians of today." Their promenade was accompanied by the White Earth School Band and the White Earth Cornet Band. People in this group wore Euroamerican-style clothing and celebrated the transformation of Anishinaabe culture.

The "Grand Parade" had something for everyone, and members of both ethnic groups could find an acceptable niche. Events of the past fifty years that retained prominence in the collective Anishinaabe memory found a place in the pageantry of the June 14 Celebration. Those who orchestrated the parade shared the evolutionary, progressive interpretation of history popular among U.S. policymakers. The parade symbolically represented the demise of the "traditional" way of life and the ushering in of a new, "modern" order. There is no doubt that U.S. policy-makers viewed changes in Anishinaabe culture in this way, but whether all celebration participants shared this perspective is open to question.

Social activities familiar to each ethnic group filled the afternoon. Those skilled at lacrosse, pony races, and foot races were given a chance to compete. Spectators watched Indian men perform "war, scalp, skull and pipe dances" and the *shawano-gah* dance, where women joined in. Also, "bowery dances were scheduled all afternoon and evening," with a local band providing tunes. Indian "chiefs" presided, and sometimes even the governor of Minnesota made an appearance.[88]

The event truly offered an opportunity for both ethnic groups to come together. Everyone participated in a celebration replete with pageantry, contests, and revelry. Period photographs reflect the interethnic nature of the celebration. Men in derbies and women with parasols stood in their store-bought finery next to their horseless carriages, while Indians bedecked in feathers and beaded buckskin danced around center drummers, their wigwams, tipis, and tents in the background. While interethnic celebrations drew people together in a physical sense, familiar divisions were yet apparent.[89]

In the early twentieth century, Anishinaabeg came to the June 14 Celebration not only as members of the Mississippi band or the Otter Tail Pillager or Mille Lacs bands, but as residents of the White Earth Reservation. These interethnic celebrations demonstrated that a reservation-based consciousness had begun to displace former band affiliations. Band differences would diminish as ethnic differences grew among members of a population that were coming to think of themselves first as White Earth residents.

Conclusion

The concentration of Anishinaabe bands at White Earth created a fragmented collection of individuals accustomed to different lifeways—a community of communities, so to speak. The geography and ecology of human settlement patterns reflected these ethnic differences. Towns and villages in the eastern forests came to symbolize the conservative way of life still centered on the seasonal round, which Indians identified with the full-blood ethnic pattern. The mediating and entrepreneurial activities of the métis cultural brokers at White Earth Village and successful commercial farmers in the west formed yet another ethnic pattern, associated in peoples' minds with individuals of métis descent. Although many White Earth residents perceived these distinctions themselves, the ethnic divisions were not immutable and individuals easily deviated from the general pattern to create unique adaptations.

John Rogers's father, Pindegaygishig, best exemplified this phenomenon. Rogers had not known his father as a child; not until he had reached his teens did he learn anything about him. From acquaintances he learned that his father owned a large lumber camp near Cass Lake and employed hundreds of men. When he went to visit him, Rogers encountered a way of life far different from that which he had shared with his mother. His father lived in a large two-story house with many rooms— not a one-room cabin or wigwam. He owned many animals, tools, and machines, and hired others to cut hay and work for him. Pindegaygishig had apparently adopted many of the trappings of Western culture, and served as something of a broker, providing work for many.

Yet Rogers's father also retained a deep Anishinaabe spirituality. He frequently brought out the drum at home and instructed his family on how to communicate with the Great Spirit. Rogers never described his conservative mother engaging in such ceremonies. Furthermore, Pindegaygishig participated fully in the complex of Midéwiwin rituals as a highly respected leader.

Pindegaygishig's example serves as a reminder that human beings function as more than mere cultural containers. They can make changes in their lifeways and adopt new materials and values without simultaneously spurning analogous elements of their older, established ways. The adaptations that individuals devise can be more than mirror images of the choices they face. Symbols and stereotypes are necessarily reified concepts that can never fully reflect the melange of adaptations that individuals can make. John Rogers perceived this fact himself as he observed that "religion always came from within and all children of the Great Spirit had equal power to receive His blessings."[90]

Jack Pine, White Pine,
and Porcupine
The Alienation of Resources

Introduction

White Earth's resources adequately supported its diverse population only as long as they remainded under Indian ownership. The 1867 Treaty stipulated that the Indians were to retain all lands within the reservation's boundaries. The 1889 Nelson Act altered this arrangement by mandating allotment of the land base under terms of the 1887 Dawes Act. The population influx that occurred after passage of the Nelson Act necessitated that the entire land base be allocated, with no surplus remaining. The twenty-five year trust period established by the Nelson Act was intended to protect allotted land from alienation until Indian owners learned to manage their property and financial matters. Neither the 1867 Treaty nor the 1889 Nelson Act anticipated the wholesale loss of resources that was to follow the series of legislative acts passed in the early 1900s.

Congressional legislation, couched in a carefully worded rationale justifying reservation land loss, increasingly came to benefit outside interests that whittled away the land and timber resources at White Earth. This development paralleled a national trend in which Congress allowed local interests to determine Indian policy. Only the difficult question of determining exactly what constituted a "mixed-blood" slowed the exploitation of resources at White Earth—and then, only for a short time.

Loss of Four Eastern Pine Townships

The U.S. Chippewa Commission had anticipated securing a cession of land before they arrived to negotiate with the White Earth bands; they fully intended to proceed with their plans despite any objections the Ani-shinaabeg might raise. Persuading Wabonaquod that selling their pine lands would ultimately safeguard the full value of the timber against fire and theft only facilitated a decision that had already been made.[1]

Appraisal of the "Chippewa ceded lands" began on the four ceded townships in the fall of 1891. The Nelson Act provided for examiners to survey, examine, and appraise the lands, distinguishing between pine and agricultural lands. The lands were then to be offered for sale to the highest bidder at public auction, with any remaining land offered afterward at private sale.[2]

By early 1893, rumors of fraud regarding the White Earth pine lands were already rife. Critics accused the examiners of underestimating stands of timber near waterways, while overestimating more distant stands. This tactic produced reasonable aggregate estimates, but it clearly benefited lumber companies by underestimating the most valuable timber. The examiners furnished correct figures to a lumber syndicate, while reporting only minimum estimates to the government. Allegations that the "pine ring" had committed fraud and resorted to bribery eventually led to the dismissal of two incompetent crews of examiners who were clearly in the pockets of the lumber companies.[3]

In August of 1896, new Interior Secretary David R. Francis appointed Inspector J. George Wright to get to the bottom of the thievery on Ani-shinaabe ceded lands in northern Minnesota. The careful efforts of Inspector Wright and his competent, experienced crew produced estimates that indicated that lumber company owners knew full well that the lands they purchased contained over twice as much timber as had been estimated. Measurements had been estimated illegally; eighteen crew members had absolutely no experience in timber cruising at all; and the crew rarely followed instructions, sometimes biding their time at nearby saloons rather than cruising the plots for which they were responsible. After reviewing Wright's evaluations, Commissioner of Indian Affairs Daniel M. Browning concurred that the estimates made were "absolutely worthless . . . and that the sale of timber on the basis of those estimates would be unjust to the Indians in the extreme."[4]

Wright estimated that the work completed at that time should not have cost more than $52,000, but in reality, costs already surpassed

$150,000 by 1896. All expenses for these shoddy operations had been assessed against the "Chippewa in Minnesota Fund."[5] Seven years after passage of the Nelson Act, the tasks of surveying, examining, and appraising the ceded lands had not yet been accomplished. The "Chippewa in Minnesota Fund" showed a deficit because the ceded lands could not be sold until the surveys were completed.

These unforeseen delays persuaded policymakers to sell some land early. Pine lands were especially at risk; fires and wind storms annually damaged timber, greatly detracting from its value. In addition, lumber interests would bid only on current estimates. On 26 February 1896, proponents secured passage of a bill authorizing pine to be sold on ceded lands whenever 100,000 acres had been examined. The timber on 40-acre parcels of land would be offered at public auction to the highest bidder. Lands remaining unsold after public auction would then be offered at private sales.[6]

A third corps of examiners finished surveying the four "ceded" townships during the winter of 1899. Interior Secretary Ethan Allen Hitchcock authorized most of this land to be sold on 27 November 1900 at Crookston, Minnesota.[7]

Rumors of collusion among bidders and conspiracy to limit competition prompted Secretary Hitchcock to withhold patents that were to issue under the sale. Even though an investigation had been ordered in 1902, what had actually transpired at the 27 November 1900 Crookston sale remained obscure until a congressional investigation into White Earth affairs in 1911 and 1912.[8] The congressionally appointed Graham Commission questioned hundreds of witnesses and collected evidence proving that certain large lumber concerns in the immediate White Earth area had conspired to prevent competitive bidding, hold prices down, freeze out competitors, and divide the territory among themselves. The large number of bidders present "were in reality merely dummies acting in the interests of leading concerns in the combination." They refrained from competing with each other, but always bid aggressively to stifle any interest shown by genuine independent bidders. Through these sorts of tactics, lumber companies succeeded in securing pine for an average of $1.60 rather than $3.00 per 1,000 board feet as stipulated by the Nelson Act. What happened at the 1900 Crookston sale of the four "ceded" townships was not an isolated example of such chicanery. Selling ceded land at public auction had proven itself easy prey to land and timber grafters.[9]

At the time, some suspected that the Crookston sale had been fraudulent, but purchasers produced affidavits asserting that they had acted in good faith, as requested by Interior Secretary Hitchcock, and he caused patents to be issued in 1903. Evidence gathered by the Graham Commission eight to nine years later revealed that the rumors and allegations had been true. Plat maps and title abstracts showed that within a few years after the Crookston sale, titles had passed from the initial purchasers to the lumber companies in question. The assembled evidence showed "a clean cut and well-executed plan for the purchase of the timber lands," so that the whole territory was conveniently divided between the Nichols-Chisolm, Park Rapids, and Wild Rice lumber companies. The same companies that acquired the four "ceded" townships also secured the bulk of the timber in the remaining thirty-two townships as well.[10]

In 1899, the Minnesota State Legislature passed a law prohibiting a single corporation from owning more than 5,000 acres of land in the state, but the corruption of the 1900 Crookston sale permitted lumber concerns to evade this law. Interior Secretary Hitchcock postponed further timber sales until remedial legislation replaced public auction with the "bank scale," where logs were actually measured on the banks of waterways.[11]

Framers ostensibly designed the 1902 Morris Act, which instituted the "bank scale," to correct Nelson Act provisions by approximating more correctly the actual value of timber cut. However, the Morris Act also contained a provision allowing timber to be sold separately from the land, effectively side-stepping the 1899 Minnesota state law. In this fashion lumber companies acquired unlimited access to timber on Anishinaabe ceded lands, while evading state taxes on landholdings. Furthermore, this precedent disposed policymakers to create legislation allowing timber to be sold separately from the land on the remainder of the White Earth Reservation. Not surprisingly, the same lumber interests came to acquire most of the timber on allotted lands as well.[12]

Inherited Allotments

The initial allotment of the White Earth Reservation by the U.S. Chippewa Commission ran smoothly in comparison with what was to come. Even though most residents chafed at Congress's unilateral reduction of agricultural allotments by half in 1891, a fairly equitable allotment process mitigated internal conflict. But harmony among reservation residents was soon to shatter, as White Earth's resource base came under attack. Conditions that had prompted Bishop Whipple and others to lobby for the concentration of all the Anishinaabeg at White Earth persisted and intensified throughout the 1890s.

The first avenue by which Indian allotments were lost came through an Act of Congress in 1902 that allowed Indian heirs to sell inherited land with approval of the Secretary of the Interior. This approval transferred full and unrestricted title to allotments to heirs. The proper courts were to appoint guardians to manage minors' affairs.[13]

In 1902, Agent Simon Michelet worried that enabling inherited allotments to be sold would permit the land "to be bought up by syndicates." If that happened, he could "see no good to come from the law." His suspicions proved warranted. Such corruption attended the initial sales of inherited land that rules governing their sale had to be amended. The Commissioner of Indian Affairs observed that "to the average land speculator the Indian seems to be considered common prey." Nationally, speculators stood ready near every agency to "fleece the Indian of the last penny." Would new regulations curb such exploitative behavior? Hoping that they would, modified rules required the use of sealed bids and ninety-day notification of sales. Policymakers also instituted a ten dollar per month ceiling on the amount that might be withdrawn from individual Indians' bank funds to protect them from being "squandered."[14]

The western prairies of the Red River Valley had attracted European immigrants eager to try their hand at farming since the 1870s. After the Minneapolis, St. Paul, and Sault Ste. Marie Railway Company built the Soo Line running north-south through the western White Earth townships, towns began to grow at railroad junctions. Callaway, Ogema, Waubun, Mahnomen, and Bejou all began on a foundation of inherited Indian allotments. These centers of Euroamerican settlement came to play major roles in further alienating reservation resources.[15] The amount of inherited allotted land sold at White Earth under this act was not great (by 1905, about 5,000 acres had been sold for a total of $57,760), but this was the first step toward eroding individually owned property.[16]

The 1904 Clapp Rider and Steenerson Act

The most destructive series of legislative acts began in 1904 when an inconspicuous "rider" included at the end of the annual Indian Appropriations Act escaped attention. Since these acts were many hundreds of pages long and appropriated funds for every aspect of Indian affairs across the country, congressmen grew weary of their detail and such "riders" could slip through without close scrutiny or debate. The 1904 "Clapp Rider" (after Moses Clapp, the Minnesota senator responsible for its introduction) authorized the "Chippewa of Minnesota" to sell the timber on their allotments. The Nelson Act had prohibited pine lands from being allotted because their greater value prevented land from being apportioned equitably. Only a few allotments of this type had been made. By itself, the effect of the 1904 Clapp Rider might have been negligible, but when paired with upcoming legislation, the effects were truly disastrous.[17]

The White Earth Anishinaabeg had protested since Congress had reduced their allotments by half in 1891. Finally, in 1904, it seemed that this rank injustice would be corrected. Senator Clapp and Congressman Halvor Steenerson worked together to achieve passage of a bill providing additional acreage, which became known as the Steenerson Act. At White Earth, people celebrated. They were so pleased that some initiated proceedings to adopt Steenerson into the tribe and give him his own allotment of land.[18]

On the surface, these measures seemed designed to benefit the Anishinaabeg and there were those who regarded them in this light. However, the two measures took on an insidious quality when introduced in tandem. The Clapp Rider provided for disposition of the timber and the Steenerson Act supplied extra land from which the timber could be taken. The benefits for lumber companies were not lost on Judge Marsden C. Burch, who recognized that the two measures "were introduced one day apart and became law one week apart."[19]

Under the 1904 Steenerson Act, each Indian who had received an allotment at White Earth was to receive another 80 acres of land to total 160 acres, as provided for by the Nelson Act. If the existing unallotted land base proved inadequate to provide everyone with 80 more acres, the land was to be divided *pro rata* so that each allottee would receive an equal share. Only if the pine lands, heretofore largely unallotted, were divided could these provisions be met. Evidence collected by the Graham Commission suggests that outside lumber concerns understood full well the implications of pairing these two acts.[20]

Within these constraints, any allocation of unallotted reservation lands was bound to produce conflict. Those individuals who had already accepted agricultural lands, or who had cleared 10 acres to gain title to 40, as stipulated by the original 1867 Treaty, felt cheated before allotment procedures had even begun. Agent Simon Michelet calculated that the available acreage would suffice to provide everyone with 160 acres. However, Michelet neglected to consider that lake surfaces and swampland claimed by the State of Minnesota under an 1860 act, amounting to approximately 86,000 acres, could not be allotted. Failing to include this acreage in his estimations, he proceeded to make 80-acre additional allotments on a first-come, first-served basis on the appointed day, 24 April 1905.[21]

By the day additional allotments were to be made, enough time had elapsed to allow those who regarded land and timber as marketable resources to examine the lands and determine their preferences. Lumber companies, especially, planned well ahead and sent cruisers all through the forests.

Those who hoped to make profitable selections assembled early near the agency. When John Carl (Quaysegood) arrived at White Earth Village on that Saturday, the hotels were already filled to capacity. Luckily he was able to stay with his friend, Robert G. Beaulieu. At 7:30 on Easter Sunday morning, people began to queue at "the entrance of the agency building, outside of the fence." Carl reminded John Lynch (a man married to a woman of mixed descent), who was "walking up and down acting as kind of a bodyguard," that allotments were not to be made until 9 A.M. the following morning. Lynch replied, "Well, we are going up here anyhow and get our first chance." By two o'clock in the afternoon, about a hundred people had gathered with intentions of camping in line over night. Neighboring friends supplied extra food, blankets, and pillows. Demonstrating their familiarity with surveyors' techniques, many had taken the trouble to secure "minutes," or descriptions of land.

A crowd composed of many who were not White Earth residents gathers early at the agency hoping to be among the first to receive their choice of additional allotments in 1905 under the 1904 Steenerson Act. *Photo courtesy of Minnesota Historical Society.*

Some also sold these "minutes" to Indians who understood neither surveyors' marks nor profitable methods of dealing in real estate. Among the crowd were nonresident individuals of Anishinaabe descent who had journeyed from Duluth, Minneapolis, St. Paul, St. Louis, Chicago, and "everywhere" who clearly intended to turn a profit rather than take up residence.[22]

When others arrived on the scene and saw the crowd that had assembled a day early, they reacted with alarm. How could so many apparent strangers, people whom they derisively referred to as "white Indians," threaten to acquire the best reservation pine lands? When Mezhucegeshig arrived, he attempted to enter the agency office to speak to the agent and chief of police, but was brusquely shoved aside by John Lynch, as if he had been trying to butt in line. As John Carl rebuked him for treating an honored *ogimaa* so poorly, Lynch sarcastically retorted, "Is he any better than anybody else?" The situation was getting ugly. Duane Porter, an Anishinaabe Episcopalian minister, surveyed the crowd and the length of the line and "got disgusted . . . and . . . went away," figuring that "the Indian was not going to get fair play; the mixed bloods were all going to get the pine, so [he] didn't bother to get any." Meanwhile, a group of dissatisfied conservative Indians "were really angry at that time" and withdrew to a nearby hill to discuss strategy. Some believed that the potential for bloodshed existed on that day. Hopeful of averting such an outbreak, the Indian police captain approached the group and, at the recommendation of Agent Michelet, suggested that they form another line for "full-bloods." The allotting would proceed two by two, one from each line simultaneously.[23]

But the formation of a "mixed-blood" and "full-blood" line, a move that was not at all required by the Steenerson Act, would not placate those who felt they were being cheated. Conservative Indians complained of the large number of strangers present whom they claimed had no rights on the White Earth Reservation. A nine-year-old girl, Margaret Lynch, received the first allotment from the "mixed-blood" line, and became a symbol for the disgruntled. As the niece of the Indian police captain, she was an easy target for the charge of favoritism. Criticism became even more strident when the captain selected his sister to receive the second allotment.

Agent Michelet, acting on the spur of the moment, attempted to defuse the situation by authorizing a new line to be formed and by offering to record all objections made to each individual receiving an allotment. A committee of eight, five "full-bloods" and three "mixed-bloods," sat in the allotment room to oversee the entire operation. These measures proved insufficient to quell the escalating controversy, especially when available land proved inadequate to supply everyone with an additional 80-acre allotment.[24]

Conservative leaders, believing that the allotment process had favored those whom they called "mixed-bloods," complained to the Indian Office and persuaded others to represent their cause as well. The Commissioner of Indian Affairs responded by appointing Special Inspector Thomas Downs to investigate. Downs confined his recommendations to general corrective points that might have gone far toward ameliorating the unrest, especially among those who had received no allotments. Wisely, he represented conflicting opinions without attempting to justify one perspective over all others.

While he supported Agent Michelet's actions in coping with the immediate crisis, Downs nonetheless believed that mixed-bloods had secured an unfair advantage. His investigation bore out Duane Porter's observations that more conservative Indians could not comprehend surveyors' marks or section corners and, "fairly gave up when the rest was up there running out lines." Inspector Downs's report blamed the inequitable allotment process on Indians' unfamiliarity with the U.S. public land system.[25]

B. L. Fairbanks and Gus H. Beaulieu defended the manner in which the additional allotments had been made, arguing that those in the line "composed very largely of non-resident mixed bloods" simply aimed to follow the "recognized method" established by land office precedents whenever unusual efforts were being made to secure choice tracts. The two men argued that these enterprising citizens were simply acting on their prior experience with U.S. Land Office policy and should be viewed as examples of the success of U.S. assimilation policy. This behavior was to be encouraged. Beaulieu and Fairbanks had no sympathy for full-bloods who failed to scout out the best land ahead of time and criticized them for ignoring "the advice of the officials of the Government and the educated mixed bloods to go and examine the lands" and then finding fault with those who did. From this perspective, the full-bloods appeared "lazy" and "neglectful" for refusing to heed good advice.[26]

These observers described long-standing cultural differences among White Earth residents. In a sense, both criticisms were correct depending on individual ethnic perspective. The "wily" mixed-bloods had taken pains to secure the best possible advantage for themselves, and the "lazy" full-bloods simply ignored good advice. A more balanced interpretation might have recognized that these traits were rooted in basic cultural differences, and refrained from castigating one group or the other.

Special Inspector Downs targeted Agent Michelet's actions for special censure. Because he ignored the *pro rata* clause in the Steenerson Act, several hundred Indians had received no allotments at all. On this ground alone, Downs recommended that the allotments be annulled and a new allotting undertaken. His concern for equity under the law and his empathy for those who had been disadvantaged underlay his recommendations: "These allotments mean much to these poor Indians, as it is the last opportunity they will have to be allotted land on this reservation." Ultimately, Downs favored neither group's perspective, accepting the legitimate rights of both mixed-bloods and full-bloods and arguing only for equity and a fair chance for all to receive what was due them. Had such a course been adhered to, the escalating factionalism that was to follow might have been minimized.[27]

Commissioner of Indian Affairs Francis Leupp accepted Inspector Downs's evaluation and annulled the allotments made under the Steenerson Act on 16 July 1905. New allotments would be made by Agent Michelet with Inspector Downs's aid. But this proposed remedy was short-lived. Those who felt satisfied with the allotments as they stood protested to Senator Clapp, who, in turn, convinced Commissioner Leupp that the conflict really stemmed from a factional dispute rather than arising from inequitable allotting procedures. Instead of annulling the allotments that had been made, Leupp decided instead to send another Indian Office inspector to determine the wishes of a majority of the Indians.[28]

When U.S. Indian Office Inspector James McLaughlin arrived at White Earth on 17 September he posted notice of a council to be held on 25 September in the post office and sent announcements to a number of leaders. The assembly voted 130 to 5 to allow allotments made by Michelet to stand. McLaughlin reported that 54 of those who supported the Michelet allotments were full-blood leaders, among them Mezhucegeshig, Taycumegeshig, Maheengaunce, Naytahwaush, Odubenaunequay (a woman, "queen," or *kitchiogimaakwe* of Manidowab's lineage), Ishquaygahbow, Joseph Charette, and Waweyeacumig. Pleased with the turnout, McLaughlin praised the council as "the largest representative gathering that has been assembled in conference on the reservation in many years." However, he did not disclose how he ascertained this, having spent no time at White Earth himself.

McLaughlin attached no lists of names with signatures and thumbprints, and made no effort to determine the number of eligible voters reservationwide or how representative those in attendance were. Furthermore, when requested by representatives of substantial constituencies to allow more time for news of the council to circulate so that outlying Indians might attend, McLaughlin refused their entreaties. He felt that a week was adequate notice, but did not consider the fact that ricing season was upon the Indians of the eastern forests.

After observing the council proceedings, McLaughlin dismissed conservative Indians' complaints, claiming that they simply wanted all full-bloods to have preference in selecting allotments. From this perspective, conservative Indians cared not for equity, but for having first choice. The upshot, of course, was that those who received no land were given no consideration.

McLaughlin blamed Reverend Charles Wright, son of Wabonaquod (Chief White Cloud), for instigating the entire conflict because of his own displeasure at not having been recognized as head chief after his father's death. McLaughlin simply dismissed the objections of individuals like Pindegaygeshig, saying that he had received a choice allotment himself and had nothing to complain about. McLaughlin seemed unwilling to entertain the possibility that individuals might consider more than their own welfare when voicing criticisms. Feeling that he fully comprehended the nature of political decision making at White Earth, McLaughlin concluded that Michelet had allotted the lands as fairly as possible. However, McLaughlin had ignored the letter of the law, making no mention either of the *pro rata* clause in the Steenerson Act or of those who would receive no land.[29]

On 25 November 1905, Reverend Charles Wright appeared in Washington, D.C., with a petition signed by 376 Indians charging that irregularities had occurred in the allotment process: 300 people with no rights at White Earth had received allotments; valuable pine allotments were concentrated within certain families; and more "mixed-bloods" had secured pine lands, while "full-bloods" found themselves in possession of cut-over lands. Wright gained no audience with governmental officials even though he presented letters of introduction from Senator Knute Nelson and Minnesota Governor John A. Johnson.[30]

Early in December, Commissioner Leupp sent a lengthy reply to the Wright Petition, stressing, above all, the need for concrete charges and proof of wrongdoing. He indignantly demanded, "Where were your 376 petitioners when that vote was taken?" Leupp was not persuaded that Indians at their rice camps had not received notice of the council in time to attend: "That is a rather lame excuse. . . . They did have a chance, and they deliberately threw it away."

Leupp's tone toward Wright then took an acerbic turn and he minced few words. He spoke of the "rule of the world and of nature" when he praised those who had slept in line overnight. They had taken the trouble to help themselves and did not "stand in so much need of help from others." The "full-bloods" should learn lessons from such behavior rather than sitting still and waiting for "the good things of life to come to them." Furthermore, Leupp chastised Wright's assumption of his father's title of "Chief White Cloud of the Chippewa Indians," charging that its hereditary basis ran counter to the U.S. government's preference for popular suffrage and made his attitude "even more emphatically hostile to the Government's endeavors." Delivering a written slap on the wrist, Leupp further reproached Wright, saying that his assumption of the title of chief "detracts from, rather than adds to, the weight of your signature."[31]

Clearly, Leupp held little sympathy for injustices that had occurred as a result of transgressions in the allotment process. After receiving this type of treatment, Wright and his associates could do little more than retreat and devise new strategies. After all their efforts, none of their grievances would be remedied.

Evidence gathered by the Graham Commission in 1911 and 1912 proved that those who complained of fraud and corruption in the assignment of additional allotments had been correct. As a man experienced in matters relating to Indian lands, Special Agent John H. Hinton examined the tract books where allotments were recorded and immediately noticed irregularities. Many entries bore evidence of tampering: names had been penciled in and later erased; names in ink were scratched out; entries had been penciled in early and then traced over with ink on allotment day. These irregularities occurred in suspicious patterns, and no Indian Office correspondence explained them as legitimate alterations. Hinton was forced to conclude that "wherein it had been charged that certain allotments had been changed by certain individuals, the erasures on the tract books bore evidence that it was true."[32] More than mere coincidence had created these patterns.

The Graham Commission demonstrated irrefutably that a veritable conspiracy had existed in which Agent Michelet cooperated with lumber corporations so that certain approved individuals acquired valued pine lands. Individuals testified that allotments had been switched to favor those willing to do business with land and timber corporations. Unfortunately, investigators discovered these instances of fraud too late to remedy them. By 1911, attention had turned toward charges of fraud in the sale of allotments, rather than irregularities in their initial assignment.[33] Government officials' fixation on transforming native cultures prevented them from securing legal justice in allotting White Earth's remaining land base. That Indian people should learn the value of capitalistic acquisitiveness was deemed more important than equity and accurate implementation of laws passed by Congress.

The Aborted 1905 Sale of Timber on Allotments

Passage of the 1904 Clapp Rider and the 1904 Steenerson Act cleared the way for lumber corporations to gain access to timber on newly allotted lands simply by bargaining with Indian owners. Recognizing the potential for fraud inherent in this arrangement, the Indian Office moved to offer all the timber for sale on sealed bids at the same time. Departmental regulations mandated that the designated company should erect sawmills on the site to employ Indian workers. Revenue so generated was to be deposited in local banks to the credit of Indian owners.

To prepare for the sale, the Indian Office sought estimates of the timber's value. A professional forester objected to the plan to offer the timber for sale on one sealed bid, arguing that Indian owners would not receive fair market value. He criticized an earlier estimate given by a totally unqualified supervisor of Indian schools and recommended that the lands be classified by township, type of timber, and proximity to waterways. The Commissioner of Indian Affairs paid the forester's advice little heed, and authorized the planned sale to proceed. The interests of Indian owners clearly were not at the top of the agenda.[34]

Circumstances surrounding the attempted sale of allotment timber left no doubt about how far lumber companies would go to secure the timber as cheaply as possible. Powerful men in the state such as Thomas Shevlin had vested interests in several lumber companies in the area. When his tactic of offering deceptive bids failed, he pressured congressmen to have the sale blocked so that a Wisconsin lumbermen would not be recognized as the highest bidder. After consulting with Senator Clapp and Commissioner Leupp and receiving protests from several White Earth Indians, Interior Secretary Hitchcock rejected all bids on 28 November 1905.[35]

When the plan to sell all allotted timber at once fell through, individual allottees were left with the options of cutting the timber themselves or seeking permission from the Indian Office to contract with someone else to do it. Each contract required departmental approval—an unwieldy proposition that lumbermen would just as soon have avoided.[36] Upcoming legislation would soon remedy this situation.

The 1906 Clapp Rider

The dilemma over sale of allotted timber coincided with a period in the nation at large when policymakers had begun to ease restrictions on allotted lands. Market-oriented Indians at White Earth argued that they had demonstrated their ability to look after their own affairs and complained that the twenty-five year trust period was an imposition on their property rights. Gus Beaulieu urged the government through *The Tomahawk* to "set aside every restrictive rule which applies to . . . these allotments, and give them [the Indians] the right to use their own judgments."[37] Protective restrictions kept them from managing their resources to turn a profit and threatened to prevent elderly Indians from realizing any benefit from their allotments before they died.

This type of sentiment emanating from some of the White Earth Indians dovetailed with a shift in the overall thrust of U.S. assimilation policy. Whereas a heady optimism regarding Indian capabilities had fueled national legislation like the Dawes Act and its Minnesota counterpart, the Nelson Act, after the turn of the century, policymakers pared down their expectations. Full-blown rhetoric about unlimited Indian potential metamorphosed into a more pragmatic approach born of a pessimistic appraisal of what Indians had actually achieved—or had failed to achieve. The appointment of Francis Leupp as Commissioner of Indian Affairs in 1904 put in place a man who favored the accelerated control of Indian resources by Euroamericans "for their own good." Historian Frederick Hoxie wrote that Leupp "believed the Indians' racial traits could not be overcome" and "recast the meaning of assimilation to allow for the expansion of white control over Indian resources."[38] The relaxation of restrictions embodied in the 1902 Inherited Allotment Act and the 1904 Clapp Rider represented the first legislative attempts to achieve this end among the White Earth Anishinaabeg. Further efforts in this direction would follow.

In the nation at large, passage of the Burke Act in May of 1906 was aligned with these goals. The Burke Act addressed policymakers' desire to allow those who were prepared to manage their own affairs to do so, while safeguarding the interests of those not yet "competent." Most important, the Burke Act postponed citizenship conferred by the Dawes Act with the assignment of allotments, until after the trust period for those allotments made after 8 May 1906. To differentiate between Indians who were capable of seeing to their own economic interests and those who were not, the Burke Act contained a clause allowing the Secretary of the Interior to terminate the trust period and issue fee patents whenever he was convinced of an allottee's "competence." Through this "competency clause" allottees might acquire unrestricted title to their allotments and attain citizenship upon application. Tribal members who chafed under intrusive U.S. policies could support this loosening of restrictions.[39]

Commissioner of Indian Affairs Leupp believed that, in combination with legislation designed to divide the tribal funds, the Burke Act would make "industry" the standard by which officials could gauge "competence," and they would "use this as a lever to force Indians to earn their

bread by labor." However, by 1907, the commissioner had already identified as a major flaw the difficulty of ascertaining individual applicants'
capabilities: "Each agent or superintendent has his individual point of
view, which, no matter how sincerely he may strive to carry out the spirit
of the law, colors his reports and recommendations."[40] Commissioner
Leupp thought that determining "competence" was problematic, but he
had not yet considered that the Indian Office would soon find itself
involved in an even more difficult task, that of determining blood status.

Despite his concerns, the commissioner praised the Burke Act for filling a national void. Before its passage, "The only way in which an
intelligent and self-dependent Indian could obtain relief from the shack-
les of wardship . . . was by special legislation, and the evils of encouraging that practice . . . are too obvious."[41] Unwittingly, the commissioner had foretold events that were about to unfold at the White Earth
Reservation.

Early in 1906, Congressmen Clapp and Steenerson collaborated to
secure inclusion of yet another rider to that year's Indian Appropriations
Act designed to remove protective restrictions on allotted lands at White
Earth. They claimed to have acted in the best interests of the Indians.
Allotment of pine lands under the 1904 Steenerson Act had created an
inequitable situation where those who received pine allotments stood to
gain a great deal more than those who had not. Removing restrictions
from the land as well as the timber would allow everyone the same
advantage; everyone would have something to sell.

On 21 June 1906, only a month and a half after the Burke Act was
passed, the second Clapp Rider passed Congress with little notice. It
removed all restrictions governing "sale, incumbrance, or taxation" of
allotted land within the White Earth Reservation held by "adult mixed
bloods." The text of the Clapp Rider and its further elaboration in 1907
were carefully drawn to achieve the broadest possible application. Its
terms would apply "heretofore" and "hereafter" to adult mixed-bloods
and to those full-bloods declared "competent" by the Secretary of the
Interior. However, no one thought to define "mixed-blood" or to specify
some way to determine an individual's status to enable the act to be
carried out.[42]

The Commissioner of Indian Affairs opposed the 1906 Clapp Rider for two main reasons. First, Leupp protested that drawing a line based on blood distinctions was "unAmerican." Second, he feared that since most Indians of mixed descent at White Earth were not competent to manage their own affairs, the law held out "a perilous suggestion to unscrupulous persons to take advantage of Indians and procure their lands for less than value."[43] The terms of the 1906 Clapp Rider ran counter to the Burke Act, which, with its emphasis on "competence" and "industry," had been designed to avoid the sort of problems that the structure of the Clapp Rider was bound to create. That the two laws should pass Congress within such a short span of time, is curious. When the events that followed are considered, the suggestion that politicians and business concerns in Minnesota drafted the legislation with their own interests in mind is unavoidable.

So quickly did fraud follow on the heels of the 1906 Clapp Rider, that the Commissioner of Indian Affairs commented on both within the same annual report. The situation that followed amply bore out his fears. On 18 July 1906, the *Minneapolis Journal* reported that the townspeople of Detroit Lakes immediately south of the reservation had given themselves over to exploiting the newly "liberated" allottees. The newspaper reported that the town had been filled with "drunken Indians" since 21 June when the act became law. Saloons capitalized on the situation and many Indians had temporarily encamped near Detroit Lakes. Charlatans and hawkers of secondhand merchandise also joined the revelry.[44]

Reports of rampant fraud notwithstanding, Agent Michelet dismissed most of the newspaper charges. Michelet reported that many Indians had, indeed, taken advantage of the new law, and that many had squandered their money on whiskey. However, he found no evidence that speculators were exchanging liquor for land deeds.[45] In the same report where the commissioner warned of the consequences that enactment of the Clapp Rider would have, Agent Michelet welcomed its passage. Adopting the rhetoric of many of his contemporaries, Michelet ignored a centuries-old pattern of Anishinaabe self-support and praised the Clapp Rider: "The sooner they learn the value of money or property by being compelled to earn it by hard labor, the better will it be for all concerned."[46] Yet Michelet did not consider the serious consequences that dispossession would have for the White Earth Anishinaabeg. His earlier

partnership with lumber companies in the assignment of additional allotments under the 1904 Steenerson Act is sufficient cause for suspicion.

Agent Michelet never reported any questionable practices following
implementation of the 1906 Clapp Rider. And yet, reports of many
government investigators and testimony of reservation residents over
the years clarified the sort of fraud that had actually occurred by discern-
ing patterns among individual experiences.

Land and lumber companies had anticipated the Clapp Rider's passage
and hired métis cultural brokers Gus Beaulieu, B. L. Fairbanks, John
Carl, and others to arrange mortgages with individual allottees that
would become legal once it passed. These men skirted the fact that no
mechanism had been established to determine mixed-blood status by
preparing witnessed affidavits attesting to individuals' blood status, and
securing allottees' signatures well before the act was passed. These affidavits carried no force of law, but they do illustrate how eager corporate
interests were to acquire Indian lands. Typically, twenty-five dollars
sufficed to "reserve" an allotment until after the law took effect, when
allottees were to receive the remainder. Mortgages were to accrue 10
percent interest, to be collected in advance and run for ten years. Lenders
then quickly called these debts in, foreclosing on property in short order. During the first three weeks the Clapp Rider was in effect, Becker
County alone recorded more than 250 mortgages. Some policymakers
believed that Indians would benefit from this removal of restrictions so
that they might sell their resources. But the real beneficiaries proved to
be land and lumber companies and banks which employed cultural
brokers of mixed descent from White Earth to gain access to the best
farm and timber land.[47]

For many Indians whose thoughts fastened on their next meal instead
of advantageous real estate transactions, the promise of immediate cash
was seductive. The subsistence economy pursued by most Indians made
some act as accomplices in alienating their resources. Fraud and inequity
in the allotment process meant that many allottees possessed land that
they would not have chosen for themselves. In fact, the White Earth
Anishinaabeg had not moved onto their allotments in great numbers.
The U.S. policymakers, by imagining that individuals would move onto
their land allotments and farm them, created impossible goals at the out-

set. Not only was the policy estranged from the realities of geography and environment, but it made no allowance for communities that already existed at White Earth. It would have entirely disrupted existing reservation social relations for individual family members to move discretely onto their land allotments. Under these circumstances, opting to mortgage allotments that many had never even seen for cash to be used for horses, furniture, sewing machines, or groceries can be seen as an entirely rational decision. Resentment over Indian Office restrictions on both their individual and collective tribal funds was widespread. To many, the 1906 Clapp Rider seemed to provide only "mixed-bloods" with an immediate means to acquire large sums of money. So appealing was the promise of ready cash, no matter how inequitable, that many naively cooperated in signing affidavits declaring themselves to be "mixed-bloods" so that they too might sell land that had little intrinsic value for them. In at least two instances, minor children testified that their parents had taken them to the bank to meet with land dealers and instructed them to represent themselves as mixed-bloods who were old enough to sell their land. Some paid fees to the brokers who worked for the corporations for engineering their land transfers. In one sense, métis cultural brokers aided those who were disadvantaged in communication skills in mortgaging when they desired. On the other hand, they also participated in shady dealings that victimized naive full-blood and mixed-blood allottees alike.[48]

Members of the Graham Commission collected evidence between 1911 and 1912 that revealed how the Clapp Riders and Steenerson Act had actually operated. Participants and observers testified that fraud and corruption had characterized every stage of the management and sale of Anishinaabe land and timber. Irrefutable evidence indicted certain key individuals of mixed descent at White Earth, Gus Beaulieu, Ben Fairbanks, and John Carl in particular, for their instrumental roles in facilitating the alienation of both allotted land and timber. Many allottees, mixed- and full-blood alike, claimed that they had not known what they were signing. Reservation residents testified that the contents of documents had been misrepresented to them and that they had been plied with liquor. Some recited promises of large amounts of money that they had never received; others signed away valuable land for only a trifle of

its worth. Corporate employees of mixed descent had knowingly prepared "applications," complete with affidavits attesting to their blood
status, for minors who were ineligible to sell. Investigators reported that
Gus Beaulieu had falsified records of a dead person to acquire the land,
posed as a guardian to orphans, and even visited the far-off boarding
schools at Haskell and Carlisle to persuade underage school children to
relinquish their allotments.[49] These illegal transfers became the basis of
complex land fraud claims at White Earth that are still pending in the
courts today.

Not only did unsuspecting Indians find that they had bound themselves to unfair agreements, but local Euroamericans also took advantage
of their naiveté by giving them worthless substitutes instead of cash.
Some received tin tokens from land buyers that could only be redeemed
for goods at specific company stores. Lumber companies issued duebills
marked "non-negotiable" which merchants cashed only at substantial
discounts.[50]

Some Indians used part of the total due them to make utilitarian
purchases that contributed to the domestic economy. Exploitative Euroamericans stood ready to fleece them at every turn. Secondhand sewing
machines and dilapidated pianos threatened to disintegrate, and nag
horses died, leaving the owners with worn-out harnesses and wagons
that they could not use. Agent Michelet informed the Commissioner of
Indian Affairs that Messrs. Kolb and Bohmer "were obtaining deeds and
mortgages from mixed-blood Indians and trading them horses in return . . . at an exorbitant price."[51] Those with an interest in Indian lands
at White Earth conceived of every imaginable scheme to take unfair
advantage of recently "freed" allottees.

The 1906 Clapp Rider also established the means by which lumber
companies might acquire allotted pine timber, a question that had been
left undecided after the aborted 1905 sale. They would negotiate with
individual Indian owners, a task they also assigned to White Earth métis
brokers. Gus Beaulieu advertised in *The Tomahawk* to buy pine timber
for the Nichols-Chisolm Lumber Company.[52] Corporate interests and
individual allottees alike were aware of the mediating roles played by
these enterprising cultural brokers.

The same local lumber companies that had shown an interest in earlier sales of pine timber acquired the vast majority of allotted pine at White Earth in the three years following the Clapp Rider. Their land purchases divided especially the forested southeastern townships according to watersheds and proximity to their manufacturing mills. They also colluded to stifle competition, reducing prices paid for timber to below those established for the 1905 sale. The Nichols-Chisolm Company operating out of Frazee bought most of the timber, approximately 150 million feet. The Park Rapids Company acquired 38 million feet, while the Wild Rice Company sent 20 million feet down the Wild Rice River to Ada, Minnesota. Their well-established infrastructures, complete with equipment and experienced personnel, gave these companies the edge in acquiring White Earth pine timber. This should have been expected for they had figured prominently in all prior sales of timber there.[53]

Callaway, Ogema, Waubun, Mahnomen, and Bejou along the Soo Line as well as nearby off-reservation towns of Detroit Lakes, Park Rapids, Frazee, Bagley, Fosston, and Crookston all supported the activities of local banks and land companies that speculated in and "developed" White Earth's resources. They had welcomed the railroad line because it promised to raise the value of their property, and they supported removal of restrictions on allotted reservation resources for similar reasons. Certain key individuals, for example L. S. Waller and Fred Sanders, were often members of boards of directors of local banks and land companies, and were repeatedly implicated in land fraud claims. A few powerful businessmen in the area formed interlocking directorates, serving in high positions in several companies in which all shared an interest. H. A. Krostue simultaneously served as cashier for the First National Bank of Detroit and as vice-president of the Waubun State Bank, and had an interest in the Waubun Land and Implement Company. The Becker County Land and Loan Company did a great deal of business with J. B. Schermerhorn, an oil producer based in Chicago. "Schermerhorn Farms" would come to comprise the largest acreage held by one owner—he was *the* "bonanza" farmer on the reservation. Most of those who dealt in White Earth lands came from the local area, but more distant speculators also showed an interest.[54]

The Donnafred Oil Company (named after Fred and Donna Sanders), with a letterhead from Okmulgee, Oklahoma, best illustrates how those involved with local business interests speculated in White Earth resources. Members of the corporation's board of directors all hailed from towns near White Earth, where they oversaw their business interests. Fred Sanders and C. A. Baker of Detroit Lakes served as president and secretary, respectively, of the Becker County Land and Loan Company. Fred Sanders figured prominently in stories that allottees recounted about being cheated by those who offered mortgages. M. J. Kolb of Bagley, Minnesota, had a major interest in the Ogema Land and Timber Company, and was charged in the first major equity case, the Kolb-Perrault case. This same M. J. Kolb had also sold inferior horses to recently "liberated" allottees at exorbitant prices, and was expelled from the reservation by the Indian Police. These men, who came together to form the Donnafred Oil Company, clearly intended to speculate in White Earth lands. Oil was one resource that did not draw investors' attention at White Earth.[55]

Investigating and Litigating Land Fraud Claims

So the situation remained until the summer of 1909, when Warren K. Moorehead, a scholar from Andover, Massachusetts, with an interest in Indian affairs, reported on his visit to the reservation. With the cooperation of government officials, Moorehead, recently appointed by Theodore Roosevelt to the Board of Indian Commissioners in 1908, engineered a special commission to investigate conditions at White Earth because of rumors he had heard about undue suffering there.

Moorehead was aghast at the state of affairs he found when he arrived in the more isolated area of Pine Point in March of 1909. He wrote to the Commissioner of Indian affairs that "the thing is so big that it may be necessary . . . to have a national commission . . . restore these lands to the poor people." He referred to Gus Beaulieu as the "leader of the wolf pack" and to the Nichols-Chisolm Lumber Company as the "king of the forest, for which the wolf-pack hunts." Moorehead was overwhelmed by what he learned: "I have never been so moved, and I am not much given to sentiment."

The nearby town of Ponsford had experienced a short economic boom period immediately after passage of the 1906 Clapp Rider, as business interests feverishly dealt in Indian lands. Moorehead witnessed the aftermath of this unimpeded rush on allotted resources. Poverty and a worsened disease environment were the more obvious consequences. Moorehead arranged for a doctor to treat tuberculosis and trachoma, which threatened to consume the population. As he assembled affidavits to determine what had happened to the White Earth experiment, Moorehead became persuaded that "the Indians had been swindled out of the major portion of their property."

Moorehead spent most of his time at the Pine Point settlement, composed predominantly of Otter Tail Pillager and some Leech Lake band members. He went to White Earth Village only after he had been at Pine Point for some time; other inspectors or special agents had spent their time solely with the agent at White Earth Village "rather than visiting the Indian cabins or hearing Indian evidence, so the Indians claimed."

Moorehead collected much evidence pointing toward land fraud and the opposition immediately took notice of his activities. He had assembled 117 affidavits representing more than a million dollars' worth of property fraudulently taken from Indians, and worried "that the lumber and land interests would attempt to prevent [him] from taking these affidavits East." Such a state of affairs forced Moorehead to be especially on his guard. He sent an emissary to the Park Rapids train station with a false departure time so that he might elude his detractors and escape via the Soo Line out of Ogema. With the aid of an armed escort, Moorehead was finally able to deliver the affidavits to Commissioner of Indian Affairs R. G. Valentine. Moorehead can be credited with spearheading efforts to investigate White Earth land fraud claims; his persistence helped to keep the issue at the fore.

The results of Moorehead's probing horrified Commissioner of Indian Affairs Valentine and he authorized Moorehead and Edward B. Linnen, a regular experienced Indian Office inspector, to undertake another investigation in July of 1909. The Moorehead and Linnen report, completed in September, rehearsed in greater detail all of Moorehead's original findings. In less than three years since passage of the 1906 Clapp Rider, fully 90 percent of land allotted to full-bloods had been mortgaged or sold; 80 percent of all reservation land had passed into private ownership. Fifteen to twenty years earlier, the White Earth Anishinaabeg had been far more industrious, sober, and engaged in agricultural pursuits. The report lamented that "they have no lands, no money, and must now either go to work or be paupers on the counties . . . or on the State of Minnesota." They attached hundreds of witnessed affidavits attesting to the manner in which the lands of full-bloods had been lost, and included a list of full-bloods' names, compiled by talking to older leaders.[56]

Linnen's and Moorehead's findings left little to the imagination. Finally, the voices of men respected by the Indian Office were added to those of the White Earth conservatives "who had dared to defy Indian agent Simon Michelet."[57] Ahbowegeshig from Pine Point had known what they would find all along: "A good many of the Indian people here are losing their property on account of . . . foreclosures and censure by the creditors."[58] Such sentiments emanating from both Indian Office inspectors and Indian leaders at White Earth meant that the dire developments could no longer be ignored. Even Indian Commissioner Valentine was finally moved to vow, "I want to go to the bottom of the thieving that has been carried out in the White Earth Country, without regard to whom we hit."[59]

By year's end, Special Attorney Marsden C. Burch and a corps of assistants from the Indian Office and the Department of Justice were in the field and collected testimony for several months in the winter and spring. Nearly every Indian Office official sent to look into the matter was scandalized by the ways Indians had lost their lands; Burch was no exception. He likened the métis cultural brokers who had expedited land transfers to the "traitor steer," used in the beef-packing establishments of Chicago and the west. Drawing an analogy to the steer that led the other cattle to the slaughter, only to be turned aside as the others "go to their doom," he chastised the brokers for the role they played: "They have led their kith and kin into the trap and induced them to part with their land."[60]

Burch began a process of filing complaints of equity in the U.S. District Court at Fergus Falls. The suits aimed to recover lands from corporations and individuals who had acquired them illegally from classes of allottees at White Earth ineligible to sell. Within a year, Burch had filed more than 1,000 suits covering 142,000 acres, $2,000,000 in land, and $1,755,000 in timber.[61]

The equity suits languished, however. Several factors hampered

Burch's efficiency: directing the Graham Commission in 1911 consumed much of his time; corporations (the "pine cartel") that stood to benefit from land transfers already made worked to impede investigation of land fraud claims;[62] and, perhaps most difficult of all, pursuing equity suits depended on establishing the blood status of reservation residents. In addition to these impediments, Burch was less than energetic in his prosecution of the equity suits and never even "requested injunctions to halt the logging of disputed lands." Historical geographer Holly Youngbear-Tibbets suggests that his laxity may have been due to his close association with the pine cartel, having found them "very tractable and decent in every way."[63]

Since the 1906 Clapp Rider freed "adult mixed bloods" to sell, Burch concerned himself only with identifying full-bloods and minor mixed-bloods. Special Agent John H. Hinton aided Burch in making sense of the thorny issue of blood quotas, which was no easy task. Hinton exercised creativity in his attempt. First he combed agency records and completed cards for each allottee, recording all vital information he could find. Since most Indians showed no inclination to travel to Detroit Lakes where Burch was headquartered, Hinton considered traveling about the reservation as Moorehead and Linnen had done. Finally, he decided to attend the annuity payment that fall and, through consultation with Indian leaders, record each individual's status to the sixteenth fraction of white blood. Several Indian leaders accompanied him on the annuity circuit and provided extensive genealogical information about the ancestry and family relationships of younger individuals. At each location "Indians in family groups and from particular neighborhoods or well acquainted with each other were permitted to enter together." The "Hinton Roll," constructed from these cards, was approved by the Secretary of the Interior on 31 December 1910. Burch and Hinton took pride in their product, confident that it reflected professional care and an unprecedented concern with Indian family groups.[64]

Even as the equity cases went forward, the "land sharks continue[d] to ply their nefarious trade." Members of the Graham Commission traveled to see the situation for themselves. The terrible social consequences of dispossession were everywhere evident. Committee members visited "one desolate hut" where "three women who, although blind, were about to be ejected on a mortgage deal."[65]

Clear-cut evidence collected by the Graham Commission prompted five individuals to confess. Lucky S. Waller, M. J. Kolb, J. E. Perrault, Andrew Vanoss, William Uran, and Louis D. Davis were charged with conspiracy to induce "United States officials to issue land patents to full-blood Indians." Civil charges were filed against the Nichols-Chisolm Lumber Company, but former agent Simon Michelet, who had been implicated in the scams, escaped without censure. The Graham Commission forwarded 1,529 cases of illegally sold trust allotments to the Department of Justice.[66]

The 1913 Roll Commission

The pine cartel and their political allies in northwestern Minnesota, some of whom were defendants in the equity cases, met in the fall of 1912 to discuss the land fraud investigations. At this meeting, they devised another new twist to their usual delaying tactics. By this time, everyone knew that establishing the blood status of individual allottees was the linchpin in these cases. Claiming that errors of judgment seriously flawed the Hinton Roll, they urged their political cronies to submit a bill to Congress for the creation of a roll commission to fix the blood status of White Earth allottees more accurately. Conveniently, their motion would also undermine Judge Burch's efforts in the equity cases by delaying adjudication, a situation certainly favorable to their interests.[67]

Congressmen Clapp and Steenerson, who always figured prominently in legislative remedies for White Earth land issues, attended the 1912 meeting in Detroit Lakes and set out to see to the wishes of their voting constituents. After a series of legislative shuffles, Congress passed a provision for a roll commission as part of the Indian Appropriations Act of 30 June 1913 calling for the appointment of two commissioners to determine individuals' blood status and create a roll.[68]

Gordon Cain, recommended by the Justice Department, and Ransom J. Powell, a local attorney, were promptly appointed. Powell's appointment put in place a man who had served as counsel for many Minnesota lumber companies over the past ten years. He represented the largest of them all, the Nichols-Chisolm Lumber Company. In their behalf, he had opposed the 1905 sale of allotted timber, and he went on to become chief solicitor for many defendants in Judge Burch's equity suits.

An incredulous Interior Secretary Franklin Lane recognized how Powell's vested interests would prejudice the roll commission's work, because he served as attorney "for all of the people interested in the White Earth Reservation; some of them lumbermen, . . . bankers, . . . real estate dealers, . . . merchants, . . . farmers, . . . and many mixed-blood Chippewa Indians . . . are among his clients as well."[69] Decisions about blood status made by the roll commission would expedite the very cases for which Powell served as chief defense. Powell himself had drafted the roll commission bill and was confident that the man appointed by the Justice Department would be "satisfactory to the parties I represent" and that "I shall be the other Commissioner."[70] Although the conflict of interests could not have been more apparent, Powell fulfilled his commission with no further notice from federal officials. Political and economic interests in northwestern Minnesota were obviously on quite cozy terms.

While involved in his duties as roll commissioner, Powell continued to advise his clients of the viability of their claims to allotments at White Earth. He capitalized on his position and even "initiated a $50 service for interested public officials charged with preparing titles of record."[71] Powell informed them that neither the roll currently being made nor a Supreme Court decision would dispose of the cases pending; the blood status of individuals had to be determined "by proof or by agreement."[72] Since no "proof" existed prior to the development of a roll, Powell engineered such "agreements" himself. His dual capacities as roll commissioner and counsel for the defense eased his task immeasurably. Adequate monetary compensation was his chief concern; if enough money had changed hands, he could be absolutely cavalier in his judgments. He advised Ponsford merchant J. W. Nunn that his payment of $1,400 for a piece of allotted land would probably suffice to get the sale approved. Then Powell offered further aid of the sort that only *he* could give: "In consideration of such a settlement the government will agree that the Indian is a mixed blood, and eventually give you a fee simple patent." In the meantime, he advised Nunn to "go ahead and improve the property and get as much out of it as you can."[73] News of the imaginative approaches undertaken by the roll commission had circulated widely among interested parties in northwestern Minnesota. Theodore H. Beaulieu, whose stationery read "Garden Spot of Minnesota Lands, Exclusive

Lake Shore Lots, White Earth, Minnesota," had received "some encouraging information about the blood status of the woman, 'Quod-aince'" from Mrs. Waweyeacumig or Nawajibigokwe, but the government now questioned his purchase of this land.[74] Beaulieu anxiously turned to Powell for advice, having learned of the inventive arrangements he had orchestrated. Powell was not above magically altering birth dates to legalize a minor child's allotment transfer. Just how many of these creative "deals" Powell engineered cannot be determined, but, clearly, the commissioners took considerable liberty in executing their responsibilities.

Powell himself recognized how irregular his extralegal deals were as he explained to Fred Sanders, a man who played a prominent role in buying and selling Indian lands, that establishing blood quotas ought to settle land claims and not represent merely the opinion of the roll commissioners. White Earth Agency officials should mediate full-bloods' land claims and mixed-bloods should be free to do as they please. He feared that "we will find ourselves in all sorts of trouble" if the deals arranged by the roll commission were ever contested.[75]

Serving on the roll commission also afforded Powell opportunities to dispense patronage and he tried to take good care of his clients. Julius Brown, usually allied with Gus Beaulieu and B. L. Fairbanks, sought employment through Powell as an interpreter for the roll commission. He spoke very candidly about his former employment as an agent for the Nichols-Chisolm Lumber Company through Gus Beaulieu, as if he knew to expect a sympathetic ear from Powell: "Since there is no work for me from the Lumber Co., I have been without employment."[76] Powell assured him that he would try to take care of him.

Powell also protected some of the métis brokers, shielding them from potential punishment for their roles in the land fraud cases. Gus H. Beaulieu transferred title to his personal property to others, Powell among them, to protect it from attachment for debt. As he wrote to Powell, he planned to shift some land titles from Powell's name to J. N. Nichols of the Nichols-Chisolm Lumber Company, Beaulieu's benefactor. He confided, "I signed a deed this week transferring to Fairbanks for my parents' allotment. I do not know exactly how my own allotment stands since I could do nothing with it while in your name." Powell served a similar function for Ed Tanner.[77]

Other Indians from White Earth who wanted to mortgage their property wrote to Powell to find out how the roll commission viewed their status. Shoneyahquay or Mrs. Jane Buckanaga made such a query: "I have some land north of Mahnomen county and I can sell it but they do not think I am a mixed blood. Please tell me what I am [*sic*] I think I am all right." Powell replied, "I think you will probably be fixed as a mixed-blood but not right away." The same request from Eugene Bird elicited a similar response: "I cannot tell you yet whether you are a full-blood or a mixed-blood. Some people say you are one thing and others say the other."[78] Clearly, everyone concerned eagerly awaited resolution of the blood status issue.

Producing a White Earth roll satisfactory to all parties was an impossible task. Previous attempts by Linnen and Moorehead and by Hinton involved community participation to an unprecedented extent, but the larger number of "full-bloods" they identified were unacceptable to the pine cartel. Powell himself oversaw compilation of a lengthy genealogy, only to be advised that it lacked substantive legal proof. As he editorialized to the *Minneapolis Tribune*, "It is much easier to determine a legal proposition relative to what constitutes a mixed-blood . . . than it is to determine who are the mixed bloods."[79]

Adjudication of the equity cases still proceeded slowly although Charles C. Daniels, Burch's replacement, was a far more "articulate advocate" and "aggressive prosecutor." Daniels immediately recognized that the title disputes involved private property, the owners of which "were entitled to due process of law." Unfortunately, he was one of the only litigators involved in the land fraud claims who ever held firm to this belief. He won his first case, where "M. J. Kolb, president of the Ogema Land and Timber Company," was charged "with criminal conspiracy and inducing federal officials to issue land patents to full-blood Indians." But his momentum was undermined as defense attorneys, Ransom J. Powell among them, exploited nuances of judicial and congressional strategy to accomplish delays that worked to their clients' advantage. As Youngbear-Tibbets observed, "Powell's strategy had always been to outwait rather than outwit federal prosecutors."[80]

The 1913 roll commission had been effectively hamstrung by judicial wrangling over a definition of the term "mixed-blood"; such a determination was necessary before it could begin its work in earnest. Exactly how much white blood made an Indian a mixed-blood? Equity suits filed thus far had assumed that mixed-bloods possessed one-half or more white blood. Lawyers submitted three cases to test the principle. Judge Page Morris of the U.S. District Court ruled that a mixed-blood had at least one-eighth fraction of white blood. The U.S. Circuit Court of Appeals then overruled the decision, defining a "mixed-blood" as an Indian with any amount of "white blood," no matter how small. Finally, on 8 June 1914, the Supreme Court upheld the decision of the Circuit Court of Appeals. This decision represented the broadest possible construction of the term "mixed-blood," had absolutely no relation to the nationally focused Burke Act's emphasis on "competence," and immediately loosened the legal underpinnings of many of the pending equity suits.[81]

By September of 1915, the government had lost most cases it brought to trial where blood status was not the issue.[82] The new government attorney, Francis J. Kearful, surveyed the situation at White Earth and surmised that pressing the claims in court was futile because of the time that had elapsed: chief witnesses had moved or died and could not be relied upon to appear, and the statute of limitations had expired, prohibiting criminal prosecutions. Kearful abandoned Daniels's commitment to due process and sought an out-of-court compromise.

Kearful contacted Powell and the two lawyers framed the following agreement. All land transferred from "true" full-bloods should be restored to them. Cases involving transfers from mixed-bloods judged competent to sell would be dismissed. However, these cases represented only a fraction of those remaining. Defendants involved in the remaining cases were to pay the difference between what they had actually paid and the fair market value, plus 6 percent interest. Anyone not satisfied with this compromise could continue to seek redress in court. No means were established to recover lands fraudulently acquired from mixed-bloods. The attorneys' chief concern was adequate monetary compensation, not reestablishing an economic foundation of individually allotted land. Such individuals faced the prospect of costly court battles and would labor against the same obstacles that had prompted Kearful and Powell to compromise in the first place.[83]

In terms of blood status, this compromise meant that only full-bloods need be identified, but attorneys still needed "substantive legal proof" for their determinations to carry any weight in court. So they turned to two scientific experts whose testimony regarding blood status had been used in several equity cases. Dr. Aleŝ Hrdliĉka, director of anthropology at the Smithsonian Institution, and Dr. Albert E. Jenks, an anthropologist at the University of Minnesota, claimed to have devised certain scientific tests capable of distinguishing between mixed-bloods and full-bloods. The roll commissioners hoped that these scientists' expertise might enable them to complete their task in timely fashion.

Initially, the anthropologists had only testified about characteristics that they believed differentiated full- from mixed-bloods. Hrdliĉka had made a formal statement to the Justice Department laying out what he proposed full-blood features to be. Influenced by eugenic ideas of his day, Hrdliĉka founded his determination of blood status on distinguishing physical characteristics. Both men referred to this deposition as an authority for their subsequent work in Minnesota. Powell also used it when advising individuals of their status. Jim Jugg was impatient to learn the results of his visit with "that Doctor who knows what Indians are."[84] When Julius Brown asked about his blood status, Powell relied on the anthropologists' opinion, saying with assurance that an Indian could not possibly be a full-blood unless he "is fairly dark complected, has coarse straight black hair, very dark brown eyes, amounting practically to black, and a scarcity of hair on the body, other than the hair of the head."[85]

In 1916, Dr. Hrdliĉka traveled to the White Earth Reservation with Commissioner Robert C. Bell to gather further evidence for his anthropometric inquiry. They drove from home to home to examine individual Indians whose status was in question, directing special attention to "the skin of the body, especially that of the chest, to the hair and eyes, physiognomy and a number of other features, such as the nails, gums and teeth."[86] One test Hrdliĉka employed "consisted of drawing with some force the nail of the fore-finger over the chest" which created a "reddening, or hyperaemia, along the lines drawn."[87] Supposedly, mixed bloods' skin reacted more vividly—unless they were anemic.

By theorizing that the Pima Indians of Arizona represented "the most Indian of all Indians," Hrdliĉka hoped to construct a "full-blood" physical standard against which Anishinaabe samples might be compared.[88] Hal Downey of the Department of Animal Biology at the University of

Minnesota aided Hrdliĉka in his efforts by constructing a standard for differentiating hair quality. He "made several measurements along each hair at distances of one half centimeter" and recommended that at least ten hairs per person were necessary to construct a scientific standard.[89] The racist overtones of these efforts grew increasingly blatant.

In the course of this work Hrdliĉka and Jenks had cause to question the results of their "scientific" measurements. Jenks reported with surprise that among their findings, they had discovered that "both Hrdliĉka and myself have hair of most typical negro type, and the Scandinavians have hair more circular in cross section than our pure blood Pima Indians." Puzzled by the failure of their methods, Jenks was forced to conclude that "Dr. Hrdliĉka and I are related to the negro, and the Scandinavians are simply bleached out Mongolians." Mired in confusion, the anthropologists had to admit that classifying human races by hair texture was proving to be a far more problematic undertaking than they had initially imagined.[90]

Anishinaabe informants called to testify about individuals' genealogical backgrounds understood genetic variations better than did the anthropologists. Mezhucegeshig grew impatient with repetitive questioning about distinctive "mixed-blood" genetic characteristics: "It wouldn't make any difference if [someone] was curly-headed. My hair is curly. . . . Some Indians are blacker than others, and some are lighter." Mahdosayquay concurred: "Generation after generations in the Indian, sometimes there is one lighter than the others . . . it just happens." These informants objected to establishing fixed physical standards by which to differentiate among Indians because of variations they observed among themselves. Aydahwaycumigoquay offered a practical suggestion to his interrogator, who was distressed to find that his informant could offer no help in determining a deceased man's status: "He is dead long ago. I don't know exactly what he was. You can go dig him out of his grave, and then you can find out."[91] The U.S. examiners had more reason to determine blood status than did most Indian informants.

Such doubts did little to hinder the anthropologists. As Youngbear-Tibbets observed: "This was a heady era for the newly emerging social sciences, which embraced staggering doctrines of environmental determinism. Among the social sciences, anthropology found itself playing center stage to devoted professional and lay audiences—and nowhere did the limelight shine more brilliantly than on the work of the physical anthropologists." After examining 696 of approximately 800 Indians who claimed full-blood status, the scientists felt sure enough of their observations to go beyond identifying what they believed to be general racial characteristics to testify as to individuals' status. Through spurious methods of this sort, Hrdlička and Jenks lent their professional, scientific expertise to attempts to resolve White Earth land fraud claims. Their efforts directly contributed to formulation of the 1920 Blood Roll, and outright racism received the imprimatur of academia.[92]

Although the opinions of Jenks and Hrdlička persuaded Powell and Bell, they could not incorporate the results without a legislative amendment. The 1913 act creating the roll commission required a fractional delineation of blood status. The 1917 Indian Appropriations Act remedied the situation, providing that the roll should record only full-blood or mixed-blood status, rather than fractions thereof. With this alteration, Powell and Bell used the experts' findings to complete the Blood Roll in 1917. Once all the equity suits were dispensed with, Judge Page Morris of the U.S. District Court approved the Blood Roll on 12 November 1920.[93]

The 1920 Blood Roll enrolled 5,173 allottees of the White Earth Reservation. Only 104 full-bloods of 126 identified by Hrdlička survived to be recorded. The commissioners agreed that 282 allottees who had died should be included as full-bloods. Thus, a total of 408 full-bloods had been identified.[94]

Although all the rationale offered by government officials at the national level emphasized "competence" as the criterion justifying termination of the trust relationship, such consideration did not prevail at the White Earth Reservation. Federal officials interpreted the 1906 Clapp Rider literally, and set out to ascertain the genetic makeup of individuals. The legitimacy of the 1920 Blood Roll rested on a methodological foundation devised by experts who pioneered the science of eugenics. As such it was an inherently racist document.[95]

The 1920 Blood Roll resolved the White Earth controversy only in the short run. The most important issue, that of individual allottees' right to due process of law, had not been tried in the courts. At White Earth, individuals had never been persuaded of its validity. "Full-blood" children were attributed to "mixed-blood" parents. The experts adjudged siblings with exactly the same parents differently. Louisa Fineday complained to the Chippewa Enrollment Commission: "All the Finedays are the same. And some are on the roll as full blood Indians and some are mixed blood Indians. . . . Who is the one that put this on the roll that some are full and some mix [*sic*]?"[96] No solution could have pleased everyone. The real beneficiaries, however, were the land and pine cartel, their political benefactors, and their métis agents who had awaited such a resolution for fourteen years.

Conclusion

Land alienation and resource exploitation at White Earth closely paralleled trends among the "Chippewa in Minnesota" and Indian people in the United States at large. White Earth's wealth of timber and farmland and the proximity of an expansive Euroamerican population guaranteed that it would become an early target for both allotment legislation and removal of the protective trust relationship.

By 1920, most of the reservation land base had transferred to Euroamerican hands. The framework for this outcome had been in place immediately following passage of the 1906 Clapp Rider, but questions about blood status postponed resolution until 1920. Corporate and business interests used every means imaginable, including employing métis agents, to gain access to allotted resources at White Earth. Politicians pressured government officials to render decisions favorable to these business interests. Only Charles C. Daniels emerged, like Bishop Whipple in an earlier period, to help spotlight the cause of the White Earth Anishinaabeg, but his tenure was short-lived. Their leaders struggled largely alone.[97]

Many different government inspectors investigated what had occurred at White Earth over the years. The history appalled almost everyone and persuaded them that fraudulent transactions had, indeed, occurred among both full-bloods *and* mixed-bloods. Yet decisions made at the upper echelons of the Interior Department hierarchy, more often than not, benefited outside economic interests. The observations and recommendations of the 1911 Graham Commission, an expensive, time-consuming, and comprehensive investigation producing over 3,000 pages of evidence, had little effect on Indian policy. Judicial maneuvering delayed final resolution of the claims cases until the statute of limitations had expired, barring criminal prosecutions from being made.

None of the investigators used Indian definitions or understandings of the terms "mixed-blood" and "full-blood," even though later interpretations of treaty rights established this as a fundamental consideration when adjudicating claims. Inspectors Linnen, Moorehead, and Hinton probably came closest to capturing a larger proportion of those who would have been encompassed by Anishinaabe categorizations. Judicial decrees favored a broad construction of the term "mixed-blood" in its literal, genetic sense. The 1920 Blood Roll, based upon so-called scientific standards, restricted the pool of full-bloods even further. Not accidentally, these legalities continually reduced the number of pending equity cases.

The rationale offered for passage of the 1906 Clapp Rider flew in the face of contemporaneous national legislation such as the Burke Act that emphasized competence rather than blood status as the determining factor in the removal of the U.S. government's trust responsibility. Although the term "competent" surfaced repeatedly in discussions of legislation affecting White Earth, criteria for competence were not the final test for abrogation of the trust relationship. Policymakers interpreted blood status literally at White Earth . . . with absurd consequences. The U.S. society at large easily accepted this racist reasoning at a time when discrimination against other racial and ethnic minority groups was on the rise.

At the national level, federal officials assessed Indians' competence and issued fee patents at an accelerating speed, removing the government's trust responsibility in the process.[98] What happened at White Earth accomplished this end with even greater facility. Events at White Earth did not follow the national trend—they helped to set it. Legislative, judicial, and political haggling over blood status masked the fact that the vast majority of White Earth Anishinaabeg were declared mixed-bloods and were therefore free to sell and/or be taken advantage of. By 1920, most reservation resources lay effectively beyond Indian control.

⌐4⌐

Warehousers and Sharks

The Social and Economic Bases
of Political Factionalism

Introduction

Immigrant Anishinaabeg continued to observe band ties after relocating to White Earth. Treaty relationships, residence patterns, and family and community ties all contributed to the perpetuation of band affiliations. Blood status had meant little to the Anishinaabeg, many of whom recognized some Euroamerican ancestry. As they explained themselves, the terms "mixed-blood" and "full-blood" indicated basic cultural or ethnic differences—not solely genetic ones. After the turn of the century, however, leaders transformed these cultural terms into political symbols. Two pivotal events prompted a realignment among reservation political leaders. First, the hotly contested additional allotments issued under the 1904 Steenerson Act polarized reservation residents. Through this controversy, the *mixed-blood* and *full-blood* cultural symbols took on political meaning. Ensuing land fraud claims and investigations generated by the 1906 Clapp Rider exacerbated this conflict and cemented factional (not political party) divisions.[1] Overall ethnic orientation eclipsed band affiliations in determining factional alliances, although band ties continued to influence political preferences.

More conservative Anishinaabeg, calling themselves "full-bloods," united across band lines to oppose policies advocated by those whom they called "mixed-bloods." Key métis leaders favored loosening restrictions on allotted resources and then positioned themselves to serve as agents for land and lumber companies anxious to acquire White Earth's wealth; as such, they presented easy political targets for conservative leaders. Through a formal petition directed at specific individuals, the "full-bloods" contested métis leaders' right to reside at White Earth and to participate in distributions of tribal funds. Ultimately, despite opposition from the "Full Blood Faction," government investigators, and Indian Office personnel, Interior Department officials decided in favor of those whose status had been questioned.

The same leaders who bore the brunt of this criticism went on to found the "General Council of the Chippewa" in 1913. Though the council intended to address issues that should have been of great concern to all Minnesota Anishinaabeg, delegates transplanted the factional struggle from White Earth to the tribal level. Unable to find a way around the factional dispute, Indian Office officials supported the push for inter-reservation tribal government.

Administrators demanded that disgruntled petitioners resolve their differences in a representative council. At the tribal level, this strategy saw some success as an authentic majority eventually came to overwhelm those individuals accustomed to dominating political affairs. Before 1920, however, contending factions at White Earth thwarted attempts to convene a genuinely representative council. By the time elective structures were in place, far higher numbers of Franco- and Anglo-Anishinaabeg assured that the proportional representation from more conservative bands would decline. Elective structures imposed by the Indian Office brought a degree of stability to the political situation, but they also spelled the end of the more flexible process of splintering and amalgamation that had characterized Anishinaabe polity.

Political factions at White Earth espoused two different strategies for managing and distributing reservation resources. Assimilationist leaders urged the U.S. government to rescind its trust responsibility and lift restrictions on allotted resources. They also advocated distributing the tribal funds *pro rata*, in essence liquidating them. Conservative leaders opposed these policies largely because of the exploitative behavior of key métis leaders. They had witnessed the damage wrought by placing individual interests above those of the reservation community. With their capitalistic ethic, assimilationists had moved away from more conservative Anishinaabe values emphasizing greater concern for equity among community and kin.

Several active métis leaders from White Earth again moved toward broader political involvement to become active in national pan-Indian organizations as their status was questioned among the Minnesota Anishinaabeg at large. White Earth representatives joined other formally educated cultural brokers like themselves from across the country in pan-tribal organizations where they espoused their laissez-faire approach to Indian policy.

While political conflict played a central role in temporarily safeguarding Anishinaabe resources, it also tried the fabric of Indian society at White Earth. Lack of consensus hampered resolution of land fraud claims and hindered the operation of stable government. At a time when protecting reservation assets against a common foe required a united front, the White Earth Indians had never been more divided. And yet, without opposition from the Full Blood Faction, assimilationist leaders might have expedited the dissipation of White Earth resources in a much shorter period of time.

The Full-Bloods' Critique

Inspector McLaughlin's dismissal of all charges of wrongdoing in making additional allotments, charges that were eventually borne out by a later congressional investigation, accentuated conservative band leaders' growing sense that they were losing control over their lives. Fraud that followed the 1906 Clapp Rider added tinder to their smoldering resentment. Individuals who had once played positive broker roles, shielding more conservative Indians from extensive Euroamerican contact, had extended their mediating skills beyond activities that served useful social functions for the Anishinaabeg. The fact that the most notorious land and pine cartel agents, Gus Beaulieu and Ben Fairbanks, were descended from Lake Superior and Wisconsin bands provided conservative leaders with the final element necessary for them to elaborate on familiar cultural symbols and mobilize them in the political arena. Although many people told stories about being tricked and cheated, patterns of fraud in allotted land transfers were not immediately apparent. Nevertheless, groups of Anishinaabeg gathered whenever government investigators took testimony, sometimes traveling as far as Washington, D.C., to attend. They listened to one another's accounts and learned what government investigators like Moorehead, Linnen, and Hinton filed in their reports. Together, conservative Indians and government investigators pieced together what had happened and, between 1909 and 1913, a clearer picture began to emerge. There is little wonder that conservative band leaders grew increasingly incensed as they became aware of the fraud and exploitation being perpetrated by individuals among them who professed to have their best interests at heart.

In an earlier era, substantial differences in outlook that could not be compromised were likely to splinter the group. But under the 1889 Nelson Act, all assets and resources of the "Chippewa in Minnesota" contributed to a general fund held in common by all Anishinaabeg. It became clear to conservative band leaders that their acquiescence in the U.S. government's recognition of "elective" councils held by assimilationist leaders was tantamount to abdicating any control over administering their tribal funds, leaving these important decisions to those who did not share their ethics.

Charles Wright, eldest son of Wabonaquod, emerged as a leader during the conflict over additional allotments. Wright served as an Episcopal minister who preached solely in the Anishinaabe language at Cass Lake, Minnesota. Although Wright was enrolled at the White Earth Reservation, he had not lived there for some time. Wright lent his name and influence when requested by conservative band leaders, many from Pine Point, who felt cheated by the allotment process. Given his assumption of his father's position as the paramount *ogimaa*, he believed that he had both the authority and responsibility to intercede. Wright explained that in the past a band *ogimaa* had acted as a diplomat: "They council among themselves. When they have decided . . . they give me the petition to take . . . to Washington, so I do that since my father died."[2]

Wright's intervention in the allotment controversy merely presaged the full political onslaught to come. As White Earth's valuable resources passed into the hands of lumber companies from the east and speculators and settlers from the Red River Valley to the west, Charles Wright and other conservative leaders mounted a political attack against the capitalists among them who favored these exploitative policies. Conveniently, the fact that many of the most visible, offensive leaders of mixed descent were descended from Lake Superior and Wisconsin bands gave conservatives a legal tool for challenging their right to enrollment as "Chippewa of Minnesota."

To enhance his authority, Charles Wright instructed the Indian Office to recognize his status as *ogimaa* in 1909. Wright's demand was more complicated than it seemed on the surface. Several supporters bolstered Wright's claim, attesting that Wabonaquod had appropriately designated him as his successor on a public occasion. Others believed Wabonaquod had chosen the son of a Christian marriage, William, to assume the role. Perhaps observers meant to emphasize that Wabonaquod had selected the son of a *Catholic* marriage, rather than simply a Christian one, for Charles was an Episcopalian Christian. The BIA censuses list William as a chief, but his name never appears on any official correspondence; he did not have a significant political role on the reservation. Some even suggested that he was "simple-minded," making him Gus's and B.L.'s choice to assume Wabonaquod's position because of the ease with which they might manipulate him. Significantly, questions about the legitimacy of Charles Wright's claims emerged just as he began to lodge his complaints. Since hereditary leadership lines were waning in significance, the issue has relevance largely in relation to the escalating factional conflict.

In response to Wright's appeal, an assistant to the Commissioner of Indian Affairs informed him that "the policy of the Department has been and is not to recognize or create chiefs of Indian tribes, and to cause the Indians as soon as possible to break up their tribal relations and assume responsibilities as individuals." Wright was told that as far as the United States was concerned, his title was purely honorary; in official political and diplomatic matters he could act only as an individual.[3]

The refusal of the Indian Office to acknowledge Wright's claim was in keeping with its policy, in the late nineteenth and early twentieth centuries, of undermining the strength of tribal bonds. Their idealistic vision of cultural evolution called for the complete reordering of native cultures. The sooner the "chiefs" were gone, they reasoned, the sooner the masses of Indians would learn to forsake their tribal ways and become totally self-reliant. Although government representatives had created and supported "chiefs" to smooth their assimilation programs in the past, it no longer suited their purposes. Instead, the Indian Office began to recognize political gatherings purporting to be elective councils at White Earth, where assimilationists dominated. Since Indians insisted on organizing politically, federal administrators more easily tolerated elective structures that resembled U.S. institutions.

Although U.S. approval would have enhanced his authority, failing to receive it did not interfere with Wright's intention to serve as an *ogimaa* of the Anishinaabe people. He and other conservative leaders were dogged in their determination. They had witnessed the headlong exploitation of Anishinaabe land and timber and were angered by the duplicitous actions of a greedy few.

In 1911, sixteen White Earth Indians petitioned the Indian Office to remove eighty-six individuals from the tribal rolls and prevent them from sharing any further in the resources and assets of the "Chippewa Indians of Minnesota." Among the signers of the Wright Petition were Charles Wright (Nashotah), Mezhucegeshig, Wahweyeacumig, Ahbowegeshig, George Walters (Kahgondaush), James Bassett (Mayzhuckegwonabe), Taycumegeshig, Pindegaygeshig, and Duane Porter. Not surprisingly, most of these men had been upset by the way additional allotments had been handled. In their words, such a move would "purify the tribal rolls" by eliminating members of three families whom they claimed had no legal right to reside on the White Earth Reservation or to participate in distributions of tribal funds.

Included among the eighty-six individuals were Gus Beaulieu and Ben Fairbanks, very active metis leaders whose actions had drawn criticism from more conservative reservation leaders. Charles Wright led the movement and proceeded to hire a lawyer to press their claims because of their inability to gain satisfaction through regular Indian Office channels. They had been instructed to make their charges explicit so that they might be investigated. Wright and his associates hoped that leveling their charges in this fashion would give them their day in court.[4]

The men who advocated "purification" of the tribal rolls intended the petition as a political ploy. If their primary aim had been to purge the rolls of all those descended from "Lake Superior bands," there were many other people that they knew full well should have been included. The Warrens, Morrisons, Bellangers, Beaupres, Bellecourts, and others were all descended from trading families located near Lake Superior. An accurate determination of those descended from Lake Superior and Wisconsin bands would have required extensive genealogical research into *all* White Earth families, not just the eighty-six people listed. Instead the petition targeted only selected members of the Beaulieu, Fairbanks, and Bellefeuille families for special censure, not entire families. For example, Benjamin L. Fairbanks was included—but neither his brothers nor his uncles were. Theodore H. Beaulieu, Gus's cousin, was not listed; his efforts to distance himself from Gus may have contributed to his exclusion. Charges embodied in the Wright Petition represented a further elaboration of the mixed-blood symbol, emphasizing the Lake Superior and Wisconsin band origins of the métis political leaders who most offended conservative leaders.

It is easy enough to understand why the petitioners would target Gus Beaulieu and Ben Fairbanks on such a list. Yet it remains a mystery why so many members of the Bellefeuille family, representing forty-three or exactly half of those listed, were included. No one with the surname "Bellefeuille" was ever politically involved in a highly visible way. Given some Bellefeuille first names, Euzebe, Cassimer, Euchare, Zephine, Leopold, and Tellephore, it is unlikely that they were using Anishinaabe names instead. Their names are not represented in any of the thousands of pages of testimony produced by various White Earth investigating committees. It is tempting to surmise that members of the Bellefeuille family had absolutely no legitimate connection to Minnesota Anishinaabe bands whether determined by American kinship terms or by *the Indian way*, and that conservative band leaders knew it. People continually recounted stories of people who had been "rounded up" and added to the tribal rolls without sufficient justification. The overwhelming preponderance of Bellefeuilles on the list may indicate that their presence was symbolic, just as the *absence* of certain members of the Beaulieu and Fairbanks families was symbolic.

It is also surprising that the Indian Office took this petition so seriously, eventually suspending all eighty-six individuals from the tribal rolls. This was not the first time such complaints had been made and they had never before produced any action. Knowledge gained from investigating and prosecuting the land fraud claims had fomented animosity on the part of both conservative band leaders and Indian Office representatives toward the métis cultural brokers for the roles they had played and continued to play. These sentiments probably provoked the unprecedented amount of attention given to this petition.

Once motivated to act, conservative leaders dedicated themselves to their cause with a relentless fervor. They wanted nothing more to do with the mixed-bloods and demanded that they take their fee simple patents and go to "be as the whites." Ahbowegeshig's complaints reflected the ethical basis of their criticisms: "The half-breeds have been . . . taking pine lands and they have prevented the full blood Indians from taking them. . . . They have become wealthy on account of these allotments."[5] Conservative band leaders denounced every move the métis brokers made—every word they spoke—and decried delegations of their opponents as not truly representative of the "Chippewa of Minnesota."

Land fraud claims at White Earth came, in the minds of conservative band leaders, to be inextricably bound up with actions of descendants of "Lake Superior mixed-bloods." Complaints about the targeted families surface with dizzying frequency in the correspondence that conservative leaders sent to various officials in Washington, D.C. For these angry men, all of the greed and evil associated with the land fraud claims came to be embodied in the ethnic heritage and personas of the Lake Superior mixed-blood brokers. Their articulation and development of this symbol allowed them to focus on what they perceived as the source of their grievances and to rally support to their cause.

Use of the symbolic terms "mixed-blood" and "full-blood" masks the fact that culturally determined values, especially economic ones, were most important in establishing factional affiliations. Several conservative leaders insisted that ethnic heritage—not genetic makeup—determined the value orientation of individuals. Since the fur trade era, intermarriage between the Anishinaabeg and Euroamericans had been widespread, so that many Indians had some French, Scottish or British ancestry. Waweyeacumig explained that "a person born of white and indian blood raised in the custom and costume of the indian is an indian mixed blood." Similarly, those of mixed descent brought up in the "custom and costume" of Euroamerican society were "white mixed bloods."[6]

In reality, political leaders recognized that each faction contained individuals of both genetic groups. Allied conservative leaders insisted that they did *not* mean to imply "that the full blood faction [is] composed entirely of full bloods, and mixed bloods entirely of mixed bloods." They emphasized their economic agenda, explaining that they relied on the wisdom of "conservative men, safeguarding the interest of the tribe as a whole without any regard to personal interest or private gain," whereas the mixed-bloods cared only for self-gain in the name of "progressivism." Conservative leaders described mixed-bloods as "shrewd," and complained that they could not "compete" with them.[7] Money and a denunciation of economic ethics figured prominently in nearly all of their references to mixed-bloods. Some complaints centered on land fraud claims, others on expenses of delegations to both Washington, D.C., and council meetings, and still others on funds for the annual June 14 Celebration (who should receive the funds and, therefore, the authority to organize the party?).

Conservative leaders of what they eventually labeled the "Full Blood Faction" had not always used "full-blood" so freely. Although the two terms were widely used, conservative band leaders more often referred to their opposition as "mixed-bloods" and themselves as "Indians" or "real Indians." Their use of the term "full-blood" increased over time. Similarly, métis cultural brokers did not refer to themselves as "mixed-bloods"; instead, they used descriptive phrases such as "progressive Indians" or "educated Indians." Their adversaries were sometimes "full-bloods," but just as often were described as "the warehouse faction" or "warehousers," an insulting reference to their reliance on food distributed from agency warehouses. The oppositional use of *mixed-blood* and *full-blood* owes its full elaboration largely to conservative band leaders, but Euroamericans also picked up the terms. Euroamericans associated the same sorts of cultural connotations with the terms, but believed they could be measured genetically.

The notion that the *real Indians* were being exploited and that *mixed-bloods* grew wealthy at their expense clearly emerged from conservative band leaders' complaints. Mezhucegeshig protested that "some of the mixed bloods are the white man's chief helpers in cheating their people." His comments went on to reveal just as much about the behavior of "full-bloods": "My people don't realize what a mortgage is and the white people easily persuade them to give one for a small bit of money for they know they are sure to get the land then on a foreclosure."[8] Whereas in an earlier era, mixed-bloods were simply described as having different cultural values and customs, now the phrase had taken on political overtones and the inequitable economic ethics of certain leaders drew censure. When they intended *mixed-blood* to have political connotations, they were referring only to specific individuals—not to all people of mixed descent. Years later, Josephine Warren Robinson explained that "the Indians didn't think too much of" certain people of mixed descent: "They were so grabby, you know. They had to be first in everything."[9]

Prior to Charles Wright's petition to remove the "Lake Superior mixed bloods" from the tribal rolls, assimilationist leaders had paid little attention to their adversaries' claims. Their criticisms had been reserved for the U.S. government, and the Indian Office in particular. They argued that U.S. paternalism prevented Indians from learning to manage their resources, dissipated tribal funds for incompetent Euroamerican employees and misguided policies, and sanctioned the wholesale confiscation of Anishinaabe resources. And they were right. Modern scholars routinely level the same sorts of criticisms at U.S. Indian policy in the late nineteenth and early twentieth centuries. At the time, however, the assimilationists' rhetoric rang hollow in light of their exploitative activities, and conservative leaders refused ever again to trust them.

Once the Indian Office suspended their names, those targeted adopted a defensive posture.[10] Whenever Gus Beaulieu took the stand as a witness, he was sure to recite an extended genealogical discourse to try to establish some legitimate kinship link with the Minnesota Anishinaabeg—tenuous though it may have been. Knowing that he would have a hard time making his case using American kinship terminology, he always emphasized *the Indian way* of reckoning kin, which accorded kinship distinctions to more far-flung relatives. As the accused articulated justifications for their position on the White Earth Reservation, they also revealed their nonchalant attitudes toward impoverished reservation residents whom they tended to call "warehousers." Overall, they favored reducing social welfare expenditures from the "Chippewa in Minnesota Fund." In keeping with this stance, they recommended abolishing the warehouse system that provided for distributions of flour and pork to Indians in need because it encouraged Indians to remain "idle and

indolent" and made "cringing, lazy cowards" of them.[11] "Lazy," "idle,"
and "indolent" are descriptive terms that métis cultural brokers emphasized when referring to economic behavior that they found objection-
able. They were familiar enough with U.S. society to know that they
were pushing the right buttons when they argued that the so-called
warehousers had garnered more than their fair share of tribal resources
and ought to be "turned loose to fend for themselves" rather than receiving welfare gratuities from the tribal funds. Sick, elderly, and indigent
Indians would face bleak prospects under those circumstances. At no
time did the accused acknowledge that "the 'warehouse faction' . . .
were those Anishinaabeg made landless by the thefts and frauds of allotment." Concern for the welfare of genuinely needy warehousers was
never expressed.[12]

Members of both factions evaluated each other on the basis of economic criteria that transcended family, community, and band relationships. Although all these considerations influenced alliances that
individuals formed with each other and with the organized factions,
participants cited economic indicators as determining one's political
identity as a mixed-blood or a full-blood.

Members of the Full Blood Faction wrote numerous letters to the
Indian Office protesting the recognition of any mixed-blood organization
between 1907 and 1913. Family, band, and community ties continued to
determine the particular political groupings through which individuals
expressed themselves. However, conservative leaders eschewed band labels in favor of "mixed-blood" and "full-blood" to differentiate their
political affiliations.

This change was most evident among Mississippi band leaders. Conservative band leaders who had once supported the mixed-bloods now
broke away to criticize them. Mezhucegeshig was one of the first to
change affiliations after the land fraud claims; Waweyeacumig hesitated,
and then also switched loyalties. Among more conservative Indians,
band ties persisted, attitudes and political ideology remained constant,
but political affiliations changed. Their ethics gave the full-bloods common cause and contributed to the development of a true, interband,
reservation-based political consciousness.[13]

The full-bloods were faced with a difficult transition. Their leaders

Some men in this 1899 delegation to Washington, D.C., would later become bitter
factional opponents in the twentieth century. *Left to right, bottom:* Wahmaywenew,
Mahjigshig, unknown, Mezhucegeshig, Joseph Charette. *Middle:* Charles Beaulieu,
Bidegaygishig, Gus H. Beaulieu, Darwin Hall (U.S. Chippewa Commissioner). *Top:*
Maydwaygohnonind, William T. Campbell (interpreter), Joe Morrison (interpreter),
Benjamin Casswell (interpreter), Mayzhuckkeaywong. *Photo courtesy of DeLancey
Gill of the Bureau of American Ethnology, Minnesota Historical Society.*

confronted the task of developing their own independent "voice." For
years they had relied on key métis cultural brokers to represent their
concerns. Now, knowledge of their complicity in land fraud had engendered in conservative leaders a deep-seated mistrust of those who had
conspired to secure their reservation lands. The leaders' initial efforts
were clumsy and they apologized for their crude attempts to correspond
in the English language. Characteristic lists of thumbprints attached to
full-blood petitions attest to the magnitude of the linguistic gulf they
had to cross to communicate with their "guardian."

Some early spokespeople transmitted their resolutions to the agent orally for want of a secretary or interpreter. Older leaders turned to their young, formally educated relatives to compose letters for them. Isabel Schneider, a frequent interpreter, was repulsed by the assimilationists' tactics and made her services available to conservative leaders. Eventually, a number of "returned students," such as Ben Casswell, came to perform as competent and respected interpreters. A new generation of brokers emerged who were inclined to pay more attention to the concerns of conservative reservation residents, and less to lining their own pockets.[14]

Conservative leaders may have succeeded in developing a voice, but they had yet to construct a distinctive agenda beyond expressing concern for equity and full-blood welfare. Some council resolutions requested agricultural implements. However, most of their entreaties consisted of scathing denunciations of the mixed-bloods, accompanied by requests to send their own full-blood delegation to Washington, D.C. At times their stated platforms represented little more than point-by-point refutations of resolutions passed by the assimilationists. Since many in the conservative camp hailed from Pine Point, the full-bloods often protested any exceptional services directed toward White Earth Village, where many of the most offensive métis leaders lived.

In their defense, their efforts to stay abreast of their opponents' activities occupied much of their time. Safeguarding their individual and tribal property against exploitation by both internal and external interests assumed paramount importance. No one from either faction articulated any carefully conceived plans for reservation development. Assimilationists lobbied against the administration of their affairs by the Indian Office, just as conservatives lobbied against the administration of their affairs by the assimilationists. Even though the federal government had confiscated thousands of acres of Anishinaabe land, the mixed-bloods loomed as the larger threat in the full-bloods' minds. They cast their lot with the Indian Office as their only defense against the mixed-bloods, whose ethics they rejected.[15]

More conservative band leaders from the eastern forests took action when Gus Beaulieu, Ben Fairbanks, and other members of their coalition joined with representatives from several other Minnesota Anishinaabe reservations to form the General Council of the Chippewa in May of

1913. The conservatives allied across band lines, styled themselves the official Full Blood Faction, and immediately denounced the "Cass Lake Council organized by the White Earth suspendees."[16] White Earth land fraud claims had prompted a fundamental political realignment among band leaders.

Mixed-Bloods and the General Council of the Chippewa

Word of the impending council to be held at Cass Lake worried conservative band leaders at White Earth. Several announced their intention to boycott the organizational meeting scheduled for 4 February 1913. A group of Pine Point Indians disapproved of the incipient organization, certain that its members intended to "obstruct, and hamper all efforts that are being made by the Indian Dept. . . . in investigating, and prosecuting the Land [sic] fraud cases on the White Earth Reservation." Learning that their adversaries were among the initiators of the General Council did nothing to allay their skepticism: "Many of the mixed-bloods at these councils were those who have been suspended from our rolls and the others generally were mixed bloods who had been told that they would be on the next list to be suspended." Their distrust was total and unequivocal. From the first hint of a call for a general council, conservative band leaders at White Earth associated the move with the factional dispute. When métis cultural brokers assembled at White Earth on 23 April to elect delegates to the upcoming General Council, conservative leaders conducted an intrareservation gathering a week later to counter them. Even though James Coffey, a Fond du Lac Indian from Duluth, originated the call, conservative leaders attributed the idea to their "Lake Superior mixed-blood" adversaries.[17]

Those who attended the Cass Lake General Council from 6 to 8 May 1913 shared a belief that the U.S. government had failed to uphold its obligations under the Nelson Act. Gus Beaulieu estimated that the U.S. government, in its role as guardian, had in effect confiscated more than $7,000,000 in Anishinaabe resources. Council members voted to appropriate tribal funds to hire a lawyer to pursue and settle their claims.[18]

The U.S. government's mismanagement of tribal funds and resources had justifiably become an issue demanding immediate attention. The list of grievances was long. Anishinaabe leaders were incensed that pine lands near Leech Lake had been confiscated to create the Minnesota National Forest. Repeatedly waiving homestead fees on ceded lands denied the Anishinaabeg a vital source of revenue. The State of Minnesota had claimed swampland on all Anishinaabe reservations under much-belated authority of the 1860 Swamp Land Act. The Anishinaabeg had received compensation for none of these claims. And all of this legislative poaching coincided with the land fraud that had impoverished so many Indians. At the same time that the "Chippewa in Minnesota Fund" received no revenues, the U.S. government charged against it costs of its assimilation programs, forwarding cash as stipulated by legislation. Anishinaabe leaders scoffed at the idea that Indians were little more than beggars who were a burden on the U.S. government; how could they be held responsible for operating in the red under such circumstances?[19]

All of the Anishinaabeg, mixed- and full-blood alike, should have been able to rally around these issues, for all shared an interest in the tribal resources. The General Council represented the first attempt by the Anishinaabeg to organize statewide. The "Chippewa in Minnesota Fund," to which all Anishinaabe band members shared an equal right, provided a focus for establishing an interreservation organization. Without such a political structure, it was impossible for the Anishinaabeg to influence U.S. officials in their administration of tribal assets. As the U.S. government repeatedly transgressed in its role as guardian, the impetus to form such a pan-reservation organization grew. Special Inspector John H. Hinton agreed with Indian leaders that the U.S. government should shoulder its responsibility: "As the Indians are wards of the United States . . . the government owes them . . . to take the matter of adjusting the alleged claims of the Minnesota Chippewa in hand, and settle it for all time."[20]

Internal dissension had hindered earlier attempts to pursue claims against the U.S. government. Encouraged by Indian Office representatives, some Anishinaabe leaders envisioned using the General Council to offer a unified voice in their dealings with federal and state officials. Mille Lacs band chief Wahweyeacumig offered timorous support for the General Council as a way to gain some measure of control over "this thing that they are keeping from us [the "Chippewa in Minnesota Fund"] . . . so we can feed our children and clothe them too." Most Anishinaabeg felt the constricting noose of federal guardianship, but

escalating factional dissension had prevented them from acting in con-
cert. Now Waweyeacumig urged those assembled to "get together and be
of one mind on this proposition."[21] Unfortunately, this would prove to be
a nearly impossible task.

As tensions escalated, members of rival White Earth factions deluged
exasperated Indian Office personnel with complaints. Although petitions from the Full Blood Faction usually appended more signatures and
thumbprints than those from so-called representative councils, the Indian Office had no way to determine which faction was most representative of the general reservation population. Once it was decided to support
elective tribal government as the key to a unified Anishinaabe voice, the
Indian Office remained deaf to demands by both factions to be considered the official governing body. Admonishing both groups to resolve
their differences in a representative council, the Indian Office supported
the "White Earth suspendees'" push for tribal government among the
Anishinaabeg in Minnesota at large. E. P. Holcombe, chief supervisor of
the first General Council meeting, observed that "a few of the delegates
controlled the convention," a pattern that had become very familiar at
White Earth. Still, he emphasized the need for a unified voice and urged
delegates to refrain from cynicism and maintain their commitment to
the elective ideal, saying, "No righteous object is bad because it is advocated by some designing individuals. If it were so, most righteous objects
would be killed by design."[22]

In keeping with its paternalistic policy, the Indian Office designated
"supervisors" to oversee authorized elective councils. These supervisors
were committed to see that proper elective procedures were followed,
but they brought their own biases regarding key métis cultural brokers
with them. The factional conflict had deep ethnic roots with which
many were familiar. Additionally, on an almost daily basis ongoing land
fraud litigation brought unseemly details of the past behavior of métis
pine cartel agents to light. As early as 1909, White Earth agent John
Howard candidly described his preferential treatment of full-bloods. La-
boring under the misconception that the 1906 Clapp Rider, by conferring
citizenship with fee patents, had severed mixed-bloods' relationship
with the U.S. government, he reasoned that they retained only a right to
participate in distributions of tribal funds, not in reservation political

organizations. He, therefore, recognized a "Full Blood Business Committee" ("tribal governments" were discouraged) at Pine Point where, according to him, the "real Indians" who needed U.S. assistance lived. From Graham Commission disclosures and his own observations, Howard had developed a distaste for the métis cultural brokers.[23] It was a sentiment that most Indian Office representatives shared. In their struggle to oust their adversaries, conservative band leaders had the Indian Office on their side.

But conservative leaders refused to tolerate the involvement of their symbolic enemies, the Lake Superior mixed-bloods, in organizations that would have the right to make decisions for the Anishinaabeg. Past misdeeds of the assimilationists remained fresh in their minds. In time-honored fashion, they presented their own Full Blood Faction as an alternative to the General Council that had convened at Cass Lake between 6 May and 8 May, only to be informed that their views would receive a hearing only in a representative general council. Complaining that they appeared to have little control over their own political structures, leaders of the Full Blood Faction acquiesced long enough to elect their own delegates in opposition to those "selected" by an "executive committee" of the assimilationist faction at White Earth.[24] Reflecting no attempt to cooperate at all, two delegations from White Earth prepared to attend the next meeting of the General Council of the Chippewa.

Restoration of the White Earth Suspendees

Soon after Charles Wright filed his petition questioning the tribal rights of the eighty-six Lake Superior mixed-bloods, the assimilationist faction began to demand that the tribal funds be liquidated by distributing them in equal *pro rata* payments. They criticized the Indian Office for using unreasonably large amounts of their funds for "useless employees," schools that benefited only a few, and administering individual Indians' accounts who had been classed as "incompetent" to manage their own affairs. They charged that these expenses benefited them in no way, and feared that the Indian Office would expend all of their funds in its slipshod assimilation program before they could be distributed to everyone's advantage. Besides, they reasoned, doling out money in such small increments prevented more "progressive" Indians from making capital investments. Those who spearheaded these recommendations had their own best interests at heart and spoke from an overarching capitalistic philosophy that they had favored for years. The métis cultural brokers espoused values that were very "American"; the United States celebrated an avowedly capitalistic economy. Criticizing them for espousing values that paralleled those of U.S. society at large holds them up to standards that had no relevance for them. Their most recent demands did, however, represent a departure from the past. Previously, métis cultural brokers had pressed for the right to administer their tribal funds. Failing in this, they now advocated that tribal assets be liquidated and distributed in *pro rata* payments. However, it may be more than mere coincidence that key leaders of mixed descent began to lobby for tribal funds to be apportioned and disbursed just as their rights to those funds were attacked by the Full Blood Faction.[25]

Although many could agree that pressing their claims against the U.S. government was in their best interest, conservative leaders still reacted adversely to the presence of the Lake Superior mixed-bloods, with their capitalistic ethic. Given their hard-learned experience with the way opportunistic assimilationists did business, their fears were justified. On 28 May 1914, a full-blood Indian council held at Pine Point condemned General Council officers for taking the position that Indians should be "freed" from the virtual bondage of governmental control. Conservative leaders now saw the situation in a different light; to them, "freeing the Indian" meant removing government protections so that they might become "easy prey of land sharks and timber speculators," with "mixed-bloods" expecting to share the spoils.[26] Their perspective had shifted from complaining about government "bondage" to emphasizing government "protection." Graham Commission disclosures had made clear to everyone that while Gus Beaulieu and Ben Fairbanks may have had good reason to criticize governmental restrictions on the Anishinaabeg, they also had their own plans for allotted resources, and perhaps for the tribal funds, which they were careful not to disclose. Conservative leaders welcomed the involvement of the Indian Office and Justice Department to counteract the influence of exploitative métis assimilationists.

Despite the supporting testimony and legal advice mustered by Indian Office inspectors, on 29 January 1916, conservative band leaders were

informed of the Interior Secretary's decision to reinstate the eighty-six
Lake Superior mixed-bloods who had been suspended from the tribal
rolls. The courts had ruled that proper jurisdiction for the question lay
not with the U.S. judicial system, but with the Interior Department.
Even though government investigators supported conservative leaders'
accusation that these individuals had no legal rights "through treaty or
act of Congress" to reside on the White Earth Reservation, the Indian
Office accepted the action taken by the U.S. Chippewa Commission in
enrolling them during the late nineteenth century. Attorneys for the full-
bloods pointed out that the U.S. Chippewa Commission had not been
instructed to determine eligibility for enrollment. At the time, a three-
person committee had been appointed to pass on individuals' eligibility
and the Indian Office maintained that ample opportunity had been given
to all concerned to raise such questions.[27] However, establishing the
committee ran counter to instructions the commission had received and
was another example of ad hoc Indian Office decisions that stretched the
bounds of legality.

The 1889 Nelson Act made no distinction between "mixed-bloods"
and "full-bloods," but neither did it include individuals from Wisconsin
bands of Anishinaabeg. Close ties between business and government in
Minnesota and the nation at large may have ensured that conservative
Indian leaders' pleas would fall on deaf ears. Lumbering, railroads, and
land speculation were big businesses in Minnesota. Networks of men in
influential positions stood to lose a great deal if the credibility of certain
métis brokers was undermined. After the 1916 ruling, the Indian Office
restored the suspendees' rights and initiated steps to resume payments
and services to which they were entitled as enrolled members of the
"Chippewa of Minnesota."

When delegates of the Full Blood Faction at White Earth went to
Washington, D.C., in March of 1916 to confer with officials in the Interior Department, the decision to reinstate the Lake Superior mixed-
bloods was uppermost on their minds. Ahbowegeshig protested that
"before this action was taken the Indians should have been consulted."
Assistant Commissioner of Indian Affairs E. B. Merrit explained that the
suspended individuals had "acquired a certain property right" and that
"the funds and . . . property can not now be taken away from them."

Although Merrit's explanation made clear that the decision rested more on the fact that the suspendees had acquired substantial property on the reservation than on their legal right to be enrolled, he told the full-blood delegates that "It was purely a legal question."

Evidence offered by attorneys for conservative leaders amply illustrated the validity of their claims. According to laws and treaties, only bands of "Chippewa Indians in Minnesota" were entitled to enrollment under the 1889 Nelson Act. Losing patience with these seemingly capricious institutional "rulings," Ahbowegeshig reminded the commissioner of treaty terms governing "the separation of the Lake Superior Chippewa from those of the Mississippi" accomplished in the 1854 Treaty, and of compensation ("half-breed scrip") previously given to the mixed-bloods to "leave the tribe." Members of the Full Blood Faction understood full well the treaty provisions and laws governing their relationship with the U.S. government. Policy directives that deviated from these terms usually resulted from ad hoc Indian Office decisions of questionable legality. After struggling to persuade the Indian Office to allow a full-blood delegation to come to Washington, D.C., they were disappointed in the audience they had received. Ahbowegeshig was bitter in his displeasure, and complained that "the Indians are not satisfied at all." But Merrit remained emphatic that the "highest authority" had ruled that "those mixed blood Indians have just as much right on the rolls." Realizing that his guests had not received the decision well, he urged them to "consider the matter as closed," recommending that it would be more productive for them to "try to get the two factions together and dwell in harmony on the reservation"—advice that did not make much of an impression. Dejected and at a loss for an appropriate response, Ahbowegeshig had to recognize their powerlessness in the situation: "From this it is evident that the Indians have no voice in the matter."[28]

The Contest for Control

The decision to reinstate the suspendees may have fulfilled the Indian Office's responsibility in the matter, but it did little to resolve factional differences among the White Earth Anishinaabeg. Two factions assembled separately at White Earth during June of 1916 to elect delegates to the General Council to be held at Bemidji in July. Neither group gave much concern to ensuring representation beyond their own contingent, and neither convened on the first Tuesday in June as specified in the Constitution of the General Council. Conservative leaders met at Pine Point, while assimilationists gathered at White Earth Village. Familiar patterns were yet apparent in the manner in which the council at White Earth Village was conducted. Theodore H. Beaulieu criticized his cousin Gus for dominating through a "steam-roller process" where sixty "henchmen" were selected by a mere thirty participants. Indian Office Inspector C. M. Knight concurred that Gus Beaulieu and Benjamin Fairbanks controlled the council for the purpose of selecting as delegates those who "would work in harmony with them so that they would have the controlling vote in the General Council."[29] The contest was under way.

When two contending delegations from White Earth appeared at the General Council meeting in Bemidji on 11 July 1916, they were instructed to select only one delegation from their combined numbers. This limited the number of delegates from the assimilationist faction to only half. Nonetheless, among the resolutions passed by the interreservation General Council was a demand that the common tribal funds be divided *pro rata*. Apparently, there was more political consensus among the Minnesota Anishinaabeg than appeared on the surface, for the majority of delegates composed of members of both factions lent support to the call to liquidate the tribal funds.[30]

The Indian Office remained unresponsive to the demand carried forward by Gus Beaulieu and Ben Fairbanks to divide the tribal funds, but the threat worried those concerned about the White Earth situation all the same. Earlier, the two men had convened a local White Earth council on 1 December for the express purpose of sending a delegation to Washington, D.C., to pursue this end. Theodore H. Beaulieu reacted with alarm. In the interests of "myself, members of my family and the greater majority of the progressive, self-supporting people of the reservation," Beaulieu protested the expenditure of "one cent of the tribal funds" for this delegation. He warned Warren K. Moorehead that the White Earth Anishinaabeg were still being "hounded by 'evil forces.'" Beaulieu and Moorehead remembered the past ten years' land fraud and saw broader implications in the actions of assimilationist leaders. Their past success in the face of so many critical investigations confounded those anxious to contain their influence. With characteristic indignation, Moorehead pointed out that no one had ever denied the "facts published and spoken," so that there was "no earthly reason why the real Indians (not the French-Canadians) [sic] should not control affairs at White Earth." But thousands of pages of evidence and allegations produced by numerous official investigations always reached a dead end at the upper echelons of the Interior Department. Beaulieu and Moorehead surmised that Senator Moses Clapp and the land and pine cartel were behind the "mixed-bloods' " political success. Although investigators had failed to produce a "smoking gun," the evidence collected led many to envision an "invisible hand." As objects of such suspicion, assimilationist leaders would not have an easy time achieving support for their agenda through normal procedures.[31]

Resolutions passed by the General Council that met in July of 1917 elaborated on the theme established the previous year. The tenor of the proceedings was decidedly antagonistic toward the Indian Office; delegates urged its outright abolition because its "ultra-paternal . . . minute supervision" had caused Indians to "deteriorate shamefully and to become a pauperized, degenerated race." Access to tribal funds again emerged as a central concern. The refusal of the Indian Office to allow Indians a primary role in administering their tribal property made every request for funds ring with protest. According to Inspector H. S. Taylor, they maneuvered "to secure as rapidly as possible for immediate dissipation all moneys which they now have in the treasury or ever hope to have," with no articulated plans for tribal development. The rhetoric was familiar and paralleled many concerns shared by prominent assimilationist leaders from White Earth. And yet, Inspector Taylor noted a novel development. Surprisingly, in the midst of passing resolutions that opportunistic assimilationists from White Earth had been championing for years, General Council delegates "wholly denounced, chastised and branded [Gus Beaulieu, Ben Fairbanks, and others] as the greatest grafters and thieves of this generation." Support for the liquidation of tribal funds had apparently gained widespread favor among delegates to the General Council from across northern Minnesota. Although they shared the delegates' sense that their autonomy had been compromised, this development should have worried conservative White Earth leaders.[32]

In early December, John G. Morrison, Jr., as president of the General Council, appointed a Legislative Committee months after the council had adjourned. Henry D. Warren, Frank D. Beaulieu, Benjamin L. Fairbanks, James I. Coffey, and Nathan J. Head proceeded to Washington, D.C., to represent the General Council, even though the General Council had not authorized them to do so.

Legislative Committee members came to lobby for passage of H.R. 11410, "A Bill: For the classification of members and preparation of correct tribal rolls, the completion of allotments, and the disposal of all remaining property of the Chippewa Indians of Minnesota in conformity with the agreement of 1889." The bill contained several related components. (1) Any remaining restrictions on allotments were to be removed, except for their nontaxable status for the original Indian owner. (2) All tribal property would be sold and the tribal funds consolidated into the "Chippewa in Minnesota Fund." (3) All school lands and buildings would be given to the State of Minnesota, with tribal funds financing tuition for Indian children whose parents did not pay taxes. (4) Townsites would be laid out and the property sold. The bill proposed sweeping changes in current land tenure arrangements that were consistent with the plank that assimilationists had been developing for years. However, it had not been discussed or approved by the 1917 General Council.[33]

The bill put forward by the Legislative Committee reflected only a portion of their overall platform. The leaders claimed that a "spirit of rebellion" existed among the Anishinaabe people of northern Minnesota; most yearned to throw off the yoke of federal guardianship. They insisted that fully 90 percent of all of the Anishinaabeg were "not Indians in the ordinary acceptation of the term," but were "competent citizens of the state and nation, performing all the obligations and duties of citizenship performed by our white neighbors." The allotment acts had "elevated them to the plane of citizenship" and tribal relations had, "for most purposes, ceased to exist."[34] This overblown rhetoric gave the impression that U.S. assimilation programs had totally succeeded and that maintaining any vestiges of the system was counterproductive and threatened its success. In essence, they recommended that U.S. assimilation policy be intensified and the timetable stepped up.

Predictably, Legislative Committee members recommended abolishing the Indian Office along with its retinue of programs and employees, complaining that it virtually created positions for itself to be financed by Anishinaabe tribal funds. Taken together, their recommendations aimed to settle all outstanding tribal affairs, to consolidate all tribal funds, and, ultimately, to distribute all of the assets of the "Chippewa of Minnesota." They made no nationalistic plans to conserve land or timber or to use tribal funds for reservation development. If federal officials had followed the framework suggested by the Legislative Committee, all past treaty rights and legislative terms would have been terminated and the "Chippewa of Minnesota" as an economic, political, and diplomatic entity would, for purposes of the U.S. government, have ceased to exist. Members of the two opposing factions might have continued to affiliate and struggle, but they would have been distinctly disadvantaged, much as federally nonrecognized tribes are today.[35]

The first inkling that anything was amiss in Washington came from James Coffey, himself a member of the Legislative Committee. He informed the Commissioner of Indian Affairs in January of 1918 that Fairbanks and Webster Ballinger, an attorney, had arranged a deal where "one would get the control of the tribal common property while the other is turned loose upon the unrestricted Indian allotments." Coffey warned that the "gang of schemers" aimed to "GAIN CONTROL OF ALL THE TRIBAL PROPERTY OF THE CHIPPEWA INDIANS IN MINNESOTA, by deception and fraud."

Coffey was the only Legislative Committee member to protest this course of action. He tried to persuade them that they had no authority from the General Council, but was told that "they *were* the General Council." John G. Morrison, Jr., proceeded to sign papers drafted by Attorney Ballinger that conferred unlimited powers on the Legislative Committee over all the common tribal property of the Anishinaabeg. Coffey protested this ad hoc attempt to seize power and claimed to be "the only member of the legislative committee here in the city having the support of the mass of the Chippewa Indians in Minnesota." Other members of the Legislative Committee attempted to expel him because of his intransigence.[36]

Determined to thwart the actions of the Legislative Committee in Washington, Coffey returned to Minnesota to sound the alarm and convene a special session of the General Council. On 25 April 1918, seventy-seven Anishinaabe representatives from across northern Minnesota assembled at the village of Ball Club on the White Oak Point Reservation. They shared Coffey's alarm and voted to unseat the entire outlaw Legislative Committee. They resolved that the Legislative Committee had violated the Constitution and By-Laws of the General Council by promoting legislation injurious to the Anishinaabeg, and voted to replace John G. Morrison, Jr., with James Coffey as president. Government inspectors praised this special session of the General Council as representing the sentiments of the "real Indians."[37]

Ben Fairbanks quickly charged Coffey with libel. The charge held up in court, but most predicted that Coffey would win an appeal. Although defending himself against the libel charge consumed much of his time, Coffey pressed ahead with his opposition, confident that the majority of the tribe supported him. E. P. Wakefield, sure that Fairbanks had made the charges simply to discredit Coffey, defended Coffey, saying, "If Mr. Coffey is 'crooked' why didn't Ben Fairbanks gather him into his camp?"

Factional differences cut across ties of family, band, and community. Theodore H. Beaulieu became a harsh critic of his cousin Gus. Friendships were damaged, too. E. P. Wakefield chose to remain loyal to his ethics rather than his friend, Henry Warren, and chastised him for his behavior as a Legislative Committee member: "Certainly through friendship's sake, I regret very much to have you included with the White Earth Contingent, but . . . you chose your associates."[38]

By the summer of 1918, Henry Warren and John Broker had renounced the Legislative Committee and severed ties with it. Broker reconsidered its platform and admitted that it exaggerated reality to claim that fully 90 percent of the Anishinaabeg were "competent." Warren agreed, "This is like throwing them into the lake and letting them that can't swim sink."[39] Very little difference existed between the White Earth assimilationists' ideology and the capitalistic philosophy that guided U.S. economic policy.

And the contest raged on, both at White Earth and at the state level. Across the state, factions met separately to choose delegates, and that July, the city of Bemidji hosted two competing General Councils. James Coffey found the doors to City Hall locked when he came to prepare for the delegates' arrival. Instead of honoring his prior commitment to Coffey, the mayor had given the keys to John G. Morrison, Jr. Nevertheless, both councils met that day, each convinced of its legitimacy.[40]

The Morrison Council convened with sixty to seventy delegates, but their numbers were quickly depleted. The contingent from Red Lake Reservation had decided beforehand to withdraw from the General Council because Morrison's allies favored allotting the Red Lake Diminished Reservation, selling the large acreage that would remain, and depositing the money in the "Chippewa in Minnesota Fund" as originally specified in the 1889 Nelson Act. This would have provided even more money to be divided. Peter Graves, a spokesman for the Red Lake band, recommended that the "clamoring mixed bloods" be given their proportional share of the tribal funds so that they might "cease to be tribal Indians." But he felt that they did not accurately represent the true conditions of most of the "Minnesota Chippewa." As he saw it, "The Indians need protection from the Government from their own people who have taken control of their Council."[41]

Red Lake band members were not about to relinquish their hard-won right to hold their land in common. Legislation passed in 1904 guaranteed them sole possession of their reservation. They had secured the legislation they preferred, avoided taking allotments, and cared little for the Nelson Act, which stipulated that the sale of unallotted lands at Red Lake should provide the bulk of the "Chippewa in Minnesota Fund." Red Lake leaders spoke from the perspective of hindsight, not caring to replicate the process of dispossession that had occurred at White Earth. They turned their backs on the General Council of the Chippewa and formed their own "General Council of the Red Lake Band."[42]

Delegates from Nett Lake, Leech Lake, and White Earth Village also withdrew from the Morrison Council and joined those from Pine Point who attended the Coffey Council, which drew more than a hundred delegates espousing conservative values. Council members unanimously voted to affirm the election which had replaced John G. Morrison with James Coffey as president and resolved that Coffey's legal expenses from fighting the libel charge should be paid from tribal funds. They went on to identify members of the wayward Legislative Committee as "mixed bloods of the White Earth reservation" and resolved that they had no right to "usurp the power and privileges of the 'Chippewa Indians of

Minnesota.' " In the face of such firm resolve, it is a wonder that the 1917 Legislative Committee could ever have suggested that tribal relations had ceased to exist among the Anishinaabeg.[43]

Indian Office inspectors and Anishinaabeg throughout northern Minnesota supported the Coffey Council and censured the Legislative Committee's unconstitutional activities. Inspectors Linnen and Moorehead reported that council after council renounced the rule of the "mixed-bloods," and upheld "full-bloods" for demonstrating more sincerity and commitment to Indians' welfare, and supporting policies that were "constructive and not destructive."[44]

After the 1918 debacle, federal supervisors vowed that the 1919 General Council would finally settle the factional dispute. In an attempt to give conservative leaders every advantage, they ignored the constitution and by-laws and convened the White Earth local council in the Pinehurst Pavilion at Twin Lakes on 17 June. For the first time since the conflict had erupted, both factions attended the same local council. Delegates were obviously uncomfortable and argued over every matter of procedure. But conservatives faced the greatest dilemma; in a representative council convened on their home turf, they comprised only a minority of the delegates instead of the majority that they and policymakers had anticipated. In an elective framework, they were sure to lose.[45]

Recognizing their predicament, conservative leaders began to request special consideration. Since their ancestors had originally determined Indian property rights, they argued that they should be entitled to half the delegates sent to the next General Council at Cass Lake. In reply, Frank Beaulieu extolled majority rule as the "law of all nations."[46] When conservatives failed to secure this concession, they rose in a body and left. Unable to persuade them to return, the others proceeded to elect their slate of candidates.

The local council in 1919 clarified some misconceptions that policymakers held about Anishinaabe polity at White Earth. Several inspectors had predicted that "full-bloods" would predominate in a truly representative council. In 1919, despite exceptional measures designed to give them every advantage, conservative band leaders failed to constitute a majority. Superintendent W. F. Dickens judged that the vote taken for chair of the special meeting, 417 for Frank Cajune and 255 for Scott

Porter, most closely approximated relative factional strength. Conservatives realized that they would be unable to prevail, and responded in
typical Anishinaabe fashion by leaving.[47] But the tried-and-true tactic of
splintering the group would not work this time.

Demographic trends at White Earth had worked against the interests
of conservative band leaders. Larger population and household sizes
among people of métis descent meant that they would overwhelm their
opposition in elective councils. Superintendent Dickens understood that
as long as political affairs at White Earth were determined "by a majority
vote of its enrolled members . . . it will continue to be dominated by the
mixed bloods." Patterns of intermarriage, mortality, and child-spacing
ensured that full-bloods would "rapidly diminish" while mixed-bloods
"rapidly increased." Instituting elective reservation and tribal government among the Anishinaabeg had produced a permanent conservative
minority, much as the later 1934 Indian Reorganization Act would.[48]
Once again, events that transpired at White Earth presaged national
trends. In the process of finding a "voice" and gaining experience with
the mechanistic operations of elective government, conservative leaders
simultaneously suffered further restrictions on their political autonomy.
The contest had by no means ended, but the context had metamorphosed.

Conclusion

Among some Indian groups, factionalism has been described as a
contest between mixed-bloods and full-bloods. On the White Earth Reservation in the first two decades of the twentieth century, leadership
factions had more to do with economic behavior, attitudes toward economic development, and experience with U.S. institutions than with
blood quotas. Factionalism on the White Earth Reservation reflected a
clash of economic ethics and world view, rather than genetic differences
alone. Assimilationist métis leaders always identified themselves as
"Indians," but their accumulation of wealth and alignment with the land
and pine cartel drew fire from the conservative faction. Their exploitative activities elevated their individual prosperity above the interests of
the reservation community as a whole. Perhaps their ethnic heritage of
brokerage influenced their economic orientation.

Actually the métis cultural brokers had succeeded as small-scale capitalists. Although neither sufficient capital nor opportunities were present for them to behave as venture capitalists by reinvesting profits continually to expand their enterprises, they nonetheless had achieved the standards of U.S. society by means acceptable in the U.S. marketplace. It is ironic that U.S. policymakers still intended that Indians should become small-scale yeoman farmers rather than the capitalistic entrepreneurs who represented success in the contemporary United States. Those individuals of Anishinaabe descent who achieved success in the capitalistic mode were described as "white" by conservative Indians and local government investigators alike.

More conservative Anishinaabe leaders launched a critique of the capitalistic values of the assimilationist faction that emphasized concern for equity and the welfare of community and kin. They transformed the meanings of *mixed-blood* and *full-blood* into potent political symbols that encapsulated a conservative understanding of the social and economic processes that had changed the structure of their lives.

Divisions apparent at White Earth paralleled divisions among other Anishinaabe reservation populations in the state. The movement toward elective tribal government crystallized these factional differences statewide. Participants transplanted the *mixed-blood* and *full-blood* symbols to the tribal level and resumed their contest.

But demographic and economic trends combined to muffle the "voice" that conservative leaders had nurtured. Individuals of mixed descent proliferated as intermarriage and market demands further impinged on more conservative Anishinaabe lifeways. Elective tribal government subjected the contrasting values and world views of competing factions to a representative vote . . . and the conservatives ultimately lost.

Assimilationist leaders tested their political expertise in ever-wider arenas. During the early reservation period, they had served as articulate defenders of Anishinaabe resources. The skills they gained by working within U.S. institutions served them well in the future. They performed invaluable services for the Anishinaabeg, and yet they took full advantage of their relationships in the process. When congressional investigations revealed the blatantly self-serving activities of key métis leaders, conservative leaders moved to expel them at both the reservation and tribal levels.

In Washington, D.C., White Earth assimilationist leaders encountered

Indian lobbyists from all over the United States. Sharing similar backgrounds as formally educated cultural brokers, they often found that
they could agree on matters of national policy that would potentially af-
fect them all. National pan-Indian organizations that flourished during
the early 1900s drew on this core group for their membership. Several
métis leaders from White Earth became active in such organizations. By
the early 1920s, however, the most famous of these, the Society for
American Indians, had lost much of its earlier reforming zeal. Men
who came to the fore as leaders during this period, like Thomas Sloan,
espoused a more distinctive capitalistic ideology of tribal dissolution.
Founding leaders like Arthur Parker grew disillusioned with the society's
activities and broke ties with it. John Carl, Theodore Beaulieu, and
Henry Warren from White Earth were among those who presided during
the denouement of the Society for the American Indian.[49]

The White Earth métis cultural brokers directed their political organizing efforts ever outward as their identity was questioned at home.
Their move to establish the General Council in 1913 coincided with the
suspension of key leaders of mixed descent from the tribal rolls. The
tribal arena might have offered some respite from attack had participants
not transplanted the factional conflict. In the long run, assimilationist
leaders found greater acceptance of their ethics and world view among
national pan-Indian leaders than among the conservative Anishinaabeg
of Minnesota.

"We Can Not Get a Living as We Used To"

Assimilation Gone Awry

Introduction

White Earth residents could not foresee the long-term consequences of the alienation of allotments at the time the 1906 Clapp Rider was passed. Both ethnic groups at the reservation continued to pursue familiar economic strategies. Those who lived in the eastern forest and lake country continued for a while to derive most of their subsistence directly from the land, while those in the western prairies relied more on wage labor and less on the seasonal round. Band ties persisted to some degree, but intermarriage across both band and racial lines helped to blur these distinctions. Overall ethnic orientation replaced band as the primary determinant of social and political affiliations.

Pressures on reservation resources continued unabated throughout the first two decades of the twentieth century. State claims to swampland and the destructive practices of lumber companies threatened the way of life that had been sustained in the eastern forests. Allotments continued to pass out of Indian ownership through further sales and tax forfeiture proceedings. The shift to state control of Indian education reduced the number of schools at White Earth and restricted access to formal education, especially for more conservative Indians. On many fronts White Earth's natural and human resources continued to come under attack. Increasing property restrictions reduced access to seasonal food resources and contributed to declining health among the Indian population. Under such circumstances, diseases took a more deadly toll. The way of life that had developed in the eastern woodlands bore the brunt of these changes.

Those who mastered a more market-oriented way of life fared best, for they learned to bend with the circumstances and maximize their options. Various types of participation in the local market economy characterized life in the western part of the reservation. Wage laborers, farmers, small-scale entrepreneurs, and owners of banks and corporations all congregated near the centers of commerce. Some managed meager resources to get by; others turned a profit. Meanwhile, a steadily rising population meant that relatively few Anishinaabe families would realize any long-term benefits from these changes. Alienation of land and resources reduced available opportunities for everyone at White Earth, both in the immediate sense and in terms of future economic development.

Postponement of the Effects of Dispossession

Divisions between east and west persisted among White Earth residents. The subsistence-oriented pattern, still tied to the land, and market-oriented options were the only two choices for those who wished to remain on the reservation. Most people tried to meld the two.

Major settlements in the eastern lake country at Round Lake, Elbow Lake, Pine Point, Twin Lakes, Gull Lake, Wild Rice River, and points in between continued to serve as bastions of conservatism. As in earlier periods, observers and the Indians themselves described inhabitants of the eastern lakes and forests as more "full-blooded" and more conservative. The seasonal round remained the economic backbone of their way of life. Residents still left the main settlements for days and weeks at a time to harvest seasonal produce, the major portion of which went toward their subsistence with the rest being traded for groceries and other utilitarian items.

Government inspectors affirmed that the eastern lake country was still "Grand Medicine Territory," where Midé priests and priestesses and the moccasin game held sway. Inspector W. H. Gibbs lamented that "the Indians seem to think they are safe from punishment and hark back to tribal custom with impunity."[1] At the passage of the 1906 Clapp Rider, the context of life had changed only minimally for those who lived to the east.

Wage labor came to play a larger role at White Earth. Prosperous agricultural enterprises in the Red River Valley and lumber camps in the forests to the east continued to draw Indian men and some women.

Typically, Indians preferred working in groups, a form of labor organization rooted in past patterns.[2] Lumber camps and log drives provided opportunities to continue in this fashion. Whole families sometimes moved to the camps where men cut and hauled logs and women laundered clothes and cooked. Although these positions generally afforded low wages, experienced woodsmen could rely on a fairly steady source of income. The seasonality of temporary employment allowed wage labor to remain a flexible complement to the circuit of activities comprising the industrial year. But the Anishinaabeg approached this economic option with their own objectives in mind and not all were eager for wage work. Indian Office employment supervisors were dismayed that young Anishinaabe women displayed little enthusiasm at the prospect of working as domestics in whites' homes in the Twin Cities, noting that they would rather dig snakeroot. Young men, however, had come to accept these employment conditions as the way of the future, and loggers and farmworkers pieced together decent livelihoods.

Employers sometimes complained that Indian workers were unreliable and intimated that they could more often be found in the saloons than in the forests. However, as lumber companies moved into Anishinaabe ceded lands, owners resented regulations requiring them to hire Indians instead of Euroamerican loggers with whom they were more familiar. Inspectors reported that northern Minnesota lumber companies discriminated against Indian workers, paying them lower wages. Labor historians have interpreted similar comments about workers' unreliability as evidence of a "premodern" workers' mentality that prevented "traditional" workers from behaving in a timely, industrial fashion. Supposedly, traditional patterns tied to the ebb and flow of the seasons were not easily transferred to a regimented, daily work routine that paid hourly wages. Nevertheless, employers' complaints also reflect their frustration at not getting the work done quickly enough and do little to clarify Indians' motivations.

The persistence of the seasonal round provided a context for wage labor that did not require regularized daily work routines. Requirements of the household economy determined choices made regarding wage labor, not an inherent inability to adjust to time discipline. Logging was a seasonal occupation by nature, with most work done in the winter. Most wage laborers in the lumber industry had to find other means of subsistence during the off-season. The same can be said about farm work. Conveniently, the seasonal requirements of each complemented the annual round of harvesting activities at White Earth.[3]

The persistence of the seasonal round coupled with the availability of wage labor helped to ease the transition conservative Anishinaabeg faced as the primacy of the fur trade passed. With wage labor as an alternative, male roles suffered less dislocation as the hunting and trapping economy was undermined. In addition, gender roles bent to provide men with more prominent roles in the traditionally female spheres of provisioning such as ricing and sugar making. While gender and age divisions persisted, men participated more frequently in these activities which had grown in importance as hunting and trapping declined and opportunities to market these products to the surrounding Euroamerican population increased. Early twentieth-century ethnographers captured these transitional gender roles in their many photographs.[4]

As noted earlier, most Indians had declined to move onto their land allotments, a fact that continually frustrated federal officials. Given the manner in which many allotments had been assigned and the escalating land alienation, this should not have been surprising. Even so, White Earth agents regularly used this fact to deny Indians access to funds in their individual accounts or to government services. Many of those who did retain their allotments could not be induced to take up residence even when homes were built for them; some rented them to others. Each government farmer reported the number of families in his district actually living on their allotments; the numbers were always small, more so in the eastern area.

By 1910, forests once blanketing White Earth's eastern townships had been "cut-over" and their poor soil, wetlands, and tree stumps posed special problems for potential farmers. Even the Euroamerican "bonanza farmers" on the western prairies would have been hard-pressed to operate profitable farms under such conditions. Conservative Indian leaders blamed the unfair allotment process for the poor quality land they had come to own, complaining that all they received were "stone hills, swamps, lakes, and pine stumps." Under these worsening conditions, the agricultural option had even less power to entice conservative Indians in the east to alter familiar patterns.

Instead of establishing homesteads on their allotments, most conservative Indians in the east congregated in small villages of 200 to 300 people. They lived on cut-over lands along lake shores in homes ranging from cloth tipis and bark wigwams to tarpaper shacks and log cabins, with few dwellings of any more substance. Many were "squatters" in the eyes of the law, living in areas convenient to meet their economic and social needs without regard to "legal" ownership. Boarding schools located at Pine Point, Wild Rice River, and White Earth Village served as focal points for families to relocate to be closer to their children. Others established themselves on uncontested areas such as school, government, and church reserves. Some found space on cut-over lands owned by lumber companies. Occasionally, absentee Euroamerican landowners allowed Indian families to encamp on their land. Indian Office inspectors were reluctant to encourage landless families to do more than establish garden plots because any developments would likely be lost when land titles cleared.

Escalating land alienation prompted creative living strategies. So many landless individuals shared quarters with friends and relatives that "during the winter several additional persons . . . crowded into nearly every house." It was common for several families to cluster together on a minor child's allotment, since it remained in trust until the minor came of age. Mille Lacs *ogimaa* Waweyeacumig welcomed many families onto his own allotment near Elbow Lake. These flexible arrangements were in keeping with Anishinaabe values that stressed hospitality and concern for relatives. Indians in the east continued to adapt to changing conditions they encountered, secure in custom if not in land tenure.[5]

In 1913, policymakers instituted the "Reimbursable Plan" to make loans available to Indians to develop their allotments and avoid supplying "gratuities" from the tribal funds. Allottees had only to agree to repay the loans within several years, but clouded titles made the Reimbursable Plan a risky proposition because any improvements would pass with the land when the titles cleared. Some Indians believed the Reimbursable Plan was just another scheme to seize more of their property; others knew they could not generate enough capital to pay off a loan. Their experiences with mortgages had taught them that much.[6]

From his vantage point in the eastern forests, Inspector Oscar Lipps observed in 1912, "There is as much difference between this portion of the reservation and that portion contingent to the agency as there is between Minnesota and Mexico." What Lipps saw troubled him, for he knew that the customary way of life could no longer sustain the population. The remedy he outlined had an eerie familiarity to it. Five farmers would distribute "teams, farming implements and seeds" to Indians and would assist them in "clearing their lands, planting and cultivating their crops, [and] marketing the surplus." Roads and telephone lines would be constructed and "everything possible done to infuse new life and interest in all the Chippewa communities."[7] The currents of Yankee ideology ran deep, but the rhetoric was no longer appropriate for the White Earth Reservation.

As Anishinaabe resources enriched the Euroamericans who increasingly populated Callaway, Ogema, Mahnomen, Waubun, and Bejou along the western Soo Line, these towns surpassed White Earth Village, Beaulieu (Wild Rice River), and Ponsford in economic importance. People of means still resided in the towns where métis cultural brokers had chosen to live, but train stations sustained more involved commercial activities. These railroad towns resembled other rural, agricultural centers, except for their proximity to a reservation population having rights to millions of dollars' worth of tribal funds and resources.

White Earth Village, the location of the agency complex, boarding school, hospital, and Episcopal mission buildings, retained a preeminent position among White Earth's interior towns, but all began to decline in importance. Their transitory prosperity had stemmed from the removal of restrictions on mixed-bloods' allotted land. Ponsford and Beaulieu experienced a brief boom period as land and timber sales fueled a burst of economic activity. Indians were able to avoid transportation costs by marketing their produce to nearby lumber crews. Banks, real estate offices, lumber camps, and fly-by-night charlatans came and went with the passage of the land titles.

Evidence compiled by the Graham Commission made clear the magnitude of fraud and exploitation rampant at White Earth since passage of the 1906 Clapp Rider. Charges of corruption instantly threw land transactions into confusion. As long as land titles remained in question, new owners feared to develop the land and were unable to borrow money against their holdings. These questionable transactions postponed development of reservation land by Euroamericans until judicial determination cleared most titles. In essence, the land fraud that occurred between 1906 and 1915 delayed actual legal conveyance of land parcels that would have interfered with the seasonal subsistence cycle. This ironic quirk impressed Inspector Oscar Lipps, who noted that "so far, those who have sold their allotments have experienced no inconvenience thereby as the purchasers have not yet disturbed them." This confusion allowed conservative Indians to continue to reside where they pleased and pursue their familiar way of life.[8]

Continued Alienation of Resources

Through fraud, manipulation of legal loopholes, and mismanagement, resources of the White Earth Anishinaabeg continued to come under attack. Allotted land, timberland, and swamplands all passed from Indian control, and revenue that should have bolstered the tribal funds was repeatedly denied to the "Chippewa in Minnesota Fund." A gradual, long-term assault was directed against Anishinaabe resources on all fronts.

Allotted landholdings continued to attract speculators. Once the greater number of adult mixed-bloods' allotted lands had been transferred, land companies turned their attention to the lands of minor mixed-bloods. According to Minnesota state law, girls reached the age of majority at eighteen—boys at twenty-one. A veritable barrage of speculators "camp[ed] upon the trail of minors," waiting to pounce on them as they came of age. "In many, if not most instances, a conveyance during minority" preceded the actual mortgage arrangement which simply ratified the earlier act.[9] Minors posed easy targets as the last significant category of allottees that land dealers could readily identify.

To complicate matters further, the federal government neglected its responsibilities in probating trust lands and determining heirs, causing these cases to "drift along undetermined." When in 1915, the U.S. government created a vacuum of authority by totally abandoning these cases, county and state governments stepped in to fill the void. This ad hoc illegal arrangement further contributed to the economic miasma on the reservation, with implications that persist to the present time.[10]

For those mixed-bloods who managed to retain their allotments despite all odds, tax forfeiture proceedings loomed as a threat. Policymakers had interpreted the 1906 Clapp Rider to mean that White Earth mixed-bloods had been declared U.S. citizens and were liable to support public services. Newly organized Mahnomen County, with a high proportion of tax-exempt trust land, had to provide many services (such as roads and schools) on a limited tax base. John Carl, a prominent métis agent for the land and pine cartel and a realtor in his own right, became Mahnomen County auditor. His involvement, and that of other métis mediators, followed logically from their pitch for self-government. Mahnomen and Becker county officials levied high taxes and increasingly seized remaining allotted lands in tax forfeiture proceedings, which came to be the primary method of obtaining allotted lands. All of this happening only a year after passage of the 1906 Clapp Rider seemed more than coincidental to Agent John R. Howard who surmised that "the levying of such a high rate of taxes is a scheme put up by land dealers to enable them to purchase tax titles . . . and finally get possession . . . with but a small outlay." By increasingly complicated means, dispossession was forced upon even those few mixed-bloods who had maintained their allotted land holdings.[11]

As in most areas, the Anishinaabeg could exert little control over administration of their timber. Prior to allotment of the pine lands, the dead and down logging policy permitted Indians to earn wages by cutting damaged timber. Arrangements entered into under this policy reflected ethnic differences on the reservation. Prominent cultural brokers of mixed descent and Euroamericans who had married into the tribe were able to monopolize applications to cut dead and down timber. Some cut the wood themselves, but most contracted with outside lumber firms to do the actual logging. These lumber companies in turn hired young men, sometimes Indians, to work for wages. Applicants skimmed a mediating fee from the transaction, but lumber companies gained the most. That the Anishinaabeg would receive only wages and no chance to process and manufacture wood products did not concern Indian Office personnel, who were satisfied that wage labor would build "character" in line with their goal of assimilation.

Lumbermen flouted provisions of the dead and down logging policy by trying to make off with large amounts of green, living timber. Those familiar with the logging business insisted that all dead and down timber had long since been removed and that "evidences of the clean cutting of everything merchantable were abundant everywhere." They criticized unscrupulous lumbermen who "(by some occult means) . . . can tell about how long a tree will live," and proceed to harvest it even though it is "standing and growing and ha(s) green boughs." Furthermore, lumber companies cut roads and skidways through prime living timber in their quest for dead and downed trees. They torched Anishinaabe forests so that mysterious fires blazed throughout northern Minnesota creating stands of slightly damaged pine timber that could be bought at "fire sale" prices. Effective surveillance was impossible in the vast northwoods. Phony dead and down logging perpetrated great frauds against the Anishinaabeg at White Earth and in Minnesota at large, robbing them of the value of their growing pine timber.

As early as the spring of 1901, Round Lake Indians had had enough. Many Indians worked as expert drivers who floated logs to the Shevlin mills at Frazee for the Commonwealth Lumber Company (predecessor of the Nichols-Chisolm). During the drive they noticed that many logs were oozing sap, a sure sign that they had been green and alive when cut. When they discovered they were being cheated, they held a council and decided to demand compensation. "So one day some sixty or seventy Indians . . . armed with rifles, shotguns, etc., appeared at the Round Lake dam and ordered the drive to halt under the threat of blowing up every dam within the reservation." They threatened death to the first man who tried to put a log through. Other employees on the drive and merchants from Ponsford supported the dissidents and provided supplies for their four-day showdown. Offers of provisions from the lumber company and a promise to re-scale the logs placated the Round Lakers and they agreed to let the drive proceed.[12]

In the first two decades of the twentieth century, neither the Anishinaabeg nor U.S. government administrators regarded timber as a renewable resource. Policies mandating that timber simply be sold off in bulk denied the Anishinaabeg a chance to capitalize on their timber. White Earth residents were fortunate if lumber companies erected portable mills so that Indians might earn wages. Even the 1902 Morris Act, which instituted the "bank scale" to correct abuses in the appraisal and auction of timber, made no provision for manufacturing wood products as at La Pointe or Menominee, Wisconsin. Had U.S. administrators managed Anishinaabe timber according to principles of conservation and sustained yield, principles not unheard of at the time, they might have derived greater benefit from this revenue-generating resource. The U.S. assimilationists foolishly intended that the Anishinaabeg should become small-scale yeoman farmers, not successful lumbermen. The U.S. administrators did not apply principles of conservation and sustained-yield management to Anishinaabe timber until 1916 when the Red Lake Indian Forest was established. By that time, most timber on Anishinaabe ceded lands had simply been clear-cut by Euroamerican lumbermen. Ironically, the U.S. government had confiscated Anishinaabe ceded lands, "forest reserve" lands near Leech Lake originally set aside by the 1891 Morris Act, to create the Minnesota National Forest (now the Chippewa National Forest) in 1908. The Indians protested this theft of land and timber until they received monetary compensation (not the land) in 1925. Conservationists were apparently no more attuned to Anishinaabe interests than were lumber companies.[13]

In 1895, the State of Minnesota claimed the swampland on all Anishinaabe reservations under authority of the 1860 Swamp Land Act. The act had been intended to provide new states (specifically Minnesota and Oregon) with a source of revenue. On behalf of the Anishinaabeg, Indian Office officials challenged the state's action in waiting thirty-five years to make its claim. Not only had Anishinaabe tribal funds financed surveys that allowed swampland parcels to be identified, but state claims conflicted with about 200 allotments that had already been made at White Earth. In 1896 in the *State of Minnesota vs. Craig*, the court questioned Minnesota's right to make such a claim: "A grant must have definiteness and precision. . . . To say that thirty-five years after a grant of swamplands had passed . . . that a State can assert title . . . is to say that there is actually no bar of time . . . and there would be no . . . quiet, peaceable possession of real estate inside the State of Minnesota." Despite allegations of improper procedure and violation of treaty rights, the Interior Department sustained state contentions and issued patents to swampland between 1910 and 1912. Ultimately, the Supreme Court ruled in the state's favor in 1926, but no compensation was awarded to the Indians until 1936.

It took so long to resolve the State of Minnesota's claims to White Earth swampland that they had little immediate effect on subsistence patterns. The contested area lay mostly within the eastern townships at White Earth where conservative Indians clung tenaciously to the seasonal round. The state claimed the entire shoreline of Rice Lake, which had long been one of the most important ricing centers on the reservation. While conservative Indians in the east may not have felt its effects, state jurisdiction over crucial wild rice fields and marshes remained a latent threat to their subsistence base.[14]

Created by the 1889 Nelson Act to be held in trust by the U.S. government, the "Chippewa in Minnesota Fund" represented a considerable resource for all Minnesota Anishinaabeg. Sales of ceded land and timber were to provide the bulk of its revenue, which would then be used to finance U.S. assimilation programs. Anishinaabe tribal funds financed schools, hospitals, social welfare programs, agricultural instruction, and the development and maintenance of rudimentary economic foundations on the reservations. Facile generalizations about Anishinaabe dependence on welfare outlays from the U.S. government mask the fact that the Anishinaabe essentially financed their own "assimilation." And yet, Indian Office policy effectively barred Anishinaabe people from exercising any control over these funds. The U.S. government acted as guardian of all Anishinaabe resources, including the tribal funds.

In its role as guardian, U.S. administrators mismanaged the "Chippewa in Minnesota Fund" almost from its inception. Even though individual Anishinaabe clearly had the legal right to elect *not* to move to the White Earth Reservation, U.S. Chippewa commissioners illegally spent thousands of dollars traveling through northern Minnesota to persuade them to do so. Mismanagement in the care and sale of timber cost the Anishinaabeg millions. Legislation repeatedly commuted homestead fees for settlers on ceded lands, denying revenue to tribal funds. Policymakers ignored objections of tribal leaders and slated money from the "Chippewa in Minnesota Fund" to cover some costs associated with ditching and draining wetlands on ceded lands north of Red Lake. Compensation for confiscated land—swampland claimed by the State of Min-

nesota and timberland taken for the Minnesota National Forest—was
not forthcoming for twenty to forty years. Under these circumstances,
the "Chippewa in Minnesota Fund" often showed a deficit, and the U.S.
government was forced to forward money to carry out its assimilation programs. The Anishinaabeg were often in debt to the government because of actions taken by federal officials in their role as guardian of Indians' resources. The tribal funds were yet another resource that
the government failed to administer to serve the best interests of the
Anishinaabeg.[15]

Closing both day and boarding schools at White Earth also deprived
some Anishinaabeg of an important resource. Market-oriented families
had long taken advantage of educational opportunities. Formal education had played a significant role in creating the bilingual métis cultural
brokers and enabled them to succeed within the market economy. Conservative Indians had also developed a greater appreciation of the benefits
of education in Euroamerican ways. Though by no means a panacea,
formal education enabled young Anishinaabe men and women to cope
with the transition they faced and to define new social and economic
roles for themselves. Formal education especially aided Indian women to
adapt their usual social roles to the reservation system. They found
places among school and hospital personnel and as field matrons. Nurses
helped to combat disease in the post-1909 health crisis. Increasingly, as
their resources and way of life came under attack, Indians came to
recognize the advantage of being able to function within and to manipulate U.S. institutions. Returned students Benjamin Casswell, Isabel
Schneider, Margaret Warren, Josephine Parker, and others assumed key
mediating roles on the reservation and helped to displace Anishinaabe
dependence on those métis cultural brokers who had exploitation on
their minds. In this sense, education became a political tool.

Schools at White Earth were never adequate for all those who wished
to attend, but by 1910, Indian schools had become thoroughly integrated
on the reservation. Although complaints about abuses in the schools,
especially about undue child labor, had become commonplace, White
Earth residents had grown accustomed to the system. Knowing that their
people faced a difficult transition, Indian political leaders had done their
best to make sure that these schools would benefit present and future

generations of Anishinaabe children. For growing numbers of children, this had become the normative experience.[16]

Although twentieth-century policymakers maintained an overall commitment to educating Indian students, they adopted a more pragmatic, less optimistic approach than their evangelical, reform-minded predecessors. As their enthusiasm dampened, they blamed the allotment policy's failure to produce desired changes on Indians' inherent "backwardness"; earlier reformers had simply expected too much from them. This new generation of social engineers stressed vocational or industrial education to aid Indians in their adjustment to wage labor, and argued that higher courses of education would only estrange them from their home environment. Educators had scaled back their aspirations for Indian students, and their programs reflected this. Charles Dagenett, Supervisor of Employment for the Indian Office, quashed the dreams of several White Earth boys who hoped to learn auto mechanics. He recommended only a brief exposure to auto repair, so that they would "appreciate their limitations." Later, he assured them, "the Office will be glad to place them in factories for thorough training." Doubts about Indians' ability to "advance" and congressional concern over the ballooning budget combined to provide Indian children with a second-rate education that would consign them to the fringes of U.S. society.[17]

Since the 1890s, officials had anticipated the day when Indian children would be integrated into public schools. Financial considerations alone made this an attractive objective, but policymakers also reasoned that rubbing shoulders with Euroamericans was "the most rapid process for civilization." Aware that the Indian Office used Anishinaabe tribal funds to mete out a substandard education, métis leaders at White Earth took up the public school crusade. They argued that Indian schools wasted tribal funds and did not benefit "progressive" Indians.

By 1900, administrators had already begun closing government-operated schools at White Earth and paying tuition at nearby public schools for Indian pupils. Special arrangements transferred buildings financed by Anishinaabe tribal funds directly to the State of Minnesota to use in the public school system. Local discrimination against Indians had undermined earlier efforts to integrate Indian students into public schools; the tuition payments were intended to sweeten the proposition. Because tuition payments for Indian students helped finance education for the others, public school systems in counties with much trust land and high tax rates welcomed the payments—but not the Indian children.

It was commonly assumed that mixed-bloods at White Earth had gained U.S. citizenship under the 1906 Clapp Rider. A few administrators understood the implications of this fact. Legally, most Indians were "entitled to such privileges [a public school education] without the payment of the [tuition] bonus," which came from tribal funds.

School officials and assimilationist leaders pointed out that many Indian citizens at White Earth paid no taxes because they had lost their lands and argued that tuition payments should offset the cost to the county school systems of educating landless citizen Indians. They argued, in effect, that property holding should determine an Indian's right to a free public education. Anishinaabe tribal funds went to finance school buildings and material plants utilized by the public schools and then covered tuition for the children of Indians who were U.S. citizens to attend the very schools that their tribal funds had helped to build.

By 1920, a firm foundation had been laid for a cooperative relationship between the State of Minnesota and the Indian Office in regard to educating Indian children in public schools. Anishinaabe tribal funds and state school district funds were slated for the construction of schools to be located near Indian children. Even so, local public school boards, like that of Becker County District 124 where the Pine Point school was located, "refuse[d] to take over the responsibility of educating the Indian children in that district." Supervisor P. R. Wadsworth thought that if sufficient "pressure [was] brought to bear they will consent to operate it, especially when offered adequate tuition." But others affirmed that few public schools reached the children of the eastern cut-over district.

Conservative Indians had lost the "Indian schools" where their presence was not greeted with scorn and derision. The Indian Office may have offered only a second-rate curriculum, but many had come to regard the schools as "theirs." The Commissioner of Indian Affairs received numerous complaints about closing the Indian schools, but pushed forward with his plan to utilize public schools, however unwilling those schools might prove to be. The Anishinaabeg at White Earth felt the effects of this policy differentially. Those in the west found the public schools accessible and of better quality than the old Indian schools. In the east, these changes restricted conservative Indians' access to the formal education that many had come to value.[18]

Undermining the Seasonal Round

While the lengthy process of adjudicating land fraud claims effectively postponed the effects of dispossession for the White Earth Anishinaabeg, other factors were undermining the seasonal round. As early as 1900, crucial subsistence resources in the eastern forest and lake country were threatened. Policymakers did not recognize how integral the seasonal round was to Anishinaabe well-being and they failed to protect it. In actuality, the integrity of the subsistence base served as a barometer for the overall health and viability of the White Earth population.

Logging methods were environmentally destructive. Because rivers were too shallow, lumbermen constructed a series of dams to catch the spring rains and snow melt to float logs downstream. They chose Rice Lake, a major center for harvesting wild rice, as their main reservoir. The technique worked well enough for the lumber companies, allowing them to transport timber to towns where their milling operations were based. The effect on the Anishinaabeg, however, was anything but benign. Damming the eastern waterways flooded the swamps and marshes that supplied crucial subsistence resources. Wild rice requires a certain water depth and a mild, regular current. At times, dams completely washed out the wild rice crop. Floodwaters also engulfed low-lying Indian gardens on river bottom land. Clear-cutting timber caused erosion and muddied streams, choking aquatic life. Piles of brush and "stumpage" created prime conditions for fires, which destroyed vegetation, further contributing to erosion. This manipulation of White Earth's waterways sometimes scoured lakes of silt and sediment, which posed an additional threat to the rice crop. What lumber companies regarded as nothing more than a necessary right-of-way took a decided toll on the subsistence economy.

Those Indians who suffered most directly protested immediately. Agent John H. Sutherland relayed the Gull Lake band's demand for reimbursement because they depended "largely on the wild rice crop for subsistence of their families." Although the Wild Rice Lumber Company contracted to provide what it considered to be adequate restitution ("flour, pork, tea, and sugar for 85 to 90 families"), this did not prevent Gull Lakers from taking matters into their own hands in 1901. Forty armed themselves, destroyed one dam and tried to break up another, engaging in a stand-off with lumber company employees "for the best part of a day." Company officials expected "every minute a battle," which only skillful negotiation by the foreman averted. Gull Lake leader Pindegaygeshig hoped to drive home the point that "the streams on this reservation are not public highways . . . and that the consent of the Indians must be obtained."

If lumbermen comprehended the severe consequences of flooding the rice beds, their actions did not reflect it. The Wild Rice Lumber Company sent a communiqué to *The Tomahawk*, assuring its readers that the dam would be used only "for a short time each Spring, and no harm can come from it if used in this way." They completely misunderstood the problem. John Johnson, Jr., Enmegahbowh's son, grumbled that Agent Michelet did little to mediate this conflict: "He don't care to do business with Indians and don't pay any attention to their complaints." But worst of all, he feared that "the Indians some day are liable to make a mistake in taking matters in their hands." In 1903, Pindegaygeshig still threatened that "the Indians are going to . . . hold the logs now in Rice Lake and break the dam immediately." Issuance of a small amount of provisions could not begin to compensate for the destruction of a primary subsistence resource.

As late as 1916, conservative Indians still threatened guerrilla resistance against the dams and "other obstruction of fish ways" which had rendered some of the rice fields "entirely barren." When the Wild Rice Lumber Company offered to sell the dam to the Indian Office as a valuable tool for regulating Rice Lake's water level, officials took a hard look at the situation. What they found underscored the gravity of the Indians' complaints: "Prior to the construction of the dam . . . there were immense rice fields covering hundreds of acres." Realizing that there would be more rice without the dam, they recommended dismantling it before it caused another "Johnstown disaster" for Euroamerican farmers downstream who had also lodged complaints against the lumber companies. Ultimately, repeated rice failures prompted agency employees to recommend reseeding the rice beds to increase the yield. Unfortunately, suggestions of this sort were tacit recognition that the subsistence round had suffered immeasurably.[19]

In the early twentieth century, state game laws further circumscribed Indian activities and established seasons for hunting that ran expressly counter to their treaty rights. A number of men had been "arrested for hunting 'out of season,'" causing Mezhucegeshig, a prominent Mississippi band leader, to lament that "the law seems against us . . . so we can not get a living as we used to do." Law enforcement officials had a difficult time monitoring this inconspicuous activity. Indians withstood accusations of poaching and proceeded to harvest game on which they had depended for generations. They found more than enough moose meat and venison to meet their subsistence needs, enough to sell a surplus. Under these circumstances, they must have considered state demands that they reduce their take to be irrational and unreasonable. Yet the threat of enforcement necessitated that they proceed surreptitiously and move some of their processing activities indoors.[20]

Lumber companies' destructive practices, state control of swampland, and state game laws all worked to erode the seasonal round. But the greatest disaster stemmed from land alienation. The lengthy process of resolving land fraud claims postponed its impact—but long-term observers knew that clouded land titles were only a temporary impediment. The assault on White Earth's resources on all fronts portended dire consequences for the Anishinaabeg. Soon Indians would "not be permitted to use either the waters adjacent thereto or to trespass upon the lands." And, sure enough, Indians began to encounter fences and "No Trespassing" signs as they continued their harvesting. With keen foresight, agents predicted that the alienation of allotted land would "condemn [the Indians] to destitution and beggary."[21]

The Social Consequences of Dispossession

Both subsistence-oriented Indians and those who were more involved in the market economy coexisted in relative harmony during the early years at the reservation when resources were still abundant. As already noted, rising population, the alienation of resources, and environmental degradation strained remaining resources for both groups. Always the backbone of the subsistence economy, seasonal activities increasingly were unable to sustain the growing population. Euroamerican land ownership restricted conservative Indians' access to lake fronts and other areas encompassing seasonal resources. Disruption of hunting and gathering fostered poverty and disease at White Earth as resources decreased, causing poor nutrition and declining health. As a consequence, Agent John R. Howard predicted that "there will be an increasing number of destitute Indians . . . from now on for several years."[22]

Agent Howard had augured correctly. The 1909 Linnen and Moorehead report forced national attention to diseases that ravaged the White Earth population. Pulmonary infections were a plague, with tuberculosis, "the coughing sickness," the primary killer. Thousands suffered from trachoma, or "sore eyes," which caused blindness in its advanced stages. Responding to the emergency, federal officials converted the boarding schools to hospitals and sanatoriums to house the diseased. Doctors ordered a special diet to bolster the strength of children in eastern schools who had grown weak from hunger and infection. In an effort to find something positive to say, Inspector F. D. Cooke commented in October of 1910 that the general health of the population had improved "by the natural process by which the diseased ones are eliminated."

White Earth gained national notoriety for its abysmal disease conditions. Between 1910 and 1920, the Indian Office redoubled its efforts to stem communicable diseases. Administrators increased the number of hospitals, built barracks to house diseased adults, and constructed specialized sanatoriums to treat severe cases. Inspectors conducted house-to-house examinations of Indians to gauge the extent of sickness more accurately and determine what effect home life had on Indians' health. Especially in the eastern forests and cut-over areas, they found deplorable conditions, uprooted people, and congested living arrangements, especially in winter. Communicable diseases thrived under such conditions. In one home the diseased inhabitants just sat and stared. Inspector Warren K. Moorehead pointed out, "We cannot expect the Indians to be healthy if they continue to live as they do." Land loss and environmental degradation had sapped the very life-blood of the people.

Health inspectors were convinced that poor sanitation and ignorance of proper nutrition and methods to combat disease could only be remedied through educational measures. Physicians began a series of evening lectures to acquaint Indians with the nature of the diseases that afflicted them, how to treat them, and how to stop their spread. Field matrons began regular rounds in which they instructed Indian women on hygiene, nutrition, child care, and housekeeping. Health officials embarked on a "Save the Babies" campaign in response to the alarmingly high infant mortality rate. By 1920, their efforts had met with some success, but conditions that spawned diseases worsened, and poor health continued to plague Indians at White Earth.[23]

The extent of alcohol abuse is difficult to gauge. Contemporary comments create the impression that most of the proceeds from land and timber sales passed through the neck of a whiskey bottle. However, consumption of alcohol was a standard morality charge, just as were "fornication" and dipping into the tribal funds. No one was immune. Factional battles and dissatisfaction with Indian Office personnel elicited charge after charge of drunkenness or illegal trafficking in alcohol. This atmosphere and its impact on documentation complicates efforts to view alcohol consumption in its historical context.

To come to grips with this important yet elusive historical issue, scholars must attempt to historicize alcohol consumption to determine the conditions that contributed to chronic abuse. In this vein, anthropologist Jack O. Waddell analyzes one fur trader's journal that recorded the amount of alcohol distributed to specific numbers of Indians. His analysis makes clear that fur trading posts were social centers where otherwise sober and productive Indians expected to drink. Given the demands of hunting, he concludes that they could not possibly have simultaneously been perennial drunkards and successful hunters. Insights from his work are instructive for historical analyses of alcohol consumption in general. Scholars need to be attuned to differences in amounts of alcohol consumed, by whom, and how frequently. They must consider whether charges of alcohol consumption were morality charges, stereotyped racial epithets, or accurate reflections of social conditions. Dispossession and economic and spiritual depression have certainly been shown to contribute to chronic alcoholism, as the work of Anthony F. C. Wallace for the Iroquois, R. David Edmunds for the Shawnee, and Richard White for the Choctaw amply demonstrate. But native groups were not incapable of regulating their experience with alcohol, as White's discussion of the Pawnee shows. Unfortunately, available documentary evidence is often inadequate to address this issue in a refined fashion.

Conditions at White Earth between 1910 and 1920 were certainly ripe for an increase in chronic alcoholism. By the twentieth century, the Anishinaabeg had had long-standing experience with alcohol. Their leaders had insisted on specific treaty provisions to curtail its distribution in Indian country. In the early years at White Earth, Episcopalian Anishinaabe leaders had urged their associates to sign official oaths "to abstain from fire-water." Antialcohol rhetoric ran high, but so too did consumption. Law enforcement officials and Indian leaders were sure that traders supplied it to "blind piggers," who sold it on the sly. Most complaints about Indian drunkenness centered on larger towns where saloons lured Indians to drink. During Prohibition, observers commented that women store owners served as fronts for the illegal distribution of liquor. Alcoholism was likely on the rise as rising landlessness and decreasing opportunities restricted options available to young adults, who composed the "wild" element witnessed in towns. But historians may never be able to gauge alcohol consumption with precision.[24]

Alienation of land and resources eliminated the Indian-owned land base necessary to their autonomy and future development. By 1915, only 300 Indians were farming, and the acreage cultivated had fallen from a high of 9,125 in 1984 to a mere 2,400. Agriculture no longer seemed to be a worthwhile option for most. Indian Office Inspector H. S. Taylor recommended abandoning the White Earth experiment because it was "impossible to have a constructive policy upon this reservation. . . . The land is gone."[25]

Demographic processes alone ensured that a progressively smaller proportion of Indians would be able to farm. A rising Indian population (see Figure 7) coupled with a steadily shrinking land base accompanied the demise of Indian farming at White Earth. Equally important was the influx of Euroamericans to White Earth's western townships where agricultural promise beckoned. Land companies and speculators who bought Indian allotments at ridiculously low prices further profited from a state campaign to attract northern European immigrants to the Red River

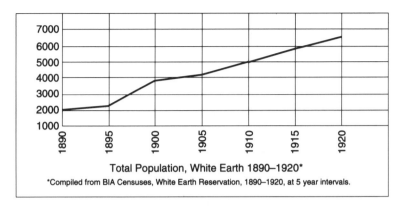

Figure 7. Total population of White Earth, 1890–1920. Compiled from Bureau of Indian Affairs censuses, White Earth Reservation, 1890–1920, at five-year intervals.

Valley. If agriculture had once been a viable economic option for market-oriented Indians, it became increasingly difficult for them to sustain their endeavors or for new farmers to break in. A few individual families managed to retain their holdings, but this alternative remained beyond the reach of most Indians.[26]

Those who remained on the reservation could meet only part of their subsistence needs from seasonal gathering. Greater numbers of people turned to some type of market involvement, relying more on agricultural wage labor and lumber work as long as they were available. As the boom period for the extractive lumber industry passed, Indian loggers had to venture farther from home to find work. For others, increased dependence on Anishinaabe tribal gratuities or the U.S. government resulted as the number of people receiving rations and housed in the Indigents' Home steadily increased.[27]

As available resources and economic opportunities constricted, White Earth residents increasingly opted to leave the reservation to make their ways in nearby towns and cities. In 1915, Inspector Taylor bemoaned the failure of the White Earth experiment, noting, "Its people . . . are now scattered to the four winds with no interest in it." White Earth enrollees received their annuity checks "in hundreds of post offices from Canada to the Gulf of Mexico and from the Pacific to the Atlantic." Rather than a gradual process where population outstripped resources, this change was an abrupt one in which loss of resources made it increasingly difficult for people to adapt and remain on the reservation.[28]

By 1916, Inspector W. H. Gibbs actually celebrated the process of dispossession that had unfolded at White Earth. To him, the impoverishment of the Anishinaabeg was but an unfortunate by-product of "the metamorphosis of an Indian reservation into a civilized, cultivated country." "Individual cases of hardship, suffering and wrong" were simply concomitants of the fulfillment of a "higher human destiny."[29] Similar experiences at reservations across the country would be interpreted in the same way.

But Indian people did not see it this way. Many folks, like Josephine Warren Robinson, had not mastered the detailed labyrinth of congressional legislation and investigations pertaining to White Earth. In their understandings, individuals symbolized the larger processes that had changed their lifeways, and chronology and "facts" were confused. This is the story Josephine Warren Robinson told:

> This old chief [Hole-in-the-Day] didn't think it's right that the Indians should sell the allotment. Because he has already seen how much the Indians have lost to the white people coming into our country. And he was afraid that there wouldn't be any hunting rights for the Indians if they ever opened up the reservation, which he was right. And fishing rights maybe, all that he had, he was a pretty smart man. . . .
> So that's where all the trouble began. They wanted to get rid of him. . . . After this old chief was killed, well then the reservation was wide open. They were allowed to sell their property. And there was a lot of rich, rich Indians. Especially these mixed bloods they called half-breeds, these Fairbanks and Beaulieus. And boy, they did a lot of land buying themselves. They turn around and sell their property and turn around and buy some poor Indian's property for maybe half or one-third of what they got for theirs. And they turn around and sell that and that's how they made money. . . . After all the land . . . was sold on the reservation, . . . that's when they begin to leave.[30]

The Anishinaabeg could agree with this folk rendition of White Earth's history more than the version offered by Inspector Gibbs.

Conclusion

The rhetoric of assimilation and allotment policies emphasized independent, small-scale market agriculture as the salvation of Indian people
nationwide. The policies failed to achieve this goal. Government policy
also encouraged Indians to adopt American cultural patterns. Some inclined in that direction on their own; others used the means supplied in
ways that policymakers had not intended. The Anishinaabeg adapted to
changing circumstances more through their own efforts than through
congressional largess or coercion. The expansion of market capitalism
was a more powerful agent of change than U.S. assimilation policy.

Minnesota congressmen and business interests did succeed in incor-
porating White Earth's material resources into the U.S. economy, despite
their mistakes in phrasing legislation. In the process, they also made it
impossible for the majority of White Earth Indians to remain a land-
based people. The policies put in place brought about dispossession
of both ethnic groups, whether individuals understood the workings of
the market or not. The U.S. policymakers' chief accomplishment was
Anishinaabe "assimilation"—but only as a marginalized group since the
Anishinaabeg, and many other native peoples, found themselves at the
bottom of the American social and economic hierarchy, where hundreds
of thousands of southern freed slaves and transoceanic immigrants had
begun. Only elite entrepreneurs of mixed descent fared well. A few
profited directly from the dispossession process. Others had the knowledge and wherewithal to migrate, adapt, and eventually prosper. But
most Indians entered the mainstream of U.S. society from a landless and
impoverished position.

Before dispossession, the Anishinaabeg had been able to adapt and do
well at White Earth. In terms of world-systems theory, the reservation lay

in a "region of refuge" or "marginal-peripheral" area.¹ Its geographic isolation retarded extensive market development or Euroamerican settlement. Moreover, the streams at White Earth drain into the Red River to the west, which flows north to Hudson Bay, which meant that favorable marketing arrangements awaited better transportation links.

White Earth's ecological diversity supported multiple strategies for making a living. Anishinaabeg from north-central Minnesota were able to escape limitations of dwindling game populations and a lack of arable land. White Earth was situated in a previously uninhabited buffer zone over which Dakota and Anishinaabeg had competed for generations, creating a sort of game preserve. Although furred animals were not abundant, game animals, the most important of which was the white-tailed deer, had not been depleted. The prairies of the western reservation also provided excellent land for cultivating crops. White Earth sustained the seasonal round and made farming possible.

The expanding market economy, which offered opportunities for selling seasonal produce, wage labor, and commercial farming, also eased the adjustment immigrants faced. Métis cultural brokers mediated between conservative Anishinaabeg and agents of American society, activities characteristic of such "regions of refuge." By 1907, the White Earth Anishinaabeg were well on their way toward establishing an economic and social structure that would allow residents with different ways of life to remain on the reservation and prosper.

For a time, two ethnic groups at White Earth coexisted in relative harmony. But when U.S. policymakers intensified their emphasis on privatizing and alienating reservation resources, which allowed those with acquisitive values to gain full sway at the expense of their unsuspecting neighbors, things changed. Nothing offended conservative Anishinaabeg more than inequitable accumulation by a few of what had once been collective resources, and they contested political domination by those who had profited unfairly. But the political faction espousing capitalistic values gained ascendancy, which undermined the entire social and economic fabric of the reservation.

Dispossession destroyed the White Earth experiment, and a larger view of economic conditions may help explain why dispossession occurred when it did. The rising price of wheat in the late nineteenth and early twentieth centuries served as the initial incentive to develop rich agricultural lands in the Red River Valley. Completion of the Minne-apolis, St. Paul, and Sault Ste. Marie Railroad through the western town-ships at White Earth linked the area to Twin Cities markets, reduced transportation costs, and was a magnet for Euroamerican settlement. Lumbermen stood ready at White Earth's eastern borders, having worked their way through forests from the east. White Earth's "undeveloped" resources looked attractive to these local business interests. Indeed, the protective restrictions of the Nelson Act were designed to combat pre-cisely this type of threat.

These conditions arose just as support for the agrarian ideal on reser-vations was waning. Blaming the failure of programmatic directives to assimilate Indians on the Indians themselves and their inherent "back-wardness," policymakers lost interest in social engineering, lifted re-strictions from "competent" Indians, and tolerated an accelerated aliena-tion of allotted reservation lands. At White Earth, a powerful clique of state politicians and local business interests accomplished dispossession even more effectively by enabling "mixed-bloods" to sell their land and by dispensing with any philanthropic justification. Allotment of the land base had occurred first on reservations where resources were most valuable.[2] Removal of protective restrictions probably followed a similar pattern. In the case of White Earth, events did not follow the national pattern—they helped to set it.

If left to their own devices to live out their lives under the Nelson Act, the White Earth Anishinaabeg might have continued to adapt. Of course, protective restrictions would have been lifted when the twenty-five year trust period ended, but that would have occurred in the early 1930s when a widespread depressed rural economy might have produced a different outcome. Instead, Euroamerican farmers replaced Indian landowners and White Earth timber went to fuel urban development in Chicago, Minneapolis, and cities to the west. Through resource extraction, White Earth passed from being a "region of refuge" to a "dependent" or "full-blown periphery."[3] Its people were marginalized. Most scattered, hoping to find niches elsewhere as day-laborers. Despite productive attempts by members of both ethnic groups to adapt to the expanding market econ-omy, the close partnership between political and corporate interests in Minnesota doomed their efforts to failure.

The particular constellation of circumstances reviewed here explains the timing of dispossession for the White Earth Anishinaabeg. Their experiences, however, parallel those of other dispossessed Indian groups. In most cases, population growth elsewhere generated demands for resources that had little to do with the needs or desires of indigenous people. The related processes of incorporation of resources and marginalization of people account for similarities in the White Earth experience, dispossession of eastern coastal tribes in the late seventeenth century, removal of southeastern tribes in the 1830s, and the exploitation of Indian coal, gas, and uranium after World War II. Potential illustrations are legion. Echoing those who came before her, Lucy Thompson, born at White Earth in 1906, reflected on changes that had occurred during her lifetime, "Now the white people claim everything that the Indians used to use in the olden days. . . . If they could do it, they'd take everything. . . . The only thing they'd leave us is our appetites."[4]

Epilogue

"White Earth Is Not for Sale"

Today only 7 percent of White Earth's land base remains under Indian control. Federal, state, and county governments and private landowners share title to the remaining 93 percent. The White Earth rolls carry the names of more than 11,000 official members of the White Earth Band, but only about 4,000 people actually live there. Many reside in neighboring towns, the Twin Cities, Duluth, and all over the country. Some return to the reservation periodically to renew ties of family, community, and culture that have changed but are not forgotten.

All is not well upon the White Earth Reservation. Bitter conflict over contested land titles, a legacy of dispossession, has produced "open sores of community disruption."[1] Heirs of allottees whose private property was illegally conveyed have faced off against well-organized Euroamerican landowners whose titles are "clouded." Due to their varying interests, Indians have not reached consensus among themselves. Had litigators handled these cases properly in the first place, this strife might have been avoided. Blame for this ugly situation lays squarely with the federal government for failing to carry out its trust responsibilities.

On 24 March 1986, congressional leaders representing northwestern Minnesota succeeded in passing legislation through Congress to resolve outstanding land claims on the reservation. They achieved this in a manner reminiscent of a not-so-bygone era. Always a very controversial bill, the White Earth Land Settlement Act (WELSA) initially prompted two full days of congressional debate. When it failed to pass, Representative Arlan Stangeland introduced it to a handful of congressmen under a suspension of the rules intended to apply only to "non-controversial" measures (pension benefits, military awards, and the like). This bill was hardly "non-controversial," yet it was attached to a wild rice license requirement bill and slipped through the Minnesota House of Representatives four days later. The plan offered only 10,000 acres of state-owned land (about 10 percent of all White Earth lands confiscated by the state) and an $11 million cash settlement (to be paid to the Reservation Business Committee, *not* to rightful heirs) to clear titles clouded by fraud over the past eighty years.[2]

Beginning in 1978, tribal researchers working under the federally funded "2415 Land Claims Project" had discovered that the titles of more than 200,000 acres of reservation land were questionable, and this was after having investigated only one-third of the land parcels. The success of the project's researchers made Reagan-era politicians uncomfortable. Interior Secretary James Watt canceled the project in 1982 short of its allotted time. At that point, the Minnesota Chippewa Tribe had submitted 1,198 White Earth claims and 25 percent of the case files had yet to be reviewed. Given the amassed evidence, concessions contained in the White Earth Land Settlement Act seemed paltry compensation to those who believed that White Earth heirs were legally entitled to a much larger acreage. The act required all claims to be filed within six months, when reservation boundaries would be dissolved and tribal control restricted to the remaining checkerboarded acreage. The White Earth Land Settlement Act had far-reaching implications for individual Indian property rights and for tribal jurisdiction and sovereignty.

The effort by state politicians to force a bill through congress that virtually ignored individual Indian property rights came only five years after White Earth heirs had won a major Minnesota Supreme Court decision. In 1977, in the *State vs. Zay Zah* decision, the court ruled that removal of the U.S. government's trust responsibility under the 1889 Nelson Act should not have occurred unless the allottee *applied* for such removal. This contemporary interpretation of the 1906 Clapp Rider runs expressly counter to the assumption by U.S. officials at the time that all restrictions had been removed from mixed-bloods' allotted resources and it opened a Pandora's box for White Earth heirs. George Aubid's victory in defending his grandfather's allotment against illegal tax forfeiture proceedings in *Zay Zah* gave hope to many landless urban Indians that there was yet a chance to save their reservation.[3] Ironically, land fraud claims generated during the early twentieth century have, in a sense, protected parcels of contested land from absolute alienation. Many White Earth enrollees realize that this is their last chance to reclaim what is rightfully theirs.

But the *Zay Zah* decision also made Euroamerican landowners at White Earth tremble. When they began to receive notices that their land titles were "clouded," they organized. The United Township Association utilized extensive governmental connections at the county, state, and federal levels. Not coincidentally, these interests were also implicated in past transgressions involving Indian land titles; it was a natural alliance. In addition, they allied with anti-Indian organizations across the nation that had galvanized to abrogate treaty rights. The United Township Association borrowed from them the argument that treaty rights were unfair benefits granted to a privileged few, and claimed the moral high ground as innocent, exploited victims. In their careful construction of a public image, it mattered little that the White Earth cases involved *individual property* rights—*not* treaty rights. Sadly, simmering anti-Indian sentiment in towns on and adjacent to the White Earth Reservation boiled over into blatant racism, alleviated only by members of several liberal churches who begged for understanding as they watched their communities torn asunder.[4]

A grass-roots group of heirs of allottees whose land had been alienated came together in 1984, calling themselves "Anishinabe Akeeng" (The People's Land), and committed themselves to work to restore land titles. Many had attended college, some had participated in the 2415 Land Claims Project, and others had had radicalizing experiences with the American Indian Movement and the International Indian Treaty Council that gave them a broader perspective. They understand the importance of a land base to economic development and political and cultural autonomy, and are determined to recover as much fraudulently conveyed land as possible. Given the forces that inveigh against guaranteeing Indian property owners due process under the Fifth Amendment to the Constitution, their crusade has taken on a tone of urgency. They know that determination of White Earth land fraud cases will decide not only the fate of the reservation, but will set a precedent for similar land fraud cases nationwide.[5]

Their task is complicated by the very nature of these claims. They involve individual property rights—not claims to which all reservation enrollees are party. Therefore, tribal attorneys and Indian Legal Services staff cannot help them. Indeed, the Reservation Business Committee has powerful reasons not to support them and to accept the compromise bill which offers substantial rewards for them to do so. Also, Anishinabe Akeeng is organizationally handicapped in comparison to the United Township Association. They have had to cultivate a network of expertise from within and they have no ready political allies. White Earth's history is fraught with community discord and some who are descendents of exploitative individuals would prefer that the painful past not be dredged up. All of these factors prevent White Earth Indians from achieving a united perspective.

Despite these drawbacks, Anishinabe Akeeng does have the force of morality and constitutional legality on its side. With these, they have been able to galvanize a substantial base of support. When the White Earth Reservation Business Committee succumbed to pecuniary considerations and endorsed WELSA, Anishinabe Akeeng's supporters turned out in a show of force. Between 700 to 1,000 gathered to ask why the reservation leadership had compromised White Earth's future. Children from the "Heart of the Earth Survival School, who had staged a 'Run for the Land' earlier in the day, were a poignant symbol of the legacy that would be denied to future generations." Since a major part of their task involves educating and organizing other White Earth heirs, Anishinabe Akeeng leaders were heartened. Not only do they help impoverished Indians attend meetings on the reservation, but they have extended their organizing to urban areas where White Earth heirs now live. They raise funds, work with sympathetic local church groups, and teach university classes about White Earth's history. Their lobbying activities have taken them from Minnesota Chippewa tribal headquarters at Cass Lake, to St. Paul, the state capital, to Washington, D.C. When verbal appeals failed to produce results, they resorted to civil disobedience, risking arrest to occupy tribal offices and demonstrate at the state capitol building or at legislators' offices. Anishinabe Akeeng affiliate Winona La Duke has even established the White Earth Land Recovery Project with the goal of soliciting funds to buy back reservation land; several purchases have

Police arrest an Anishinaabe woman participating in a sit-in demonstration protesting the 1986 White Earth Land Settlement Act outside Senator Rudy Boschwitz's office in St. Paul. *Photo courtesy of Randy Croce.*

already been made. Most important, Anishinabe Akeeng members have formulated court cases to test the constitutionality of the White Earth Land Settlement Act. Taken together, these test cases, including *Little Wolf vs. Hodel* and *Manypenny vs. U.S.*, have made little headway, but not because they do not have merit. Attorneys for Anishinabe Akeeng surmise that "it was simply never envisioned that as citizens, Indians too, are entitled to due process under the law"; "the emphasis has always been on their 'Indianness' rather than on their individual property rights as citizens."[6] Indeed, it seemed to many that history was repeating itself.

Along with a number of others, Marvin Manypenny has often been a spokesperson on behalf of Anishinabe Akeeng. In 1985, Marv and Karen Manypenny and their family moved back to White Earth from the predominately Indian Franklin Avenue neighborhood in Minneapolis to work full time trying to overthrow the White Earth Land Settlement Act and reclaim the reservation land base. Many others cooperate to accomplish these objectives and most have stories to tell about how they or their friends or relatives lost land through questionable transactions. Anishinabe Akeeng leaders live the struggle. In this sense, Marv's story is only one of many, and yet it illustrates the legal and moral morass into which these claims have fallen.

Marv's grandfather, George Manypenny or Wahbonaquod (no relation to Wabonaquod, the Mississippi band *ogimaa*), was a Mississippi band member listed on the 1890 Bureau of Indian Affairs census as a six-year-old boy with his mother Jane. Various censuses capture his life cycle as he grew into adulthood, married, and raised his own family. Inspectors Linnen and Moorehead listed George as a full-blood on their 1909 roll. As such, George would have been ineligible to authorize the sale of his allotment. Any transaction that had occurred would have been illegal. Inspector Hinton also listed George as a full-blood in 1910. These inspectors based their judgments on testimony of Indian elders and relatives. But on the 1920 Blood Roll, George Manypenny appeared as a mixed-blood. Racist methods used by the Roll Commission had legitimated the transfer of George Manypenny's land with a quick scratch of his chest.

Manypenny has questions about the determination of his grandfather's blood status, and yet the transaction was completely legal in the eyes of the law. George Manypenny had been declared a "mixed-blood" and was free to convey his property. In the course of pursuing what he believes to be a legitimate claim, Marv Manypenny must engage in the same kind of racist reasoning used by the roll commissioners. He must argue that his grandfather was a "full-blood."[7]

Furthermore, records of land transfers were not kept up. Probate work will take years to complete. Ironically, the U.S. government recorded the number of allotments issued, but not the amount of allotted land retained by Indians, leaving policymakers no way to evaluate whether their programs were effective. This inattention to detail has created a quagmire of paperwork that has hamstrung determination of these cases.

As Marv Manypenny continues to work with other members of Anishinabe Akeeng to restore White Earth's land base, he sees parallels with the past. Again, local Euroamericans are reluctant to acknowledge the legitimacy of Indians' claims; the ramifications are too far-reaching for them to consider. Settlers in the area, many of them descended from recent European immigrants, were themselves victims of land speculators who bought Indian land at ridiculously low prices and made a killing selling it to immigrants. Again, local representatives in Congress and state politicians concern themselves with their more numerous Euroamerican constituents. When asked in 1985 if state policymakers had ever considered a plan that would create a fund to be used gradually to buy out Euroamerican owners and return lands to Indians, Minnesota Attorney General Hubert "Skip" Humphrey III simply said "No."[8]

Many contemporary Indians in Minnesota blame poverty, disease, domestic violence, and chemical dependency ultimately on the processes of dispossession that snowballed in the late nineteenth and twentieth centuries. The stereotype of the irresolute, drunken Indian grew out of these conditions. Contemporary stereotypes and misunderstandings conceal historical processes that have created current conditions. Marv Manypenny and others recognize this as they urge all of us to remember that "the history is everything."[9]

Notes

Abbreviations

BIA	Bureau of Indian Affairs
CCF	Consolidated Central Files
CIA	Commissioner of Indian Affairs
CGLO	Commissioner of the General Land Office
E	Entry
GLO	General Land Office
KCFRA	Kansas City Federal Regional Archives
LR	Letters Received
MCTRHP	Minnesota Chippewa Tribe Reservation History Project
MHS	Minnesota Historical Society
MHSA	Minnesota Historical Society Archives
NARS	National Archives and Records Service
OIA	Office of Indian Affairs
RCGLO	Annual Report of the Commissioner of the General Land Office
RCIA	Annual Report of the Commissioner of Indian Affairs
RG	Record Group
RSI	Annual Report of the Secretary of the Interior
WEA	White Earth Agency
WEOHP	White Earth Oral History Project

Introduction

1. Quotation from "Chippewa Indians in Minnesota," House Executive Documents 2747, no. 247, 51 Congress, 1 Session, (1890): 109 (hereafter "Report of the U.S. Chippewa Commission"). John Nichols and Earl Nyholm translate *anishinaabe/g* as "Indian person," in *Ojibwewi-Ikidowinan: An Ojibwe Word Resource Book* (St. Paul: Minnesota Archaeological Society, 1979), 11. Reverend R. R. Bishop Baraga translates *Anishinabe* as "Man, (human being, man, woman or child); . . . also, Indian," in *A Dictionary of the Otchipwe Language, Explained in English*, 2 parts (Minneapolis: Ross & Haines, 1966),

part 2, 38. "Anishinaabe" is used here in preference to the terms "Chippewa" or "Ojibwe." For the synonyms of *ojibwa*, see E. S. Rogers, "Southeastern Ojibwa," in Bruce Trigger, ed., *Handbook of North American Indians: Northeast* (Washington, D.C.: U.S. Government Printing Office, 1978), 768–69. J. N. B. Hewitt in "Ethnological Researches among the Iroquois and Chippewa," *Explorations and Field-Work of the Smithsonian Institution in 1925*, Smithsonian Miscellaneous Collections 78: 1 (1926): 116, conjectured that the name *Ojibwa* derived from their word *ojibweg*, meaning those who make pictographs. See also Christopher Vecsey, *Traditional Ojibwa Religion and Its Historical Changes* (Philadelphia: American Philosophical Society, 1983), 85. Baraga translates *Ojibiwa* as "I write or mark on some object" (p. 319). Nichols and Nyholm translate "he writes" as *ozhibii'ige* (p. 243).

2. Loring Benson Priest, *Uncle Sam's Stepchildren: The Reformation of U.S. Indian Policy, 1865–1887* (New Brunswick, N.J.: Rutgers University Press, 1942); Robert A. Trennert, Jr., *Alternative to Extinction: Federal Indian Policy and the Beginnings of the Reservation System, 1846–1851* (Philadelphia: Temple University Press, 1975); Frederick E. Hoxie, *A Final Promise: The Campaign to Assimilate the Indians, 1880–1920* (Lincoln: University of Nebraska Press, 1984); D. S. Otis, *The Dawes Act and the Allotment of Indian Lands*, ed. Francis Paul Prucha (Norman: University of Oklahoma Press, 1973); Francis Paul Prucha, *American Indian Policy in Crisis: Christian Reformers and the Indian, 1865–1900* (Norman: University of Oklahoma Press, 1976); Henry E. Fritz, *The Movement for Indian Assimilation, 1860–1890* (Philadelphia: University of Pennsylvania Press, 1963); Robert Mardock, *The Reformers and the American Indian* (Columbia: University of Missouri Press, 1971); Leonard Carlson, *Indians, Bureaucrats, and Land: The Dawes Act and the Decline of Indian Farming* (Westport, Conn.: Greenwood Press, 1981); H. Craig Miner, *The Corporation and the Indian: Tribal Sovereignty and Industrial Civilization in Indian Territory, 1865–1907* (Columbia: University of Missouri Press, 1976); Janet A. McDonnell, "Competency Commissions and Indian Land Policy, 1913–1920," *South Dakota History* 11 (1980): 21–34; Janet A. McDonnell, "The Disintegration of the Indian Estate: Indian Land Policy, 1913–1929," Ph.D. Dissertation, Marquette University, 1980; Janet A. McDonnell, *The Dispossession of the American Indian, 1887–1934* (Bloomington: Indiana University Press, 1991). For discussions of the U.S. economy at this time, see Martin J. Sklar, *The Corporate Reconstruction of American Capitalism, 1890–1916* (Cambridge: Harvard University Press, 1971); Stephen Skowronek, *Building a New American State: The Expansion of National Administrative Capacities, 1877–1920* (Cambridge: Harvard University Press, 1982).

3. Classic treatments using world-systems theory are Immanuel Wallerstein, *The Modern World System: Capitalist Agriculture and the Origins of Euro-*

pean World-Economy in the Sixteenth Century (New York: Academic Press, 1974); Immanuel Wallerstein, *The Capitalist World Economy* (Cambridge: Cambridge University Press, 1979); Christopher Chase-Dunn, "Core-Periphery Relations: The Effects of Core Competition," in B. H. Kaplan, ed., *Social Change in the Capitalist World Economy* (Beverly Hills: Sage, 1978), 159–75; Christopher Chase-Dunn, "The Development of Core Capitalism in the Antebellum United States: Tariff Politics and Class Struggle in an Upwardly Mobile Semiperiphery," in A. Bergesen, ed., *Studies of the Modern World System* (New York: Academic Press, 1980), 189–230; Ronald H. Chilcote and D. L. Johnson, *Theories of Development: Modes of Production or Dependency?* (Beverly Hills: Sage, 1983); Daniel Chirot and Thomas D. Hall, "World Systems Theory," *Annual Review of Sociology* 8 (1982): 81–106; Andre Gunder Frank, *Capitalism and Underdevelopment in Latin America: Historical Studies of Chile and Brazil*, rev. ed. (New York: Monthly Review, 1969); Andre Gunder Frank, *Latin America: Underdevelopment or Revolution* (New York: Monthly Review, 1969); Joseph G. Jorgensen, "Indians and the Metropolis," in Jack O. Waddell and O. Michael Watson, eds., *The American Indian in Urban Society* (Boston: Little, Brown and Co., 1971), 67–113; Joseph G. Jorgensen, "A Century of Political and Economic Effects on American Indian Society, 1880–1980," *Journal of Ethnic Studies* 6 (1978): 1–82.

4. Among those world-systems theorists who devote greater attention to indigenous peoples are Thomas D. Hall, *Social Change in the Southwest, 1350–1880* (Lawrence: University of Kansas Press, 1988); Thomas D. Hall, "Patterns of Native American Incorporation into State Societies," in C. Matthew Snipp, ed., *Public Policy Impacts on American Indian Economic Development* (Albuquerque: Native American Studies, University of New Mexico, 1988), 23–38; Thomas D. Hall, "Incorporation in the World System: Toward a Critique," *American Sociological Review* 51 (1986): 390–402; Thomas D. Hall, "Change and Assimilation: Native Americans under Spain and the United States," *Free Inquiry* 13 (1985): 173–77; Thomas D. Hall, "Is Historical Sociology of Peripheral Regions Peripheral?" *California Sociologist* 8 (1985): 281–304; Thomas D. Hall, "Peripheries, Regions of Refuge, and Nonstate Societies: Toward a Theory of Reactive Social Change," *Social Science Quarterly* 64 (1983): 582–97; C. Matthew Snipp, "The Changing Political and Economic Status of American Indians: From Captive Nations to Internal Colonies," *American Journal of Economics and Sociology* 45 (1986): 145–57; C. Matthew Snipp, "Old and New Views of Economic Development in Indian Country," in *Overcoming Economic Dependency,* Occasional Paper Series, no. 9 (Chicago: D'Arcy McNickle Center for the History of the American Indian, Newberry Library, 1988); Gary C. Anders, "The Internal Colonization of Cherokee Native Americans," *Development and Change* 10 (1977): 41–55; Gary C. Anders, "Theories of Underdevelopment and the American

Indian," *Journal of Economic Issues* 39 (1985): 681–702; Gary C. Anders, "The Reduction of a Self-Sufficient People to Poverty and Welfare Dependence: An Analysis of the Causes of Cherokee Indian Underdevelopment," *American Journal of Economics and Sociology* 40 (1981): 225–38; Cardell K. Jacobsen, "Internal Colonialism and Native Americans: Indian Labor in the U.S. from 1871 to World War II," *Social Science Quarterly* 65 (1984): 158–71.

5. Hall, "Patterns of Native American Incorporation"; Hall, *Social Change*, chaps. 1 and 2.

6. Melissa L. Meyer, "Signatures and Thumbprints: Ethnicity among the White Earth Anishinaabeg, 1889–1920," *Social Science History* 14 (1990): 305–45; Melissa L. Meyer, "The Red Lake Ojibwe," in H. E. Wright, Jr., Barbara A. Coffin, and Norman E. Aaseng, eds., *The Patterned Peatlands of Minnesota* (Minneapolis, Minn.: University of Minnesota Press, 1991) 251–61; Fred Eggan, *Social Organization of the Western Pueblos* (Chicago: University of Chicago Press, 1950); Elsie Clews Parsons, *Pueblo Indian Religion* (Chicago: University of Chicago Press, 1939); Edward Dozier, *The Pueblo Indians of North America* (New York: Holt, Rinehart, and Winston, 1970); Peter Whiteley, *Deliberate Acts: Changing Hopi Culture through the Oraibi Split* (Tucson: University of Arizona Press, 1988).

7. Melissa L. Meyer, "'We Can Not Get a Living as We Used To': Dispossession and the White Earth Anishinaabeg, 1889–1920," *American Historical Review* 96 (1991): 368–94; Albert Hurtado, *Indian Survival on the California Frontier* (New Haven: Yale University Press, 1989); Richard White, *The Roots of Dependency: Subsistence, Environment, and Social Change among the Choctaw, Pawnee, and Navajo* (Lincoln: University of Nebraska Press, 1984); Edward H. Spicer, *Cycles of Conquest: The Impact of Spain, Mexico, and the United States on the Indians of the Southwest, 1533–1960* (Tucson: University of Arizona Press, 1962).

8. Robert F. Berkhofer, Jr., "Native Americans," in John Higham, ed., *Ethnic Leadership in America* (Baltimore: Johns Hopkins University Press, 1978), 128.

9. See Meyer, "Signatures and Thumbprints." Exceptions are Loretta Fowler, *Shared Symbols, Contested Meanings: Gros Ventre Culture and History, 1778–1984* (Ithaca, N.Y.: Cornell University Press, 1987); Loretta Fowler, *Arapaho Politics, 1851–1978: Symbols in Crises of Authority* (Lincoln: University of Nebraska Press, 1982); Loretta Fowler, "Political Middlemen and the Headman Tradition among the Twentieth-Century Gros Ventres of Fort Belknap Reservation," *Journal of the West* 23 (1984): 54–63; Loretta Fowler, "Local-Level Politics and the Struggle for Self-Government," in *Struggle for Political Autonomy*, Occasional Papers in Curriculum, no. 11 (Chicago: D'Arcy McNickle Center for the History of the American Indian, Newberry Library, 1989); Rebecca Kugel, "Factional Alignment among the Minnesota

Ojibwe, 1850–1880," *American Indian Culture and Research Journal* 9 (1985): 23–47; David Rich Lewis, "Reservation Leadership and the Progressive-Traditional Dichotomy: William Wash and the Northern Utes, 1865–1928," *Ethnohistory* 38 (1991): 124–48; James A. Clifton, ed., *Being and Becoming Indian: Biographical Studies of North American Frontiers* (Chicago: Dorsey Press, 1989).

Chapter 1. Anishinaabe Migrations and White Earth Communities

1. When possible, all Anishinaabe words other than proper names have been spelled in accordance with the Nichols and Nyholm orthography. *Miigis* (*megis* in many historical sources), translates as "shell; sacred shell" in Nichols and Nyholm, eds., *Ojibwewi-Ikidowinan*, 207. See also William Whipple Warren, *History of the Ojibways Based upon Traditions and Oral Statements* (St. Paul: Minnesota Historical Society Press, 1970).

2. *Midéwiwin* translates as "Grand Medicine Lodge; Medicine Dance," in Nichols and Nyholm, eds., *Ojibwewi-Ikidowinan*, 62; See also Walter J. Hoffman, "The Midéwiwin or 'Grand Medicine Society' of the Ojibwa," *Annual Report of the Bureau of American Ethnology* 7 (1885–86): 149–306 (Washington, D.C.: U.S. Government Printing Office, 1891); Walter J. Hoffman, "Pictography and Shamanistic Rites of the Ojibwa," *American Anthropologist* 1 (1888): 209–29.

3. Harold Hickerson, *The Southwestern Chippewa: An Ethnohistorical Study,* American Anthropological Association, Memoir 92 (Menasha, Wisc.: American Anthropological Association, 1962), 82.

4. Both quotes, ibid., 77. Harold Hickerson, *The Chippewa and Their Neighbors: A Study in Ethnohistory* (New York: Holt, Rinehart, and Winston, 1970), 47; Ruth Landes, *Ojibwa Sociology,* Columbia University Contributions to Anthropology, vol. 29 (New York: Columbia University Press, 1937); Nichols and Nyholm, eds., *Ojibwewi-Ikidowinan*, 106, 230.

5. Quotations from Fred Eggan, ed., *Social Anthropology of North American Tribes* (Chicago: University of Chicago Press, 1955), 532, and G. D. Scull, ed., *Voyages of Peter Esprit Radisson, Being an Account of His Travels and Experiences among the North American Indians, from 1652 to 1684* (New York: Peter Smith, 1943), 217, 219. See also Hickerson, *Southwestern Chippewa,* 65–86; Harold Hickerson, "The Feast of the Dead among the Seventeenth Century Algonkians of the Upper Great Lakes," *American Anthropologist* 62 (1960): 81–107; Hickerson, *The Chippewa and Their Neighbors,* 37–63; Harold Hickerson, "The Genesis of Bilaterality among Two Divisions of Chippewa," *American Anthropologist* 68 (1966): 1–26; A. Irving Hallowell, "Cross-Cousin Marriage in the Lake Winnipeg Area," *Publications of the Philadelphia Anthropological Society* 1 (1937): 95–110; Harold Hickerson,

"Some Implications of the Theory of Particularity or 'Atomism' of Northern Algonquians," *Current Anthropology* 8 (1967): 313–43; Bernard James, "Some Critical Observations Concerning Analyses of Chippewa 'Atomism' and Chippewa Personality," *American Anthropologist* 56 (1954): 283–86.

6. Lyle M. Stone and Donald Chaput, "History of the Upper Great Lakes Area," in Bruce G. Trigger, ed., *Handbook of North American Indians: Northeast* (Washington, D.C.: Smithsonian Institution, U.S. Government Printing Office, 1978), 602–9; Bruce G. Trigger, *The Children of Aataentsic: A History of the Huron People to 1669*, 2 vols. (Montreal: McGill-Queen's University Press, 1976); Bruce G. Trigger, "The Destruction of Huronia: A Study in Economic and Cultural Change, 1609–1650," *Transactions of the Royal Canadian Institute* 33 (1960): 14–45; Elisabeth Tooker, "An Ethnography of the Huron Indians, 1615–1649," *Bureau of American Ethnology Bulletin* 190 (Washington, D.C.: U.S. Government Printing Office, 1964); George Hunt, *The Wars of the Iroquois: A Study in Intertribal Trade Relations* (Madison: University of Wisconsin Press, 1940); William N. Fenton, "The Iroquois in History," in Eleanor B. Leacock and Nancy O. Lurie, eds., *North American Indians in Historical Perspective* (New York: Random House, 1971); Francis Jennings, *The Ambiguous Iroquois Empire: The Covenant Chain Confederation of Indian Tribes with English Colonies* (New York: W. W. Norton, 1984); James A. Clifton, *The Prairie People: Continuity and Change in Potawatomi Indian Culture, 1665–1965* (Lawrence: Regents Press of Kansas, 1977); Richard White, *The Middle Ground: Indians, Empires, and Republics in the Great Lakes Region, 1650–1815* (Cambridge: Cambridge University Press, 1991).

7. Foregoing quotations from Hickerson, *Southwestern Chippewa*, 66, 82; see also 65–69 and 85; and Stone and Chaput, "History of the Upper Great Lakes," 603.

8. Emma H. Blair, trans. and ed., *The Indian Tribes of the Upper Mississippi Valley and the Region of the Great Lakes as Described by Nicolas Perrot, French Commandant in the Northwest; Bacqueville de la Potheri, French Royal Commissioner to Canada; Morrell Marston, American Army Officer; and Thomas Forsyth, United States Agent at Fort Armstrong*, 2 vols. (Cleveland: Arthur H. Clark Co., 1911), 1:277; Hickerson, *Southwestern Chippewa*, 85; Warren, *History of the Ojibways*, 49.

9. Blair, *Indian Tribes*, 1:182, 358–59; 2:28, 34–35, 68, 112; Warren, *History of the Ojibways*, 96–97; Hickerson, *Southwestern Chippewa*, 66–67. Tim E. Holzkamm, "Eastern Dakota Population Movements and the European Fur Trade: One More Time," *Plains Anthropologist* 28 (1983): 225–33; White, *The Middle Ground*, 1–49.

10. La Chauvignerie in *Documents Relating to the Colonial History of the State of New York*, vol. 9 (Albany: n.p., 1853–87), 1053–58; Hickerson, *South-*

western Chippewa, 67; Warren, *History of the Ojibways,* 96–97; Blair, *Indians Tribes,* 1:182; Helen Hornbeck Tanner, "The Glaize in 1792: A Composite Indian Community," *Ethnohistory* 25 (1978): 15–39.

11. Warren, *History of the Ojibways,* 96–97; quotations from 99; see also Hickerson, *Southwestern Chippewa,* 67.

12. Hickerson, *Southwestern Chippewa,* 73–86; Hickerson, "Genesis of Bilaterality"; James G. E. Smith, "Proscription of Cross-Cousin Marriage among the Southwestern Ojibwa," *American Ethnologist* 1 (1974): 751–67; Harold Hickerson, "The Sociohistorical Significance of Two Chippewa Ceremonials," *American Anthropologist* 65 (1963): 67–85; Hickerson, *Chippewa and Their Neighbors,* 51–63.

13. Quotations from Warren, *History of the Ojibways,* 100. The origin of the Midéwiwin is a topic of debate. See Hickerson, *Chippewa and Their Neighbors,* 51–63; Hickerson, *Southwestern Chippewa,* 67; Hickerson, "Sociohistorical Significance"; Harold Hickerson, "Notes on the Post-contact Origin of the Midéwiwin," *Ethnohistory* 9 (1962): 404–23; Hoffman, "The Midéwiwin or 'Grand Medicine Society' of the Ojibwa," 143–300; W. Vernon Kinietz, *Indians of the Western Great Lakes, 1615–1760,* Occasional Contributions from the Museum of Anthropology of the University of Michigan, no. 10 (Ann Arbor: University of Michigan Press, 1940); Vecsey, *Traditional Ojibwa Religion;* Robert A. Brightman, "Toward a History of Indian Religion: Religious Changes in Native Societies," in Colin Callaway, ed., *New Directions in American Indian History* (Norman: University of Oklahoma Press, 1988), 223–49.

14. Quotation from Hickerson, *Southwestern Chippewa,* 69. See also Henry A. Innis, *The Fur Trade in Canada,* rev. ed. (Toronto: University of Toronto Press, 1956), 84–118; Stone and Chaput, "History of the Upper Great Lakes," 604.

15. For debates about "Sioux" migrations away from northeastern Minnesota, see Hickerson, *Southwestern Chippewa,* 69–70; Hickerson, *Chippewa and Their Neighbors,* 64–79; Holzkamm, "Eastern Dakota Population Movements"; Gary C. Anderson, "Early Dakota Migration and Intertribal War: A Revision," *Western Historical Quarterly* 11 (1980): 17–36; Gary Clayton Anderson, *Kinsmen of Another Kind: Dakota-White Relations in the Upper Mississippi Valley, 1650–1862* (Lincoln: University of Nebraska Press, 1984), 29–57; White, *The Middle Ground,* 142–85.

16. Alexander Henry, *Travels and Adventures in Canada and the Indian Territories between the Years 1760 and 1776* (Boston: Little, Brown and Co., 1901), 187–89; Hickerson, *Southwestern Chippewa,* 68–70.

17. Harold Hickerson, "The Virginia Deer and Intertribal Buffer Zones in the Upper Mississippi Valley," in Anthony Leeds and Andrew Vayda, eds., *Man, Culture, and Animals: The Role of Animals in Human Ecological Adjust-*

ments (Washington, D.C.: American Association for the Advancement of
Science, Publication 78, 1965); Charles Watrall, "Virginia Deer and the Buffer
Zone in the Late Prehistoric-Early Protohistoric Periods in Minnesota,"
Plains Anthropologist 13 (1968): 81–86; Anthony M. Davis, "The Prairie-
Deciduous Forest Ecotone in the Upper Middle West," *Annals of the Asso-
ciation of American Geographers* 67 (1977): 204–13; Hickerson, *Southwest-
ern Chippewa,* 12–29, 70–71; Hickerson, *Chippewa and Their Neighbors,*
64–119.

18. Warren, *History of the Ojibways,* 39–40, 242–47; Hickerson, *Southwestern
Chippewa,* 35–39; Henry R. Schoolcraft, *Discovery of the Sources of the
Mississippi, or Narrative of an Expedition through the Upper Mississippi to
Itasca Lake, the Actual Source of this River; Embracing an Exploratory Trip
through the St. Croix and Burntwood (or Broule) Rivers; in 1832* (New York:
Harper and Brothers, 1834), 128–30, 221; Henry R. Schoolcraft, *Informa-
tion, Respecting the History, Condition and Prospects of the Indian Tribes of
the United States; Collected and Prepared under the Direction of the Bu-
reau of Indian Affairs,* 6 vols. (Philadelphia: J. B. Lippincott, 1851–57), 1:468;
Michel Curot, "A Wisconsin Fur Trader's Journal, 1803–1804," *Collections
of the State Historical Society of Wisconsin,* Reuben G. Thwaites, ed., 20
(Madison: Wisconsin Historical Society, 1911): 410, 429, 442–44; C. M.
Gates, ed., *Five Fur Traders of the Northwest, Being the Narrative of Peter
Pond and the Diaries of John Macdonell, Archibald N. McLeod, Hugh Faries,
and Thomas Connor* (Minneapolis: University of Minnesota Press, 1933),
255–56; Lawrence Taliaferro, "Journals," 2: 7 April 1822, 4: 16 January 1828,
5: 30 May 1829, 10: 20 July 1836, 4 August 1836, 12: 26 October 1838,
Minnesota Historical Society Archives, St. Paul (hereafter MHSA); M. L.
Williams, ed., *Narrative Journal of Travels through the Northwestern Re-
gions of the United States Extending from Detroit through the Great Chain
of American Lakes to the Sources of the Mississippi River in the Year 1820,*
Henry R. Schoolcraft (East Lansing: Michigan State College Press, 1953),
159, 165, 169, 438–40; Aitkin to Boutwell, 25 April 1838, "Papers of Henry
Hastings Sibley," MHSA; *U.S. Statutes at Large* 7:536–38, 591–93; "David
Bushnell Census," *Congressional Document Series* 354:488; 577:14, 23;
N. H. Winchell, *The Aborigines of Minnesota, a Report Based on the Collections of Jacob V. Brower, and on the Field Notes of Alfred J. Hill and Theodore H. Lewis* (St. Paul: Minnesota Historical Society Press, 1911), 646–47;
Charles J. Kappler, comp., *Indian Affairs: Laws and Treaties,* 5 vols., (Washington, D.C.: U.S. Government Printing Office, 1904–41), 2:685–90; D. D.
Owen, *Report of a Geological Survey of Wisconsin, Iowa, and Minnesota;
and Incidentally of a Portion of Nebraska Territory. Made under Instructions from the United States Treasury Department* (Philadelphia: Lippincott, Crambo and Co., 1852), xxvii–xxviii.

19. Quotations from Henry Rowe Schoolcraft, *The Indian in His Wigwam or Characteristics of the Red Race of America* (Buffalo, N.Y.: W. H. Graham, 1848), 73. See also Priscilla K. Buffalohead, "Farmers, Warriors, Traders: A Fresh Look at Ojibway Women," *Minnesota History* 48 (1983): 236–44.

20. On leadership, see Hickerson, *Southwestern Chippewa*, 46–64; quotations from 97; Nichols and Nyholm, eds., *Ojibwewi-Ikidowinan*, 78, 127, 196; Buffalohead, "Farmers, Warriors, Traders," 36; Pauline Colby Papers, "Reminiscences," 1931, MHSA, 92; James G. E. Smith, *Leadership among the Southwestern Ojibwa*, National Museums of Canada, Publications in Ethnology 7 (Ottawa: National Museums of Canada, 1973); Frances Theresa Densmore Papers, "Chippewa Chiefs," Radio talk, 2 March 1932, MHSA; Rebecca Kugel, "Factional Alignment among the Minnesota Ojibwa, 1850–1880," *American Indian Culture and Research Journal* 9 (1985): 23–48. References to various *ogimaag* (the singular form is *ogimaa*) are scattered throughout Warren, *History of the Ojibways*.

21. Hickerson, *Southwestern Chippewa*, 30–64; Warren, *History of the Ojibways*, 193.

22. Quotation from Eggan, ed., *Social Anthropology*, 85. See also Hickerson, *Southwestern Chippewa*, 42–45; Warren, *History of the Ojibways*, 97–98; Blair, ed., *The Indian Tribes*, 1:106–7; W. Vernon Kinietz, *Chippewa Village: The Story of Katikitegon*, Cranbrook Institute of Science Bulletin 25 (Bloomfield Hills, Mich.: Cranbrook Press, 1947), 51–52; J. B. Tyrrell, ed., *David Thompson's Narrative of His Explorations in Western America* (Toronto: Champlain Society, 1916), 281; Williams, ed., *Narrative Journal*, 183; M. Inez Hilger, *Chippewa Child Life and Its Cultural Background*, Bureau of American Ethnology Bulletin 146 (Washington, D.C.: U.S. Government Printing Office, 1951), 122; Eleanor Leacock, *The Montagnais 'Hunting Territory' and the Fur Trade*, American Anthropological Association, Memoir 78 (Menasha, Wisc.: American Anthropological Association, 1954); Margaret Mead, ed., *Cooperation and Competition among Primitive Peoples* (New York: McGraw-Hill, 1937).

23. Quotations from Buffalohead, "Farmers, Warriors, Traders," 31; and Blair, ed., *Indian Tribes*, 1:69.

24. Quotations in the preceding paragraphs from Blair, ed., *Indian Tribes*, 1:69; Buffalohead, "Farmers, Warriors, Traders," 240; Pauline Colby Papers, "Reminiscences," 1931, MHSA, 50, 53; Williams, ed., *Narrative Journal*, 120–21; Hickerson, *Southwestern Chippewa*, 81; Henry Rowe Schoolcraft, *Archives of Aboriginal Knowledge*, 2 vols. (Philadelphia: n.p., 1860), 2:63; Schoolcraft, *The Indian in His Wigwam*, 179. See also Nichols and Nyholm, eds., *Ojibwewi-Ikidowinan*, 58, 176; Frances Densmore, *Chippewa Customs*, Bureau of American Ethnology, Bulletin 86 (Washington, D.C.: U.S. Government Printing Office, 1929), 22–28, 39–43, 119–30, 137, 163–64; John Rog-

ers (Way Quah Gishig/Chief Snow Cloud), *Red World and White: Memoirs of a Chippewa Boyhood,* rev. ed. (Norman: University of Oklahoma Press, 1974), 15–61, 80–82, 94–99, 105–27, 146; Frances Densmore, *How Indians Use Wild Plants for Food, Medicine and Crafts* (New York: Dover Publications, 1974); Joseph A. Gilfillan, "The Ojibways in Minnesota," *Minnesota Historical Society Collections* 9 (1898): 70–72; Ignatia Broker, *Night Flying Woman: An Ojibway Narrative* (St. Paul: Minnesota Historical Society Press, 1984).

25. Janet D. Spector, "Male/Female Task Differentiation among the Hidatsa: Toward the Development of an Archaeological Approach to the Study of Gender," in Patricia Albers and Beatrice Medicine, eds., *The Hidden Half: Studies of Plains Indian Women* (New York: University Press of America, 1983), 77–99; Buffalohead, "Farmers, Warriors, Traders," 236–44; Walter L. Williams, *The Spirit and the Flesh: Sexual Diversity in American Indian Culture* (Boston: Beacon Press, 1986); Stephen Gudeman, *Economics as Culture: Models and Metaphors of Livelihood* (London: Routledge and Kegan Paul, 1986).

26. Innis, *The Fur Trade in Canada;* George Quimby, *Indian Culture and European Trade Goods* (Madison: University of Wisconsin Press, 1966); Lewis Saum, *The Fur Trader and the Indian* (Seattle: University of Washington Press, 1965); Marshall Sahlins, *Stone Age Economics* (Chicago: Aldine, 1972); Arthur J. Ray and Donald Freeman, *Give Us Good Measure: An Economic Analysis of Relations between the Indians and the Hudson's Bay Company before 1763* (Toronto: University of Toronto Press, 1978); Philip D. Curtin, *Cross-Cultural Trade in World History* (Cambridge: Cambridge University Press, 1984); George Dalton, "The Impact of Colonization on Aboriginal Economics in Stateless Societies," *Research in Economic Anthropology* 1 (1978): 113–84; Christopher L. Miller and George R. Hamell, "A New Perspective on Indian-White Contact: Cultural Symbols and Colonial Trade," *Journal of American History* 73 (1986): 311–28; Stephen Gudeman, "Anthropological Economics: The Question of Distribution," *Annual Review of Anthropology* 7 (1978): 347–77; Charles Cleland, "The Inland Shore Fishery of the Northern Great Lakes: Its Development and Importance in Prehistory," *American Antiquity* 47 (1982): 761–84; Carolyn Gilman, *Where Two Worlds Meet: The Great Lakes Fur Trade* (St. Paul: Minnesota Historical Society Press, 1982); Patricia Albers, "Sioux Women in Transition: A Study of Their Changing Status in a Domestic and Capitalist Sector of Production," in Albers and Medicine, eds., *The Hidden Half,* 175–234; Alan Klein, "The Political-Economy of Gender: A 19th Century Plains Indian Case Study," in Albers and Medicine, eds., *The Hidden Half,* 143–73; John H. Moore, "The Developmental Cycle of Cheyenne Polygyny," *American Indian Quarterly* 15 (1991): 311–28.

27. Quotations in this and the preceding paragraphs from Jacqueline Peterson, "Ethnogenesis: The Settlement and Growth of a 'New People' in the Great Lakes Region, 1702–1815," *American Indian Culture and Research Journal* 6 (1982): 23–64, esp. 26, 28–29, and 52–53. See also Jacqueline Peterson, "Many Roads to Red River: Métis Genesis in the Great Lakes Region, 1680–1815," in Jacqueline Peterson and Jennifer S. H. Brown, eds., *The New Peoples: Being and Becoming Métis in North America* (Lincoln: University of Nebraska Press, 1985); Jacqueline Peterson, "Prelude to Red River: A Social Portrait of the Great Lakes Métis," *Ethnohistory* 25 (1978): 41–67; Jacqueline Peterson, "The People in Between: Indian-White Marriage and the Genesis of a Métis Society and Culture in the Great Lakes Region, 1702–1815," Ph.D. Dissertation, University of Illinois, Chicago Circle, 1981; Clifton, *The Prairie People*; Anderson, *Kinsmen of Another Kind*; Gary Clayton Anderson, "Joseph Renville and the Ethos of Biculturalism," in Clifton, ed., *Being and Becoming Indian* 59–81; James M. McClurken, "Agustin Hamlin, Jr.: Ottawa Identity and the Politics of Persistence," in Clifton, ed., *Being and Becoming Indian*, 82–111; James A. Clifton, "Personal and Ethnic Identity on the Great Lakes Frontier: The Case of Billy Caldwell, Anglo-Canadian," *Ethnohistory* 78 (1978): 669–94; Innis, *The Fur Trade in Canada*; E. E. Rich, *The Fur Trade and the Northwest to 1857* (Toronto: McClelland and Stewart, 1967); Louise Phelps Kellogg, *The French Regime in Wisconsin and the Northwest* (Madison: State Historical Society of Wisconsin, 1925); Louise Phelps Kellogg, *The British Regime in Wisconsin and the Northwest* (Madison: State Historical Society of Wisconsin, 1935); G. C. Davidson, *The Northwest Company* (Berkeley: University of California Press, 1918); Wayne E. Stevens, *The Northwest Fur Trade, 1763–1800* (Urbana: University of Illinois Press, 1928); Kenneth W. Porter, *John Jacob Astor, Business Man* (Cambridge: Harvard University Press, 1931).

28. Julia Warren Spears Papers, "Interesting Reminiscences of Early Frontier Days," MHSA, 8.

29. Ransom J. Powell Papers, Microfilm Rolls 9 and 10, "Book of Families," Microfilm Roll 8, "Indian Genealogies: Paul H. Beaulieu Family," Microfilm Rolls 11 and 12, "Genealogies of Allottees," MHSA; M444, U.S. Office of Indian Affairs (OIA), "Records of Investigation of White Earth Mixed Bloods, 1911–1915," MHSA: 27, 73, 93, 111, 123, 125–26, 128, 133, 138, 151–52, 171, 190–93, 233, 283, 391–409, 411–12, 417, 419–24, 440–42, 463, 467–69, 481–82, 553–54, 597–98, 621–22, 629, 643, 645–46; "Report of Special Investigator Thomas Shearman," 1912, Bureau of Indian Affairs (hereafter BIA) Record Group (hereafter RG) 75, Central Classified Files (hereafter CCF), White Earth Agency (hereafter WEA), National Archives and Records Service, Washington, D.C. (hereafter NARS); "Report of Thomas G. Shearman, Asst. Attorney, Visit to and Conference with certain full-blood Indians, ordered by

the Dept., April 15, in connection with the White Earth controversy," 6 May
1913, BIA RG 75, CCF 150, WEA, NARS; "Report of Thomas C. Shearman,
Investigation of the enrollment of certain mixed blood Chippewa Indians on
the White Earth Reservation in Minnesota," 11 December 1913, BIA RG 75,
CCF 211, WEA, NARS.

30. Peterson, "People in Between"; Sylvia Van Kirk, *Many Tender Ties": Women
in Fur-Trade Society, 1670–1870* (Winnipeg: Watson and Dwyer, 1980); Jennifer S. H. Brown, *Strangers in Blood: Fur Trade Company Families in
Indian Country* (Vancouver: University of British Columbia Press, 1980);
Jennifer S. H. Brown, "Fur Traders, Racial Categories, and Kinship Networks," in William Cowan, ed., *Papers of the Sixth Algonquian Conference,
1974* (Ottawa: National Museum of Man, Mercury Series, Canadian Ethnology Service no. 23, 1975), 210–22; Jennifer S. H. Brown, "People of Myth,
People of History: A Look at Recent Writings on the Métis," *Acadiensis* 17
(1987):150–62; Julia Harrison, *Métis: People between Two Worlds* (Van-
couver: Douglas and McIntyre, 1985); Trudy Nicks, "Mary Anne's Dilemma:
The Ethnohistory of an Ambivalent Identity," *Muse* 3, 4 (1986): 52–55;
Peterson and Brown, eds., *The New Peoples: Being and Becoming Métis in
North America*; John C. Ewers, "Mothers of the Mixed-Bloods: The Marginal
Woman in the History of the Upper Missouri," in Ross Toole et al., eds.,
Probing the American West: Papers from the Santa Fe Conference (Santa Fe:
Museum of New Mexico Press, 1962); Tanis Chapman Thorne, "People of the
River: Mixed-Blood Families on the Lower Missouri," Ph.D. Dissertation,
University of California, Los Angeles, 1987.

31. Quotations from Sr. Bernard Coleman, Sr. Verona LaBud, and John Humphrey, *Old Crow Wing: History of a Village* (Duluth: College of St. Scholastica, 1967), 6, and "Report of the U.S. Chippewa Commission," 105, 108. See
also Ransom J. Powell Papers, Microfilm Roll 9, "Book of Indian Families,"
Microfilm Rolls 10 and 11, "Genealogies of Allottees," MHSA; Warren, *History of the Ojibways*, 115, 145, 228, 381–83; Alvin H. Wilcox, *A Pioneer
History of Becker County, Minnesota* (St. Paul: Pioneer Press Company,
1907), 220, 266–71, 640–41, 742.

32. Quotations in this and the preceding paragraphs are from Rhoda R. Gilman,
Carolyn Gilman, and Deborah M. Stultz, *The Red River Trails: Oxcart
Routes between St. Paul and the Selkirk Settlement, 1820–1870* (St. Paul:
Minnesota Historical Society, 1979), 64–68, and Coleman, LaBud, and Hum-
phrey, *Old Crow Wing*, 3, 9, 10, 22. See also 1847 Treaty at Fond du Lac, in
Kappler, comp. *Indian Affairs* 2:567–69; U.S. Congress, Senate Committee
on Indian Affairs, *An Investigation of Affairs at White Earth Reservation to
Investigate the Conduct of Agents and Their Subordinates* (Washington,
D.C.: U.S. Government Printing Office, 1887) (hereafter "1887 Investiga-
tion"); Peterson, "Prelude to Red River"; Peterson, "Many Roads"; Peterson,

"Ethnogenesis"; Peterson, "People in Between"; Tanner, "The Glaize in 1792"; Peterson and Brown, eds., *The New Peoples*; Brown, *Strangers in Blood*; Van Kirk, *"Many Tender Ties"*; Olive P. Dickason, "From 'One Nation' in the Northwest to 'New Nation' in the Northwest: A Look at the Emergence of the Métis," *American Indian Culture and Research Journal* 6 (1982): 1–21; Kugel, "Factional Alignment."

33. Quotation in preceding paragraph from Reginald Horsman, "American Indian Policy in the Old Northwest, 1783–1812," *William and Mary Quarterly*, 3d series, 18 (1961): 35–53. See also Francis Paul Prucha, *The Great Father* (Lincoln: University of Nebraska Press, 1984); Wilcomb E. Washburn, *Red Man's Land/White Man's Law: A Study of the Past and Present Status of the American Indian* (New York: Macmillan, 1971); Felix S. Cohen, *Handbook of Federal Indian Law* (Washington, D.C.: U.S. Government Printing Office, 1942); Reginald Horsman, *Race and Manifest Destiny* (Cambridge: Harvard University Press, 1981); Reginald Horsman, *Expansion and American Indian Policy, 1783–1812* (East Lansing: Michigan State University Press, 1967); Francis Paul Prucha, *American Indian Policy in the Formative Years: The Indian Trade and Intercourse Acts, 1790–1834* (Cambridge: Harvard University Press, 1962).

34. Quotations from Warren, *History of the Ojibways*, 38, 39, 85. For specific treaties and executive orders pertinent to the history of the White Earth Reservation, see Kappler, comp., *Indian Affairs*, 29 July 1837 Treaty of St. Peters, 1:491–93; 4 October 1842 Treaty of LaPointe, 2:542–45; 2 August 1847 Treaty at Fond du Lac, 2:567–69; 21 August 1847 Treaty with the Pillager Band, 2:569–70; 30 September 1854 Treaty of LaPointe, 2:648–52; 22 February 1855 Treaty, 2:685–90; 11 March 1863 Treaty, 2:839–42; 2 October 1863 Old Crossing Treaty, 2:853–55; 12 April 1864 Treaty, 2:861–62; 7 May 1864 Treaty, 2:862–65; 7 April 1866 Bois Forte Treaty, 2:916–18; 19 March 1867 Treaty, 2:974–76; 3 March 1873 Executive Order, 1:143–49; 29 October 1873 Executive Order, 1:854; 4 November 1873 Executive Order, 1:851; 26 May 1874 Executive Order, 1:852; 18 March 1879 Executive Order, 1:853; 20 December 1881 Executive Order, 1:853; 30 June 1883 Executive Order, 1:850; 13 July 1883 Executive Order, 1:853. See also Edmund J. Danziger, Jr., *The Chippewas of Lake Superior* (Norman: University of Oklahoma Press, 1979).

35. Preceding quotations from Charles Breck, comp., *The Life of the Reverend James Lloyd Breck D.D.*, (New York: E. & J. B. Young, 1886) 326, Coleman, LaBud, and Humphrey, *Old Crow Wing*, 23, and John Johnson Enmegahbowh to Henry B. Whipple, 29 November 1862, Henry Benjamin Whipple Papers, Box 3, MHSA (hereafter Whipple Papers). See also "1887 Investigation"; "Report of U.S. Chippewa Commission"; Kugel, " 'To Go About on the Earth,' " 170–83; Densmore, *Chippewa Customs*, 180–83; Edmund Danziger, "They

Would Not Be Moved: The Chippewa Treaty of 1854," *Minnesota History* 43 (1973): 175–85; William Watts Folwell, *A History of Minnesota,* 4 vols. (St. Paul: Minnesota Historical Society Press, 1930; rev. ed. 1969), 1:305–8; Ronald N. Satz, *American Indian Policy in the Jacksonian Era* (Lincoln: University of Nebraska Press, 1975); Paul Stuart, *The Indian Office:* Growth and Development of an American Institution (Ann Arbor: University of Michigan Research Press, 1979).

36. Kappler, comp., *Indian Affairs,* 2:567–69 (Article 4), 685–90 (Article 6), 861–62 (Article 7); *U.S. Statutes at Large,* 10:219–25 (Article 2); 16:1–4 (Article 4); "Chippewa Half-Breeds of Lake Superior," House Executive Documents 1513, no. 193, 42d Congress, 2d Session; Coleman, LaBud, and Humphrey, *Old Crow Wing;* "1887 Investigation"; Danziger, "They Would Not Be Moved"; Folwell, *A History of Minnesota,* 1:470–78.

37. Quotation in previous paragraph from Kugel, " 'To Go About on the Earth,' " 235; see also 233–365. See "The Story of Enmegahbowh's Life," in Henry Benjamin Whipple, *Lights and Shadows of a Long Episcopate* (New York: Macmillan, 1899), 145–47, 497–98; John Johnson Enmegahbowh, "Reminiscences," n.d., Whipple Papers, MHSA; Donald B. Smith, *Sacred Feathers: The Story of the Rev. Peter Jones (Kahkewaquonby) and the Mississauga Indians* (Lincoln: University of Nebraska Press, 1987); John H. Pitezel, *The Life of Rev. Peter Marksman, an Ojibwa Missionary, Illustrating the Triumphs of the Gospel among the Ojibwa* (Cincinnati: Western Methodist Book Concern, 1901); George Copway, *The Life, History and Travels of Kah-ge-ga-gah-bowh, (George Copway) a Young Indian Chief of the Ojebwa Nation, a Convert to the Christian Faith, and a Missionary to His People for Twelve Years; With a Sketch of the Present State of the Ojebwa Nation, in Regard to Christianity and Their Future Prospects,* 2d ed. (Philadelphia: J. Harmstead, 1847); George Copway, *The Traditional History and Characteristic Sketches of the Ojibway Nation* (London: C. Gilpin, 1850); Peter Jones, *History of the Ojebway Indians; with Especial Reference to Their Conversion to Christianity* (London: A. W. Bennett, 1861); Peter Jones, *The Life and Journals of Kah-ke-wa-quo-na-by (Rev. Peter Jones): Wesleyan Missionary* (Toronto: A. Gree, 1860).

38. Martin N. Zanger, " 'Straight Tongue's Heathen Wards': Bishop Whipple and the Episcopal Mission to the Chippewas," in Clyde A. Milner II and Floyd A. O'Neil, eds., *Churchmen and the Western Indians, 1820–1920* (Norman: University of Oklahoma Press, 1985), 177–214; Whipple, *Lights and Shadows;* Henry Benjamin Whipple, "Civilization and Christianization of the Ojibways in Minnesota," *Collections of the Minnesota Historical Society* 9 (1889–1900); Harold Hickerson, "The Chippewa of the Upper Great Lakes: A Study in Sociopolitical Change," in Eleanor Burke Leacock and Nancy O. Lurie, eds., *North American Indians in Historical Perspective* (New York:

Random House, 1971), 182, 186–89; Kugel, "'To Go About on the Earth,'" 251–53; Kappler, comp., *Indian Affairs*, 2:862–65, 974–76; *U.S. Statutes at Large*, 16:1–4.

39. Hickerson, *Southwestern Chippewa*, 21, 24, 36–38, 46, 49; Warren, *History of the Ojibways*, 47, 49, 353–54; Rev. Alfred Brunson, "Sketch of Hole-in-the-Day," *Collections of the State Historical Society of Wisconsin* 5 (1868): 387–99; Lyman C. Draper, "A Note on Hole-in-the-Day," *Collections of the State Historical Society of Wisconsin* 5 (1868): 401; Julia Warren Spears Papers, "Reminiscences of a Short History of the Chippewa Chief Hole-in-the-Day," written July 1922, MHSA; Coleman, LaBud, and Humphrey, *Old Crow Wing*, 24–31; Zanger, "'Straight Tongue's Heathen Wards,'" 201–4; Stephen P. Hall, "The Hole-in-the-Day Encounter," *Minnesota Archaeologist* 36 (1977): 77–96; "An Account of the Flight of the Rev. Ottmar Cloeter and His Family from Gabitawe'egama Mission Station to Fort Ripley during the Indian Uprising in 1862," 15 October 1936, Ottmar Cloeter and Family Papers, MHSA; Kugel, "'To Go About on the Earth,'" 164–210.

40. Quotations in the preceding paragraphs from Julia Warren Spears Papers, "Reminiscences of a Short History of the Chippewa Chief Hole-in-the-Day," MHSA, and U.S. Office of Indian Affairs, "Records of Investigation of White Earth Mixed Bloods, 1911–1915," Microfilm Roll M444, MHSA, 133, 144, 222, 273; see also 111, 138, 164, 187, 240, 407, 442, 453, 494, 593, 623; Coleman, LaBud, and Humphrey, *Old Crow Wing*, 24–31; Kappler, comp., *Indian Affairs*, 2:862–65, 974–76; Kugel, "'To Go About on the Earth,'" 164–210.

41. All quotations from Julia Warren Spears Papers, "History of White Earth," MHSA. See also Kugel, "'To Go About on the Earth,'" 199–202, 238–43.

42. Quotations in the preceding paragraph from Joseph Alexander Gilfillan and Family Papers, "A Novel Trip," MHSA, 11. See also Indian Office *Reports* 1867: 397; 1868: 301; 1870: 305; 1871: 588, 592; 1872: 210; 1874: 195; 1875: 53, 298; 1876: 84; 1877: 129; 1878: 81; Folwell, *History of Minnesota* 4:196–97; *U.S. Statutes at Large* 17:189, 534; 18, pt. 3:173–74.

43. Quotation from "Communication from the Secretary of the Interior, with Papers Relating to Chippewa Indians in Minnesota," Senate Executive Document 2449, no. 115, 49 Congress, 2 Session (1887), 10, 53 (hereafter "Northwest Indian Commission Report"). See also Theodore Blegen, *Minnesota: A History of the State* (Minneapolis: University of Minnesota Press, 1963), 320, 338–58; Folwell, *History of Minnesota*, vol. 3; Edward V. Robinson, *Early Economic Conditions and the Development of Agriculture in Minnesota* (Minneapolis: University of Minnesota, Studies in the Social Sciences no. 3, 1915); William Cronon, *Nature's Metropolis: Chicago and the Great West* (New York: W. W. Norton, 1991), esp. chaps. 3 and 4; Whipple, *Lights and Shadows*, 29, 314; George C. Tanner, *Fifty Years of Church Work in the*

> *Diocese of Minnesota, 1857–1907* (St. Paul: n.p., 1909), 299–301, 511–15; "A Communication from the Secretary of the Interior, Relative to Legislation for the Chippewa Indians in Minnesota," Senate Executive Documents 2333, no. 44, 49 Congress, 1 Session (1886), 6.

44. *U.S. Statutes at Large* 24:44; Senate Executive Documents 2333, no. 44, 49 Congress, 1 Session (1886); "Northwest Indian Commission Report," 1, 2, 12–22, 39–41, 50–82; Folwell, *History of Minnesota,* 4:204–7.

45. *U.S. Statutes at Large,* 4:388–91. See also Hoxie, *A Final Promise;* Otis, *The Dawes Act;* Prucha, *American Indian Policy in Crisis;* Fritz, *The Movement for Indian Assimilation;* Mardock, *The Reformers and the American Indian.*

46. *U.S. Statutes at Large,* 25:642–43.

47. Quotations in preceding paragraphs from "Report of the U.S. Chippewa Commission," 1, 85, 88, 129. For all the various negotiations, see pp. 1–193. See also Smith, "Leadership among the Southwestern Ojibwa."

48. BIA Census, 1900, Microfilm Roll 653, NARS.

49. Quotations from William M. Campbell, Chairman, Chippewa Commission, to J. M. Smith, Chippewa Commission, 15 December 1893, BIA RG 75, CCF 150, WEA, NARS; Chairman, Chippewa Commission, to T. J. Morgan, Commissioner of Indian Affairs, 11 December 1891, BIA RG 75, CCF 150, WEA, NARS; and Wa we i e cumig to Commissioner of Indian Affairs, 5 March 1903, BIA RG 75, Letters Received (hereafter LR) 1903, NARS. See also RCIA 1895: 29; 1902: 224, 225; 1904: 223; Chairman, Chippewa Commission, to J. W. Noble, Secretary of the Interior, 21 January 1893, BIA RG 75, CCF 150, WEA, NARS; U.S. Citizens on former Mille Lacs Indian Reservation to Commissioner of Indian Affairs, 20 February 1891, BIA RG 75, LR 1891, NARS; "Record of the Minutes of a Council of the Mille Lac Band of Chippewa Indians Held at Lawrence, on the Mille Lac Indian Reservation, in the State of Minnesota, on the 27th Day of May, 1900, for the Purpose of considering Legislation Now Pending in Congress Affecting their Interests," Senate Documents 3878, no. 446, 56 Congress, 1 Session (1900): 1–3; "Mille Lac Chippewa Indians of Minnesota," Senate Reports 3890, no. 1089, 56 Congress, 1 Session (1900): 1–6; "Mille Lac Chippewa Indians of Minnesota," Senate Reports 4259, no. 340, 57 Congress, 1 Session (1902): 1–2; "Mille Lac Chippewa Indians of Minnesota," House Reports 4405, no. 1784, 57 Congress, 1 Session (1902): 1–7; *U.S. Statutes at Large,* 32:268; BIA Censuses for White Earth Reservation, 1898–1907, Microfilm Rolls 653–55, NARS. A packet of correspondence produced by Charles H. Beaulieu as allotting agent: Charles H. Beaulieu to William Campbell, U.S. Chippewa Commission, 30 October 1893; 4 December 1893; 6 January 1894; 26 February 1894; 1 March 1894; 29 March 1894; 1 April 1894; 25 April 1894; 2 May 1894; 3 May 1894; 10 May 1894; 14 May 1894; 14 June 1894; 14 July 1894; 27 July 1894; 6 August 1894; 7 August 1894; 9 August 1894; 11 August 1894; 16 August 1894; 20 August 1894, BIA RG 75, CCF 150, WEA, NARS.

50. Quotations from Charles H. Beaulieu to B. D. Williams, Chippewa Commission, 26 January 1895, BIA RG 75, CCF 150, WEA, NARS. See the following for Charles H. Beaulieu's activities as allotting agent in the Leech Lake area: Charles H. Beaulieu to B. D. Williams, Chippewa Commissioner, 24 January 1895; 26 January 1895; 31 January 1895; 28 February 1895; 16 March 1895; 19 March 1895; 9 April 1895; Charles H. Beaulieu to M. R. Baldwin, Chairman, Chippewa Commission, 11 May 1895, BIA RG 75, CCF 150, WEA, NARS. See also D. M. Browning, Commissioner, to M. R. Baldwin, Chairman, Chippewa Commission, 9 June 1896, BIA RG 75, CCF 150, WEA, NARS.

51. "Memorial from the Indian Rights Association Relating to Timber Lands on the Chippewa Indian Reservation in Minnesota," Senate Documents 3728, no. 49, 55 Congress, 3 Session (1899): 3–4; RCIA 1896: 33.

52. RCIA 1895: 29–30.

53. Removal statistics are drawn from "Records of the Chippewa Commission," Register of Arrivals, 1890–1899, BIA RG 75, Entry (hereafter E) 1305, NARS. See also RCIA 1892:276; 1893:34; 1894:29; Reverend Joseph A. Gilfillan, "The Ojibways in Minnesota," *Minnesota Historical Society Collections* 9 (1889): 55–86; Records of the Chippewa Commission: Correspondence 1889–1900, BIA RG 75, E 1297, NARS; Letters Sent by the Chairman, 1892–1900, BIA RG 75, E 1298, NARS; Letters Sent by the Chairman to the Secretary of the Interior, May–December 1892, BIA RG 75, E 1300, NARS. This migration pattern represents the norm. See Arthur Margon, "Indians and Immigrants: A Comparison of Groups New to the City," *Journal of Ethnic Studies* 4 (1977): 17–28; John Bodnar, *The Transplanted: A History of Immigrants in Urban America* (Bloomington: Indiana University Press, 1985); John Gjerde, *From Peasants to Farmers: The Migration from Balestrand, Norway to the Upper Middle West* (Cambridge: Cambridge University Press, 1985).

54. Quotations in this and the preceding paragraphs from Gus H. Beaulieu to CIA, 25 April 1901, BIA RG 75, LR 1901, NARS; C. H. Beaulieu to Mr. Campbell, 9 August 1894, BIA RG 75, CCF 150, NARS; D. H. Robbins, Vineland, Minnesota, to Commissioner of Indian Affairs, 17 February 1906, BIA RG 75, LR 1906, NARS; Simon Michelet, Agent, to Commissioner of Indian Affairs, 17 February 1906, BIA RG 75, LR 1906, NARS. Removal statistics are drawn from "Records of the Chippewa Commission," Register of Arrivals, 1890–99, BIA RG 75, E 1305, NARS. See also Charles H. Beaulieu to Mr. Campbell, 4 August 1894, BIA RG 75, CCF 150, NARS; A. C. Tonner, Acting Commissioner of Indian Affairs, to Simon Michelet, Agent, 26 March 1904, LR, Office of Indian Affairs (hereafter OIA), Kansas City Federal Regional Archives (hereafter KCFRA); Records of the Chippewa Commission: Correspondence 1889–1900, BIA RG 75, E 1297, NARS; Letters Sent by the Chairman, 1892–1900, BIA RG 75, E 1298, NARS; Letters Sent by the Chairman to the Secretary of the Interior, May–December 1892, BIA RG 75, E

1300, NARS; RCIA 1892: 276; 1893: 34; 1894: 29; Reverend Joseph A. Gilfillan, "The Ojibways in Minnesota," *Minnesota Historical Society Collections* 9 (1889): 55–86.

55. Quotation from Chairman, Chippewa Commission, to John W. Noble, Secretary of the Interior, 29 December 1892, BIA RG 75, E 1300, NARS. See also
Records of the Chippewa Commission: Correspondence 1889–1900, BIA RG
75, E 1297, NARS; Letters Sent by the Chairman to the Secretary of the
Interior, May–December 1892, BIA RG 75, E 1300, NARS; H. M. Rice, Chairman, Chippewa Commission, to Francis Campbell, Commissioner, 22 June
1891, BIA RG 75, CCF 150, WEA, NARS; Memorandum by B. D. Williams, c.
late 1893–early 1894, BIA RG 75, CCF 150, WEA, NARS; B. D. Williams,
Chippewa Commission, to William Campbell, Chippewa Commission,
13 July 1893, 2 October 1893, 17 January 1894, 8 May 1894, BIA RG 75, CCF
150, NARS.

56. Preceding quotation from RCIA, 1892: 81. See also RCIA, 1889; 1890: 470–71;
1891: 780–81; 1892: 81; 1894: 152; 1900: 52; 1901: 253; *U.S. Statutes at
Large* 26:794–96; *U.S. Statutes at Large* 33:539; *Congressional Record,* 56
Congress, 1 Session: 56, 2566; 58 Congress, 2 Session: 3660, 4413, 5546,
5825; "Allotments to Indians on White Earth Reservation in Minnesota,"
House Reports 4023, no. 493, 56 Congress, 1 Session (1900): 1–5; "Allotments to Indians on White Earth Reservation, Minnesota," House Reports
4583, no. 2460, 58 Congress, 2 Session; "Report in the Matter of the Inves-
tigation of the White Earth Reservation," House Reports 6336, no. 1336, 62
Congress, 3 Session (1913): 822–27 (hereafter "Graham Report"); Chairman,
Chippewa Commission, to T. J. Morgan, Commissioner of Indian Affairs,
1 December 1891, BIA RG 75, CCF 150, WEA, NARS; Chairman, Chippewa
Commission to John W. Noble, Secretary of the Interior, 10 December 1891,
BIA RG 75, CCF 150, WEA, NARS; Chairman, Chippewa Commission, to T. J.
Morgan, Commissioner of Indian Affairs, 1 January 1893, BIA RG 75, CCF
150, WEA, NARS; Chairman, Chippewa Commission, to T. J. Morgan, Com-
missioner of Indian Affairs, 10 January 1893, BIA RG 75, CCF 150, WEA,
NARS; Chairman, Chippewa Commission, to Commissioner of Indian Af-
fairs, 21 March 1893, BIA RG 75, CCF 150, WEA, NARS; Memorandum by B. D.
Williams, c. late 1893–early 1894, BIA RG 75, CCF 150, WEA, NARS; Arm-
strong, Acting Commissioner of Indian Affairs, to Darwin S. Hall, Chairman
Chippewa Commission, 16 May 1893, BIA RG 75, CCF 150, WEA, NARS;
B. D. Williams, Chairman, Chippewa Commission, 21 June 1894, BIA RG 75,
CCF 150, WEA, NARS; W. A. Jones, Commissioner of Indian Affairs, to
Michelet, Agent, 24 July 1903, and 30 September 1903, LR, OIA, "Land,"
KCFRA; A. C. Tonner, Acting Commissioner of Indian Affairs, to Michelet,
Agent, 26 March 1904, LR, OIA, "Land," KCFRA; "Allotment Certificates,"
1875–92, 1892–93, 1891–1907, Special Case 58, BIA RG 75, NARS; "Minutes
of a Council of the Mississippi Bands of Minnesota Chippewa Indians at

White Earth Agency to Adopt Halvor Steenerson of Crookston, Minnesota,"
9 May 1904, BIA RG 75, LR 1904, NARS; A. C. Tonner, Acting Commissioner
of Indian Affairs, to Michelet, Agent, 4 June 1904, LR, OIA, "Land," KCFRA;
The Tomahawk, 23 June 1904: 1 (MHS); A. C. Tonner, Acting Commissioner
of Indian Affairs, to Michelet, Agent, 11 July 1904, LR, OIA, "Land," KCFRA;
Charles T. Wright to Commissioner of Indian Affairs, 28 February 1905, BIA
RG 75, LR 1905, NARS; E. A. Hitchcock, Secretary of the Interior, to Commissioner of Indian Affairs, 15 April 1905, BIA RG 75, LR 1905, NARS;
Charles Wadena to Michelet, Agent, 29 May 1905, LR, OIA, "Land," KCFRA.

Chapter 2. Signatures and Thumbprints

1. Herb E. Wright, Jr., "Late Quaternary Vegetational History of North Amer-
   ica," in K. K. Turekian, ed., *Late Cenozoic Glacial Ages* (New Haven: Yale
   University Press, 1971), 425–64; Herb E. Wright, Jr., and William A. Watts,
   Glacial and Vegetational History of Northeastern Minnesota, SP11 Special
   Publication Series, Minnesota Geological Survey (St. Paul: University of
   Minnesota Press, 1969); P. K. Simms and G. B. Morey, eds., *Geology of
   Minnesota: A Centennial Volume* (St. Paul: Minnesota Geological Survey,
   1972), 515–47, 561–80; Davis, "The Prairie-Deciduous Forest Ecotone";
   John R. Borchert, *Minnesota's Changing Geography* (Minneapolis: Univer-
   sity of Minnesota Press, 1959); Carl Otto Rosendahl and Frederic K. But-
   ters, *Trees and Shrubs of Minnesota* (Minneapolis: University of Minnesota
   Press, 1928); Warren Upham, *Catalogue of the Flora of Minnesota* (Min-
   neapolis: Johnson, Smith, and Harrison, 1884); Alfred Rogosin, "Wild Rice
   (*Zizania aquatica L.*) in Northern Minnesota, with Special Reference to the
   Effects of Various Water Levels and Water Level Changes, Seeding Densities,
   and Fertilizer," M.S. Thesis, University of Minnesota, 1958; Hickerson, "The
   Virginia Deer." For policy consideration, see Horsman, *Expansion and Amer-
   ican Indian Policy, 1783–1812*; Bernard W. Sheehan, *Seeds of Extinction:
   Jeffersonian Philanthropy and the American Indian* (Chapel Hill: University
   of North Carolina Press, 1973); Prucha, *American Indian Policy in the For-
   mative Years*; Satz, *American Indian Policy in the Jacksonian Era*; Trennert,
   Alternative to Extinction; Fritz, *The Movement for Indian Assimilation*;
   Mardock, *The Reformers and the American Indian*; Loring Benson Priest,
   Uncle Sam's Step-Children; Prucha, *American Indian Policy in Crisis*;
   Hoxie, *A Final Promise.*
2. Quotations from Enmegahbowh as quoted in Kugel, " 'To Go About on the
   Earth,' " 224, and Julia Warren Spears Papers, "History of White Earth,"
   MHSA, 4.
3. All quotations are from Joseph Alexander Gilfillan and Family Papers, "The
   Spirit of Missions," January 1874, MHSA.
4. Quotations from Joseph Alexander Gilfillan and Family Papers, "The Field,

1882," Box 1, MHSA. See also Tay-cum-i-gi-shick to Timothy J. Sheehan, 3 July 1885, Timothy J. Sheehan Papers, Box 2, MHSA; Kugel, " 'To Go About on the Earth,' " 260, 306, 308.

5. Quotations from "Report of the U.S. Chippewa Commission," 90, 109, and RCIA 1893: 165, 1895: 176. Subsistence farming is common in fringe areas where capital outlays exceed profits. See David Rich Lewis, "Farming and the Northern Ute Experience, 1850–1940," in *Overcoming Economic Dependency,* Occasional Paper Series, no. 9 (Chicago: D'Arcy McNickle Center for the History of the American Indian, Newberry Library, 1988); R. D. Hurt, *Indian Agriculture in America: Prehistory to the Present* (Lawrence: University Press of Kansas, 1987); Bettye Hobbs Pruitt, "Self-Sufficiency and the Agricultural Economy of Eighteenth-Century Massachusetts," *William and Mary Quarterly* 41 (1984): 333–64; Christopher Clark, "Household Economy, Market Exchange and the Rise of Capitalism in the Connecticut Valley, 1800–1860," *Journal of Social History* 13 (1979): 169–89; Michael Merrill, "Cash Is Good to Eat: Self-sufficiency and Exchange in the Rural Economy of the United States," *Radical History Review* 4 (1977): 42–71; John Mack Faragher, *Sugar Creek: Life on the Illinois Prairie* (New Haven: Yale University Press, 1986).

6. Quotations from RCIA, 1885:342, 1901:253 and "1887 Investigation," 12. See also Julia Warren Spears Papers, "Benjamin L. Fairbanks," MHSA.

7. RCIA, 1887; 1888; 1889; 1890: 470–71; 1891: 260, 780–81; 1892: 276, 804–5; 1893: 165; 1894: 151; 1899: 586–87; 1904: 620–21. Between 1895 and 1898, Anishinaabe agricultural statistics were overaggregated, frustrating efforts to examine White Earth alone. Statistics are problematic; categories change frequently and figures often remain the same. After 1904, the lack of local agents' reports further complicates statistical analysis. Even so, broad statistical trends parallel my interpretation.

8. RCIA, 1885: 342; 1890: 112, 470–71; 1891: 22, 780–81; 1892: 276, 804–5; 1893: 165; 1894: 150–51; 1895: 175–76, 233; 1896: 170; 1899: 586–87; 1900: 662–63; 1901: 253, 712–13, 1902: 654–55; 1903: 532–33; 1904: 620–21.

9. Quotations from Gilfillan, "The Ojibways in Minnesota," 72. See also Rogers, *Red World and White,* 98; RCIA, 1890: 470–71; 1891: 260, 780–81; 1892: 276, 805–6; 1893: 165; 1894: 151; 1895: 175; 1896: 170; 1897: 500–501; 1898: 618–19; 1899: 586–87; 1900: 662–63; 1901: 712–13; 1902: 654–55; 1903: 532–33; 1904: 620–21. See also Albert E. Jenks, "Wild Rice Gatherers of the Upper Lakes: A Study in American Primitive Economics," *19th Annual Report of the Bureau of American Ethnology, 1897–98,* part 2 (Washington, D.C.: U.S. Government Printing Office, 1900): 1013–1137.

10. Quotations from Gilfillan, "The Ojibways," 71, and Pauline Colby Papers, "Reminiscences," 34.

11. Quotations in this and the preceding paragraphs from RCIA 1895: 153, 1896:

174, and *The Tomahawk*, 7 May 1903: 4, and 16 July 1903: 4, and Special Agent Charles S. McNichols to Commissioner of Indian Affairs (hereafter CIA), 15 January 1902, BIA RG 75, LR 1902, NARS.

12. These ads regularly appeared in every issue of *The Tomahawk* from 9 April 1903 to 1 September 1904.

13. Quotations from Rogers, *Red World and White*, 31, 82, and Pauline Colby Papers, "Reminiscences," 31, 33–34, 99.

14. Quotations from *The Tomahawk*, 23 April 1903: 1, and Rogers, *Red World and White*, 51, 52, 59–60. See also "Report of the U.S. Chippewa Commission," 90, 115; Densmore, *How Indians Use Wild Plants*, 336–37, 338–39, 364–65; Virgil Vogel, *American Indian Medicine* (Norman: University of Oklahoma Press, 1970), 307, 310, 372–73; Densmore, *Chippewa Music*," songs throughout.

15. Quotation from Rogers, *Red World and White*, 127. See also James L. Clayton, "The Growth and Economic Significance of the American Fur Trade, 1790–1890," *Minnesota History* 40 (1966): 219; Rhoda R. Gilman, "Last Days of the Upper Mississippi Fur Trade," in Malvina Bolus, ed., *People and Pelts: Selected Papers of the Second North American Fur Trade Conference* (Winnipeg: Pequis Publishers, 1972).

16. Rogers, *Red World and White*, 123–24; Gilfillan, "The Ojibways," 100; Sam Fullerton, Board of Game and Fish Commissioners, to Knute Nelson, Senator, 24 January 1905, and 6 March 1905, BIA RG 75, LR 1905, NARS.

17. Quotations from Rogers, *Red World and White*, 99, and *The Tomahawk*, 23 April 1903: 3, 2 July 1903: 1. See also RCIA, 1898: 181.

18. Petition from Citizens of Thief River Falls, 17 April 1893, BIA RG 75, LR 1893, NARS.

19. RCIA, "Lists of Employees," 1891: 701, 705; 1892: 834, 847–48; 1894: 513, 546–47, 566; 1895: 541–42, 560–61; 1896: 571, 611; 1897: 532, 571–72; 1898: 672–73, 693–94; 1899: 616, 636, 656; 1900: 698, 740; 1901: 763, 779; 1902: 707, 725; 1903: 590, 608; 1904: 651, 643–44; 1905: 536, 572–73; *The Tomahawk*, 28 May 1903: 4; Gilfillan, "The Ojibways in Minnesota"; Pauline Colby Papers, "Reminiscences."

20. Robert M. Allen, Agent, to CIA, 26 January 1894, BIA RG 75, LR 1894, NARS; A. J. Bisson to CIA, 1 December 1905, BIA RG 75, LR 1905, NARS; Kay-dug-gay-gwon-ay-aush, Chief, Otter Tail Indians, Pine Point District, to CIA, 27 March 1900, BIA RG 75, LR 1900, NARS.

21. RCIA, 1898:181.

22. Quotations from Pauline Colby Papers, "Reminiscences," 9, 17–20, 84, and Francis L. Palmer, "An Account of the Work of Miss Pauline Colby for Many Years among the Chippewa Indians, with some Particulars as to the Lace-Making Industry under the Direction of Deaconess Sybil Carter. This Statement is Transcribed from Notes Made from Conversations with Miss Colby,

December, 1936, March, 1937, November, 1937," Pauline Colby Papers, MHSA, 3. See also Historiographer of the Diocese of Minnesota, "Data as to the Life and Work of Miss Pauline Colby among the Chippewas Taken from Conversations with Her December, 1936, March, 1937, etc.," Pauline Colby Papers, MHSA. The lace-making schools were ultimately extended to Birch Coulee, South Dakota, and even to La Jolla, California!

23. Quotations from Gilfillan, "The Ojibways in Minnesota," 74, 122, and Special Agent Charles S. McNichols to CIA, 15 January 1902, BIA RG 75, LR 1902, NARS.

24. Quotation from Waush-ke-sid Agustin to CIA, 9 March 1905, BIA, LR, OIA, "Land," KCFRA. See also RCIA, 1905: 82; C. F. Larrabee, Acting CIA, to Michelet, Agent, 18 March 1905, BIA, LR, OIA, "Land," KCFRA.

25. Quotations from Ah-bow-ah-ge-shig to CIA, 16 January 1905, BIA LR, OIA, "Land," KCFRA and Special Agent Charles S. McNichols to CIA, 15 January 1902, BIA RG 75, LR 1902, NARS. See also Jacob Folstrum to Department of Interior, 18 February 1902, BIA RG 75, LR 1902, NARS; Simon Michelet, Agent, to CIA, 11 March 1902, BIA RG 75, LR 1902, NARS; Louis Charette to Jones, Assistant CIA, 30 October 1901, BIA, LR, OIA, "Accounts," KCFRA; A. C. Tonner, Acting CIA, to S. Michelet, 7 November 1901, BIA, LR, OIA, "Accounts," KCFRA; A. C. Tonner, Acting CIA, to Michelet, 16 November 1901, BIA, LR, OIA, "Land," KCFRA; A. C. Tonner, Acting CIA, to Michelet, 29 January 1902, BIA, "Accounts," KCFRA; Simon Michelet to CIA, 13 February 1902, BIA RG 75, LR 1901, NARS; Simon Michelet to CIA, 18 April 1902, BIA RG 75, LR 1902, NARS; Chief Way-we-yay-cumig to CIA Jones, 14 July 1902, BIA RG 75, LR 1902, NARS.

26. Quotations from Gilfillan, "The Ojibways," 125, and "Inspection Report of Elsie E. Newton on the Work of the Field Matron at Pine Point," 22 September 1911, BIA RG 75, CCF 917.1, WEA, NARS. See also B. D. Williams, Chippewa Commission, to William Campbell, Chairman Chippewa Commission, 12 July 1894, BIA RG 75, CCF 150, WEA, NARS; Charles Wadena to CIA, 19 June 1912, BIA RG 75, CCF 150, WEA, NARS; Louise M. Fairbanks to CIA, 21 September 1914, BIA RG 75, CCF 150, WEA, NARS; Louise M. Fairbanks to CIA, 21 September 1914, BIA RG 75, CCF 155, WEA, NARS; John R. Howard, Superintendent, to CIA, 2 November 1909, BIA RG 75, CCF 820, WEA, NARS; Interview with Fred Burnett Weaver, born 1900, c. 1982, interviewer unknown, cassette tape, WEOHP.

27. Quotations from *The Tomahawk*, 30 April 1903: 1, and 7 May 1903: 1.

28. Coleman, LaBud, Humphrey, *Old Crow Wing*; Kappler, comp., *Indian Affairs* 2:567–69 (Article 4), 685–90 (Article 6), 861–62 (Article 7); "Chippewa Half-Breeds of Lake Superior," House Executive Documents 1513, no. 193, 42 Congress, 2 Session; Danziger, "They Would Not Be Moved," 184–85; Folwell, *History of Minnesota* 1:470–78.

29. *The Tomahawk*, 9 April 1903 to 1 September 1904. See also photographs in the audiovisual collection of the Minnesota Historical Society.

30. Information on the daily lives of women of mixed descent is limited. See *The Tomahawk* 9 April 1903–1 Sept. 1904, 25 Nov. 1915–27 Dec. 1917, 3 Jan. 1918–25 Dec. 1919; Alvin H. Wilcox, *A Pioneer History of Becker County Minnesota* (St. Paul: Pioneer Press Co., 1907); Rev. Benno Watrin, *The Ponsfordian, 1880–1930: A Collection of Historical Data dealing especially with Pioneer Days of Ponsford, Becker County, Minnesota* (Park Rapids, Minn.: Press of the Park Rapids *Enterprise*, 1930); "Voices from the Past: Louis Edward Brunette and Caroline Bisson Norton Family History," no date, spiral bound. A copy can be found at the Becker County Historical Society, Detroit Lakes, Minnesota. Interview with Winnifred Jourdain, born 1898, c. 1982; Interview with Bessy Bertha Martinson, born 1897, c. 1982; Interview with Irene CeCelia Vizenor, born 1903, c. 1982, MCTRHP.

31. See Maria Campbell, *Half-Breed* (Lincoln: University of Nebraska Press, 1982); Harrison, *Métis*; Nicks, "Mary Anne's Dilemma"; Brown, "People of Myth."

32. Quotation from "Report of the U.S. Chippewa Commission," 95. See also Kugel, " 'To go About on the Earth,' " 238–39.

33. Quotation from Joseph Alexander Gilfillan and Family Papers, "Ojibway Personal Names, White Earth 1890," compiled by Gilfillan, 21 August 1908, p. 44. See also U.S. OIA, "Records of Investigation of White Earth Mixed Bloods, 1911–1915," Microfilm Roll M444, MHSA, 91–110, 205–6, 266–93; "Report of the U.S. Chippewa Commission," 165; "Voices from the Past: Louis Edward Brunette and Caroline Bisson Norton Family History," n.d.; Becker County Historical Society; Kugel, " 'To Go About on the Earth,' " 240–41.

34. "Minutes of Council of the Mississippi and Otter Tail Pillager Bands," 27 December 1895, BIA RG 75, LR 1895, NARS; Pembina Band to CIA, 8 January 1896, BIA RG 75, LR 1896, NARS; Mississippi Chippewa Delegates to CIA, 3 February 1896, BIA RG 75, LR 1896, NARS; Mississippi Bands to CIA, 3 February 1896, BIA RG 75, LR 1896, NARS; Pembina Band to CIA, 17 March 1897, BIA RG 75, LR 1897, NARS; Letter 7357 (Pembina band members), 27 January 1900, BIA RG 75, LR 1900, NARS; "Minutes of a Council of the Otter Tail Band of Pillager Chippewa Indians of Minnesota," 30 January 1900, BIA RG 75, LR 1900, NARS; Mille Lacs band (at Lawrence) to Knute Nelson, 15 March 1900, BIA RG 75, LR 1900, NARS; "Chiefs of Mississippi Bands" to CIA, 12 February 1902, BIA RG 75, LR 1902, NARS; "Pembina Band of Chippewa" to Simon Michelet, 26 November 1903, BIA RG 75, LR 1903, NARS; "Minutes of a Council of the Chiefs of the Mississippi Bands," 29 July 1904, BIA RG 75, LR 1904, NARS; "Mississippi Chippewa

of White Earth," 22 February 1905, BIA RG 75, LR 1905, NARS; "Minutes of Council of Mississippi Bands," 19 June 1905, BIA RG 75, LR 1905, NARS.

35. Quotation from Wah bah nah quod, Song way way, Mah kah keence, Sha day, and Robert Morrison to CIA, 21 March 1892, BIA RG 75, LR 1892, NARS. See also Chief Mah eng aunce et al., to CIA, 9 April 1894, BIA RG 75, LR 1894, NARS.

36. Chiefs and Members of Chippewa Tribe of Indians to CIA, 18 June 1897, BIA RG 75, LR 1897, NARS.

37. Quotations from T. J. Morgan, CIA, to B. P. Shuler, Agent, 12 October 1889, BIA, LR, OIA, "misc.," KCFRA; Me-zhuc-e-ge-shig's Testimony, 14 April 1914, Ransom J. Powell Papers, Box 5, Folder 29, MHSA, 725. U.S. OIA "Records of Investigation of White Earth Mixed Bloods, 1911–1915," Microfilm Roll M444, MHSA, 543–44. See also U.S. General Land Office, Crookston Land District, "Register of Indian Allotment Entries: Nelson Act," 1901, Minnesota State Archives, MHSA.

38. "1887 Investigation," 6; Mezhuc e ge shig's Testimony, 14 April 1914, Ransom J. Powell Papers, Box 5, Folder 29, MHSA, 750–54.

39. Quotations from W. A. Jones, CIA, to Temperance Chief, Park Ridge, Minnesota, 10 January 1900, BIA RG 75, LR 1900, NARS, and W. A. Jones, CIA, to Michelet, Agent, 8 January 1902, BIA RG 75, OIA, "Land," KCFRA.

40. Joseph Alexander Gilfillan and Family Papers, "The Spirit of Missions," January 1874; "Notes Written by my Mother, Harriet Cook Gilfillan"; "Material Progress"; "A Novel Trip"; taken from *Minnesota Missionary*, June 1879 "Shay-day-ence: A Little Sketch"; "Some Indians I Have Known—Nabi-quan (The Ship) or Rev. Samuel Madison, the Faithful," by J. A. Gilfillan, from *The Redman*, December; "Domestic Missions: The Indian Deacons at White Earth," by the Rev. Joseph A. Gilfillan, 5 December 1888; "Chippewa Missions," printed in the *Detroit Record*, 25 October 1895; J. A. Gilfillan to Mr. Bradbury, 24 July 1900, sent from Sweet Springs, West Virginia; J. A. Gilfillan to Mr. Friedman, Carlisle School, Penn., 13 September 1911 "Indians I Have Known—Na-bi-quan (The Ship)," MHSA; J. A. Gilfillan to Mr. Friedman, Carlisle School, 14 September 1911 "Indians I Have Known—An-i-mi-ki-wi-qwon (the feather of the bird of thunder)"; J. A. Gilfillan to Mr. Friedman, Carlisle School, 15 September 1911 "Indians I Have Known—Nebun-esh-kunk"; J. A. Gilfillan to Mr. Friedman, Carlisle School, n.d. "Indians I Have Known—Ke-zhi-ash (he who sails very fast)." See also Joseph Alexander Gilfillan, Letters, 1883–1913, Microfilm Roll M168, MHSA. See also Kugel, " 'To Go About on the Earth,' " 287–300.

41. Quotations from Pauline Colby Papers, "Reminiscences," 80.

42. Quotations from "Graham Report," 166, 569, and "Report of the U.S. Chippewa Commission," 26, 37, 41, 43, 49, 52, 55; Baraga, *Dictionary of the*

Otchipwe Language, 291; U.S. General Land Office, Crookston Land District, "Register of Indian Allotment Entries: Nelson Act, 1901," Minnesota State Archives, MHSA.

43. Quotation from Me-zhuc-e-ge-shig's Testimony, 14 April 1914, Ransom J. Powell Papers, Box 5, Folder 29, p. 1, MHSA. See also Densmore, *Chippewa Customs*, 9–10; Warren, *History of the Ojibways*, 41–53.

44. Julia Warren Spears Papers, "Interesting Reminiscences of Early Frontier Days," MHSA; "Robert Fairbanks Dead," *Detroit Record*, 12 April 1904, p. 7; "Voices from the Past: Louis Edward Brunette and Caroline Bisson Norton Family History"; "Graham Report," 673, 1516, 1578.

45. Julia Warren Spears Papers, "Some Notes on B. L. Fairbanks," MHSA; "Graham Report," 1645.

46. Quotations from "Graham Report," 1787–1800, 1804, and Interview with Naomi Warren LaDue, born 1906, 24 July 1968, interviewed by Cynthia Kelsey, ms. 222, American Indian Oral History Research Project, University of South Dakota, New York Times Oral History Program, transcription of cassette tape (Sanford, N.C.: Microfilming Corporation of America, 1979), 16.

47. Quotations from "Graham Report," 674, 678.

48. Ibid., 673–79 (quotation on p. 674); U.S. OIA, "Records of Investigation of White Earth Mixed Bloods, 1911–1915," Microfilm Roll M444, MHSA; Timothy J. Sheehan Papers, "Diary," vol. 2, Box 4, MHSA.

49. "Report of the U.S. Chippewa Commission," 105, 108; Me-zhuc-e-ge-shig's Testimony, 14 April 1914, Ransom J. Powell Papers, Box 5, Folder 29, MHSA; "Report of Thomas G. Shearman, Asst. Attorney, Visit to and conference with certain full-blood Indians, ordered by the Department, April 15, in connection with the White Earth Controversy," 6 May 1913, BIA RG 75, CCF 150, WEA, NARS; "Report of Thomas G. Shearman, Investigation of the enrollment of certain mixed blood Chippewa Indians on the White Earth Reservation in Minnesota," 11 December 1913, BIA RG 75, CCF 211, WEA, NARS; C. C. Daniels, Counsel for Respondents, "In the Matter of the Petition of Charles T. Wright et al. for the Purification of the White Earth Roll: Request for Findings of Fact & Brief of Petitioners," 1914, BIA RG 75, CCF 155, WEA, NARS: 115; Council Proceedings at Pine Point, 20–22 January 1915, BIA RG 75, CCF 054, WEA, NARS; Pay kin ah waush, Joseph Critts (Wain che mah dub), Me zhak-ke-ke-shig, and Ojibway, with interpreter Paul H. Beaulieu to CIA, 2 March 1889, BIA RG 75, LR 1889, NARS; Fred Weaver, c. 1982, interviewed by Winona LaDuke, WEOHP, Bemidji State University.

50. "Report of the U.S. Chippewa Commission," 105, 108; Me zhuc-ege shig's Testimony, 14 April 1914: 750, Ransom J. Powell Papers, Box 5, Folder 29, MHSA; U.S. OIA, "Records of Investigation of White Earth Mixed Bloods,

1911–1915," Microfilm Roll M444, MHSA, esp. testimony beginning on pp. 266, 463, 479, and 591.

51. "Report of the U.S. Chippewa Commission," 108.

52. Ibid., 105.

53. Quotations from Pay kin ah waush, Joseph Critts (Wain che mah dub), Me zhak-ke-ke-shig, and Ojibway, with interpreter Paul H. Beaulieu to CIA, 2 March 1889, BIA RG 75, LR 1889, WEA, NARS. See also Council Proceedings at Pine Point, 20–22 January 1915, BIA RG 75, CCF 054, WEA, NARS; Inspection Report of Warren K. Moorehead, 9 August 1909, BIA RG 75, CCF 150, WEA, NARS; Coleman, LaBud, and Humphrey, *Old Crow Wing*, 30–32; "Report of Thomas J. Shearman"; C. C. Daniels, "In the Matter of the Petition of Charles T. Wright," 115. Interview with Fred Weaver, born c. 1900, interviewed by Winona LaDuke, c. 1982, WEOHP, Bemidji State University.

54. Quotations from John R. Howard and John Hinton to Cato Sells, CIA, 11 June 1914, BIA RG 75, CCF 054, WEA, NARS; "Graham Report," 107; C. F. Larrabee, Acting CIA, to Agent, 10 April 1906, BIA, LR, OIA, "Land," KCFRA.

55. Quotations from Affidavit of Mrs. Ella Beaulieu, 18 January 1919, BIA RG 75, CCF 155, WEA, NARS; "Report of Inspector C. M. Knight on the Annual Meeting of the General Council of the Chippewa," at Bemidji, 11–15 July 1916, BIA RG 75, CCF 054, WEA, NARS.

56. Quotation from RCIA, 1894:152. Joseph Alexander Gilfillan and Family Papers, "The Spirit of the Missions," January 1874; "Material Progress"; "The Bishop's Visitation to White Earth Reservation, 1873"; "A Novel Trip," taken from *Minnesota Missionary*, June 1879; "Shay-day-ence: A Little Sketch"; "Notes Written by my Mother, Harriet Cook Gilfillan"; "Some Indians I Have Known: Na-bi-quan (The Ship) or Rev. Samuel Madison, the Faithful," by J. A. Gilfillan, from *The Redman*, December; "Domestic Missions: The Indian Deacons at White Earth," by the Rev. Joseph A. Gilfillan, 5 December 1888; "Chippewa Missions," printed in the *Detroit Record*, 25 October 1895; J. A. Gilfillan to Mr. Bradbury, 24 July 1900; J. A. Gilfillan to Mr. Friedman, Carlisle, Penn., 14 September 1911: "Indians I Have Known: An-i-mi-ki-wi-gwun (the feather of the bird of thunder); J. A. Gilfillan to Mr. Friedman, Carlisle School, 13 September 1911: "Indians I Have Known—Na-bi-quan (The Ship); J. A. Gilfillan to Mr. Friedman, Carlisle School, 15 September 1911, "Indians I Have Known—Ne-bun-esh-kunk; J. A. Gilfillan to Mr. Friedman, Carlisle School, n.d.: "Indians I Have Known—Ke-zhi-ash (he who sails very fast)," MHSA; Joseph Alexander Gilfillan, Letters, 1881–1913, Microfilm Roll M168, MHSA; Zanger, " 'Straight Tongue's Heathen Wards.' "

57. Preceding quotation from "1887 Investigation," 117. See also pp. 45, 64–65, 127, 176, 220, 225–26, 229, 230; RCIA, 1887: 210; 1888: 147; 1894:152; Sister Carol Berg, "Climbing Learners' Hill: Benedictines at White Earth, 1878–1945," Ph.D. Dissertation, University of Minnesota, 1983, 46, 63; Carol J.

Berg, "Agents of Cultural Change: The Benedictines at White Earth," *Minnesota History* 48 (1982): 158–70; John C. Scott, "'To Do Some Good Among the Indians': Nineteenth-Century Benedictine Missions," *Journal of the West* 23 (1984): 26–36.

58. Quotations from Vecsey, *Traditional Ojibwa Religion*, 62, 72, 75. See also Nichols and Nyholm, eds., *Ojibwewi-Ikidowinan*, 58.

59. Warren, *History of the Ojibway*; Ruth Landes, *The Ojibwa Woman* (New York: Columbia University Press, reprint, 1969), 5; A. Irving Hallowell, *Contributions to Anthropology* (Chicago: University of Chicago Press, 1976); A. Irving Hallowell, "Ojibwa World View," in Roger Cowen, ed., *The North American Indians* (New York: Macmillan, 1967); A. Irving Hallowell, "Ojibwa Ontology, Behavior, and World View," in Dennis Tedlock and Barbara Tedlock, eds., *Teachings from the American Earth: Indian Religion and Philosophy* (New York: Liveright, 1975), 141–78; Hallowell, *Culture and Experience*, 112–84; Ruth Landes, *Ojibwa Religion and the Midewiwin* (New York: AMS Press, 1969; reprint of 1938 ed.); Densmore, *Chippewa Customs*, 44–48, 78–97, 175–76; John A. Grim, *The Shaman: Patterns of Siberian and Ojibway Healing* (Norman: University of Oklahoma Press, 1983); Vecsey, *Traditional Ojibwa Religion*.

60. Quotations from Densmore, *How Indians Use Wild Plants*, 322; Vecsey, *Traditional Ojibwa Religion*, 144; Hoffman, "The Midewiwin," 167 (also 149–306). See also Densmore, *Chippewa Customs*, 44–48, 78–97, 175–76; Densmore, *Chippewa Music*, 25, 60, 27, 37, 49, 79, 80, 91, 92, 95, 112, 113.

61. RCIA, 1899: 216.

62. Quotations from Rogers, *Red World and White*, 45, 86.

63. All quotes regarding education from RCIA, 1890; 1892: 151; 1893: 171; 1895: 175; 1896: 170, 172; 1897: 158, 160; 1898: 181; 1899: 215; 1900: 262; 1901: 255; 1905: 235–36; Interview with Evangeline Critts Fairbanks, born 1905, 31 July 1968, interviewed by Cynthia Kelsey, ms 243, 23, American Indian Oral History Research Project, University of South Dakota, New York Times Oral History Program, transcription of cassette tape; Interview with Naomi Warren LaDue, born 1906, 11 July 1968, interviewed by Cynthia Kelsey, ms. 221, American Indian Oral History Research Project, University of South Dakota, New York Times Oral History Program, transcription of cassette tape. See also Sally McBeth, "Indian Boarding Schools and Ethnic Identity: An Example from the Southern Plains Tribes of Oklahoma," *Plains Anthropologist* 28 (1983): 119–28; Diane T. Putney, "Fighting the Scourge: American Indian Morbidity and Federal Policy, 1897–1928," Ph.D. Dissertation, Marquette University, 1980, 78–109; Russell Thornton, *American Indian Holocaust and Survival: A Population History since 1492* (Norman: University of Oklahoma Press, 1987).

64. Rogers, *Red World and White*, 8.

65. U.S. Census Office, 1900 Census Schedules, Microfilm Collection T623: 756, 798; U.S. Census Office, 1910 Census Schedules, Microfilm Collection T624: 689, 710; White Earth Reservation, BIA Census, 1930, Indian Census Rolls, 1885–1940, Microfilm Collection M595, no. 65, BIA RG 75, NARS microfilm publication.

66. Baraga, *Dictionary of the Otchipwe Language,* 124, 421; Nichols and Nyholm, eds., *Ojibwewi-Ikidowinan,* 179.

67. Ke-che-mah-quah's Testimony, September 1914, Testimony taken before C. F. McNamara, Notary Public at Ogema, Ransom J. Powell Papers, Box 6, Folder 34, p. 24, MHSA.

68. Wah-way-zho-o-quay's Testimony, 15 January 1914, Testimony taken at Pine Point, Ransom J. Powell Papers, Box 5, Folder 21, p. 103, MHSA.

69. Ay-dow-ah-cumig-o-quay's Testimony, 15 January 1914, Testimony taken at Pine Point, ibid.

70. Mezhuc-e-ge-shig's Testimony, 14 April 1914, Ransom J. Powell Papers, Box 5, Folder 29, p. 650, MHSA.

71. Quotation from Bay-bah-daung-ay-yaush's Testimony, 15 January 1914, Testimony taken at Pine Point, Ransom J. Powell Papers, Box 5, Folder 21, p. 442, MHSA. See also Nichols and Nyholm, eds., *Ojibwewi-Ikidowinan,* 106. The plural form is *doodemag.*

72. Gah-mah-nah-che-wah-nay's Testimony, 4 February 1914, Ransom J. Powell Papers, Box 5, Folder 26, MHSA.

73. Shin-ow-waince's Testimony, 15 January 1914, Ransom J. Powell Papers, Box 5, Folder 21, p. 458, MHSA.

74. George Morrison's Testimony, September 1914, Testimony before C. E. McNamara, Notary Public at Ogema, Ransom J. Powell Papers, Box 6, Folder 24, p. 51, MHSA.

75. Bay-bah-daung-ay-aush's Testimony, 27 July 1914, Ransom J. Powell Papers, Box 6, Folder 32, p. 1044. MHSA.

76. Quotations from Me-zhuc-e-ge-shig's Testimony, 14 April 1914, Ransom J. Powell Papers, Box 5, Folder 29, pp. 675, 739, 761, MHSA. See also "Report of Thomas G. Shearman, Asst. Attorney, Visit to and Conference with certain full-blood Indians, ordered by the Dept., April 15, in connection with the White Earth controversy," 6 May 1913, BIA RG 75, CCF 150, WEA, NARS; "Report of Thomas J. Shearman, Investigation of the enrollment of certain mixed blood Chippewa Indians on the White Earth Reservation in Minnesota," 11 December 1913, BIA RG 75, CCF 211, WEA, NARS.

77. Quotations from Mah-do-say-quay's Testimony, 9 March 1914, Ransom J. Powell Papers, Box 5, Folder 28, pp. 565, 567, MHSA.

78. Ke-zhe-wash's Testimony, 15 January 1914, Testimony taken at Pine Point, Ransom J. Powell Papers, Box 5, Folder 21, p. 428. MHSA; Shin-ow-aince's Testimony, 15 January 1914, Testimony taken at Pine Point, Ransom J. Powell Papers, Box 5, Folder 21, p. 200, MHSA.

79. "1887 Investigation," 6.

80. 1837 Treaty of St. Peter's, in Kappler, comp., *Indian Affairs*, 2:482–86; 2 August 1847 Treaty at Fond du Lac, in 2:567–69; Interview with Fred Weaver, born 1900, c. 1982, interviewed by Winona LaDuke, WEOHP; Interview with Mary Bellanger, born 1914, c. 1982, interviewer unknown, hand-written synopses of answers to questionnaires, MCTRHP; Interview with Francis Keahna, born 1905, c. 1982, interviewer unknown, hand-written synopses of answers to questionnaires, MCTRHP. Bald eagle translates as *migizi*. Sugar maple translates as *ininaatig*, and leaf as *aniibiish*. Nichols and Nyholm, eds., *Ojibwewi-Ikidowinan*, 63, 170, 176.

81. Densmore, *Chippewa Customs*, 52–53; Ritzenthaler, "Acquisition of Surnames," 175–77; Nichols and Nyholm, eds., *Ojibwewi-Ikidowinan*, 120, 242.

82. Sister Bernard Coleman, *Where the Water Stops: Fond Du Lac Reservation* (Superior, Wisc.: Arrowhead Printing Co., 1967); Harold Hickerson, "The Genesis of a Trading Post Band: The Pembina Chippewa," *Ethnohistory* 3 (1956): 289–345; Alexander Ross, *The Red River Settlement: Its Rise, Progress, and Present State, With Some Account of the Native Races and Its General History, to the Present Day* (London: Smith, Elder and Company, 1856); Peterson, "Many Roads"; Peterson, "Ethnogenesis"; Peterson, "Prelude to Red River"; Peterson, "The People in Between"; Willoughby Babcock, "With Ramsey to Pembina: A Treaty-Making Trip in 1851," *Minnesota History* 38 (1962):1–10; Ella Hawkinson, "The Old Crossing Chippewa Treaty and Its Sequel," *Minnesota History* 15 (1934): 282–300; Gilman, Gilman, and Stultz, *The Red River Trails*; Coleman, LaBud, and Humphrey, *Old Crow Wing*; Edmund Danziger, *The Chippewas of Lake Superior* (Norman: University of Oklahoma Press, 1979).

83. Hickerson, *The Chippewa and Their Neighbors*; Hickerson, "The Southwestern Chippewa"; Warren, *History of the Ojibway*; Roger Buffalohead and Priscilla Buffalohead, *Against the Tide of American History: The Story of the Mille Lacs Anishinaabe* (Cass Lake: Minnesota Chippewa Tribe, 1985); "Report of Thomas G. Shearman, Asst. Attorney, Visit to and Conference with certain full-blood Indians, ordered by the Dept., April 15, in connection with the White Earth controversy," 6 May 1913, BIA RG 75, CCF 150, WEA, NARS; "Report of Thomas J. Shearman, Investigation of the enrollment of certain mixed blood Chippewa Indians on the White Earth Reservation in Minnesota," 11 December 1913, BIA RG 75, CCF 211, WEA, NARS.

84. Quotations from Gilfillan, "The Ojibways," 82; Rogers, *Red World and White*, 130.

85. "Local and Personal," *The Tomahawk*, 9 April 1903 to 1 September 1904.

86. Quotations from *The Tomahawk*, 23 April 1903: 4; RCIA, 1901: 225.

87. Gilfillan, "The Ojibways," 122.

88. The foregoing description is drawn from accounts contained in *The Toma-*

hawk, 21 May 1903: 4; 28 May 1903: 1; 4 June 1903: 4. Quotations from 11 June 1903: 1; 14 June 1903: 1; 15 June 1903: 1.

89. For historical photographs of the June 14 Celebration, see Audio-Visual Archives, MHS.

90. Quotation from Rogers, *Red World and White*, 145, and see 131–53 in general. See also Fredrik Barth, "Introduction," in Fredrik Barth, ed., *Ethnic Groups and Boundaries: The Social Organization of Culture Difference* (London: George Allen and Unwin, 1969), 9–38; Malcolm McFee, "The 150% Man, a Product of Blackfeet Acculturation," *American Anthropologist* 70 (1968): 1096–1107; Ronald L. Trosper, "Native American Boundary Maintenance: The Flathead Indian Reservation in Montana, 1860–1970," *Ethnicity* 3 (1976): 256–74; Karen I. Blu, *The Lumbee Problem: The Making of an American Indian People* (Cambridge: Cambridge University Press, 1980); Clifton, "Alternate Identities"; James A. Clifton, "Culture, Identity, and the Individual," in P. Whitten and D. Hunter, eds., *The Study of Anthropology* (New York: Harper & Row, 1975); Ann McElroy, "Oopeeleeka and Mina: Contrasting Responses to Modernization of Two Baffin Island Inuit Women," in Clifton, ed., *Being and Becoming Indian*, 290–318; Ann McElroy, *Alternatives in Modernization: Styles and Strategies in the Acculturative Behavior of Baffin Island Inuit* (New Haven: HRAFlex Books, ND 5-001 Ethnography Series, 1977); Abner Cohen, *Two-Dimensional Man: An Essay on the Anthropology of Power and Symbolism in Complex Society* (Berkeley: University of California Press, 1974); Steven Polgar, "Biculturation of Mesquakie Teenage Boys," *American Anthropologist* 62 (1960): 217–35; George L. Hicks and P. E. Leiss, eds., *Ethnic Encounters: Identities and Contexts* (Boston: Duxbury Press, 1977).

Chapter 3. Jack Pine, White Pine, and Porcupine

1. "Report of the U.S. Chippewa Commission," 85–115.
2. Reports of the Secretary of the Interior (hereafter RSI), 1891: xliii; *U.S. Statutes at Large* 24:388–91.
3. RSI 1895: xi, 1896: xx, 1898: xxxiii; *Mississippi Valley Lumberman*, 28 April 1893: 6; *Crookston Times*, 27 April 1893: 3; 22 May 1893: 3; Folwell, *History of Minnesota*, 4:236–37.
4. Quote from "The Report of Indian Inspector J. George Wright, together with Accompanying Papers, Relative to Pine Lands and Pine Timber on the Red Lake Reservation, in the State of Minnesota," Senate Document 3562, no. 85, 55 Congress, 1 Session (1897): 2, 5 (hereafter "Wright Report"); RSI 1896: iii, xxi, cxxxi; "Correspondence Relating to Timber on Chippewa Indian Reservations," Senate Documents 3731, no. 70, 55 Congress, 3 Session (1899): 2–12; Folwell, *History of Minnesota*, 4:239.

5. "Wright Report," 11.
6. "Chippewa Indians in Minnesota," House Report 3269, no. 459, 53 Congress, 2 Session (1894); "Chippewa Indians in Minnesota," House Report 3457, no. 119, 54 Congress, 1 Session (1896); *U.S. Statutes at Large* 29:17.
7. RSI 1900: lvi; 1901: lxxiii.
8. RSI 1901: lxxiii; 1902:29.
9. "Graham Report," i–xxvi, quote from 241.
10. Ibid., 276–313; Folwell, *History of Minnesota*, 4:242–43.
11. Minnesota, *Laws* 1899: 131.
12. *U.S. Statutes at Large* 32:400–404; Folwell, *History of Minnesota*, 4:249–53.
13. *U.S. Statutes at Large* 32:275.
14. RCIA 1902: 225; 1904: 62, 63, 66; 1905: 30, 61; 1906: 94; RSI 1903: 34, 202–6; 1904: 36; Folwell, *History of Minnesota*, 4:263–64.
15. "Graham Report," 54, map opposing 1112; Railroad and Warehouse Commission *Reports* 1905: 15; Folwell, *History of Minnesota*, 4:264–65.
16. RCIA 1905: 61.
17. *U.S. Statutes at Large* 33:209; "Sale of Pine Timber on White Earth and Red Lake (diminished) Reservation," House Reports 4023, no. 492, 56 Congress, 1 Session (1900); *Congressional Record*, 56 Congress, 1 Session: 56, 2566; 58 Congress, 2 Session: 700; Acting CIA to D. S. Hall, Chairman of Chippewa Commission, 31 August 1892, BIA RG 75, CCF 150, WEA, NARS; Folwell, *History of Minnesota*, 4:265–66.
18. *U.S. Statutes at Large* 33:539; "Allotments to Indians on White Earth Reservation in Minnesota," House Reports 4023, no. 493, 56 Congress, 1 Session; *Congressional Record*, 56 Congress, 1 Session: 56, 2566; 58 Congress, 2 Session: 3660, 4413, 5546, 5825; Theodore H. Beaulieu to Frank M. Eddy, 29 January 1900, "The Land Allotment Question of the Chippewas of the Mississippi on the White Earth Reservation, Minnesota," Detroit, Minnesota, 1900, MHS; "Graham Report," 822–27; Wah bah nah quod, Song way way, Mahkah keence, Shaday, Robert Morrison (interpreter) and witnesses Fred Smith, Charles Wright, Theo. H. Beaulieu, Gus H. Beaulieu to CIA, 21 March 1892, BIA RG 75, LR 1892, NARS; "Minutes of a Council of the White Earth Bands of Mississippi Chippewa," 12 January 1904, BIA RG 75, LR 1904, NARS; Simon Michelet to CIA, March 2, 1904, BIA RG 75, LR 1904, NARS; "Minutes of a Council of the Mississippi Bands of Minnesota Chippewa Indians at White Earth Agency to adopt Halvor Steenerson of Crookston, Minnesota," 9 May 1904, BIA RG 75, LR 1904, NARS; *The Tomahawk*, 14 April 1904: 4; 24 April 1904: 1; 28 April 1904: 1; 23 June 1904: 1; Secretary of the Interior Hitchcock to CIA, 15 April 1904, BIA RG 75, LR 1904, NARS.
19. "Graham Report," 242.
20. *U.S. Statutes at Large* 33:539.
21. "Graham Report," 525–41.

22. Ibid., 34, 543–44, 547–51, 586–91, 619, all quotes from 1521–22; Folwell, *History of Minnesota*, 4:267–68; Interview with Maggie Hanks, born 1888, c. 1982, WEOHP, Bemidji State University.

23. "Graham Report," 586–91, all quotes from 587–88 and 1522; Folwell, *History of Minnesota*, 4:268.

24. "Graham Report," 555–59, 560–62, 568–79, 586–91; Oh-bow-we-ge-shik, Pen-de-ga-ge-shik, Pe-do-se-dey, John W. Stephens to CIA, May 23, 1906, BIA RG 75, LR 1906, NARS.

25. "Graham Report," 555–59, quote from 589; Folwell, *History of Minnesota*, 4:269.

26. All quotes from "Graham Report," 560–62.

27. Ibid., 555–59; quote from 558.

28. Ibid., 560–67; Folwell, *History of Minnesota*, 4:270.

29. "Graham Report," 568–74, 800; quote from McLaughlin, 569; Folwell, *History of Minnesota*, 4:271.

30. "Graham Report," 800–802, 815–18.

31. All quotes from ibid., 805–6.

32. Ibid., 548–49.

33. Ibid., 618–23.

34. Ibid., 646–51; Folwell, *History of Minnesota*, 4:273–74; C. F. Larrabee, Acting CIA, "Regulations as to the sale of Timber on White Earth," 3 August 1905, BIA RG 75, CCF 339, WEA, NARS; "Notice as to Proposals for Purchase of Indian Timber," Department of the Interior, U.S. Indian Service, August 1905, BIA RG 75, CCF 339, WEA, NARS; J. R. Farr, General Superintendent of Logging, to CIA, 28 October 1905, BIA RG 75, CCF 339, WEA, NARS. "Indian Timber May Go Cheap," *Minneapolis Journal*, 22 August 1905; "Protest Filed by Delegation," *Minneapolis Journal*, 23 August 1905.

35. "Graham Report," 646–62; Folwell, *History of Minnesota*, 4:273–76.

36. "Graham Report," 1843–47.

37. *The Tomahawk*, 17 May 1903: 1; George Bellanger to James Garfield, Secretary of the Interior, Received by OIA 28 August 1907, BIA RG 75, CCF 306, WEA, NARS.

38. Hoxie, *A Final Promise*, 164.

39. *U.S. Statutes at Large* 34:182–83; McDonnell, *The Dispossession of the American Indian*, 87–102; Carlson, *Decline of Indian Farming*; Leonard A. Carlson, "Federal Policy and Indian Land: Economic Interests and the Sale of Indian Allotted Land, 1900–1934," *Agricultural History* 52 (1983): 33–45.

40. Quotes from RCIA 1906: 30, and 1907: 64.

41. RCIA 1906: 30.

42. *U.S. Statutes at Large* 34:353, 1034; *Congressional Record*, 59 Congress, 1 Session: 5784, 6463, 7424, 8264, 8348, 9157; "Graham Report," 665–70; Folwell, *History of Minnesota*, 4:276–77.

43. RCIA 1906: 148.

44. RCIA 1906: 147–48; "Graham Report," 721–25, 2652–53, 2660, 2667; *Minneapolis Journal*, 17 July 1906: 1; 18 July 1906: 1; 21 July 1906: 2; *Fergus Falls Weekly Journal*, 26 July 1906: 2; *Crookston Times*, 18 July 1906: 8; Warren K. Moorehead, *The American Indian in the United States, 1850–1914* (Andover, Mass.: Harvard University Press, 1920), 77–78.

45. "Graham Report," 2752.

46. RCIA 1906: 250.

47. "Graham Report," 246–48, 730–32, 767–68.

48. Ibid., 72, 93, 113, 246–48, 730–32; "Report on White Earth Schools and Reservation by L. F. Michael, Supervisor," Section 3, Lands, 5 December 1913, BIA RG 75, CCF 300, WEA, NARS; Gus H. Beaulieu to Kenneth S. Murchison, 21 July 1906, BIA RG 75, LR 1906, NARS.

49. "Graham Report," 40, 113, 730–32; Warren K. Moorehead to CIA, Received by Indian Office (10), 8 April 1909, BIA RG 75, CCF 150, WEA, NARS; Warren K. Moorehead to CIA, 8 April 1909, BIA RG 75, CCF 150, WEA, NARS; R. S. Connell, Special Agent, to CIA, October 1906, BIA RG 75, LR 1906, NARS; C. F. Larrabee, Acting CIA, to Agent, White Earth Agency, 15 August 1906, BIA RG 75, LR 1906, NARS.

50. "Graham Report," 74, 99.

51. Simon Michelet to CIA, 28 August 1906, BIA RG 75, LR 1906, NARS.

52. "Graham Report," 70; *The Tomahawk*, 24 February 1910.

53. "Graham Report," 246–48, 2224–76, map opposing 1112.

54. Ibid., 1044–46.

55. See letterheads scattered through Boxes 1 and 2, Ransom J. Powell Papers, MHSA; John Vig to Secretary of the Interior, 31 July 1906, BIA RG 75, LR 1906, NARS; Kolback Lumber Co., Oskaloosa, Iowa, to Secretary of the Interior, 21 August 1907, BIA RG 75, CCF 310, WEA, NARS; Benjamin E. Reynolds, Winnebago, Minnesota to Secretary of the Interior, 27 September 1909, BIA RG 75, CCF 310, WEA, NARS; C. F. Hanke to C. A. Baker, State Bank of Ogema, 10 March 1910, BIA RG 75, CCF 310, WEA, NARS; A. F. Richardson, Gilman, Montana, to U.S. Land Officer, 11 February 1914, BIA RG 75, CCF 300, WEA, NARS. See equity case files contained in the Ransom J. Powell Papers, Microfilm Roll 4, MHSA. See also Holly Youngbear-Tibbets, "Without Due Process: The Alienation of Individual Trust Allotments of the White Earth Anishinaabeg," *American Indian Culture and Research Journal* 15 (1991): 93–138; Cronon, *Nature's Metropolis*, especially part 2, "Nature to Market," 97–259.

56. All quotes so far from "Graham Report," 731–32, 2039–41, 2045–47; Warren K. Moorehead to CIA, 8 April 1909, BIA RG 75, CCF 150, WEA, NARS; Watrin, *The Ponsfordian*, 14; Folwell, *History of Minnesota*, 4:281–82. See

also "Graham Report," 1005–49, 1817; "Inspection Report of Warren K. Moorehead re. Full Bloods at White Earth," 9 August 1909, BIA RG 75, CCF 050, WEA, NARS; "Report of E. B. Linnen and W. K. Moorehead," 30 September 1909, BIA RG 75, CCF 150 and 310, WEA, NARS; "Records Relating to Investigation of Allotments—W. E. Agency," BIA RG 75, E 1260, WEA, NARS; Youngbear-Tibbets, "Without Due Process," 100–101.

57. Youngbear-Tibbets, "Without Due Process," 97.

58. Ah-bow-we-ge-shig to CIA, 14 December 1909, BIA RG 75, CCF 310, WEA, NARS.

59. Memo attached to R. G. Valentine, CIA, to R. A. Ballinger, Secretary of the Interior, 10 December 1909, BIA RG 75, CCF 150, WEA, NARS; J. Weston Allen to CIA, 19 September 1909, BIA RG 75, CCF 150, WEA, NARS; Warren K. Moorehead to CIA, December 1909, BIA RG 75, CCF 150, WEA, NARS; John R. Howard to CIA, 6 December 1909, 7 February 1910, BIA RG 75, CCF 310, WEA, NARS.

60. "Graham Report," 40.

61. Ibid., 19–21.

62. John R. Howard to E. B. Linnen, 15 January 1910, BIA RG 75, CCF 150, WEA, NARS; Gus H. Beaulieu to President of U.S.A., 1 May 1912, BIA RG 75, CCF 150, WEA, NARS; "Report of Thomas G. Shearman, Asst. Attorney, Visit to and conference with certain full-blood Indians, ordered by the Department, April 15, in connection with the White Earth Controversy," 6 May 1913, BIA RG 75, CCF 150, WEA, NARS; C. C. Daniels to E. Marvin Underwood, Asst. Atty. Gen., 19 June 1914, BIA RG 75, CCF 154, WEA, NARS; Youngbear-Tibbets, in "Without Due Process," coined the term "pine cartel."

63. Quoted in Folwell, *History of Minnesota*, 4:285 footnote. Both quotes appear in Youngbear-Tibbets, "Without Due Process," 103.

64. Quote from Marsden C. Burch to Attorney General, 23 December 1910, BIA RG 75, CCF 150, WEA, NARS. See also "Lists Showing the degree of Indian Blood of Certain Persons Holding Land upon the White Earth Reservation in Minnesota and a List Showing the Date of Death of Certain Persons Who Held Land upon Such Reservation" (Washington, D.C.: U.S. Government Printing Office, 1911); "Graham Report," 55–57, 1300–20.

65. Quotes from "Graham Report," xx. Also quoted in Youngbear-Tibbets, "Without Due Process," 102.

66. *Minneapolis Journal*, 16 January 1913: 1, 13 November 1913: 1; Youngbear-Tibbets, "Without Due Process," 102.

67. *Congressional Record*, 61 Congress, 3 Session, 1411, 2657–2660; *Detroit Record*, 29 November 1912: 1; Folwell, *History of Minnesota*, 4:286; Attorney General to Secretary of the Interior, 19 March 1910, BIA RG 75, CCF 150, WEA, NARS.

68. House Reports 6334, no. 1459, 62 Congress, 3 Session; *Congressional Record*, 62 Congress, 3 Session: 2014, 2762; 63 Congress, 1 Session, indexed under

House Bill 1917; *U.S. Statutes at Large* 38:88; 39:36; Folwell, *History of Minnesota*, 4:286–87.

69. Enclosure contained in R. J. Powell to Daniel B. Henderson, 27 May 1913, Ransom J. Powell Papers, Box 4, Folder 13, MHSA.

70. Powell to N. B. Hurr, 30 April 1913, Ransom J. Powell Papers, Box 1, item 132, MHSA, also quoted in Youngbear-Tibbets, "Without Due Process," 104.

71. Youngbear-Tibbets, "Without Due Process," 114.

72. R. J. Powell to R. L. Smith Land Co., 16 April 1917, Ransom J. Powell Papers, Box 1, MHSA.

73. R. J. Powell to J. W. Nunn, 24 May 1917, ibid.

74. Theodore H. Beaulieu to R. J. Powell, 17 January 1916, ibid.

75. R. J. Powell to Becker County Land and Loan Company, 6 January 1919; R. J. Powell to Fred Sanders, 16 January 1919, ibid.

76. Julius H. Brown to R. J. Powell, 30 January 1915; R. J. Powell to Julius H. Brown, 17 February 1915, ibid.

77. Gus H. Beaulieu to R. J. Powell, 10 May 1916; R. J. Powell to Mrs. Mary English, 11 July 1918, ibid.

78. All quotes from Sho-ne-yah-quay to R. J. Powell, 27 October 1917; R. J. Powell to Sho-ne-yah-quay, 22 November 1917; Eugene Bird to R. J. Powell, 12 March 1919; R. J. Powell to Eugene Bird, 9 April 1919, ibid.

79. Quote from R. J. Powell to Editor, *Minneapolis Tribune*, post–April 1917, Ransom J. Powell Papers, Box 4, Folder 14, MHSA. See also *U.S. Statutes at Large* 38:88; 39:136; RCIA 1914: 64, 72; 1915: 35; "The Book of Families," Ransom J. Powell Papers, MHSA; Folwell, *History of Minnesota*, 4:291; J. H. Hinton, Special Indian Agent, to CIA, 24 April 1914, BIA RG 75, CCF 300, WEA, NARS; Gordon Cain, Commissioner, to CIA, 18 May 1914, BIA RG 75, CCF 300, WEA, NARS; Memorandum from C. C. Daniels "Relative to the Chippewa Commission Appointed under Act of June 30, 1913," no date, BIA RG 75, CCF 300, WEA, NARS; E. B. Meritt, Assistant CIA, to Secretary of the Interior, 21 August 1915, BIA RG 75, CCF 300, WEA, NARS.

80. All quotes from Youngbear-Tibbets, "Without Due Process," 106–7.

81. RCIA 1914: 64, 72; 1915: 35; Attorney General *Reports* 1913: 44; *Minneapolis Journal*, 5 April 1914: 6; "Graham Report," 1308; Folwell, *History of Minnesota*, 4:288; Decision of Judge Morris, U.S. District 4, District of Minnesota, 6th Division, in equity suits: *U.S. vs. First National Bank of Detroit*, no. 356; *U.S. vs. Nichols-Chisolm Lumber Co. et al.*, 234 U.S. 245 (1914); J. H. Hinton, Special Agent, to CIA, 24 November 1913, BIA RG 75, CCF 150, WEA, NARS.

82. *Minneapolis Journal*, 19 June 1914: 13; 19 December 1915: 6; 24 December 1915: 1–2; 19 January 1916: 18; 27 January 1916: 2; Folwell, *History of Minnesota*, 4:288–89; R. J. Powell to J. T. Van Metre, 8 March 1916, Ransom J. Powell Papers, Box 1, MHSA; Youngbear-Tibbets, "Without Due Process," 107–11.

83. *Minneapolis Journal*, 1 May 1918: 1, 5 May 1918: 12; Folwell, *History of Minnesota*, 4:290–91.

84. Jim Jugg to R. J. Powell, 6 February 1919, Ransom J. Powell Papers, Box 4, Folder 14, MHSA.

85. R. J. Powell to Julius Brown, 12 March 1915, Ransom J. Powell Papers, Box 1, MHSA.

86. Aleŝ Hrdliĉka, "Trip to Chippewa Indians of Minnesota," *Smithsonian Miscellaneous Collections* 66, 3 (1915): 73.

87. Aleŝ Hrdliĉka, "Anthropology of the Chippewa," in F. W. Hodge, ed., *Holmes Anniversary Volume: Anthropological Essays* (Washington D.C.: U.S. Government Printing Office, 1916), 202–3.

88. Youngbear-Tibbets, "Without Due Process," 134, note 36.

89. Hal Downey to R. J. Powell, 25 February 1916, Ransom J. Powell Papers, Box 1, MHSA.

90. Both quotes from A. E. Jenks to R. J. Powell, 21 March 1917, ibid.

91. Quotes from Mezhucegeshig's Testimony, 14 April 1914, Ransom J. Powell Papers, Box 5, Folder 29, MHSA; Mah-do-say-quay's Testimony, 9 March 1914, 567, Ransom J. Powell Papers, Box 5, Folder 28, p. 567, MHSA; Ay-dah-way-cumig-o-quay's Testimony, 15 January 1914, Ransom J. Powell Papers, Box 5, Folder 21, p. 72, MHSA.

92. Quote from Youngbear-Tibbets, "Without Due Process," 111. See also Aleŝ Hrdliĉka, "Physical Anthropology in America: An Historical Sketch," *American Anthropologist* n.s. 16 (1914): 508–54; Hrdliĉka, "Trip to the Chippewa"; Hrdliĉka, "Anthropology of the Chippewa," 198–227; Aleŝ Hrdliĉka, "Anthropological Work among the Sioux and Chippewa," *Smithsonian Miscellaneous Collections* 66, 17 (1915); Albert E. Jenks, *Indian White Amalgamation: An Anthropometric Study*, Studies in the Social Sciences no. 6 (Minneapolis: University of Minnesota Press, 1916); David L. Beaulieu, "Curly Hair and Big Feet: Physical Anthropology and Land Allotment on the White Earth Chippewa Reservation," *American Indian Quarterly* 8 (1984): 281–314; Folwell, *History of Minnesota*, 4:292.

93. *U.S. Statutes at Large* 38:88; 39:136; 379; RCIA 1918: 61; *Minneapolis Tribune*, 1 November 1920, 13 November 1920; *Detroit Record*, 10 May 1918: 1, 31 May 1918: 2, 2 May 1919: 1; *Fergus Falls Daily Journal*, 12 November 1920: 1, 13 November 1920: 1; Folwell, *History of Minnesota*, 4:293–94.

94. "Roll of Chippewa Allotted Land in White Earth Reservation, 1917," BIA RG 75, Consolidated Chippewa, Oversize Documents, KCFRA; Folwell, *History of Minnesota*, 4:294.

95. Marvin Harris, *The Rise of Anthropological Theory: A History of Theories of Culture* (New York: Crowell, 1968); Curtis M. Hinsley, *Savages and Scientists: The Smithsonian Institution and the Development of American Anthropology, 1846–1910* (Washington, D.C.: Smithsonian Institution Press, 1981). Hoxie, *A Final Promise*; Stephen Jay Gould, *The Mismeasure of Man*

(New York: W. W. Norton, 1981); Kathleen Gough, "Anthropology: Child of Imperialism," *Monthly Review* 19: 11 (1967): 12–27.

96. Louisa Fineday to Chippewa Enrollment Commission, 3 March 1920, Ransom J. Powell Papers, Box 2, MHSA.

97. Folwell, *History of Minnesota*, 4:295–96.

98. McDonnell, *Dispossession and the American Indian*; Hoxie, *A Final Promise*; Thomas M. Holm, "Indians and Progressives: From Vanishing Policy to the Indian New Deal," Ph.D. Dissertation, University of Oklahoma, 1978; McDonnell, "The Disintegration of the Indian Estate"; Carlson, *Indians, Bureaucrats, and Land*.

Chapter 4. Warehousers and Sharks

1. Mancur Olson, *The Logic of Collective Action: Public Goods and the Theory of Groups* (Cambridge: Harvard University Press, 1965); Pierre Clastres, *Society against the State: Essays in Political Anthropology* (New York: Zone Books, 1987).

2. "Graham Report," 795.

3. Quote from C. F. Hauke, 2d Assistant CIA to John R. Howard, 23 November 1910, BIA RG 75, CCF 050, WEA, NARS. See also Charles T. Wright to C. E. Richardson, 28 October 1909, BIA RG 75, CCF 050, WEA, NARS; C. E. Richardson to CIA, 28 February 1910, BIA RG 75, CCF 050, WEA, NARS; CIA to C. E. Richardson, post-28 February 1910, BIA RG 75, CCF 050, WEA, NARS; John R. Howard to CIA, 11 November 1910, BIA RG 75, CCF 050, WEA, NARS; Charles T. Wright to John R. Howard, 2 May 1910, BIA RG 75, CCF 050, WEA, NARS; John R. Howard to Charles T. Wright, 8 May 1910, BIA RG 75, CCF 050, WEA, NARS; Charles T. Wright to John R. Howard, 11 May 1910, BIA RG 75, CCF 050, WEA, NARS; Affidavit of O-my-ah-be-tung, 17 June 1910, BIA RG 75, CCF 050, WEA, NARS; Affidavit of Kah-gon-daush or George Walters, 17 June 1910, BIA RG 75, CCF 050, WEA, NARS; C. F. Hauke, 2d Assistant CIA to John R. Howard, 23 November 1910, BIA RG 75, CCF 050, WEA, NARS.

4. Charles T. Wright, "In the Matter of the Petition of Charles T. Wright et al. for the Purification of the White Earth Indian Roll Brief of Petitioners (Washington, D.C.: U.S. Government Printing Office, 1914).

5. Ah-bow-ege-shig's remarks, Report of a "Full Blood" Delegation to Washington, D.C." Received by Indian Office 8 February 1911, BIA RG 75, CCF 050, WEA, NARS.

6. Both quotes from Wah-we-yea-cumig or Round Earth, Head Chief of the Mille Lacs Chippewa, to Francis Leupp, CIA, 24 January 1909, BIA RG 75, CCF 050, WEA, NARS.

7. Both quotations from Proceedings of a Council called by the "Full Blood Faction," 21 May 1913, BIA RG 75, CCF 156, WEA, NARS.

8. Both quotes from May-zhuc-ke-ge-shig to CIA, 10 May 1909, BIA RG 75, CCF 050, WEA, NARS.

9. Interview with Josephine Warren Robinson, born c. 1894, 9 August 1968, interviewed by Cynthia Kelsey, ms. 190, transcription of cassette tape, American Indian Oral History Research Project, part 2, University of South Dakota, New York Times Oral History Program (Sanford, N.C.: Microfilming Corporation of America, 1979), 18.

10. The Indian Office issued suspension letters to each of the eighty-six individuals on 25 November 1911. R. A. Valentine, CIA, to Benjamin L. Fairbanks, 25 November 1911, BIA RG 75, CCF 211, WEA, NARS; George B. Edgerton to CIA, 25 January 1912, BIA RG 75, CCF 211, WEA, NARS. Gus Beaulieu denied the authority of the Indian Office to take such action. Gus H. Beaulieu to R. A. Valentine, CIA, 27 January 1912, BIA RG 75, CCF 211, WEA, NARS. Robert G. Beaulieu also protested. Robert G. Beaulieu to R. A. Valentine, CIA, 18 January 1912, BIA RG 75, CCF 211, WEA, NARS; C. F. Hauke, 2d Assistant CIA, to Robert G. Beaulieu, 30 January 1912, BIA RG 75, CCF 211, WEA, NARS. Many of the suspendees hired the same law firm to represent them. C. F. Hauke, 2d Assistant CIA, to Messrs. Edgerton and Edgerton, Attorneys-at-Law, 8 February 1912, BIA RG 75, CCF 211, WEA, NARS; M. C. Burch to CIA, 17 October 1911, BIA RG 75, CCF 211, WEA, NARS. Suspended individuals drew on all manner of personal and business ties to support their right to enrollment. The Indian Office received letters of support from Senators Knute Nelson and Moses E. Clapp and from such prominent businessmen as Frank B. Kellogg. A collection of such correspondence exists as BIA RG 75, CCF 211, WEA, NARS. A detailed defense of the position of the eighty-six individuals can be found in Webster Ballinger, Attorney for Respondent Beaulieu, "In the Matter of the Petition of Charles T. Wright et al. for the purification of the White Earth Roll: Brief on Behalf of Respondent Gus H. Beaulieu," received by Indian Office 1 February 1916, BIA RG 75, CCF 211, WEA, NARS.

11. Legislative Committee of the Chippewa General Council to Selden G. Hopkins, Assistant Secretary of the Interior, 18 February 1918, BIA RG 75, CCF 054, WEA, NARS.

12. Quote from Youngbear-Tibbets, "Without Due Process," 110. See also *The Tomahawk*, 20 July 1916: 1.

13. Linking names attached to council proceedings and petitions with BIA censuses for White Earth can reveal Indian leaders' band affiliations. Names of "chiefs" and "headmen" tend to represent band constituencies and are the most diagnostic. Enough linkages can be made to reveal changing political affiliations. See also Jacob Folstrum to Department of Interior, 18 February 1902, BIA RG 75, LR 1902, WEA, NARS; Charles T. Wright to CIA, 28 February 1905, BIA RG 75, LR 1904, WEA, NARS; Charles T. Wright and George Walters

to James S. Sherman, Chairman, Committee on Indian Affairs, 7 February 1908, BIA RG 75, CCF 056, WEA, NARS; May zhuc ke ge shig to CIA, 10 May 1909, BIA RG 75, CCF 050, WEA, NARS; "Chiefs of the White Earth Indian Reservation": May zhah ke ge shig, Mah eng aunce, Peter Morrison, James Rice, and J. E. Perrault to CIA, 5 April 1909, BIA RG 75, CCF 050, WEA, NARS; Isabel Schneider to Major J. R. Howard, 17 March 1909, BIA RG 75, CCF 050, WEA, NARS; Wah-we-yea-cumig or Round Earth, Head Chief of Mille Lacs Chippewa to Francis E. Leupp, CIA, 24 January 1909, BIA RG 75, CCF 050, WEA, NARS; Theo. H. Beaulieu to Warren K. Moorehead, 17 February 1910, BIA RG 75, CCF 056, WEA, NARS; Petition from "Full Blood" Council at Pine Point to Superintendent and Special Disbursing Agent, 10 March 1910, BIA RG 75, CCF 056, WEA, NARS; Isabel Schneider to the Attorney General, 13 December 1910, BIA RG 75, CCF 050, WEA, NARS; Ga je ge zhick and Peter Skippingday to Judge Long, 1 February 1911, BIA RG 75, CCF 056, WEA, NARS; Report of a "Full Blood" Delegation to Washington, D.C., Received by Indian Office 8 February 1911, BIA RG 75, CCF 056, WEA, NARS; Statements made by Indians regarding "the occurrence at their dance ring on June 16, 1911," 17 June 1911, BIA RG 75, CCF 056, WEA, NARS; Star Bad Boy to CIA, 22 December 1911, BIA RG 75, CCF 050, WEA, NARS; Theo. H. Beaulieu to Warren K. Moorehead, 15 April 1911, BIA RG 75, CCF 424, WEA, NARS; Chief May-zhuc-ke-ge-shig to CIA, 3 October 1912, BIA RG 75, CCF 056, WEA, NARS; Chief Oge-mah-woub, Chief of Mississippi band to CIA, 28 October 1912, BIA RG 75, CCF 056, WEA, NARS.

14. John R. Howard to CIA, 3 November 1913, BIA RG 75, CCF 056, WEA, NARS; May zhuc ke ge shig to CIA, 10 May 1909, BIA RG 75, CCF 050, WEA, NARS; Wah-we-yea-cumig or Round Earth, Head Chief of Mille Lacs Chippewa to Francis E. Leupp, CIA, 24 January 1909, BIA RG 75, CCF 056, WEA, NARS; Ga-je-je-ge-zhick and Peter Skippingday to Judge Long, 1 February 1911, BIA RG 75, CCF 056, WEA, NARS; Chief May-zhuc-ke-ge-shig to CIA, 3 October 1912, BIA RG 75, CCF 056, WEA, NARS; Council Proceedings at Pine Point, 20–22 January 1915, BIA RG 75, CCF 054, WEA, NARS.

15. "Council of Indians of the White Earth Reservation," at Pine Point, 1 May 1913, BIA RG 75, CCF 054, WEA, NARS; Council called by the "Full Blood Faction," 21 May 1913, BIA RG 75, CCF 056, WEA, NARS; Kay-dah-ge-gwon-nay-aush, May-zhuck-e-gwon-abe, and Ah-bow-e-ge-shig, Business Committee at Pine Point to Washington, D.C., 5 August 1913, BIA RG 75, CCF 054, WEA, NARS (The Business Committee reported on a Council at Pine Point on 7 July 1913, where they formed "a union of the full blood Indians . . . on the several reservations"); "Council at Pine Point," 3 October 1913, BIA RG 75, CCF 056, WEA, NARS; "Full blood Indian Council," at Pine Point, 28 May 1914, BIA RG 75, CCF 056, WEA, NARS; "General Council, Indians of the White Earth Reservation at Pine Point," 2 December 1914, BIA RG 75, CCF

054, WEA, NARS; Council Proceedings at Pine Point, 20–22 January 1915, BIA RG 75, CCF 054, WEA, NARS; "Full Blood Petition," 3 May 1915, BIA RG 75, CCF 054, WEA, NARS; "General Council of the Chippewa," at Ponsford, 30 September and 1, 2, and 4 October 1915, BIA RG 75, CCF 054, WEA, NARS; Ah-bow-ege-shig and the Full Blood Council, 24 January 1916, BIA RG 75, CCF 054, WEA, NARS; "General Council of Chippewa Indians," at Pine Point, 16–17 March 1916, BIA RG 75, CCF 054, WEA, NARS; Report of a Conference between Assistant CIA Meritt, William Dailey, interpreter, Ah-bow-e-ge-shig and George Walters, 25 March 1916, BIA RG 75, CCF 056, WEA, NARS; "Indians of the White Earth Reservation in Council," at Pine Point, 31 January 1913, BIA RG 75, CCF 054, WEA, NARS.

16. "Council called by the 'Full Blood Faction,'" 21 May 1913, BIA RG 75, CCF 056, WEA, NARS.

17. Quotations from "Indians of the White Earth Reservation in Council," at Pine Point, 31 January 1913, BIA RG 75, CCF 054, WEA, NARS and "Full blood Indians residing at White Earth Agency" to CIA, 17 February 1913, BIA RG 75, CCF 054, WEA, NARS. See also Charles T. Wright and Benjamin Casswell to Cato Sells, CIA, 5 January 1913, BIA RG 75, CCF 056, WEA, NARS; Joseph Northrup, Chairman of Convention, "Notice to Chippewas of Minnesota," 4 February 1913, BIA RG 75, CCF 054, WEA, NARS; "General Council of the White Earth bands," at White Earth Village, 23 April 1913, BIA RG 75, CCF 054, WEA, NARS; "Indians of the White Earth Reservation," at Pine Point, 1 May 1913, BIA RG 75, CCF 054, WEA, NARS; E. P. Holcombe, Chief Supervisor to CIA, 14 May 1913, BIA RG 75, CCF 056, WEA, NARS.

18. "Council of the Chippewa Indians of Minnesota," at Cass Lake, 8 May 1913, BIA RG 75, CCF 054, WEA, NARS.

19. The first "forest reserve" near Leech Lake was created without Anishinaabe consent from ceded lands and set aside by the Morris Act of 3 March 1891. *U.S. Statutes at Large* 32:400–404. On 23 May 1908, Congress passed an amendment to the Nelson Act creating the Minnesota National Forest out of these forestry lands. *U.S. Statutes at Large* 35:268–272. Compensation was not awarded until 1925. RCIA 1922: 17–18; "To Compensate the Chippewa Indians of Minnesota for Timber and Interest in Connection with the Settlement for the Minnesota National Forest," House Reports 8228, no. 568, 68 Congress, 1 Session (1924); "To Compensate the Chippewa Indians of Minnesota for Timber and Interest in connection with the settlement for the Minnesota National Forest," Senate Reports 8388, no. 1024, 68 Congress, 2 Session (1925). The first sales of "Chippewa ceded lands" under the Nelson Act occurred in 1896 and 1898. Commissioner of General Land Office (GLO) to Secretary of the Interior, 1922, Chippewa Logging Files, GLO, Packet no. 302. Beginning in 1896, Congress granted extensions to homestead settlers on "Chippewa ceded lands." *U.S. Statutes at Large* 29:342; 30:595; 31:241;

34:326; 36:265. On 17 May 1900 the U.S. Government assumed responsibility to pay for homestead lands under the Free Homestead Act; settlers received the land free of charge. *U.S. Statutes at Large* 31:179. Commutation rights were again granted in 1905. *U.S. Statutes at Large* 33:1005. Compensation for these lands did not come until 1924. "To Compensate Indians of Minnesota for Lands Disposed of by Free Homestead Act," House Reports 8227, no. 272, 68 Congress, 1 Session (1924); "To Compensate the Indians of Minnesota for Lands Disposed of by Free Homestead Act," Senate Reports 8388, no. 806, 68 Congress, 2 Session (1924). The issue of swamplands on Anishinaabe reservations is covered in *U.S. Statutes at Large* 9:519; 12:3; "Compensate Chippewa Indians of Minneapolis [*sic*] under Swamp Land Act," Senate Reports 9878, no. 428, 74 Congress, 1 Session (1935). Compensation was not forthcoming until 1936. *U.S. Statutes at Large* 49:321, 1765.

20. J. H. Hinton, Special Agent, to CIA, 22 July 1913, BIA RG 75, CCF 261, WEA, NARS.

21. Both quotes from Speech of Wa-we-yea-cumig, in E. P. Holcombe, Chief Supervisor, to F. H. Abbott, CIA, 15 May 1913, BIA RG 75, CCF 056, WEA, NARS.

22. Both quotes from E. P. Holcombe, Chief Supervisor to F. H. Abbott, Acting CIA, 15 May 1913, BIA RG 75, CCF 056, WEA, NARS. See also "Indians of the White Earth Reservation in Council," at Pine Point, 31 January 1913, BIA RG 75, CCF 054, WEA, NARS; Charles T. Wright and Benjamin Casswell to Cato Sells, CIA, 5 January 1913, BIA RG 75, CCF 056, WEA, NARS; Joseph Northrup, Chairman of Convention, "Notice to Chippewas of Minnesota," 4 February 1913, BIA RG 75, CCF 054, WEA, NARS; "Full blood Indians residing at White Earth Agency, 17 February 1913, BIA RG 75, CCF 054, WEA, NARS; "General Council of the White Earth bands," at White Earth Village, 23 April 1913, BIA RG 75, CCF 054, WEA, NARS; "Indians of the White Earth Reservation," at Pine Point, 1 May 1913, BIA RG 75, CCF 054, WEA, NARS; E. P. Holcombe, Chief Supervisor to CIA, 14 May 1913, BIA RG 75, CCF 056, WEA, NARS; Council called by the "Full Blood Faction," 21 May 1913, BIA RG 75, CCF 056, WEA, NARS; Kay-dah-ge-gwon-nay-aush, May-zhuck-e-gwon-abe, and Ah-bow-e-ge-shig, Business Committee at Pine Point to Washington, D.C., 5 August 1913, BIA RG 75, CCF 054, WEA, NARS. The Business Committee reported on a council at Pine Point on 7 July 1913 where they formed a "union of the full blood Indians . . . on the several reservations." "Council at Pine Point," 3 October 1913, BIA RG 75, CCF 056, WEA, NARS; "General Council, Indians of the White Earth Reservation at Pine Point," 2 December 1914, BIA RG 75, CCF 054, WEA, NARS; Council Proceedings at Pine Point, 20–22 January 1915, BIA RG 75, CCF 054, WEA, NARS; "Full Blood Petition," 3 May 1915, BIA RG 75, CCF 054, WEA, NARS; "General Council of the Chippewa," at Ponsford, 30 September and 1, 2, and 4 October 1915, BIA RG

75, CCF 054, WEA, NARS; Ah-bow-ege-shig and the Full Blood Council, 24 January 1916, BIA RG 75, CCF 054, WEA, NARS; "General Council of Chippewa Indians," at Pine Point, 16–17 March 1916, BIA RG 75, CCF 054, WEA, NARS; Report of a Conference between Assistant CIA Meritt, William Dailey, interpreter, Ah-bow-e-ge-shig, and George Walters, 25 March 1916, BIA RG 75, CCF 056, WEA, NARS; "Indians of the White Earth Reservation in Council," at Pine Point, 31 January 1913, BIA RG 75, CCF 054, WEA, NARS.

23. "Graham Report," 116; Me sha kegeshig, Gus Beaulieu, C. H. Beaulieu, J. H. Brown, John Leecy, S. E. Mooers, B. L. Fairbanks, William Potter, R. G. Beaulieu, Michael Lachapelle, R. Ledeboer to John Howard, 26 July 1909, BIA RG 75, CCF 150, WEA, NARS; John R. Howard to CIA, 17 August 1909, BIA RG 75, CCF 150, WEA, NARS; B. L. Fairbanks to E. P. Holcombe, 23 May 1913, BIA RG 75, CCF 154, WEA, NARS.

24. "Council called by the 'Full Blood Faction,'" 21 May 1913, BIA RG 75, CCF 056, WEA, NARS; "Council of the Chippewa Indians of Minnesota," at Cass Lake, 8 May 1913, BIA RG 75, CCF 054, WEA, NARS.

25. Joseph Northrup, Chairman of Convention, "Notice to Chippewas of Minnesota," 4 February 1913, BIA RG 75, CCF 054, WEA, NARS; "Minutes of a Meeting of the General Council of the White Earth Bands," 24 October 1913, BIA RG 75, CCF 054, WEA, NARS; "General Council of Chippewa Indians of Minnesota," at White Earth Village Hall, 12–14 June 1915, BIA RG 75, CCF 054, WEA, NARS; "Minutes of the General Council of the Chippewas," at Bemidji, 11–15 July 1916, BIA RG 75, CCF 056, WEA, NARS; "Resolutions adopted by the General Council of all the Chippewas in Minnesota," 11–15 July 1916, BIA RG 75, CCF 056, WEA, NARS; George A. Berry to CIA, 4 December 1916, BIA RG 75, CCF 056, WEA, NARS; "Minutes of a meeting of the Council of the White Earth Bands," at White Earth Village, 5 June 1917, BIA RG 75, CCF 054, WEA, NARS; "Minutes of the Meeting of the General Council of the Chippewa Indians of Minnesota," at Bemidji, 10–14 July 1917, BIA RG 75, CCF 155, WEA, NARS; E. P. Wakefield to James I. Coffey, 5 June 1918, BIA RG 75, CCF 054, WEA, NARS; "List of Delegates to General Council of the Chippewa of Minnesota," at Bemidji, City Hall, 9 July 1918, BIA RG 75, CCF 054, WEA, NARS.

26. "Full blood Indian Council," at Pine Point, 28 May 1914, BIA RG 75, CCF 054, WEA, NARS.

27. "Report of a conference between Assistant Commissioner Meritt, William Dailey (acting as interpreter), Ah-bow-e-ge-shig, and George Walters, Indians from White Earth Agency, Minnesota," 25 March 1916, BIA RG 75, CCF 056, WEA, NARS; "Report of a conference between Assistant Commissioner Meritt and Ah-bow-e-ge-shig and George Walters, with William Dailey, Interpreter, Indians from the White Earth Reservation," 29 March 1916, BIA RG 75, CCF 054, WEA, NARS; E. B. Meritt, Assistant CIA, to Ah-Bow-e-ge-shig,

George Walters, and William Dailey, 31 March 1916, BIA RG 75, CCF 054, WEA, NARS; U.S. Indian Office, "Records of an Investigation of Mixed Bloods of the White Earth Reservation, 1911–1915," Microfilm Roll M444, MHSA.

28. All quotes in this and the previous paragraph from "Report of a Conference," 25 March 1916, BIA RG 75, CCF 054, WEA, NARS; "Report of a Conference," 29 March 1916, BIA RG 75, CCF 054, WEA, NARS.

29. Quotations from Theo. H. Beaulieu to Halvor Steenerson, 26 June 1916, BIA RG 75, CCF 056, WEA, NARS, and "Report of Inspector C. M. Knight on the Annual Meeting of the General Council of the Chippewa," at Bemidji, 11–15 July 1916, BIA RG 75, CCF 054, WEA, NARS, respectively.

30. "Minutes of the General Council of the Chippewas," at Bemidji, 11–15 July 1916, BIA RG 75, CCF 056, WEA, NARS; "Report of Inspector C. M. Knight on the Annual Meeting of the General Council of the Chippewa," at Bemidji, 11–15 July 1916, BIA RG 75, CCF 054, WEA, NARS; *The Tomahawk,* 20 July 1916: 1.

31. All quotations from Theo H. Beaulieu to Warren K. Moorehead, 15 February 1917, BIA RG 75, CCF 056, WEA, NARS, and Warren K. Moorehead to Theo. H. Beaulieu, 2 March 1917, BIA RG 75, CCF 056, WEA, NARS, respectively.

32. Quotations from "Minutes of the Meeting of the General Council of the Chippewa Indians of Minnesota," at Bemidji, 10–14 July 1917, BIA RG 75, CCF 155, WEA, NARS, and H. S. Taylor, Inspector, to CIA, 23 July 1917, BIA RG 75, CCF 056, WEA, NARS, respectively.

33. J. G. Morrison, Jr., "President Reports Appointment of Legislative Committee," 3 December 1917, BIA RG 75, CCF 056, WEA, NARS; H.R. 11410, "A Bill: For the classification of members and preparation of correct tribal rolls, the completion of allotments, and the disposal of all remaining property of the Chippewa Indians of Minnesota in conformity with the agreement of 1889," 65 Congress, 2 Session, 12 April 1918, BIA RG 75, CCF 054, WEA, NARS.

34. All quotes from "Legislative Committee of the Chippewa General Council:" John Carl, Frank D. Beaulieu, Henry Warren, John W. Broker, B. L. Fairbanks to Selden G. Hopkins, Assistant Secretary of the Interior, 18 February 1918, BIA RG 75, CCF 054, WEA, NARS.

35. Frank W. Porter, III, ed., *Nonrecognized American Indian Tribes: An Historical and Legal Perspective,* Occasional Papers Series, no. 7 (Chicago: D'Arcy McNickle Center for the History of the American Indian, Newberry Library, 1983).

36. Quotations in this and the preceding paragraph from James I. Coffey to CIA, 30 January 1918, BIA RG 75, CCF 056, WEA, NARS, and James I. Coffey to Julius Brown, member of Executive Committee, 15 February 1918, BIA RG 75, CCF 155, WEA, NARS.

37. Ah bow ege shig to E. B. Linnen, 31 January 1918, BIA RG 75, CCF 056, WEA, NARS; James Bassett to E. B. Linnen, 1 February 1918, BIA RG 75, CCF 056,

WEA, NARS; E. B. Linnen to CIA, 14 February 1918, BIA RG 75, CCF 056, WEA, NARS; Chief Mah een gaunce, O zhe ne nee, Joe Rock, Pah o ne ge shig, and Star Bad Boy to John H. Hinton, 5 February 1918, BIA RG 75, CCF 056, WEA, NARS; Petition from "Full blood Council," at Nay tah waush, 21 February 1918, BIA RG 75, CCF 056, WEA, NARS; James I. Coffey, Legislative Committee member to CIA, 14 February 1918, BIA RG 75, CCF 056, WEA NARS; J. H. Hinton, Supt., to Warren K. Moorehead, 23 February 1918, BIA RG 75, CCF 056, WEA, NARS; E. P. Wakefield to Henry W. Warren, 23 February 1918, BIA RG 75, CCF 054, WEA, NARS; "Proceedings of the General Tribal Council of the Chippewa Indians of Minnesota," at Ball Club, 25 April 1918, BIA RG 75, CCF 054, WEA, NARS.

38. Quotations in this and the previous paragraph from E. P. Wakefield to Henry W. Warren, 23 February 1918, BIA RG 75, CCF 054, WEA, NARS.

39. Memorandum, Inter-Office Memo, post–9 July 1918, BIA RG 75, CCF 155, WEA, NARS; Memorandum, "A.M.H.," post–9 July 1918, BIA RG 75, CCF 150, WEA, NARS; Report of E. B. Linnen and C. L. Ellis to Cato Sells, CIA, 20 September 1918, BIA RG 75, CCF 054, WEA, NARS.

40. George Walters and Chief Way-ya-gua-gi-shih for the "full bloods" to CIA, 3 June 1918, BIA RG 75, CCF 150, WEA, NARS; E. P. Wakefield to James I. Coffey, 5 June 1918, BIA RG 75, CCF 054, WEA, NARS; J. H. Hinton, Supt., to CIA, 15 June 1918, BIA RG 75, CCF 150, WEA, NARS; Cato Sells, CIA, to George Walters and Chief Way-ya-gua-gi-shih et al., 27 June 1918, BIA RG 75, CCF 150, WEA, NARS; "Proceedings of the General Council of all Chippewa Indians of Minnesota," assembled at the Elko Theatre, Bemidji, 9 July 1918, BIA RG 75, CCF 054, WEA, NARS; "List of Delegates to General Council of the Chippewas of Minnesota," at City Hall, Bemidji, 9 July 1918, BIA RG 75, CCF 054, WEA, NARS; Memorandum, Inter-Office Memo, OIA, post–9 July 1918, BIA RG 75, CCF 155, WEA, NARS; Memorandum, "A.M.H." on CIA stationery, post–9 July 1918, BIA RG 75, CCF 150, WEA, NARS; James I. Coffey to CIA, 11 July 1918, BIA RG 75, CCF 054, WEA, NARS; James I. Coffey to E. B. Linnen, 25 July 1918, BIA RG 75, CCF 054, WEA, NARS.

41. All quotations from Peter Graves to E. B. Linnen, 12 August 1918, BIA RG 75, CCF 054, WEA, NARS.

42. "Chippewas of Minnesota," Hearings before the Committee on Indian Affairs, House of Representatives, 66 Congress, 2 Session, 21 January–22 March 1920 (Washington, D.C.: U.S. Government Printing Office, 1920); "Classification of the Chippewa Indians of Minnesota," House Reports 8838, no. 1851, 69 Congress, 1 Session (1928); "Divide Funds of Chippewa Indians of Minnesota," House Reports 10085, no. 1295, 75 Congress, 1 Session (1937); "Divide Funds between Red Lake and all other Chippewa Indians of Minnesota," Senate Reports 10229, no. 1552, 75 Congress, 3 Session (1938); Peter Graves to E. B. Linnen, 12 August 1918, BIA RG 75, CCF 054, WEA, NARS;

"General Council of Minnesota Chippewas in Session, Bemidji," 13 July 1918, BIA RG 75, CCF 054, WEA, NARS; Meyer, "The Red Lake Ojibwe."

43. Quotations from "Proceedings of the General Council of all Chippewa Indians of Minnesota," assembled at the Elko Theatre, Bemidji, 9 July 1918, BIA RG 75, CCF 054, WEA, NARS. See also Report of E. B. Linnen and C. L. Ellis to Cato Sells, CIA, 20 September 1918, BIA RG 75, CCF 054, WEA, NARS.

44. Memorandum, "A.M.H." on CIA stationery, post–9 July 1918, BIA RG 75, CCF 150, WEA, NARS; Report of E. B. Linnen and C. L. Ellis to Cato Sells, CIA, 20 September 1918, BIA RG 75, CCF 054, WEA, NARS.

45. "Minutes of a Council of the White Earth Bands of Minnesota Chippewa," at White Earth Boarding School Assembly Hall, 3 June 1919, BIA RG 75, CCF 054, WEA, NARS; Report of W. F. Dickens, Supt., to CIA, 19 June 1919, BIA RG 75, CCF 054, WEA, NARS.

46. Report of W. F. Dickens, Supt., to CIA, 19 June 1919, BIA RG 75, CCF 054, WEA, NARS.

47. "Special Meeting of the Local Council of the White Earth Reservation," at Pinehurst Pavilion, Twin Lakes, 17 June 1919, BIA RG 76, CCF 054, WEA, NARS; Report of W. F. Dickens, Supt., to CIA, 19 June 1919, BIA RG 75, CCF 054, WEA, NARS.

48. Quotations from Report of W. F. Dickens, Supt., to CIA, 19 June 1919, BIA RG 75, CCF 054, WEA, NARS. For the impact of the 1934 Indian Reorganization Act on tribal governments, see Vine Deloria, Jr. and Clifford Lytle, *The Nations Within: The Past and Future of American Indian Sovereignty* (New York: Pantheon, 1984); Vine Deloria, Jr., *American Indian Policy in the Twentieth Century* (Norman: University of Oklahoma Press, 1985).

49. Hazel Hertzberg, *The Search for an American Indian Identity: Modern Pan-Indian Movements* (Syracuse: Syracuse University Press, 1971): 179–209. See also William Unrau, *Mixed Bloods and Tribal Dissolution: Charles Curtis and the Quest for Indian Identity* (Lawrence: University Press of Kansas, 1989); Nancy Shoemaker, "Urban Indians and Ethnic Choices: American Indian Organizations in Minneapolis, 1920–1950," *Western Historical Quarterly* 19 (1988): 431–47.

Chapter 5. "We Can Not Get a Living as We Used To"

1. "Report of W. H. Gibbs on Industries at White Earth Reservation," 24 October 1916, BIA RG 75, CCF 910, WEA, NARS (hereafter "Report of W. H. Gibbs").

2. See also Rolf Knight, *Indians at Work: An Informal History of Native Indian Labour in British Columbia, 1858–1930* (Vancouver: North Star, 1978).

3. For discrimination against Indian workers, see "The Report of Indian Inspector J. George Wright, together with Accompanying Papers, Relative to Pine Lands and Pine Timber on the Red Lake Reservation, in the State of Min-

nesota," Senate Documents 3562, no. 85, 55 Congress, 1 Session (1897);
"Relating to the Estimation of Timber and the Cutting of Dead and Fallen
Timber on the Chippewa Indian Reservations in the State of Minnesota,"
Senate Documents 3731, no. 70, 55 Congress, 3 Session (1899). For dis-
cussions of "premodern" mentalities, see E. P. Thompson, "Time, Work-
Discipline, and Industrial Capitalism," *Past and Present* 38 (1967): 56–97;
Herbert G. Gutman, *Work, Culture and Society in Industrializing America:
Essays in American Working-Class and Social History* (New York: Alfred
Knopf, 1976). For alternative interpretations in the western Great Lakes area,
see Patricia A. Shifferd, "A Study in Economic Change: The Chippewa of
Northern Wisconsin, 1854–1900," *Western Canadian Journal of Anthropol-
ogy* 6 (1976): 16–41; Meyer, " 'We Can Not Get a Living' "; James McClurken,
"The Way to Make a Living: Odawa Traditional Subsistence and Wage Labor
in the U.S. Economy, 1820–1940," unpublished paper, American Society for
Ethnohistory Annual Conference, Tulsa, Okla., 1991. For information on
White Earth, see E. H. Colegrove, Assistant Supervisor of Indian Employment, to Charles E. Dagenett, Supervisor of Indian Employment, 28 October
1910, BIA RG 75, CCF 900, WEA, NARS; "Inspection Report of L. F. Michaels
on White Earth Schools and Agency," 10 December 1913, BIA RG 75, CCF
806, WEA, NARS. For the seasonality of logging, see Cronon, *Nature's Metropolis*, 148–206.
4. See collections at the Minnesota Historical Society Audio-Visual Archives,
especially the Frances Theresa Densmore Collection and photographs filed
under the category "White Earth Reservation." See also Nancy Lurie, ed.,
*Mountain Wolf Woman, Sister of Crashing Thunder: The Autobiography of a
Winnebago Indian* (Ann Arbor: University of Michigan Press, 1966).
5. Quotations in this and the preceding paragraph from "Full blood" Council at
Pine Point to CIA Leupp, 28 May 1906, BIA RG 75, LR 1906, NARS, and
Warren K. Moorehead to CIA, "The White Earth Investigation: Additional
Report," 26 October 1909, BIA RG 75, CCF 150, WEA, NARS, respectively.
Information for the foregoing discussion was drawn from many sources.
John R. Howard to CIA, 30 September 1912, BIA RG 75, CCF 916, WEA, NARS;
"Report of Inspector Oscar Lipps on the Industrial, Economic and Home
Conditions of the Chippewa Indians in Minnesota," 21 October 1912, BIA RG
75, CCF 916, WEA, NARS; "Report on Clipping Submitted by Congressman
Hammond Relative to Expenditures on White Earth Reservation," 28 March
1913, BIA RG 75, CCF 916, WEA, NARS; "Report on White Earth Schools and
Reservation by L. F. Michael, Supervisor," Section 2, "Industries," 5 Decem-
ber 1913, BIA RG 75, CCF 910, WEA, NARS; "Report of L. F. Michaels on
Industries and Farming," 1 April 1914, BIA RG 75, CCF 910, WEA, NARS;
"Annual Report of Charles Johnson, Farmer, 3rd District (Elbow Lake),"
received by Indian Office 4 February 1915, BIA RG 75, CCF 916, WEA, NARS;

Thomas Jackson, Farmer at Pine Point, to CIA, 15 January 1915, BIA RG 75, CCF 916, WEA, NARS; John R. Howard, Supt., to CIA, 8 February 1915, BIA RG 75, CCF 916, WEA, NARS; "Inspection Report of H. B. Peairs on Industries and Agriculture at White Earth," 9–26 June 1915, BIA RG 75, CCF 910, WEA, NARS; "Inspection Report of L. W. Aschemeier on Industries on White Earth Reservation," 8 July 1915, BIA RG 75, CCF 910, WEA, NARS; Warren K. Moorehead to F. W. Hodge, Smithsonian Institution, 6 April 1910, National Anthropological Archives, Smithsonian Institution, Washington, D.C.; Chief Kay-dug-day-gwon-nay-aush to CIA, 14 October 1910, BIA RG 75, CCF 723, WEA, NARS; Chief Wah Wea Cumig to CIA, 2 March 1912, BIA RG 75, CCF 721, WEA, NARS; N. B. Hurr to W. K. Moorehead, 1 January 1915, BIA RG 75, CCF 723, WEA, NARS; John R. Howard to CIA, 3 May 1915, BIA RG 75, CCF 056, WEA, NARS; E. B. Meritt, Assistant CIA, to John R. Howard, 18 March 1915, BIA RG 75, CCF 056, WEA, NARS; O. H. Lipps to CIA, 9 March 1915, BIA RG 75, CCF 056, WEA, NARS; "Report of Wilma G. Rhodes on the Field Matron at White Earth Reservation," 23 September 1918, BIA RG 75, CCF 150, WEA, NARS; "Inspection Report of F. D. Cooke, M.D., on Health Conditions at Pine Point," 4 October 1910, BIA RG 75, CCF 700, WEA, NARS; "Inspection Report of Elsie E. Newton on the Work of the Field Matron at Pine Point," 22 September 1911, BIA RG 75, CCF 917.1, WEA, NARS; "Inspection Report of Thomas F. Rodwell on Health Conditions at White Earth Reservation," 31 December 1911, BIA RG 75, CCF 700, WEA, NARS; "Inspection Report of L. W. White, Supervisor of Hospitals, on Conditions on the White Earth Reservation," 18 April 1917, BIA RG 75, CCF 700, WEA, NARS; "Inspection Report of Warren K. Moorehead about the General Situation and Whiskey on the White Earth Reservation," 9 August 1909, BIA RG 75, CCF 150, WEA, NARS; "Inspection of Charles F. Peirce on the White Earth Boarding School," 2 October 1912, BIA RG 75, CCF 150, WEA, NARS; "Inspection Report of Charles F. Peirce on the White Earth Agency," 21 December 1912, BIA RG 75, CCF 150, WEA, NARS; "Inspection Report of H. S. Taylor on the White Earth Reservation," 27 October 1915, BIA RG 75, CCF 150, WEA, NARS; "Inspection Report of E. B. Linnen," 9 October 1909, BIA RG 75, CCF 806, WEA, NARS; "Inspection Report of Charles F. Peirce," 24 March 1911, BIA RG 75, CCF 150, WEA, NARS; "Inspection Report of Elsie E. Newton," 18 September 1911, BIA RG 75, CCF 806, WEA, NARS; "Inspection Report of Charles F. Peirce on White Earth Schools," 9–20 December 1911, BIA RG 75, CCF 160, WEA, NARS; Chief Education Division, "Justification for a Day School at Twin Lakes," Authority from Indian Office 2 May 1912, BIA RG 75, CCF 806, WEA, NARS; "Inspection Report of Charles F. Peirce on Elbow Lake Day School," 15 December 1912, BIA RG 75, CCF 806, WEA, NARS; "Report of L. F. Michaels," 10 December 1913; "Inspection Report of Charles F. Peirce on White Earth Schools," 21 December 1913, BIA RG 75, CCF 806, WEA,

nars; "Inspection Report of L. M. Compton on White Earth Schools," 8–
9 May 1918, BIA RG 75, CCF 150, WEA, NARS; J. H. Hinton to CIA, 7 October
1918, BIA RG 75, CCF 820, WEA, NARS; J. E. Jenkins, Special Agent, to CIA,
22 May 1900, BIA RG 75, LR 1900, WEA, NARS; Interview with Maggie
Hanks, born 1888, 19 October 1982; Interview with Lucy Thompson, born
1906, c. 1982; Interview with Dick Chesley, born 1895, c. 1982; Interview
with Mary Jane Wilson, born 1898, c. 1982; Interview with Joe Bellecourt,
born 1887, c. 1982, WEOHP. Interview with Mrs. Christine Roy, born ?, 1983;
Interview with George Roy, born 1915, c. 1982; Interview with Lucy Thomp-
son, born 1906, c. 1982; Interview with John Bush, born 1898, 1982; Inter-
view with Reuben Rock, born 1905, 1982; Interview with Fred Burnett
Weaver, born 1900, 1983; Interview with Mary Bellanger, born 1914, c. 1982;
Interview with Elizabeth Roy, born 1903, c. 1982; Interview with Frances
Keahna, born 1905, c. 1982; Interview with Irene Harris, born 1898, c. 1982;
Interview with Maggie Brown Hanks, born 1888, c. 1982; Interview with
Rosalie Susan Bellecourt, born 1910, c. 1982; Interview with Emma May
Johnson, born 1905, c. 1982, MCTRHP.

6. C. F. Hauke, Acting CIA, to John R. Howard, 10 April 1913, BIA RG 75, CCF
916, WEA, NARS; "Inspection Report of L. W. Aschemeier," 8 July 1915; E. B.
Meritt, Assistant CIA, to John H. Hinton, Superintendent, 20 October 1916,
BIA RG 75, CCF 220, WEA, NARS; "Report of W. H. Gibbs," 24 October 1916;
RCIA 1913: 9, 1914: 20, 1915: 17, 1916: 38, 1917: 37, 1918: 56, 1919: 54.

7. All quotations from "Report of Inspector Oscar Lipps on the Industrial,
Economic and Home Conditions of the Chippewa Indians in Minnesota,"
21 October 1912, BIA RG 75, CCF 916, WEA, NARS.

8. Quotation from "Report of Oscar Lipps," 18 October 1912. See also RCIA
1910: 53–54, 1911: 40–41; "The Graham Report," Majority Report; Samuel
Adams, Acting Secretary of the Interior, to Robert J. Gamble, Chairman,
Committee on Indian Affairs, 1 March 1912, BIA RG 75, CCF 150, WEA,
NARS; "Report of W. H. Gibbs," 24 October 1916; Theo. H. Beaulieu to
Halvor Steenerson, 25 April 1917, BIA RG 75, CCF 916, WEA, NARS; "Report
of Elsie E. Newton," 2 September 1911; "Inspection Report of E. B. Linnen,"
9 October 1909, BIA RG 75, CCF 150, WEA, NARS; "Report of Charles F.
Peirce," 21 December 1912; "Report of H. S. Taylor," 27 October 1915;
"Report of L. F. Michaels," 10 December 1913; Complaints and queries from
purchasers of Indian allotments are contained in Ransom J. Powell Papers,
Boxes 1 and 2, MHSA.

9. Quotations from J. H. Hinton, Special Indian Agent, to CIA, 28 October 1912,
BIA RG 75, CCF 306, WEA, NARS. See also "Report on White Earth Schools
and Reservation by L. F. Michaels, Supervisor," Section 3, Lands, 5 December
1913, BIA RG 75, CCF 300, WEA, NARS; Thomas Sloan to Cato Sells, CIA,
22 August 1913, BIA RG 75, CCF 300, WEA, NARS; Samuel Adams, Acting

Secretary of the Interior, to Robert J. Gamble, Chairman, Committee on Indian Affairs, U.S. Senate, 1 March 1912, BIA RG 75, CCF 306, WEA, NARS; "Report of Oscar Lipps," 18 October 1912; J. H. Hinton, Special Indian Agent, to C. C. Daniels, Attorney in charge of White Earth Matters, 15 April 1914, BIA RG 75, CCF 300, WEA, NARS; "Report of H. B. Peairs," 9–26 June 1915; Memorandum from ? to ?, Inter-Office Memo, post–30 June 1918, BIA RG 75, CCF 220, WEA, NARS; "Report of H. S. Taylor," 27 October 1915; "Report of L. F. Michael," 10 December 1913; Interview with Joe Bellecourt, born 1887, c. 1982, WEOHP; Interview with Lizzie Brunette, born 1888, c. 1982, WEOHP.

10. Quotation from "Report of L. F. Michael," 10 December 1913. See also RCIA 1914: 62, 1915: 38, 1916: 51, 1917: 53, 1918: 53, 1919: 3, 9–17, 55, 56; *U.S. Statutes at Large* 36:855–56.

11. Quotation from John R. Howard to CIA, 3 April 1911, BIA RG 75, CCF 806, WEA, NARS. See also W. E. Frazee to Robert G. Valentine, Secretary of the Interior, 16 February 1910, BIA RG 75, CCF 150, WEA, NARS. "The Graham Report"; RCIA 1917: 3–5, 41–42, 1918: 18, 58. Tax forfeiture transactions are recorded in Mahnomen County, District Court, "Real Estate Tax Judgment Books" 1907–72, Minnesota State Archives, MHSA; Becker County, District Court, "Real Estate Tax Judgment Books" 1874–1976, Minnesota State Archives, MHSA; Interview with Dick Chesley, born 1895, c. 1982, WEOHP. For the acceleration of "forced fee patents" nationwide, see Hoxie, *A Final Promise*; McDonnell, *The Dispossession of the American Indian*.

12. Quotations in this and the preceding paragraph from "Relating to the Estimating of Timber and the Cutting of Dead and Fallen Timber on the Chippewa Indian Reservations with the State of Minnesota," Senate Documents 3731, no. 70, 55 Congress, 3 Session (1899): 86–87, 90, 21–22, and Watrin, *The Ponsfordian*, 45–46, respectively. See also *U.S. Statutes at Large* 25:673, 30:90, 924, 929; RCIA 1885: 116, 1887: 129, 1888: 149, 1890: cii, 112, 1891: 86, 1892: 86–87, 89–90, 277, 1894: 152, 1895: 54, 176, 1896: 170, 1898: 181, 1899: 51, 209, 214, 1900: 71, 1901: 67–69, 636–637, 1904: 74, 223, 1905: 233; Chairman, Chippewa Commission, to John W. Noble, Secretary of the Interior, 3 November 1891, BIA RG 75, CCF 150, WEA, NARS; "The Graham Report," 2059; RSI 1898: xxxv, 1899: xvii, xxix, 1900: lv, lvii, 1901: liii, lxxiii, 1902: 28; RCGLO 1899: 78; *Mississippi Valley Lumberman*, 15 February 1889: 9; *Minneapolis Journal* 20 April 1901, part 2: 1; *Conference between the Secretary of the Interior and the Members of the Minnesota Delegation in Congress, to Ascertain a Better Method for the Sale and Disposal of the Pine Timber on Indian Reservations in that State, January 19 and 23, 1901* (Washington, D.C.: U.S. Government Printing Office, 1901); Logging Contracts, 1890–1908, BIA RG 75, E 1261, WEA, NARS; Timber Contracts, February 1914, BIA RG 75, E 1262, WEA, NARS.

13. RCIA 1905: 80, 233, 1906: 250, 1908: 8, 1910: 24–25, 1911: 17, 18, 192, 196,

1912: 52–53, 218, 220, 223, 1913: 3, 14, 188, 191, 1914: 42, 155, 158, 1915: 37, 168, 170, 1916: 52, 161, 1917: 43, 55, 166, 1918: 62, 181, 1919: 169, 1920: 52, 1922: 17–18; *U.S. Statutes at Large* 22:590, 24:463, 32:400–404, 35:268–72, 39:137–38; RSI 1916: 350; R. A. Ballinger, First Assistant Secretary of the Interior, to Attorney General, 17 January 1910, BIA RG 75, CCF 150, WEA, NARS; Ransom J. Powell to R. A. Ballinger, 4 January 1910, BIA RG 75, CCF 150, WEA, NARS; R. A. Ballinger to the Attorney General, 14 March 1910, BIA RG 75, CCF 150, WEA, NARS; W. E. Frazee to Robert G. Valentine, CIA, 16 February 1910, BIA RG 75, CCF 150, WEA, NARS; R. G. Valentine to John R. Howard, 24 February 1910, BIA RG 75, CCF 150, WEA, NARS; First Assistant Secretary of the Interior to Attorney General, 6 November 1909, BIA RG 75, CCF 150, WEA, NARS; Frank Pierce, First Assistant Secretary of the Interior, to Attorney General, 16 October 1909, BIA RG 75, CCF 150, WEA, NARS; "Report of H. S. Taylor"; "Report of L. F. Michael," 10 December 1913; Webster Ballinger to E. B. Meritt, Assistant CIA, 22 April 1918, BIA RG 75, CCF 150, WEA, NARS; "Minutes of a Council of the Otter Tail Band of Pillager Chippewa Indians of Minnesota held at Pine Point," 30 January 1900, BIA RG 75, LR 1900, NARS; "To Compensate the Chippewa Indians of Minnesota for Timber and Interest in Connection with the Settlement for the Minnesota National Forest," House Reports 8228, no. 568, 68 Congress, 1 Session (1924); "To Compensate the Chippewa Indians of Minnesota for Timber and Interest in connection with the settlement for the Minnesota National Forest," Senate Reports 8388, no. 1024, 68 Congress, 2 Session (1925). See also Rich Nafziger, "A Violation of Trust? Federal Management of Indian Timber Lands," *Indian Historian* 9 (1976): 15–23; Sandra L. Faiman-Silva, "Tribal Land to Private Land: A Century of Oklahoma Choctaw Timberland Alienation from the 1880s to the 1980s," *Journal of Forest History* 32 (October 1988): 191–204.

14. Quotation from Acting CIA, F. H. Abbot to CGLO, 24 March 1913, BIA RG 75, CCF 309, WEA, NARS: 5. See also *U.S. Statutes at Large* 9:519, 12:3, 49:321, 1765. *State of Minnesota vs. Craig* 23 LD 305 (1896); RCIA 1904: 218, 1908: 89, 1922: 18; Acting CIA, F. H. Abbot to CGLO, 24 March 1913, BIA RG 75, CCF 309, WEA, NARS; "Compensate Chippewa Indians of Minneapolis [*sic*] under Swamp Land Act," Senate Reports 9878, no. 428, 74 Congress, 1 Session (1935). The following citations are contained in "Islands and Swamplands," BIA RG 75, CCF 309, WEA, NARS: C. E. Richardson, Attorney for the White Earth Bands, to CIA, 20 December 1907; CIA to Chauncey E. Richardson, 7 January 1908; C. E. Richardson to Francis E. Leupp, CIA; "Minutes of the Proceedings of a Council of the White Earth Bands of Chippewa Indians in Minnesota, held at the Village of White Earth, Minnesota," 18 June 1907; "Agreement between Louis A. Pradt, Attorney, and the White Earth Bands," 20 January 1908; Acting CIA to C. E. Richardson, 7 February 1908; Acting

CIA to C. E. Richardson, 19 February 1908; F. E. Leupp, CIA, to Secretary of the Interior, 24 February 1908; Acting CIA to Chauncey E. Richardson, 27 February 1908; Acting CIA to Auditor of the Treasury for the Interior Dept., 2 March 1908; Acting CIA to Superintendent in Charge, White Earth Agency, 2 March 1908; C. F. Larrabee, Acting CIA to CGLO, 19 October 1908; C. E. Richardson to Secretary of the Interior, 13 October 1908; Assistant CIA to CIA, 26 October 1908; James R. Garfield, Secretary of the Interior, to C. E. Richardson, 19 February 1909; Halvor Steenerson, House of Representatives, to Secretary of the Interior, 24 May 1909; Acting CIA Valentine to Halvor Steenerson, 27 May 1909; C. F. Hauke, Chief Clerk to C. E. Richardson, 26 June 1909; C. E. Richardson to CIA, 6 July 1909; Assistant CIA to C. E. Richardson, 20 July 1909; C. E. Richardson to Secretary of the Interior, 4 September 1909; Halvor Steenerson to Secretary of the Interior, 11 March 1910; C. F. Hauke, Chief Clerk, to John R. Howard, 19 March 1910; Assistant CIA to CIA, 24 January 1911; R. G. Valentine, CIA, to Secretary of the Interior, 21 March 1910; C. F. Hauke, Assistant CIA, to John R. Howard, 1 February 1911; Assistant CIA to CIA, 21 February 1913; S. V. Proudfit, Assistant CIA, to State Auditor, St. Paul, 15 April 1913; F. H. Abbott, Acting CIA, to CGLO, 19 April 1913; Assistant Attorney General to Secretary of the Interior, 24 September 1913; Statement of Thomas E. Harper re. White Earth Land Fraud Case, 21 December 1913; C. C. Daniels to CIA, 8 January 1914; C. F. Hauke, Assistant CIA, to John R. Howard, 1 August 1914; John R. Howard to CIA, 4 August 1914; Halvor Steenerson to CIA, 25 November 1914; C. F. Hauke, Assistant CIA, to John R. Howard, 3 December 1914; J. H. Hinton to CIA, 21 August 1915; Assistant CIA to Register, Cass Lake, Minnesota, April 1915. Box 17 of the Ransom J. Powell Papers, MHSA, contains maps identifying swamplands claimed by the State of Minnesota in red. Boxes 14–16 contain correspondence relating to state swampland claims.

15. J. H. Hinton, Superintendent, to CIA, 28 October 1916, BIA RG 75, CCF 220, WEA, NARS; "Report of W. H. Gibbs," 24 October 1916; RCIA 1909: 36–38, 1911: 254, 259; "U.S. General Accounting Office Report re. Petitions of the Minnesota Chippewa Tribe et al., and Red Lake Band, et al.," 21 August 1950, Indian Claims Commission no. 188, 189, 189-Amended, 189-A, 189-B, and 189-C; Jay H. Hoag, Attorney of Record for Plaintiff, and Marvin J. Sonovsky, Counsel, "Plaintiff's Exceptions to the Defendant's Accounting Report," Before the Indian Claims Commission, *The Minnesota Chippewa Tribe vs. U.S.A.*, Docket 19; "Plaintiff's Additional Exceptions 31–40," filed 17 December 1969; *U.S. Statutes at Large* 25:982–84, 994–95, 26:990–92, 1003–4, 1007, 27:122–23, 134, 138, 613, 615, 626–27, 632, 28:288–90, 302, 878, 880, 891, 29:323, 325, 336, 30:64, 66–67, 77, 573, 575, 584, 592, 925–29, 937, 31:222–23, 225–26, 241, 1059–60, 1062–63, 32:246–49, 268, 982, 984–86, 33:190, 193, 221, 1048, 1050–51, 34:349, 351, 1032–33, 35:82, 792, 794,

36:276, 1065, 37:525, 38:88–90, 590–91, 39:134–37, 977–79, 40:572, 41:13, 15, 31, 419, 433–34; Theo. H. Beaulieu to Halvor Steenerson, 25 April 1917, BIA RG 75, CCF 916, WEA, NARS; Memorandum, from ? to ?, Inter-Office Memo, post–30 June 1918, BIA RG 75, CCF 220, WEA, NARS; RCIA 1909: 36–38, 116, 1911: 254, 259, 1912: 286, 291, 1913: 258, 262, 1914: 185, 1915: 199, 1916: 189, 1917: 195, 1918: 209, 1919: 199. For information on the travels of the U.S. Chippewa Commission see House Executive Documents 2747, no. 247, 51 Congress, 1 Session; Senate Reports 3890, no. 1078, 56 Congress, 1 Session; House Reports 4027, no. 1858, 56 Congress, 1 Session; Senate Documents 3728, no. 49, 55 Congress, 3 Session. For information on the mismanagement of timber see House Reports 3269, no. 459, 53 Congress, 2 Session; House Reports 3457, no. 119, 54 Congress, 1 Session; Senate Documents 3562, no. 85, 55 Congress, 1 Session; Senate Documents 3731, no. 70, 55 Congress, 3 Session; House Reports 6336, no. 1336, 62 Congress, 3 Session. For information on commutation of homestead fees see House Reports 4025, no. 1103, 56 Congress, 1 Session; House Reports 4762, no. 4618, 58 Congress, 3 Session; House Reports 5065, no. 7612, 59 Congress, 2 Session; House Reports 8227, no. 272, 68 Congress, 1 Session. For information on ditching and draining wetlands north of Red Lake see House Document 5579, no. 27, 61 Congress, 1 Session. For information on confiscation of forest and swampland see, Senate Report 9878, no. 428, 74 Congress, 1 Session.

16. "Inspection Report of E. B. Linnen and W. K. Moorehead, 30 September 1909, BIA RG 75, CCF 900, WEA, NARS; A. S. Davis to CIA, 13 July 1916, BIA RG 75, CCF 155, WEA, NARS; E. H. Colegrove Assistant Supervisor of Indian Employment to Charles E. Dagenett, Supervisor of Indian Employment, BIA RG 75, CCF 900, WEA, NARS; John R. Howard to CIA, 29 July 1913, BIA RG 75, CCF 826, WEA, NARS; "Minutes of a Council of the Otter Tail Band of Pillager Chippewa Indians of Minnesota held at Pine Point," 30 January 1900, BIA RG 75, LR 1900, WEA, NARS; Wah-we-yea-cumig to Francis E. Leupp, CIA, 24 January 1909, BIA RG 75, CCF 056, WEA, NARS; Isabel Schneider, Interpreter of General Councils to John R. Howard, 17 March 1909, BIA RG 75, CCF 050, WEA, NARS; "Report of Charles F. Peirce," 21 December 1912; J. H. Hinton to J. D. Dortch, 13 September 1911, BIA RG 75, CCF 806, WEA, NARS; "Inspection Report of Mary Johnson on Birch Cooley Day School," 27 October 1913, BIA RG 75, CCF 150, WEA, NARS; "Inspection Report of Mary Johnson on White Earth Day Schools," 20 November 1913, BIA RG 75, CCF 150, WEA, NARS; "Inspection Report of Mary Johnson on White Earth Day Schools," 1 December 1913, BIA RG 75, CCF 150, WEA, NARS; "Report of L. F. Michael," 10 December 1913; Eugene J. Warren, Archie Libby, and C. R. Beaulieu, Board of Indian Education, to CIA, 4 April 1914, BIA RG 75, CCF 806, WEA, NARS; Chief Pay no nay ke shig to C. F. Hauke, Assistant CIA,

6 January 1915, BIA RG 75, CCF 806, WEA, NARS; "Inspection Report of L. M. Compton on the White Earth Indian School," 21 February 1916, BIA RG 75, CCF 410, WEA, NARS; "Inspection Report of L. M. Compton on White Earth Day Schools," 15 June 1916, BIA RG 75, CCF 810, WEA, NARS; "Report of W. H. Gibbs, 24 October 1916; John Hinton to CIA, 20 November 1916, BIA RG 75, CCF 806, WEA, NARS; "Inspection Report of L. M. Compton on the New Course of Study in White Earth Schools," 26 December 1916, BIA RG 75, CCF 810, WEA, NARS; "Inspection Report of L. M. Compton on White Earth Day Schools," 24–30 May 1917, BIA RG 75, CCF 810, WEA, NARS; J. H. Hinton to CIA, 15 August 1917, BIA RG 75, CCF 820, WEA, NARS.

17. Quotation from Charles E. Dagenett, Supervisor, to Mr. Shipe, 7 March 1918, BIA RG 75, CCF 900, WEA, NARS. See also Hoxie, *A Final Promise.* Margaret Szasz covered the pre-1920 period only briefly in *Education and the American Indian: The Road to Self-Determination since 1928* (Albuquerque: University of New Mexico Press, 1974). For information on how this shift was implemented at White Earth, see John Hinton to CIA, 9 June 1916, BIA RG 75, CCF 810, WEA, NARS; "Report of W. H. Gibbs," 24 October 1916; "Inspection of L. M. Compton on the New Course of Study in White Earth Schools," 26 December 1916, BIA RG 75, CCF 810, WEA, NARS; RCIA 1915: 3, 7, 1916: 9, 1917: 9, 1918: 22–26.

18. Quotations in this and preceding paragraphs from RCIA 1902: 37, and P. R. Wadsworth, Supervisor, to CIA, 10 August 1921, BIA RG 75, CCF 803, WEA, NARS, respectively. See also RCIA 1904: 44, 1905: 46, 1906: 47, 1914: 7–12, 124, 1918: 27, 1919: 18; "Report of Charles F. Peirce," 2 October 1912; "Report of E. B. Linnen," 9 October 1909; "Report of Elsie E. Newton," 18 September 1911; "Report of Elsie E. Newton," 22 September 1911; "Report of Charles F. Peirce," 9–20 December 1911; "Report of L. F. Michael," 10 December 1913; "Report of L. F. Michael," 19 December 1913; John R. Howard to CIA, 2 November 1909, BIA RG 75, CCF 820, WEA, NARS; J. H. Hinton to J. D. Dortch, 13 September 1911, BIA RG 75, CCF 806, WEA, NARS; Chief Education Division, "Justification for a Day School at Twin Lakes," Authority from Indian Office, 2 May 1912, BIA RG 75, CCF 806, WEA, NARS; Lewis G. Perry to John R. Howard, 22 April 1915, BIA RG 75, CCF, 806, WEA, NARS; John R. Howard to CIA, 4 May 1915, BIA RG 75, CCF 806, WEA, NARS; E. B. Meritt, Assistant CIA, to Halvor Steenerson, 27 March 1916, BIA RG 75, CCF 806, WEA, NARS; George Berry to Gus Beaulieu, 31 March 1916, BIA RG 75, CCF 806, WEA, NARS; George Berry to CIA, 31 March 1916, BIA RG 75, CCF 806, WEA, NARS; Gus Beaulieu to William Madison, 19 April 1916, BIA RG 75, CCF 806, WEA, NARS; Gus Beaulieu to Cato Sells, CIA, 19 May 1916, BIA RG 75, CCF 806, WEA, NARS; John Hinton to CIA, 20 November 1916, BIA RG 75, CCF 806, WEA, NARS; Agent to CIA, 9 February 1917, BIA RG 75, CCF 806, WEA, NARS; P. R. Wadsworth, Supervisor, to H. B. Peairs, Chief

Supervisor of Education, 14 December 1921, BIA RG 75, CCF 803, WEA, NARS; Samples: "Public School Contracts," 1917–1920, BIA RG 75, CCF 803, WEA, NARS; Interview with Thomas "Jackie" Potter, born 1915, c. 1982, WEOHP; Interview with Irene Brisbois, born 1902, c. 1982; Interview with Elizabeth Roy, born 1903, c. 1982; Interview with Frances Keahna, born 1905, c. 1982; Interview with Irene CeCelia Vizenor, born 1903, c. 1982, MCTRHP; Interview with Maggie Hanks, born 1888, c. 1982, WEOHP. See also Irving Hendrick, "The Federal Campaign for the Admission of Indian Children into Public Schools, 1890–1934," *American Indian Culture and Research Journal* 5 (1981): 13–32.

19. Quotations so far are from Agent John H. Sutherland to CIA, 17 April 1901, BIA RG 75, LR 1901, NARS; F. L. Hampson, President Wild Rice Lumber Co., to CIA, 24 December 1901, BIA RG 75, LR 1901, NARS; *The Tomahawk*, 16 April 1903, 7 May 1903; John Johnson, Jr. to CIA, 26 April 1902, BIA RG 75, LR 1902, NARS; General Council of Chippewa Indians of various bands, at Pine Point, 16–17 March 1916, BIA RG 75, CCF 054, WEA, NARS; and E. B. Meritt, Assistant CIA, to Moses E. Clapp, U.S. Senate, 6 June 1916, BIA RG 75, CCF 341, WEA, NARS. See also "Report of Oscar Lipps," 21 October 1912; John R. Howard to CIA, 29 March 1916, BIA RG 75, CCF 341, WEA, NARS; Leslie C. Garnett, Special Assistant to the Attorney General, to John R. Howard, 21 March 1916, BIA RG 75, CCF 341, WEA, NARS; J. H. Hinton, Superintendent, to CIA, 8 May 1916, BIA RG 75, CCF 341, WEA, NARS; Charles W. Smith, Special Assistant to the Attorney General, to J. H. Hinton, 8 May 1916, BIA RG 75, CCF 341, WEA, NARS; J. H. Hinton, Superintendent, to CIA, 9 May 1916, BIA RG 75, CCF 341, WEA, NARS; Wilcox, *A Pioneer History*.

20. Quotation from May zhucke ge shig to CIA, 10 May 1909, BIA RG 75, CCF 050, WEA, NARS. See also Sam Fullerton, Board of Game and Fish Commissioners, to Frank Leupp, CIA, 24 January 1905, BIA RG 75, LR 1905, WEA, NARS; Sam Fullerton, Board of Game and Fish Commissioners to Knute Nelson, Senator, 6 March 1905, BIA RG 75, LR 1905, WEA, NARS; May zhuck ke geshig to CIA, 10 May 1909, BIA RG 75, CCF 050, WEA, NARS.

21. Quotations from RCIA 1899: 210.

22. Agent John R. Howard to CIA, Received by Indian Office 4 May 1910, BIA RG 75, CCF 723, WEA, NARS; "Inspection Report of H. B. Peairs on Industries and Agriculture at White Earth," 9–26 June 1915, BIA RG 75, CCF 910, WEA, NARS; N. B. Hurr to W. K. Moorehead, 1 January 1915, BIA RG 75, CCF 723, WEA, NARS; Warren K. Moorehead to Cato Sells, CIA, 5 January 1914, BIA RG 75, CCF 723, WEA, NARS; O. H. Lipps to CIA, 9 March 1915, BIA RG 75, CCF 056, WEA, NARS; "Report of Wilma G. Rhodes on the Field Matron at White Earth Reservation," 23 September 1918, BIA RG 75, CCF 150, WEA, NARS.

23. Quotations in preceding paragraphs from "Inspection Report of F. D. Cooke,

M.D., on Health Conditions at Pine Point," 4 October 1910, BIA RG 75, CCF 700, WEA, NARS, and Warren K. Moorehead to CIA, "The White Earth Investigation: Additional Report," 26 October 1909, BIA RG 75, CCF 150, WEA, NARS. See also Frank E. Burch, MD, to Michelet, 17 May 1906, OIA, LR, "Land," KCFRA; "Inspection Report of Warren K. Moorehead," 9 August 1909, BIA RG 75, CCF 721, WEA, NARS; "Suggested basis for Eight Months' Agreement Concerning the Hospital owned by the Episcopal Church, White Earth Agency," date unknown, Hospital to be opened 1 November 1909, BIA RG 75, CCF 721, WEA, NARS; John R. Howard to CIA, 10 March 1910, BIA RG 75, CCF 721, WEA, NARS; William W. Abbott, M.D., to John R. Howard, 10 April 1911, BIA RG 75, CCF 700, WEA, NARS; P. Richards, Agency Physician, to W. G. West, Acting Superintendent, 5 August 1911, BIA RG 75, CCF 700, WEA, NARS; Willard P. Greene, Government Physician, to W. G. West, Acting Superintendent, 1 August 1911, BIA RG 75, CCF 700, WEA, NARS; William W. Abbott, Agency Physician to CIA, 30 September 1911, BIA RG 75, CCF 700, WEA, NARS; "Report of Thomas F. Rodwell," 31 December 1911; "Inspection Report of Charles F. Peirce on the Pine Point Trachoma Hospital," 2 October 1912, BIA RG 75, CCF 721, WEA, NARS; F. H. Abbott, Acting CIA, to Henry George, Jr., House of Representatives, 26 November, 1912, BIA RG 75, CCF 721, WEA, NARS; "Inspection Report of Charles F. Peirce and Joseph A. Murphy on Sanitary Conditions at Pine Point School," 4 December 1912, BIA RG 75, CCF 710, WEA, NARS; "Report of Charles F. Peirce," 21 December 1912; "Inspection Report of L. F. Michael on Health at White Earth Reservation," 5 December 1913, BIA RG 75, CCF 720, WEA, NARS; "Report of L. F. Taylor," 10 December 1913, "Report of H. B. Peairs," 9–26 June 1915; CIA to John H. Hinton, 20 April 1916, BIA RG 75, CCF 700, WEA, NARS; L. L. Culp, Special Physician, to CIA, 3 July 1916, BIA RG 75, CCF 700, WEA, NARS; J. H. Hinton, to CIA, 26 July 1916, BIA RG 75, CCF 700, WEA, NARS; J. H. Hinton to Cato Sells, CIA, 5 July 1916, BIA RG 75, CCF 700, WEA, NARS; Joseph A. Murphy, Medical Supervisor, to CIA, July 1916, BIA RG 75, CCF 700, WEA, NARS; J. H. Hinton to CIA, 26 July 1916, BIA RG 75, CCF 700, WEA, NARS; J. H. Hinton to CIA, 19 October 1916, BIA RG 75, CCF 700, WEA, NARS; E. B. Meritt, Assistant CIA, to John H. Hinton, 28 July 1916, BIA RG 75, CCF 700, WEA, NARS; "Inspection Report of W. H. Gibbs on Health at the White Earth Reservation," 24 October 1916, BIA RG 75, CCF 700, WEA, NARS; "Inspection Report of L. W. White, Supervisor of Hospitals, on Conditions on the White Earth Reservation," 18 April 1917, BIA RG 75, CCF 700, WEA, NARS; L. L. Culp, Special Physician, to CIA, 10 August 1918, BIA RG 75, CCF 150, WEA, NARS; RCIA 1912: 173, 1913: 145, 1915: 12, 138, 1916: 3–4, 135, 1917: 16, 139, 1918: 34, 154, 334, 1919: 142, 1920: 137.

24. "Records of Parishioners, Communicants, Baptisms, Marriages, Confirmations, Burials, and Offerings, of the Parish of Saint Columba, Diocese of

Minnesota," St. Columba Parish Papers, Parish Registers, 1853–1933, MHSA;
"Report of W. K. Moorehead," 9 August 1909; "Report of L. F. Michael,"
10 December 1913; "Report of W. H. Gibbs," 24 October 1916; RCIA 1911:
34, 1912: 43. Jack O. Waddell, "Malhiot's Journal: An Ethnohistoric Assessment of Chippewa Alcohol Behavior in the Early 19th Century," *Ethnohistory* 32 (1985): 246–68; Anthony F. C. Wallace, *The Death and Rebirth of
the Seneca* (New York: Vintage, 1972); R. David Edmunds, *The Shawnee
Prophet* (Lincoln: University of Nebraska Press, 1983); Richard White, *The
Roots of Dependency: Subsistence, Environment, and Social Change among
the Choctaw, Pawnee, and Navajo* (Lincoln: University of Nebraska Press,
1984); Pauline Wold, "Some Recollections of the Leech Lake Uprising,"
Minnesota History 24 (1943): 142–48; Louis H. Roddis, "The Last Indian
Uprising in the United States," *Minnesota History* 3 (1922): 284–88.
25. Quotation from "Report of H. S. Taylor," 27 October 1915. See also RCIA
1915: 117.
26. "Report of Clipping submitted by Congressman Hammond Relative to Expenditures on White Earth Reservation," F. H. Abbott, Acting CIA, 28 March
1913, BIA RG 75, CCF 916, WEA, NARS; RCIA 1911: 49; Minnesota State
Board of Immigration, *Minnesota by Counties* (St. Paul: State Bureau of
Immigration, 1916); Louis D. H. Weld, *Social and Economic Survey of a
Community in the Red River Valley* (Minneapolis: University of Minnesota
Press, 1915).
27. John R. Howard to CIA, 25 January 1910, BIA RG 75, CCF 723, WEA, NARS; Fr.
Felix Nelles, O.S.B., to Rev. Charles S. Lusk, Secretary, Bureau of Catholic
Indian Missions, 8 September 1910, BIA RG 75, CCF 723, WEA, NARS; Chief
Kay-dug-gay-gwon-nay-aush to CIA, 14 October 1910, BIA RG 75, CCF 723,
WEA, NARS; "Report of Elsie E. Newton, 22 September 1911; "Report of
Thomas F. Rodwell," 31 December 1911; Chief Wah Wea Cumig to CIA,
2 March 1912, BIA RG 75, CCF 721, WEA, NARS; "Inspection Report of
Charles F. Peirce on the Material Plant of the White Earth Agency," 21 De-
cember 1912, BIA RG 75, CCF 150, WEA, NARS; C. F. Hauke, Acting CIA to
John R. Howard, 8 February 1913, BIA RG 75, CCF 150, WEA, NARS; "Report
of an Investigation of Financial Affairs at the White Earth Indian School,
Minnesota, by H. T. Brown, Special Indian Agent," Received by Indian Office,
31 October 1913, BIA RG 75, CCF 150, WEA, NARS; "Report of L. F. Michaels:
Industries," 5 December 1913; "Report of L. F. Michael," 10 December 1913;
Warren K. Moorehead to Cato Sells, CIA, 5 January 1914, BIA RG 75, CCF
723, WEA, NARS; E. B. Meritt, Assistant CIA, to John R. Howard, 7 August
1914, BIA RG 75, CCF 150, WEA, NARS; N. B. Hurr to W. K. Moorehead,
1 January 1915, BIA RG 75, CCF 723, WEA, NARS; O. H. Lipps to CIA, 9 March
1915, BIA RG 75, CCF 056, WEA, NARS; John R. Howard to CIA, 9 March
1915, BIA RG 75, CCF 723, WEA, NARS; "Inspection Report of H. B. Peairs,"
9–26 June 1915; "Report of H. S. Taylor," 27 October 1915; J. H. Hinton to

CIA, 26 July 1916, BIA RG 75, CCF 700, WEA, NARS; J. H. Hinton to CIA, 19 October 1916, BIA RG 75, CCF 700, WEA, NARS; "Report of W. H. Gibbs," 24 October 1916; "Affidavits re. dependence and neglect," R. W. Wheelock, Chairman, State Board of Control, to Cato Sells, CIA, 23 August 1918, BIA RG 75, CCF 155, WEA, NARS; J. H. Hinton to E. B. Linnen, Chief Inspector, and C. L. Ellis, Special Supervisor, 15 November 1918, BIA RG 75, CCF 155, WEA, NARS; Charles E. Dagenett, Supervisor, to Mr. Shipe, 7 March 1918, BIA RG 75, CCF 900, WEA, NARS; RCIA 1906: 6, 1911: 154, 166, 1912: 176, 179, 1913: 152, 1914: 128, 1915: 7, 1917: 41. See also Hoxie, *A Final Promise.*

28. Quotations from "Report of H. S. Taylor," 27 October 1915. See also P. R. Wadsworth, Superintendent, to CIA, 2 August 1922, BIA RG 75, CCF 056, WEA, NARS; Andrew Bellecourt, Albert Giard, Louis Dakota, W. J. Heisler, returned soldiers, to CIA, 26 July 1922, BIA RG 75, CCF 056, WEA, NARS; P. R. Wadsworth, Superintendent, to CIA, 8 July 1922, BIA RG 75, CCF 056, WEA, NARS; RCIA 1917: 6–7, 41, 1918: 3, 62, 1919: 338; Interview with Dick Chesley, born 1895, c. 1982; Interview with Lizzie Brunette, born 1888, c. 1982, WEOHP. Interview with Mrs. Christine Roy, born ?, c. 1982; Interview with Winnifred Jourdain, born 1898, c. 1982; Interview with Fred Burnett Weaver, born 1900, c. 1982; Interview with Irene Harris, born 1898, c. 1982; Interview with Bessy Bertha Martinson, born 1897, c. 1982; Interview with Irene CeCelia Vizenor, born 1903, c. 1982; Interview with Emma May Johnson, born 1905, c. 1982, MCTRHP.

29. Quotes from "Inspection Report of W. H. Gibbs on Industries at White Earth Reservation," 24 October 1916, BIA RG 75, CCF 910, WEA, NARS.

30. Interview with Josephine Warren Robinson, born c. 1894, 9 August 1968, interviewed by Cynthia Kelsey, ms. 190, transcription of tape, American Indian Oral History Research Project, part 2, University of South Dakota, New York Times Oral History Program, 20–21.

Conclusion

1. Hall, *Social Change in the Southwest,* 17–23; Hall, "Patterns of Native American Incorporation."
2. Hoxie, *A Final Promise;* McDonnell, *Dispossession and the American Indian;* Carlson, *Indians, Bureaucrats, and Land.*
3. Cronon, *Chicago and the Great West;* Hall, "Introduction," *Social Change in the Southwest;* Hall, "Patterns of Native American Incorporation."
4. Interview with Lucy Thompson, born 1906, c. 1982, WEOHP.

Epilogue

1. Youngbear-Tibbets, "Without Due Process," 131; St. Paul *Pioneer Press Dispatch,* 23 March 1986; *Minneapolis Star and Tribune,* 31 March 1986.

2. U.S. Statutes at Large 100: 61; *Becker County Record*, 18 August 1986; *Detroit Lakes Tribune*, 9 October 1986; *Mahnomen Pioneer*, 16 October 1986; *Grand Forks Herald*, 18 November 1986. See also Youngbear-Tibbets, "Without Due Process," 126–27.

3. *State of Minnesota vs. Zay Zah*, filed 21 October 1977; 259 *Northwest Reporter*, 2d 580.

4. *Detroit Lakes Tribune*, 20 November 1986; *Becker County Record*, 24 November 1986; *Mahnomen Pioneer*, 27 November 1986; *Becker County Record*, 30 March 1987; Youngbear-Tibbets, "Without Due Process," 117–20. For information on other antitreaty rights organizations, see Donald L. Fixico, "Chippewa Hunting and Fishing Rights and the Voight Decision," in Donald L. Fixico, ed., *An Anthology of Western Great Lakes Indian History* (Milwaukee: American Indian Studies Program, University of Wisconsin, 1987); Robert Doherty, *Disputed Waters: Native Americans and the Great Lakes Fishery* (Lexington: University Press of Kentucky, 1990).

5. *The Leading Feather: Nee-Gon-Ee-Gwun (Voice of the Anishinabe)*, vols. 1–2, produced by the White Earth Oral History Project, 1983–85, White Earth, Minnesota; *Minnesota Daily* 86, 174 (24 May 1985): 1; *Minnesota Daily* 86, 179 (31 May 1985): 8–9; *Minneapolis Star and Tribune*, 24 May 1985: 3B.

6. Youngbear-Tibbets, "Without Due Process," 120–30; quotations from 126 and 129–30. Citation for Leah J. Carpenter, "The White Earth Land Controversy: Is History Repeating Itself?" (unpublished student paper, 1985, available from the author, Rte. 1, Bemidji, Minn. 56601) from p. 134, note 46. See *Mino-Bimadiziwin (The Good Life), White Earth Land Recovery Project*, 1992–1993, P.O. Box 327, White Earth, Minnesota 56591; Louise Erdrich and Michael Dorris, "Who Owns the Land," *New York Times Magazine* 4 Sept. 1988: 32–35, 52–54, 57, 65; *Little Wolf vs. Hodel*, 681 F. Supp. 929, D.D.C., (D.C., district court 1988). Subsequently, *Little Wolf vs. Lujan*, 877 D. 2d 1058, (D.C. Cir. 1989); *Marvin Manypenny et al. vs. United States of America et al.*, no. 90-5480 MN, 8th Cir., 1990. *Detroit Lakes Tribune*, 2 October 1986; *Minneapolis Star and Tribune*, 4 October 1986; *St. Paul Pioneer Press Dispatch*, 4 October 1986; *Becker County Record*, 6 October 1986; *Fargo Forum*, 20 October 1986; *Detroit Lakes Record*, 19 March 1987; *Duluth News-Tribune & Herald*, 23 March 1987; *Minneapolis Star and Tribune*, 24 March 1987; *Bemidji Pioneer*, 24 March 1987; *Fargo Forum*, 24 March 1987; *Becker County Record*, 26 March 1987; *New York Times*, 26 March 1987; *Washington Post*, 27 March 1987; *Becker County Record*, 30 March 1987. See the documentary *Clouded Land*, 1987, which attempts to portray both sides of this conflict and has been broadcast nationwide on PBS. Available from producer Randy Croce, 1117 Churchill, St. Paul, Minn. 55117.

7. The history, current policy dimensions, and implications of measuring Indian "blood" have been explored in C. Matthew Snipp, "Who Are American

Indians? Some Observations about the Perils and Pitfalls of Data for Race and Ethnicity," *Population Research and Policy Review* 5 (1986): 237–52; William T. Hagan, "Full Blood, Mixed Blood, Generic, and Ersatz, the Persisting Problem of Indian Identity," *Arizona and the West* 27 (1985): 309–26; and Melissa L. Meyer and Russell G. Thornton, "American Indian Tribal Enrollment: The Blood Quantum Quandary," Paper presented at the Annual Meeting of the American Society for Ethnohistory, Toronto, Canada, November 1990, and at the Annual Meeting of the Pacific Coast Branch of the American Historical Association, Kona, Hawaii, August 1991.

8. Interview with Minnesota Attorney General Hubert Humphrey III, by Randy Croce, director and producer, *Clouded Land*, June 1985.

9. Conversation between Marvin Manypenny and Melissa Meyer, May 1985, White Earth, Minnesota.

Bibliographic Essay

This book began as a community study that quickly became enmeshed in economics and politics. This is as it should be. To carry off the task, I have ranged widely in source materials and methods. Attempting a social history of people who were largely not literate entails its own difficulties, but scarce documentation was not among them. An untapped wealth of serial data generated by a colonial U.S. bureaucracy that sought to monitor and remake Indian cultures makes Indian groups some of the best documented people in the world, but one must venture into the realm of quantitative history to utilize it. Russell Thornton and I discuss this in "Indians and the Numbers Game: Quantitative Methods in American Indian History," in Colin Calloway, ed., *New Directions in American Indian History* (Norman: University of Oklahoma Press, 1988). Doing social history means ferreting out obscure sources and sleuthing to discover material that has not been labeled or catalogued as "social." For example, had I neglected to survey a category of BIA documents labeled "Dams and Ditches" I would have completely missed evidence of a series of organized, armed Indian protests against dams built by lumber companies that threatened the wild rice crop on which Indians depended. Similarly, had I passed over Frances Densmore's *Chippewa Music,* 2 vols., Smithsonian Institution, Bureau of American Ethnology, Bulletin 45 and 53 (Washington, D.C.: U.S. Government Printing Office, 1910–13; reprint Minneapolis: Ross and Haines, 1974), I would not have noticed that she provided biographical information about a dozen or so Midéwiwin priests and priestesses who gave her songs fully twenty years after ethnographer Walter Hoffman predicted the imminent disappearance of this religious complex. Doing social history means slicing through aggravating racist biases to render usable tidbits of information buried in old explorers' accounts that can shed light on peoples' way of life. Unearthing such information is not sufficient in itself; there must also be a skeletal structure on which to hang more idiosyncratic, anecdotal material.

My research rests on a foundation of Bureau of Indian Affairs documents, primarily Record Group 75, housed at the National Archives in Washington, D.C., and the Kansas City Federal Regional Archives, Missouri. Edward Hill's *Guide to Records in the National Archives of the United States Relating to American Indians* (Washington, D.C.: National Archives and Records Service, General Service Administration, 1981) provides an overview as does Gaston Litton's now-dated "The Resources of the National Archives for the Study of the American Indian," *Ethnohistory* 2 (1955): 191–208. Certain files were more useful than others. "Letters Received by the Commissioner of Indian Affairs" contains all correspondence sent to the commissioner, a treasure trove for social historians. The letters compiled before the introduction of the 1907 decimal system for filing correspondence are quite cumbersome to use, in part due to arcane measures that National Archives staff members force researchers to follow. Since these rules are apt to change, I will not elaborate on them. The decimal system created categories under which incoming correspondence was filed roughly chronologically. Most instructive for my purposes were inspection and investigation reports on economic conditions, health, and education, and petitions and tribal council minutes. But again, I must caution researchers not to rely solely on labels and to cast their net widely lest they miss important information. Furthermore, the filing system was by no means perfect; items are misfiled (or mysteriously filed) throughout. Understanding the structure of the Indian Office helps to make sense of these documents. Paul Stuart's *The Indian Office: Growth and Development of an American Institution* (Ann Arbor: University of Michigan Research Press, 1979) and Laurence Schmeckebier's *The Office of Indian Affairs*, Institute for Government Research Monograph 48 (Baltimore: Johns Hopkins University Press, 1927) are helpful here.

The Annual Reports of the Commissioner of Indian Affairs are a basic resource to be used in conjunction with other government documents. The format changes over time; they are most useful for data around the turn of the twentieth century when they include narrative reports from individual agents. In fact, when these are not included, it makes interpreting statistics more difficult. The amount of appended statistical information increases over time, but changing jurisdictions complicate generating comparable statistics—making it sometimes impossible to do so. J. A. Jones's "Key to the Annual Reports of the United States Commissioner of Indian Affairs," *Ethnohistory* 2 (1955): 58–64, is useful, and Robert Kvasnicka's and Herman Viola's *The Commissioners of Indian Affairs, 1824–1977* (Lincoln: University of Nebraska Press, 1979) provides biographical information about each commissioner.

Standard collections of U.S. government documents were also surveyed. Their special relationship with the U.S. government makes American Indian groups unique among American subpopulations; no other minority group was ever the target of so much legislation and voluminous reports to Congress. Laws and Executive Orders are contained in the *Statutes at Large.* Each term Congress slated money to cover most of its obligations in regard to Indian affairs in Indian Appropriations Acts, each of which is hundreds of pages long. They can also contain important legislation that is nearly hidden ("riders"). Valuable aids are Charles Kappler's compilation *Indian Affairs: Laws and Treaties,* 5 vols. (Washington, D.C.: U.S. Government Printing Office, 1904–41), and Charles Royce's "Indian Land Cessions in the United States," *Annual Report of the Bureau of American Ethnology* 18 (1896–97) 2 vols. (Washington, D.C.: U.S. Government Printing Office, 1899). All reports sent to Congress by various branches of government (Secretary of the Interior, Commissioner of Indian Affairs, etc.) and reports generated by special commissions are contained in the enormous Congressional Serial Set. Investigation reports contained in this set were absolutely critical for my research. Often they are compendiums of all relevant documentation and contain testimony from primary participants as well. Steven Johnson's *Guide to American Indian Documents in the Congressional Serial Set, 1817–1899: A Project of the Institute for the Development of Indian Law* (New York: Clearwater Publishing Co., 1977) can help up to 1900. The congressional *Record* containing congressional debates and congressional *Hearings* on various issues are also important. Indexes make each of these essential collections more accessible, but the work is time-consuming and somewhat tedious nonetheless.

Writings of primary participants contain more personal information. From these I gleaned much anecdotal material to enliven the narrative. William Warren, the tribal historian of mixed descent, wrote *History of the Ojibway Nation* (Minneapolis: Ross and Haines, 1957, reprinted 1970) and "Notes on the Chippewas," *Minnesota Archeologist* 12 (1946): 45–91, 95–107; 13 (1947): 5–21, which provide oral histories; these works are valuable despite his odd notion that Indians were descended from the ten lost tribes of Israel. Julia Spears, John Johnson Enmegahbowh, and the families of Clement Hudon Beaulieu, Theodore Hudon Beaulieu, and John Clement Beaulieu were among the earliest White Earth immigrants and provide stories about their families, friends, and experiences in their papers housed at the Minnesota Historical Society Archives (MHSA), St. Paul. Enmegahbowh published *The Church and the Indians* (New York: 1874) and *Enmegahbowh's Story: An Account of the Disturbances of the Chippewa Indians at Gull Lake in 1857, and Their Removal in 1868* (Minneapolis: Women's Auxiliary, St. Barnabas Hospital, 1904). John Rogers wrote of his childhood in *Red World and White: Memories of a Chippewa Boyhood* (Norman: University of Oklahoma Press, 1974; first edition, *A Chippewa Speaks*, 1957). Ignatia Broker reconstructed her grandmother's reminiscences in *Night Flying Woman: An Ojibway Narrative* (St. Paul: Minnesota Historical Society Press, 1983). Finally, Ransom J. Powell, attorney for lumber companies and member of the Chippewa Roll Commission, also left his papers to the MHSA; they are a gold mine containing extensive genealogical information and testimony from individuals concerning blood status.

Episcopal missionaries Joseph Gilfillan, Pauline Colby, and Henry Whipple also left detailed personal records. Gilfillan is especially useful for White Earth, though his intention to convert the Anishinaabeg and his disdain for their culture suffuses his narratives. Whipple's writings pertain more to the period immediately preceding this study, but have occasional relevance. Not surprisingly, Colby's diary reveals more about Anishinaabe women.

As with most ethnographers of this period, those who worked at White Earth hoped to capture the old, "traditional" ways before they vanished. Adaptation and change (they tended to call it decline or decay) were not much within their purview, but sometimes slip through in their photographs. Nonetheless, their writing helps to balance federal officials' preoccupation with documenting their success at assimilating ("civilizing," they called it) the Anishinaabeg. Frances Densmore worked most extensively at White Earth and published *Chippewa Music* and *How Indians Use Wild Plants for Food, Medicine, and Crafts* (New York: Dover Publications, 1974; reprint of "Uses of Plants by the Chippewa Indians," *Bureau of American Ethnology* 44 [1926–27]: 275–397). Her papers are also at MHSA. Walter Hoffman focused on the Midéwiwin in "The Midéwiwin or 'Grand Medicine Society' of the Ojibwa," *Annual Report of the Bureau of American Ethnology* 7 (1885–86): 149–306 (Washington, D.C.: U.S. Government Printing Office, 1891), and "Pictography and Shamanistic Rites of the Ojibwa," *American Anthropologist* 1 (1888): 209–229. Catholic missionary Inez Hilger conducted research at White Earth in the 1930s and 1940s, but her findings have limited relevance nonetheless. She published *A Social Study of One Hundred and Fifty Chippewa Indian Families on the White Earth Reservation of Minnesota* (Washington, D.C.: Catholic University of America Press,

1939) and *Chippewa Child Life and Its Cultural Background*, Bureau of American Ethnology Bulletin 146 (Washington, D.C.: U.S. Government Printing Office, 1951). Many have written about Anishinaabe culture, but I must caution about deducing information about White Earth from ethnographies about the Anishinaabeg in general. As the largest culture group in North America, there was much regional variability in Anishinaabe culture. White Earth's particularities cannot be captured by reference to an overly homogenized ideal.

As with Ojibwe culture, there are also regional dialects of the language. Frederick Baraga's *A Dictionary of the Otchipwe Language, Explained in English*, 2 parts (Minneapolis: Ross & Haines, 1966; earlier ed. Montreal: Beauchemin and Valois, 1878), is the best historical dictionary, but its phonetic rendition makes it incompatible with modern orthographies. I have relied on John Nichols and Earl Nyholm's *Ojibwewi-Ikidowinan: An Ojibwe Word Resource Book* (St. Paul: Minnesota Archaeological Society, 1979) whenever possible and referred to Baraga's dictionary largely for further insight into nuanced meanings.

The timing of dispossession at White Earth makes sense only by reference to world-systems theory. By now, the literature is vast but sociologist Immanuel Wallerstein laid out the classic formulation in *The Modern World System: Capitalist Agriculture and the Origins of the European World-Economy in the Sixteenth Century* (New York: Academic Press, 1974) and *The Modern World System II: Mercantilism and the Consolidation of the European World Economy, 1600–1750* (New York: Academic Press, 1980). However, his work does not elaborate on the effects for indigenous people, a topic that anthropologist Eric Wolf examines in *Europe and the People Without History* (Berkeley: University of California Press, 1982), although he treats Indians only as superexploited victims. William Cronon in *Nature's Metropolis: Chicago and the Great West* (New York: W. W. Norton, 1991) probes Chicago's environmental impact on its surrounding hinterland and the consequences for native people. White Earth was tied more to the Twin Cities market, but the analogy applies. A trio of scholars has attempted to make world-systems theory more relevant to American Indian history. Anthropologist Joseph Jorgensen described the expansion of the United States as a unilateral, overwhelming process in "A Century of Political and Economic Effects on American Indian Society, 1880–1980," *Journal of Ethnic Studies* 6 (1978): 1–82, and "Indians and the Metropolis," in Jack O. Waddell and O. Michael Watson, eds., *The American Indian in Urban Society* (Boston: Little, Brown & Co., 1971: 67–113). See also sociologist C. Mat-

thew Snipp's "The Changing Political and Economic Status of American
Indians: From Captive Nations to Internal Colonies," *American Journal of
Economics and Sociology* 45 (1986): 145–57. Most of sociologist Thomas
Hall's work has attempted to refine world-systems theory to include Indian
groups as active historical actors rather than mere victims. He calls his work
social history, but despite his contribution his focus is on economic processes; Indian individuals and political processes are barely visible. For the
clearest statements of his position see *Social Change in the Southwest,
1350–1880* (Lawrence: University of Kansas Press, 1988) and "Incorporation
in the World System: Toward a Critique," *American Sociological Review* 51
(1986): 390–402.

I owe major debts to two scholars who laid out the historical groundwork
for my study. Despite his functionalist approach, Harold Hickerson provided
quite an example for how to uncover elusive information on American
Indians. Everyone working in the area must pay homage to *The Chippewa
and Their Neighbors: A Study in Ethnohistory* (New York: Holt, Rinehart,
and Winston, 1970) and *The Southwestern Chippewa: An Ethnohistorical
Study*, American Anthropological Association Memoir 92 (Menasha, Wisc.:
American Anthropological Association, 1962). For a man who worked in the
1920s, William Watts Folwell amazed me with his ability to regard the
Anishinaabeg as serious historical actors worthy of in-depth attention in his
A History of Minnesota, 4 vols. (St. Paul: Minnesota Historical Society Press,
1969). Richard White's new award-winning book *The Middle Ground: In-
dians, Empires, and Republics in the Great Lakes Region, 1650–1815* (Cambridge: Cambridge University Press, 1991) breaks new interpretive ground in
Indian-white relations. I have relied on the work of several scholars who
explored the decline of the fur trade in Minnesota: Rhoda R. Gilman, "Last
Days of the Upper Mississippi Fur Trade," in Malvina Bolus, ed., *People and
Pelts: Selected Papers, 2nd North American Fur Trade Conference* (Winnipeg: Pequis Publishers, 1972); James L. Clayton, "The Growth and Economic Significance of the American Fur Trade, 1790–1890," *Minnesota
History* 40 (1966): 210–20; Rhoda R. Gilman, Carolyn Gilman, and Deborah M. Stultz, *The Red River Trails: Oxcart Routes between St. Paul and
the Selkirk Settlement, 1820–1870* (St. Paul: Minnesota Historical Society
Press, 1979); and Bernard Coleman, Verona La Bud, and John Humphrey, *Old
Crow Wing: History of a Village* (Duluth: College of St. Scholastica, 1967).

Ecologically, the prairie-forest transition zone determined the character of
White Earth's landscape and set parameters for the adaptations people might
have made there. Herb Wright discussed the geological processes at work in

"Late Quaternary Vegetational History of North America," in K. K. Turekian, ed., *The Late Cenozoic Glacial Ages* (New Haven: Yale University
Press, 1971: 425–64) and in his edited volume with William A. Watts, *Glacial and Vegetational History of Northeastern Minnesota*, SP11, Special
Publication Series, Minnesota Geological Survey (St. Paul: University of
Minnesota Press, 1969). Harold Hickerson explored how the transition zone
influenced relations between the Anishinaabeg and the Dakota in his influential "The Virginia Deer and Intertribal Buffer Zones in the Upper Mississippi Valley," in Anthony Leeds and Andrew Vayda, eds., *Man, Culture,
and Animals: The Role of Animals in Human Ecological Adjustments*
(Washington, D.C.: American Association for the Advancement of Science,
Publication 78, 1965). In "Virginia Deer and the Buffer Zone in the Late
Prehistoric-Early Protohistoric Periods in Minnesota," *Plains Anthropologist* 13 (1968): 81–86, Charles Watrall carried Hickerson's reasoning further
and added archaeological substantiation. Charles Cleland, "The Prehistoric
Animal Ecology and Ethnozoology of the Upper Great Lakes Region," *An-
thropological Papers 29*, Museum of Anthropology (Ann Arbor: University
of Michigan, 1966), and Richard Yarnell, "Aboriginal Relationships between
Culture and Plant Life in the Upper Great Lakes Region," *Anthropological
Papers 23*, Museum of Anthropology (Ann Arbor: University of Michigan
Press, 1964), elaborated on resources available in the western Great Lakes
region. Anthony Davis focused more closely on the transition zone itself in
"The Prairie-Deciduous Forest Ecotone in the Upper Middle West," *Annals
of the Association of American Geographers* 67 (1977): 204–13. For Minnesota, Evadene Swanson examined the history of game animals in "The Use
and Conservation of Minnesota Game, 1850–1900," M.A. Thesis, University of Minnesota, 1940; John Nelson wrote "A Study of the Nutritive Value
of Minnesota's Fresh-Water Plants," Ph.D. Dissertation, University of Minnesota, 1939; and Alfred Rogosin wrote "Wild Rice (*Zizania aquatica L.*) in
Northern Minnesota, with Special Reference to the Effects of Various Water
Levels and Water Level Changes, Seeding Densities, and Fertilizer," M.S.
Thesis, University of Minnesota, 1958. I derived inspiration for the importance of environmental considerations from Richard White's *The Roots
of Dependency: Subsistence, Environment, and Social Change among the
Choctaw, Pawnee and Navajo* (Lincoln: University of Nebraska Press, 1984)
and William Cronon's *Changes in the Land: Indians, Colonists, and the
Ecology of New England* (New York: Hill and Wang, 1983).

Frederick Hoxie's *A Final Promise: The Campaign to Assimilate the
Indians, 1880–1920* (Lincoln: University of Nebraska Press, 1984) ranges far

beyond typical sources for policy studies and roots U.S. Indian policy in the larger social and intellectual milieu of the time. It is the best work of its kind. Janet McDonnell in *The Dispossession of the American Indian, 1887–1934* (Bloomington: Indiana University Press, 1991) has produced the best study to date of subsequent legislation that eroded the supposed benefits to come from the General Allotment Act. However, she makes only occasional references to local applications in favor of a more overarching policy analysis. The danger in this approach is misinterpreting particularities in search of generalities. Francis Prucha provides encyclopedic coverage in *American Indian Policy in Crisis: Christian Reformers and the Indian, 1865–1900* (Norman: University of Oklahoma Press, 1976) and *The Churches and the Indian Schools, 1888–1912* (Lincoln: University of Nebraska Press, 1979), but he is an apologist for the U.S. government with an aggravating paternalistic bias. Other standard works on U.S. Indian policy of the period are D. S. Otis, *The Dawes Act and the Allotment of Indian Lands*, ed. Francis Paul Prucha (Norman: University of Oklahoma Press, 1973); Wilcomb Washburn, *The Assault on Indian Tribalism: The General Allotment Law (Dawes Act) of 1887* (New York: J. B. Lippincott Company, 1975); Loring Benson Priest, *Uncle Sam's Stepchildren: The Reformation of U.S. Indian Policy, 1865–1887* (New Brunswick, N.J.: Rutgers University Press, 1942); Henry Fritz, *The Movement for Indian Assimilation, 1860–1890* (Philadelphia: University of Pennsylvania Press, 1963); and Robert W. Mardock, *The Reformers and the American Indian* (Columbia: University of Missouri Press, 1971). The historical background of contemporary legal issues at White Earth are discussed aptly by Edward Peterson in "That So-Called Warranty Deed: Clouded Land Titles on the White Earth Indian Reservation in Minnesota," *North Dakota Law Review* 59 (1983): 159–81, and Holly Youngbear-Tibbets, "Without Due Process: The Alienation of Individual Trust Allotments of the White Earth Anishinaabeg," *American Indian Culture and Research Journal* 15 (1991): 93–138.

The racial underpinnings of ideologies and policies that promoted U.S. expansion are expertly analyzed by Reginald Horsman in *Race and Manifest Destiny* (Cambridge: Harvard University Press, 1981). Studies of social Darwinism and eugenics are proliferating. The best among them are Robert C. Bannister, *Social Darwinism: Science and Myth* (Philadelphia: Temple University Press, 1988); Daniel Kevles, *In the Name of Eugenics: Genetics and the Uses of Human Heredity* (New York: Knopf, 1985); and Donald Pickens, *Eugenics and the Progressives* (Nashville: Vanderbilt University Press, 1968). Robert Bieder and Curtis Hinsley explored the implications of these ideas for American Indians in *Science Encounters the Indian, 1820–1880* (Norman: University of Oklahoma Press, 1986) and *Savages and Scientists: The Smithsonian Institution and the Development of American Anthropology, 1846–1910* (Washington, D.C.: Smithsonian Institution Press, 1981), respectively. Measuring physical characteristics for political purposes at White Earth would be almost comical if its consequences were not so tragic. See David Beaulieu, "Curly Hair and Big Feet: Physical Anthropology and Land Allotment on the White Earth Chippewa Reservation," *American Indian Quarterly* 8 (1984): 281–314. Stephen Jay Gould refuted methods used by eugenicists by demonstrating how their preconceived racist notions caused them to misinterpret their data in *The Mismeasure of Man* (New York: W. W. Norton, 1981). Two practitioners plied their disturbing techniques at White Earth. Aleš Hrdlička published "Anthropological Work among the Sioux and Chippewa," *Smithsonian Miscellaneous Collections* (1915), 66: 17; "Trip to the Chippewa Indians of Minnesota," *Smithsonian Miscellaneous Collection* 66 (1916): 263–74; and "Anthropology of the Chippewa," in F. W. Hodge, ed., *Holmes Anniversary Volume: Anthropological Essays* (Washington, D.C.: U.S. Government Printing Office, 1916). Albert Jenks contributed *Indian-White Amalgamation: An Anthropometric Study,* Studies in the Social Sciences 6 (Minneapolis: University of Minnesota Press, 1916).

Any number of tribal histories encompass the time period of this study. Loretta Fowler composed the best of the lot by coupling documentary research with field work. See *Shared Symbols, Contested Meanings: Alternate Views of Culture and History in an American Indian Society; the Gros Ventres, 1778–1984* (Ithaca, N.Y.: Cornell University Press, 1987) and *Arapaho Politics, 1851–1978: Symbols in Crises of Authority* (Lincoln: University of Nebraska Press, 1982). Although she focused more on reservation politics and political symbols, her analyses, by necessity, have a strong social cast. James Clifton's *The Prairie People: Continuity and Change in Potawatomi Culture, 1665–1965* (Lawrence: Regents Press of Kansas, 1977) is also a cut above the rest. Other insightful reservation studies are Donald Berthrong, *The Cheyenne and Arapaho Ordeal: Reservation and Agency Life in the Indian Territory, 1875–1907* (Norman: University of Oklahoma Press, 1976); Terry Wilson, *The Underground Reservation: Osage Oil* (Lincoln: University of Nebraska Press, 1985); and William T. Hagan, *United States-Comanche Relations: The Reservation Years* (New Haven: Yale University Press, 1976). All of these studies have something to recommend them, but their heavy emphasis on descriptions of exploitation left me yearning for more sophisticated analyses. I must disagree with Peter Iverson's assessment, in "Indian Tribal Histories," in William Swagerty, ed., *Scholars and the Indian Experience* (Bloomington: Indiana University Press, 1984): 223–58, that Edmund Danziger's *The Chippewas of Lake Superior* (Norman: University of Oklahoma Press, 1979) is the best example of a tribal history. James Clifton's critique, "The Tribal History—An Obsolete Paradigm," *American Indian Culture and Research Journal* 3 (1979): 81–100, is on the mark; as do numerous tribal histories, Danziger's book merely skims over a predictable course of federal legislation leaving Indian people all but invisible.

In *Economics as Culture: Models and Metaphors of Livelihood* (London: Routledge and Kegan Paul, 1986), Stephen Gudeman explains that all cultures are not organized according to Western market rationality; culture is an interface in efforts to gain a livelihood. In *Indian Agriculture in America: Prehistory to the Present* (Lawrence: University Press of Kansas, 1987), Douglas Hurt describes how U.S. policies forced the transformation of Indian farming techniques. Leonard Carlson further demonstrates the decline of Indian agriculture brought about by allotment policy in *Indians, Bureaucrats, and Land: The Dawes Act and the Decline of Indian Farming* (Westport, Conn.: Greenwood Press, 1981). Two Ph.D. dissertations—Ronald Trosper's "The Economic Impact of the Allotment Policy on the Flathead Indian Reservation," Harvard University, 1974, and James Fitch's "Economic Development in a Minority Enclave: The Case of the Yakima Indian Nation, Washington," Stanford University, 1974—address the economic impact of allotment by developing local reservation case studies. Similar tales of the consequences of unbridled corporate greed in Indian country have been told by H. Craig Miner in *The Corporation and the Indian: Tribal Sovereignty and Industrial Civilization in Indian Territory, 1865–1907* (Columbia: University of Missouri Press, 1976), H. Craig Miner and William Unrau in *The End of Indian Kansas: A Study of Cultural Revolution, 1854–1871* (Lawrence: Regents Press of Kansas, 1978), and Angie Debo in *And Still the Waters Run: The Betrayal of the Five Civilized Tribes* (Princeton: Princeton University Press, 1972). Timber fraud on Indian lands has been explored by Rich Nafziger in "A Violation of Trust? Federal Management of Indian Timber Lands," *Indian Historian* 9 (1976): 15–23, and by Sandra Faiman-Silva in "Tribal Land to Private Land: A Century of Oklahoma Choctaw Timberland Alienation from the 1880s to the 1980s," *Journal of Forest History* 32 (October 1988): 191–204. Harold Steen's edited volume on sustained yield forestry makes it clear that such principles existed prior to federal policies facilitating the clear-cutting of Indian timberlands without regard to their potential to generate long-term revenue. See *History of Sustained Yield Forestry: A Symposium* (Santa Cruz, Calif.: Forest History Society, 1984). Several studies explore how Indians worked for wages and sold seasonal produce: Rolf Knight, *Indians at Work: An Informal History of Native Indian Labour in British Columbia, 1858–1930* (Vancouver: New Star, 1978); Patricia Shifferd, "A Study in Economic Change: The Chippewa of Northern Wisconsin: 1854–1900," *Western Canadian Journal of Anthropology* 6 (1976): 16–41; Stuart Berde, "Wild Ricing: The Transformation of an Aboriginal Subsistence Pattern," in J. A. Paredes, ed., *Anishinabe: Six Studies of Modern Chippewa* (Tallahassee: University Presses of Florida, 1980): 101–25; Albert E. Jenks, "Wild Rice Gatherers of the Upper Lakes: A Study in American Primitive Economics," in *U.S. Bureau of Ethnology. Nineteenth Annual Report, 1897–98* (Washington, D.C.: U.S. Government Printing Office, 1900): 1013–1137; Thomas Vennum, Jr., *Wild Rice and the Ojibway People* (St. Paul: Minnesota Historical Society Press, 1988); Joseph Mitchell, "The Mohawks in High Steel," in Edmund Wilson, ed., *Apologies to the Iroquois* (New York: Farrar, Straus, and Cudahy, 1959): 1–36; and Daniel Usner's *Indian's, Settlers, and Slaves in a Frontier Exchange Economy: The Lower Mississippi Valley before 1763* (Chapel Hill: University of North Carolina Press, 1992). A bias toward emphasizing exploitation and dispossession has obscured the diverse adaptations that Indians made to market conditions; they have typically been portrayed as either failed hunters and farmers or languishing welfare recipients. Arguments about workers' adjustment to the demands of factory time have bearing here. See the classics: E. P. Thompson, "Time, Work-Discipline, and Industrial Capitalism," *Past and Present* 38 (1967): 56–97; Herbert Gutman, *Work, Culture and Society in Industrializing America: Essays in American Working-Class and Social History* (New York: Alfred A. Knopf, 1976); and David Montgomery, *The Fall of the House of Labor: The Workplace, the State, and American Labor Activism, 1865–1925* (Cambridge: Cambridge University Press, 1987).

Migration has figured prominently in White Earth's history. Popular folklore in Minnesota has it that the "Chippewa drove the Sioux from Minnesota" with guns they acquired from fur traders. Recently scholars have revised this simplistic explanation. The best of the challengers is Timothy Holzkamm's "Eastern Dakota Population Movements and the European Fur Trade: One More Time," *Plains Anthropologist* 28 (1983): 225–33. Those who moved to White Earth had much in common with other immigrants. Recent studies in immigration history have informed my interpretation. See especially John Bodnar, *The Transplanted: A History of Immigrants in Urban America* (Bloomington: Indiana University Press, 1985), and Jon Gjerde, *From Peasant to Farmer: The Migration from Balestrand, Norway to the Upper Middle West* (Cambridge: Cambridge University Press, 1985). Arthur Margon has also argued for comparability in "Indians and Immigrants: A Comparison of Groups New to the City," *Journal of Ethnic Studies* 4 (1977): 17–28. John Moore's "Aboriginal Indian Residence Patterns Preserved in Censuses and Allotments," *Science* 207 (1980): 201–2, inspired my consideration of the relationship between residence patterns and band migration. Finally, Elaine Neils has explored movement to urban areas in *Reservation to City: Indian Migration and Federal Relocation* (Chicago: University of Chicago, Department of Geography, Research Paper 131, 1971). However, migration from White Earth began well in advance of federal relocation policies of the 1950s.

Robert Berkhofer's recommendations for the study of American Indian political history in "The Political Context of a New Indian History," *Pacific Historical Review* 40 (1971): 357–82, have well stood the test of time. Venturing into the realms of political science and anthropology can provide instructive insights into political processes in band level societies. See especially Mancur Olson, *The Logic of Collective Action: Public Goods and the Theory of Groups* (Cambridge: Harvard University Press, 1965); Pierre Clastres, *Society against the State: Essays in Political Anthropology* (New York: Zone Books, 1987); Raymond Fogelson and Richard N. Adams, eds., *The Anthropology of Power: Ethnographic Studies from Asia, Oceania, and the New World* (New York: Academic Press, 1977). Robert Berkhofer also penned an influential piece about American Indian leadership: "Native Americans," in John Higham, ed., *Ethnic Leadership in America* (Baltimore: Johns Hopkins University Press, 1978): 119–49. James G. E. Smith and Ernestine Friedl have considered Anishinaabe leaders in *Leadership among the Southwestern Ojibwa*, National Museums of Canada, Publications in Ethnology 7 (Ottawa: National Museums of Canada, 1973) and "An Attempt at Directed Culture Change: Leadership among the Chippewa, 1640–1948," Ph.D. Dissertation, Columbia University, 1951, respectively. P. Richard Metcalf argued against the contemporary grain when he made the case that factionalism within American Indian groups probably existed before European contact in "Who Should Rule at Home? Native American Politics and Indian-White Relations," *Journal of American History* 61 (1974–75): 651–65. What now seems like an obvious argument was innovative at the time. The important points to draw from it are that native groups were not necessarily homogeneous and that scholars should consider internal political dynamics in their analyses. David Rich Lewis has challenged scholars who resort to the simplistic traditional/modern dichotomy in discussions of reservation politics in "Reservation Leadership and the Progressive-Traditional Dichotomy: William Wash and the Northern Utes, 1865–1928," *Ethnohistory* 38 (1991): 124–48. His point is well taken, but I further argue that the dichotomy, though crude, symbolizes increasing patterned heterogeneity within tribal groups brought about by similar processes. Rebecca Kugel considered factionalism among the Minnesota Anishinaabeg in "Factional Alignment among the Minnesota Ojibwe, 1850–1880," *American Indian Culture and Research Journal* 9 (1985): 23–47. This piece and her dissertation, "'To Go About on the Earth:' An Ethnohistory of the Minnesota Ojibwe," Ph.D. Dissertation, University of California, Los Angeles, 1986, are most insightful especially in regard to the differential success of various denominations of missionaries and how the Anishinaabeg used them. I disagree, however, with fine points of her interpretation of the nature of Anishinaabe band politics.

In *Community and Social Change in America* (New Brunswick, N.J.: Rutgers University Press, 1978), Thomas Bender describes community as a process characterized by a network of close, face-to-face associations, the specific nature of which changes over time. When community is construed as more than simply a geographic area, it becomes difficult for historians to document. They often cannot talk to people or use questionnaires as sociologists can and are confined to bits and pieces of documentary tailings that suggest close relationships. Family reconstitution can be helpful, but networks of friends and associates cannot be reconstructed through censuses or other typical serial sources. Under these circumstances, Bender's statement, though rather vague, is still the best. Edward Rogers and Mary Black Rogers provide a useful prototype for surname reconstruction in "Method for Reconstructing Patterns of Change: Surname Adoption by the Weagamow Ojibwa, 1870–1950," *Ethnohistory* 25 (1978): 319–45. The most outstanding example of American Indian social history is Albert Hurtado's award-winning *Indian Survival on the California Frontier* (New Haven: Yale University Press, 1988). Other good examples that, however, make no attempt to quantify serial records are James Merrell's *The Indians' New World: Catawbas and Their Neighbors from European Contact through the Era of Removal* (Chapel Hill: University of North Carolina Press, 1989), Richard White's *The Roots of Dependency: Subsistence, Environment and Social Change among the Choctaws, Pawnees and Navajos* (Lincoln: University of

Nebraska Press, 1983); and *The Middle Ground Indians, Empires, and Republics in the Great Lakes Region, 1650–1815* (Cambridge: Cambridge University Press, 1991). In the last chapter of *The Lumbee Problem: The Making of an American Indian People* (Cambridge: Cambridge University Press, 1980), Karen Blu offers the best theoretical discussion of ethnicity as it relates to American Indians. C. Matthew Snipp discusses the variability of available demographic data and the implications for American Indian identity in "Who Are American Indians? Some Observations about the Perils and Pitfalls of Data for Race and Ethnicity," *Population Research and Policy Review* 5 (1986): 237–52. The creation of a generalized "American Indian" identity by more elite, entrepreneurial Indians is the subject of Hazel Hertzberg's *The Search for an American Indian Identity: Modern Pan-Indian Movements* (Syracuse: Syracuse University Press, 1971). William Unrau suggests a connection between the adoption of capitalistic values and being of mixed descent in his biography of Charles Curtis, *Mixed-bloods and Tribal Dissolution: Charles Curtis and the Quest for Indian Identity* (Lawrence: University Press of Kansas, 1989). However, he fails to elaborate on this relationship in any meaningful fashion. The best treatments of boundary maintenance are Ron Trosper's "Native American Boundary Maintenance: The Flathead Indian Reservation, Montana, 1860–1970," *Ethnicity* 3 (1976): 256–74, and Fredrik Barth's classic "Introduction," in *Ethnic Groups and Boundaries: The Social Organization of Culture Difference,* ed. Fredrik Barth (London: George Allen and Unwin, 1969): 9–38. Malcolm McFee questioned the then prevalent assumption that acculturation was a unilinear process in "The 150% Man, a Product of Blackfeet Acculturation," *American Anthropologist* 70 (1968): 1096–1107. The best musings about constructions of Indian bicultural identities can be found in James Clifton's sometimes acerbic edited volume, *Being and Becoming Indian: Biographical Studies of North American Frontiers* (Chicago: Dorsey Press, 1989).

Studies of the Canadian Métis have proliferated in recent years. Two of the most influential works that established a baseline for future research appeared in the same year: Jennifer Brown's *Strangers in Blood: Fur Trade Company Families in Indian Country* (Vancouver: University of British Columbia Press, 1980) and Sylvia Van Kirk's *"Many Tender Ties": Women in Fur-Trade Society, 1670–1870* (Winnipeg: Watson and Dwyer, 1980). Historical conditions fostering the evolution of biculturality were examined by Olive Dickason in "From 'One Nation' in the Northeast to 'New Nation' in the Northwest: A Look at the Emergence of the Métis," *American Indian Culture and Research Journal* 6 (1982): 1–21, and Carol Judd in " 'Mixt Bands of Many Nations:' 1821–1870," in Carol M. Judd and Arthur J. Ray, eds., *Old Trails and New Directions* (Toronto: University of Toronto Press, 1980): 127–46. A series of essays in *The New Peoples: Being and Becoming Métis in North America* (Lincoln: University of Nebraska Press, 1985) edited by Jacqueline Peterson and Jennifer Brown explore the origins of biculturality and consequences of Métis identity as do Julia Harrison in *Métis: People between Two Worlds* (Vancouver: Douglas and McIntyre, 1985) and Trudy Nicks in "Mary Anne's Dilemma: The Ethnohistory of an Ambivalent Identity," *Muse* 3, 4 (1986): 52–55. Social history surveys appeared in Sylvia Van Kirk, "Fur Trade Social History: Some Recent Trends," in Carol M. Judd and Arthur J. Ray, eds., *Old Trails and New Directions* (Toronto: University of Toronto Press, 1980) and Arthur Ray, "Reflections on Fur Trade Social History and Métis History in Canada," *American Indian Culture and Research Journal* 6 (1982): 91–107. Jacqueline Peterson argued that conditions in the western Great Lakes region also generated a society of bicultural people who were, in essence, a "prelude" to the evolution of true Métis identity in Canada. See her "Prelude to Red River: A Social Portrait of the Great Lakes Métis," *Ethnohistory* 25 (1978): 41–67; "The People in Between: Indian-White Marriage and the Genesis of a Métis Society and Culture in the Great Lakes Region, 1680–1830," Ph.D. Dissertation, University of Illinois, Chicago Circle, 1981; "Ethnogenesis: The Settlement and Growth of a 'New People' in the Great Lakes Region, 1702–1815," *American Indian Culture and Research Journal* 6 (1982): 23–64; and "Many Roads to Red River: Métis Genesis in the Great Lakes Region, 1680–1815," in Jacqueline Peterson and Jennifer S. H. Brown, eds., *Being and Becoming Métis in North America* (Lincoln: University of Nebraska Press, 1985). Finally, Tanis Chapman Thorne examined the genesis of bicultural people of mixed descent in the St. Louis fur trade in "People of the River: Mixed-Blood Families on the Lower Missouri," Ph.D. Dissertation, University of California, Los Angeles, 1987. People with cultural roots analogous to these bicultural métis came to dominate White Earth political and economic affairs.

The historical literature on American Indian women is only beginning to develop. The best contemporary statement questioning the assumption that women's status declined in an unwavering downward spiral following colonization relates to Hawaiian native women. See Jocelyn Linnekin's *Sacred Queens and Women of Consequence Rank, Gender, and Colonialism in the Hawaiian Islands* (Ann Arbor: University of Michigan Press, 1990). Before Linnekin, Mona Etienne and Eleanor Leacock assembled a collection of essays that also veered from this presumption, *Women and Colonization:*

Anthropological Perspectives (New York: Praeger, 1980), and penned an introduction that offered the rudiments of an alternative theory. Patricia Albers's exploration of historical circumstances that impacted on women's roles, "Sioux Women in Transition: A Study of Their Changing Status in a Domestic and Capitalist Sector of Production," in Patricia Albers and Beatrice Medicine, eds., *The Hidden Half: Studies of Plains Indian Women* (New York: University Press of America, 1983): 175–234, is one of the best treatments. Finally, Priscilla Buffalohead provided a model for approaching early historical documents with an open mind and sharp eye to enable scholars to find women who were much more well-rounded historical actors, but who have been obscured by a double-edged androcentric bias. For further elaboration about preconceptions of native women see Rayna Green, "The Pocahontas Perplex: The Image of Indian Women in Popular Culture," *Massachusetts Review* 16 (Autumn 1975): 698–714. I modified Janet Spector's method for categorizing task differentiation archaeologically to apply to historical documents to manage more effectively tidbits of information about women and activities in which both native women and men were involved. See "Male/Female Task Differentiation among the Hidatsa: Toward the Development of an Archeological Approach to the Study of Gender," also in Patricia Albers and Beatrice Medicine, eds., *The Hidden Half* (New York: University Press of America, 1983): 77–99.

Since first contacts with Europeans and Africans, disease has been of major historical import for American Indians. For the best, most balanced general discussion of disease and depopulation for North American Indians see Russell Thornton's *American Indian Holocaust and Survival: A Population History Since 1492* (Norman: University of Oklahoma Press, 1987). Diane Putney examined federal Indian policy regarding disease in "Fighting the Scourge: American Indian Morbidity and Federal Policy, 1897–1929," Ph.D. Dissertation, Marquette University, 1980. Tuberculosis and trachoma, both highly contagious, plagued American Indian reservations across the country in the late nineteenth and twentieth centuries. For a better understanding of the nature and history of these diseases see Anthony Lowell, et al., *Tuberculosis* (Cambridge: Harvard University Press, 1969); James Allen, *May's Manual of Diseases of the Eye* (Baltimore: Williams and Wilkins, 1983); Yechiel Becker, *The Agent of Trachoma* (New York: S. Karger, 1974); Rene Dubos and Jean Dubos, *The White Plague* (Boston: Little, Brown and Company, 1952). For Minnesota specifically, see Philip Jordan, *The People's Health: A History of Public Health in Minnesota to 1948* (St. Paul: Minnesota Historical Society Press, 1953). For plants and methods used to treat illness and wounds consult Virgil Vogel's classic *American Indian Medicine* (Norman: University of Oklahoma Press, 1970). Recent classification of alcoholism as a disease means that historians must find ways to historicize alcohol consumption among American Indians. Jack Waddell provides a model for this in "Malhiot's Journal: An Ethnohistoric Assessment of Chippewa Alcohol Behavior in the Early 19th Century," *Ethnohistory* 32 (1985): 246–68.

The standard work on Anishinaabe religion is Christopher Vecsey's *Traditional Ojibwa Religion and Its Historical Changes* (Philadelphia: American Philosophical Society, 1983). Vecsey's sensitivity to historical conditions that influenced the development of the Midéwiwin is insightful. However, his readiness to interpret religious changes, especially the inroads of Christianity, as decline blurs his perspective on religious syncretism. Martin Zanger in "'Straight Tongue's Heathen Wards': Bishop Whipple and the Episcopal Mission to the Chippewas," in Clyde A. Milner II and Floyd A. O'Neil, eds., *Churchmen and the Western Indians, 1820–1920* (Norman: University of Oklahoma Press, 1985): 177–214, adroitly demonstrates how the Anishinaabeg Indianized Episcopal missions as much as the Episcopals succeeded in christianizing the Indians. Other works that elaborate on Anishinaabe world view are A. Irving Hallowell, "Ojibwa Ontology, Behavior, and World View," in Dennis Tedlock and Barbara Tedlock, eds., *Teachings from the American Earth: Indian Religion and Philosophy* (New York: Liveright, 1975): 141–78, and Mary Black, "Ojibwa Power Belief System," in Raymond Fogelson and Richard N. Adams, eds., *The Anthropology of Power* (New York: Academic Press, 1977). Catholic Benedictine missions among the Minnesota Anishinaabeg have received attention from Carol Berg in "'Climbing Learners' Hill': Benedictines at White Earth, 1878–1945," Ph.D. Dissertation, University of Minnesota, 1983, and from John Scott in "'To Do Some Good among the Indians:' Nineteenth Century Benedictine Indian Missions," *Journal of the West* 23 (1984): 26–36. An excellent review of the literature on American Indian religions, including recommendations for future research is Robert Brightman, "Toward a History of Indian Religion: Religious Changes in Native Societies," in Colin G. Calloway, ed., *New Directions in American Indian History* (Norman: University of Oklahoma Press, 1988): 223–49.

Many other primary and secondary sources influenced my interpretation in some way. Those discussed here represent only the most compelling.

Index

ethnographers, 206. *See also* Colby,
Pauline; Densmore, Frances; Hoffman,
Walter J.
eugenics, 168, 170
exogamous, 12
exploitation, xii, xiv, 10, 157–59, 176,
178, 185, 208, 214; of resources, 137,
171, 185

factional dispute(s), 106, 147, 174–202,
221
factions, 4, 22, 173–202, 226
Fairbanks, Benjamin L. (B.L.), 75, 89,
100–103, 106–7, 129, 146, 155–56,
165, 175, 177–79, 185, 190, 193–97;
Evangeline Critts, 115; family: 33,
179, 224; George, Sr., 48, 75, 101;
George, Jr., 101; John H., 33–34, 40,
44, 47; Margaret Elizabeth, 33;
Robert P., 33, 46, 48, 80, 89, 100–101;
Sarah (née Dufort), 101; Sylem, 81. *See
also* surnames, Fairbanks
Falls of St. Anthony, 51
Falls of the St. Mary's River. *See* Sault
Ste. Marie
families, 6, 46, 60–61, 63–65, 81, 85,
105, 115, 122, 129, 149, 156, 173, 179–
80, 183, 193, 197, 205, 206–7, 223,
229, 234; Anishinaabe, 20–21, 23, 25,
27, 56, 77, 101, 114, 162, 204–5, 218;
métis, 30–33, 48
family hunting territories, 23
fancy work. *See* lace making
Faribault, Minn., 97
Farling, Elizabeth, 30
farmers, 29, 38, 47, 74–77, 83, 135, 164,
218, 223, 227
farming, 10, 16, 55, 64, 66, 92, 97, 155,
171, 213; implements, 64, 74; mar-
ket(s), 1, 6, 35, 49, 69, 72–76, 79, 89,
93, 101, 115, 135, 161, 204, 206, 222,
226; subsistence, 2, 40–42, 48, 73–74
Feast of the Dead, 9, 12, 16
federally nonrecognized tribes, 196
fee simple patent. *See* land, titles
Fergus Falls, Minn., 161
field matrons, 214, 221
Fineday, Louisa, 171

First National Bank of Detroit, 158
fish, 28, 73, 76, 80, 85
Fish Lake, 62; settlement, 63
fishery, 13
fishing, 13, 16, 23, 25, 48
Flandreau Boarding School, Flandreau,
S. Dak. *See* schools, boarding
Flat Lake, 78
Flat Mouth. *See* Eshkebugekoshe
Flatmouth, Ruth, 22
Fond du Lac, Minn., 32
Fond du Lac band, 59, 61, 123–25, 128
Fond du Lac Reservation, 186
forests: coniferous, 15, 18, 70–72; decid-
uous, 18, 70–72
forts, 12
Fort Gaines, 34
Fort Ripley, 34
Fosston, Minn., 158
France, 17
Francis, David R., 138
Franco-Algonquian trade alliance, 13
Franco-Anishinaabe descent. *See* mixed
descent
Franklin Ave. neighborhood, Min-
neapolis, Minn., 234
fraud, 87, 107, 138–40, 149–50, 154–56,
171, 175–76, 183, 196, 208–9, 211,
230–31; annuity, 39
Frazee, Minn., 158, 211
Frazer, Nancy, 30
Fredonia, N.Y., 100
Fremont, William, 32
French, 10, 17, 29, 120; explorers, 11, 13,
17; heritage/ancestry, 10, 30, 180. *See*
fur traders, French
French and Indian War, 18
French-Canadian, 17, 110, 194. *See also*
women, métis
"French-Canadian mixed-bloods," 45, 89
full-blood(s), xiv, 5–6, 70, 75, 99, 106–7,
118–22, 134, 145–47, 149, 153, 156,
160–63, 165–68, 170–74, 180–81,
183–85, 187–88, 190–92, 199–200,
204, 234; symbols, 135, 201
"Full Blood Business Committee," 189
Full Blood Faction, xiv, 100, 174–75, 181,
183, 186, 188–92